The Play of Allusion in the "Historia Augusta"

Publication of this volume has been made possible, in part, through the generous support and enduring vision of **Warren G. Moon.**

 # The Play of Allusion in the *Historia Augusta*

DAVID ROHRBACHER

The University of Wisconsin Press

The University of Wisconsin Press
728 State Street, Suite 443
Madison, Wisconsin 53706
uwpress.wisc.edu

Gray's Inn House, 127 Clerkenwell Road
London EC1R 5DB, United Kingdom
eurospanbookstore.com

Copyright © 2016
The Board of Regents of the University of Wisconsin System
All rights reserved. Except in the case of brief quotations embedded in critical articles and reviews, no part of this publication may be reproduced, stored in a retrieval system, transmitted in any format or by any means—digital, electronic, mechanical, photocopying, recording, or otherwise—or conveyed via the Internet or a website without written permission of the University of Wisconsin Press. Rights inquiries should be directed to rights@uwpress.wisc.edu.

Printed in the United States of America

This book may be available in a digital edition

Library of Congress Cataloging-in-Publication Data

Rohrbacher, David, 1969-, author.
The play of allusion in the Historia Augusta / David Rohrbacher.
  pages   cm — (Wisconsin studies in classics)
    Includes bibliographical references and index.
    ISBN 978-0-299-30600-7 (cloth: alk. paper)
  1. Scriptores historiae Augustae. 2. Emperors—Rome—Biography—History and criticism. 3. Rome—History—Empire, 30 B.C.–284 A.D.—Sources. 4. Rome—History—Errors, inventions, etc. 5. Allusions in literature.
    I. Title. II. Series: Wisconsin studies in classics.
DG274.R598   2016
937'.070922—dc23
                                  2015008393

ISBN 978-0-299-32704-0 (pbk.: alk. paper)

For
JULIA and JONATHAN

Contents

	Preface	IX
	List of Abbreviations	XI
	Introduction	3
1	Allusion in the *Historia Augusta*	16
2	The *Historia Augusta* and the Ancient Reader	47
3	Religion in the *Historia Augusta*	87
4	Imperial History Reimagined	134
	Afterword	170
	Notes	177
	Bibliography	203
	Index	221
	Index Locorum	235

Preface

The most recent generation of classical scholarship has witnessed a surge of interest both in late antiquity and in allusion, but the *Historia Augusta*, although it is positioned at the intersection of these interests, has been sadly neglected. In *The Play of Allusion*, I offer a new theory of the genesis of the work that requires a new method of interpretation. Even more important, I hope to rescue the *Historia Augusta* from its current confinement to a dusty museum storeroom, where a handful of late antique historians and philologists occasionally poke and prod at its text through the thick pelt of a century of abstruse notes and speculations. The endlessly fascinating, often bizarre, and sometimes hilarious pseudo-biographies of the *Historia Augusta* deserve a place in the main collection, to be appreciated by all those interested in the ancient world. The *Historia Augusta* has much to offer anyone pursuing studies in allusion, genre, historiography and biography, late Roman religion, ancient humor and parody, reception theory, and more.

I am grateful to the many people and institutions who encouraged me and aided me in the completion of this manuscript. Much of the research and writing was done during summers in the Greek and Latin Reading Room at Memorial Library in Madison, and I thank both the helpful staff there and the Office of the Provost at New College of Florida, which provided me with summer research funds. Librarians and staff at the Jane Bancroft Cook Library at New College of Florida were endlessly helpful during the school year, and the New College Library Association purchased on my behalf some greatly appreciated Budé volumes of the *Historia Augusta* that would otherwise be out of place in an undergraduate library. My colleagues and students at New College helped in many ways. A semester research leave granted by the Division of Humanities proved crucial to completing the manuscript. Richard Miles gave me the strong encouragement I needed to begin this project. François Paschoud was kind enough to share his work with me prior to publication. Alain Gowing has been an adviser and an ally for many years. Carl Shaw read many drafts and greatly improved the manuscript in both content and style. His constant help as a colleague and a friend are greatly appreciated.

At the University of Wisconsin Press I owe thanks to the editors of the series Wisconsin Studies in Classics, Mark Stansbury-O'Donnell, Patricia Rosenmeyer,

Preface

and Laura McClure, and the executive editor of the press, Raphael Kadushin. Their efforts and the efforts of the diligent and learned anonymous readers for the press have greatly improved the manuscript. For their help in guiding me through the publication process, I would also like to thank Adam Mehring, Sheila McMahon, Matthew Cosby, Amber Rose, Carla Marolt, and Sheila Leary, and the expert copyediting of Jane Barry.

Most of all, I am grateful for the love and encouragement of my wife, Anne. She was my best editor and my greatest supporter. It could not have been done without her.

Abbreviations

In addition to the abbreviations below, citations in this book follow the ones used by the *Oxford Classical Dictionary*, 3rd edition.

Books of the *Historia Augusta* (HA)

In E. Hohl, *Scriptores Historiae Augustae*. 2 vols. Stuttgart: Teubner, 1927:

Hadr.	*Hadrian*
Ael.	*Aelius*
Pius	*Antoninus Pius*
Marc.	*Marcus Aurelius*
Ver.	*Verus*
Did. Iul.	*Didius Iulianus*
Comm.	*Commodus*
Pert.	*Pertinax*
Av. Cass.	*Avidius Cassius*
Sev.	*Severus*
Pesc. Nig.	*Pescennius Niger*
Carac.	*Caracalla*
Geta	*Geta*
Elag.	*Heliogabalus*
Diad.	*Diadumenus*
Macr.	*Macrinus*
Clod. Alb.	*Clodius Albinus*
Alex.	*Alexander Severus*
Maximin.	*The Two Maximini*
Gord.	*The Three Gordians*
Max. et Balb.	*Maximus and Balbinus*
Valer.	*The Two Valerians*
Gall.	*The Two Gallieni*

In F. Paschoud, *Histoire Auguste IV.3: Vies des trente tyrans et de Claude*. Paris: Les Belles Lettres, 2011:

Tyr. Trig.   *Thirty Tyrants*
Claud.   *Claudius*

In F. Paschoud, *Histoire Auguste V.1: Vies d'Aurélien, Tacite*. Paris: Les Belles Lettres, 1996:

Aur.   *Aurelian*
Tac.   *Tacitus*

In F. Paschoud, *Histoire Auguste V.2: Vies de Probus, Firmus, Saturnin, Proculus et Bonose, Carus, Numérien et Carin*. Paris: Les Belles Lettres, 2002:

Prob.   *Probus*
Quad. Tyr.   *Quadrigae Tyrannorum: Firmus, Saturninus, Proculus, and Bonosus*
Car.   *Carus, Carinus, and Numerian*

Volumes of the *Historia-Augusta-Colloquium*

BHAC 1963   A. Alföldi, ed. *Historia-Augusta-Colloquium*. Bonn: Rudolf Habelt, 1964.
BHAC 1964/65 A. Alföldi, ed. *Bonner Historia-Augusta-Colloquium*. Bonn: Rudolf Habelt, 1966.
BHAC 1966/67 A. Alföldi, ed. *Bonner Historia-Augusta-Colloquium*. Bonn: Rudolf Habelt, 1968.
BHAC 1968/69 A. Alföldi, ed. *Bonner Historia-Augusta-Colloquium*. Bonn: Rudolf Habelt, 1970.
BHAC 1970   A. Alföldi, ed. *Bonner Historia-Augusta-Colloquium*. Bonn: Rudolf Habelt, 1972.
BHAC 1971   A. Alföldi, ed. *Bonner Historia-Augusta-Colloquium*. Bonn: Rudolf Habelt, 1974.
BHAC 1972/74 A. Alföldi, ed. *Bonner Historia-Augusta-Colloquium*. Bonn: Rudolf Habelt, 1976.
BHAC 1975/76 A. Alföldi, ed. *Bonner Historia-Augusta-Colloquium*. Bonn: Rudolf Habelt, 1978.

Abbreviations

BHAC 1977/78   A. Alföldi, ed. *Bonner Historia-Augusta-Colloquium*. Bonn: Rudolf Habelt, 1980.
BHAC 1979/81   J. Straub, ed. *Bonner Historia-Augusta-Colloquium*. Bonn: Rudolf Habelt, 1983.
BHAC 1982/83   J. Straub, ed. *Bonner Historia-Augusta-Colloquium*. Bonn: Rudolf Habelt, 1985.
BHAC 1984/85   J. Straub, ed. *Bonner Historia-Augusta-Colloquium*. Bonn: Rudolf Habelt, 1987.
BHAC 1986/89   K. Rosen, ed. *Bonner Historia-Augusta-Colloquium*. Bonn: Rudolf Habelt, 1991.
HAC 1991   G. Bonamente and N. Duval, eds. *Historiae Augustae Colloquium Parisinum*. Macerata: Boccard, 1991.
HAC 1994   G. Bonamente and F. Paschoud, eds. *Historiae Augustae Colloquium Genevense*. Bari: Edipuglia, 1994.
HAC 1995   G. Bonamente and G. Paci, eds. *Historiae Augustae Colloquium Maceratense*. Bari: Edipuglia, 1995.
HAC 1996   G. Bonamente and M. Mayer, eds. *Historiae Augustae Colloquium Barcinonense*. Bari: Edipuglia, 1996.
HAC 1997   G. Bonamente and K. Rosen, eds. *Historiae Augustae Colloquium Bonnense*. Bari: Edipuglia, 1997.
HAC 1998   G. Bonamente, F. Heim, and J.-P. Callu, eds. *Historiae Augustae Colloquium Argentoratense*. Bari: Edipuglia, 1998.
HAC 1999   F. Paschoud, ed. *Historiae Augustae Colloquium Genevense*. Bari: Edipuglia, 1999.
HAC 2002   G. Bonamente and F. Paschoud, eds. *Historiae Augustae Colloquium Perusinum*. Bari: Edipuglia, 2002.
HAC 2005   G. Bonamente and M. Mayer, eds. *Historiae Augustae Colloquium Barcinonense*. Bari: Edipuglia, 2005.
HAC 2007   G. Bonamente and H. Brandt, eds. *Historiae Augustae Colloquium Bambergense*. Bari: Edipuglia, 2007.
HAC 2010   L. Milić and N. Hecquet-Noti, eds. *Historiae Augustae Colloquium Genevense in Honorem F. Paschoud Septuagenarii*. Bari: Edipuglia, 2010.

The Play of Allusion in the "Historia Augusta"

# Introduction

The bizarre collection of imperial biographies that we call the *Historia Augusta* contains hundreds of unusual, often humorous, details that are wholly fictitious. We read, for example, that the emperor Carinus preferred to swim in pools filled with floating apples and melons, that the usurper Proculus deflowered a hundred virgins in fifteen days, and that the emperor Elagabalus used to shave the pubic hair of his friends and courtesans, and then shave his own beard with the same razor. These particular fictions were not simply invented out of thin air but represent allusions to other literary works—to Ammianus Marcellinus, Saint Jerome, and Suetonius, respectively. The inventions found in the *Historia Augusta* are largely created by allusion, and the identification of these allusions, I believe, is one of the primary purposes for which the work was created.

The *Historia Augusta* uses allusion in an anomalous manner, as a comparison with his near contemporary, the historian Ammianus Marcellinus, makes clear. Ammianus also makes extensive use of allusion. The boundaries that moderns seek between history and fiction were, as is well known, less sharp in antiquity, and allusion in Ammianus, as in other authors, often serves to enhance his narrative in ways a modern historian would see as misleading or deceitful. But Ammianus's artistry in using allusion, along with other techniques, typically serves his broader rhetorical goals of praising his heroes, attacking his enemies, or increasing the excitement or majesty of a scene or description.[1] By contrast, scholarly attempts to explain allusions in the *Historia Augusta* as tools for promoting the author's rhetorical goals have not succeeded. Too often individual allusions have been considered in isolation, but when we consider the totality of allusion we must conclude that the work lacks an overarching political or religious agenda, as I argue in particular in chapters 3 and 4 of this book. Even individual allusions are sometimes so complex or so surprising that they approach the limits of interpretability. Their extravagance draws the reader away from the source text to the creativity of the author.

Introduction

It is not for the extravagance of allusion alone, however, that Syme called the *Historia Augusta* "the most enigmatic work that Antiquity has transmitted."[2] The most mysterious aspect of the work is the contrast between its self-portrayal and its reality. The *Historia Augusta* is, in form, a biographical collection that presents the lives of the emperors and usurpers of the second and third centuries, from Hadrian to Carinus. It consists of thirty books in all, representing considerably more than thirty individual lives, since many of the books, especially toward the end, include two or more subjects each. The individual biographies are assigned in the extant manuscripts to six different authors. In some of these lives, the emperors Diocletian and Constantine are directly addressed in familiar tones, which should date the lives to the late third and early fourth centuries. In reality, the work is not by six people but by a single author, and it was written not in the age of Constantine but at least half a century later. Ancient biographers and historians sometimes shaded the truth, or even were guilty of outright fabrication, but never on a scale so extreme.

The *Historia Augusta* was taken as an authentic, if deeply flawed, source of historical information from the first recorded instance of its use in the sixth century until the end of the nineteenth century. But although the work does preserve for us many valuable pieces of the historical tradition, it does so only incidentally to its creation of a game of allusion. The *Historia Augusta* is not a fraud but a fiction for a knowing and appreciative audience.

The study of the *Historia Augusta* has traditionally been undertaken by historians who seek to identify the authentic historical material the work contains and discard the rest.[3] I propose in this book to offer, by contrast, a literary study of the work that begins with understanding the author as a creative inventor. His inventiveness is not merely a tool for filling in the gaps in his understanding of the past, or a method of commenting, seriously or comically, on his primary interest in biographical narrative. Instead, he invents in the service of a literary program that values inventiveness for its own sake. In this introduction I offer a series of examples of creative play in the *Historia Augusta* to serve as a background to the arguments of this book.

The *Historia Augusta* Was Not Written by Six People

One of the most surprising features of the *Historia Augusta* is the single author's decision to portray himself as six different authors: Aelius Spartianus, Julius Capitolinus, Vulcacius Gallicanus, Aelius Lampridius, Trebellius Pollio, and Flavius Vopiscus Syracusanus. It is difficult to find precedents for this sort of group project in antiquity.⁴ Close reading of the text reveals the author's fiction. If we were to accept the evidence of the *Historia Augusta* itself, the six authors did not collaborate by divvying up lives among themselves. Instead, the authors claim to have written many other lives that have not survived. For example, Vulcacius Gallicanus claims to have written lives of all who have held the imperial title, back even to Julius Caesar (*Av. Cass.* 3.3). In the life of the Caesar Aelius, Spartianus announces his intention to write a life of Verus (*Ael.* 2.9), but the *Verus* in the *Historia Augusta* is attributed to Julius Capitolinus. In the *Clodius Albinus*, Capitolinus makes reference to his biography of Pescennius Niger (*Clod. Alb.* 1.4), but the *Pescennius Niger* in our collection is attributed to Aelius Spartianus. Again, the *Commodus* by Aelius Lampridius reference to a life of Marcus (*Comm.* 1.1), but our *Marcus Aurelius* is by Julius Capitolinus. If it were authentically a work of multiple authors, we would have to conjure up an unseen, unmentioned editor who united these lives, and imagine many more lives that have vanished without even being cited by the authors of the lives in the *Historia Augusta*.

The six supposedly independent authors are amazingly similar in thematic details. They all chose to write lives of the usurpers and Caesars as well as the emperors. They all refer to the unprecedented nature of their task and the difficulty they face in accomplishing it, often in quite similar language.⁵ They share a dependence on otherwise unknown historians and biographers such as Aemilius Parthenianus and Junius Cordus, and use similar language to direct the reader to these or to other sources, should more information be desired. They share many errors, such as providing the incorrect name "Diadumenus" for Diadumenianus, the son of the emperor Macrinus, and they share many peculiarities of content, such as a focus on military discipline and on women and wine, each topic described with similar language. The authors all offer their own translations into Latin of poems, inscriptions, oracles, and other Greek passages, and these passages are all fictional.⁶ All the authors are obsessed with feeble wordplay on the name of their subjects: Severus is severe, Probus displays probity, Verus wrote truthfully.

A variety of unusual stylistic features recur in the different authors.⁷ While the accumulation of stylistic parallels is striking, it can never be wholly decisive, since one might credit imitation among the authors or supposed editors for the coincidence. An argument by Adams for single authorship, however, seems irrefutable.⁸ He studied different aspects of the use of two words meaning "to kill," *occidere* and *interficere*, and found that their use was consistent among the HA-authors but idiosyncratic when compared with other authors of similar time periods and genres. For example, he finds forty-two uses of *occido* in relative clauses in the various HA-authors but only one use of *interficio*, a ratio that is not found in other writers and yet could hardly be the kind of thing that an editor would impose or a group of authors would conspire to agree upon. Similarly difficult to refute is the evidence of prose rhythm. All the lives share a preference for particular metrical sentence endings.⁹

The most certain proof of the unity of authorship of the *Historia Augusta* lies in the thorough fictionality of at least some of the lives authored by each one of the supposed biographers. It is ridiculous to imagine six different authors working independently to make extensive use of fake sources, letters, documents, inscriptions, and acclamations, to a degree unknown in classical literature, and then for excerpts from these six to be gathered into the present collection.

The *Historia Augusta* Was Not Written in the Early Fourth Century

The author audaciously claims, implicitly, to be writing decades before he actually was. The gap between the purported and actual date of composition can be proven by many anachronisms. Some of these anachronisms merely reflect the difficulty of writing historical fiction with complete accuracy, but others may well have been meant to be recognized for their incongruity by ancient readers.

The imperial addresses provide the clearest evidence of anachronism. Some of the lives in the collection (the *Aelius, Marcus, Verus, Avidius Cassius, Severus, Pescennius Niger,* and *Macrinus*) address Diocletian, who was emperor from 284 to 305. Other lives address Constantine, who succeeded him, ruling from 306 to 337 (the *Clodius Albinus, Geta, Elagabalus, Alexander Severus, Two Maximini, Three Gordians,* and the *Maximus and Balbinus*), setting a *terminus ante quem* of the early fourth century. The address to Constantius Chlorus that begins the *Claudius*, attributed to Trebellius Pollio, is particularly problematic. Constantius Chlorus, the father of the emperor Constantine, is addressed with the title Caesar, which he held between 293 and May 305. The introduction is thoroughly panegyric, celebrating Claudius as the greatest of all emperors, possessing "the virtue of Trajan, the piety of Antoninus, the leadership of Augustus" ("Traiani virtus, Antonini pietas, Augusti moderatio," 2.3). The author reveals several prophecies from the time of Claudius (*Claud.* 10) that predict that his children and grandchildren will rule the empire, and he explicitly links praise of Claudius to praise of the house of Constantine. But the house of Constantine was not actually descended from Claudius.¹⁰ In 307 the usurper Constantine first legitimized his position by marrying the daughter of the tetrarch Maximianus, but in 310, having dismissed his wife and killed his father-in-law, he was in need of a new source of legitimacy. A panegyrist was therefore authorized to reveal a newly invented piece of information:

the emperor Constantine was a descendant of Claudius.[11] So the life cannot truly be addressed to Constantius Chlorus while showing knowledge of a genealogy that was invented five years after his death.[12] The connection between Constantine and Claudius pervades the life, and so it cannot be a later addition.

In the introduction to the *Aurelian* attributed to "Vopiscus," the author has an extensive conversation with Junius Tiberianus, described as the urban prefect.[13] This conversation, the comic nature of which is underlined by its setting during the festival of the *Hilaria*, has also been shown to be historically suspect. Two men with this name served in this office, in 291–92 and 303–4, the first the father of the second. The Tiberianus of the *Historia Augusta* cannot be the prefect of 303–4, since he did not hold office during the late March setting of the conversation. But he cannot be the Tiberianus of 291–92, since their conversation includes discussion of the biographer Trebellius Pollio, who, in his preface to the *Claudius*, addresses Constantius Chlorus with the title Caesar that he did not take until 293. Tiberianus provides a ride for the author in an official state chair known as the *iudicale carpentum*. Providing this chair to the urban prefect was a new and controversial perk, according to a letter of Symmachus written in 384 (*Relat.* 4), so this too is an anachronism. Finally, the title *vir illustris* that is attached to Tiberianus is otherwise first attested in 354 (*Cod. Theod.* 11.1.6) and only becomes common toward the end of the fourth century, so it is probably yet another anachronism. Tiberianus is not the only problematic figure in the *HA*. The names of characters of dubious historicity there are often anachronistic.[14] Names from the great aristocratic families of the later fourth century, the Anicii, Ceionii, Postumii, and others, are retrojected into the family trees of emperors of the second and third centuries, as is the rare name Toxotius (*Maximin.* 27.6). And the various uses of the names Maecius and Maecia are also fantasies of the late fourth century, stemming from claims of late Roman aristocrats to be descendants of the famous republican family of the Gracchi.[15]

The *HA*-author's understanding of geography also reflects that of the later, not earlier, fourth century. The *Historia Augusta* attributes to the Thracian Maximinus a mixed barbarian ancestry, part Goth and part Alan, but these barbarian groups were not present in Thrace prior to the arrival of the Huns in 375.[16] The use of the plural *Thraciae* as opposed to the singular *Thracia* reflects a change that must be dated after 312, but the dedications to the *Pescennius Niger* and the *Aurelian* in which the plural appears would place those lives before 305 and 292, respectively.[17] The *Probus* applies the term *Getae*, which properly referred to a Thracian people, to the relatively new Germanic Goths. The term is otherwise attested only in Jerome in 390 and then in Claudian and Orosius in the early fifth century.[18] Another anachronism in ethnic geography appears in the discussion of the Samaritans as a community separate from the Jews (*Elag.* 3.5; *Quad. Tyr.* 7.5, 8.3), a distinction that Syme suggests is typical of the end of the fourth century, first specified thus in a law of 390.[19] Many anachronisms can be found in the administrative and military terminology of the *Historia Augusta*.[20] Others appear in Latin words and phrases that are otherwise found only in the later period.[21] But the most important evidence for dating the *Historia Augusta* lies in its allusions. The use of Aurelius Victor by the *HA*-author ensures that he is writing after 371, and the use of Ammianus Marcellinus and Jerome ensures a date in the 390s at the earliest.[22]

The Biographies in the *Historia Augusta* Differ Sharply in Nature

A reader of the *Historia Augusta* will quickly recognize that the lives differ sharply in the amount of sober biography and ludicrous fiction that each contains. Syme and Chastagnol offer fairly similar schemes for categorizing the lives, which my own categories reflect.[23] These conventional categories make it more convenient to discuss the work as a whole. While the differences in content between the groups of lives can in part be attributed to the sources available to the author, they are in part the result of authorial choice.

First, we can distinguish a list of primary lives: the *Hadrian, Antoninus Pius, Marcus, Verus, Commodus, Pertinax, Didius Julianus, Severus, Caracalla*. These lives are rich in names and dates that can be shown to be true by recourse to other sources or that simply meet the test of plausibility, although this is not to say that they do not contain material that is suspect or demonstrably false. The primary lives can be distinguished from the secondary lives of usurpers and Caesars. Among the secondary lives, I include the *Aelius, Avidius Cassius, Pescennius Niger, Clodius Albinus, Geta, Macrinus, Diadumenianus*. All of these lives offer little that is historically accurate. What is true in them is taken from the primary life with which they are associated; what is false is often grossly or comically exaggerated. The *Elagabalus* and the *Alexander Severus*, which stand near the middle of the *Historia Augusta*, deserve a category of their own. They are a matched pair, the comic-book villain Elagabalus balanced by the fantasy hero Alexander. The *Elagabalus* contains some reliable passages, including some places where the author quotes the extant Greek historian Herodian as his source, while the *Alexander* contains almost nothing factual, but in both the amount of fiction is large. The extent and the thoroughness of the fiction differentiate them from the scattered inventions that were typical of the much shorter secondary lives.

Introduction

The next three biographies—the *Two Maximini*, the *Three Gordians*, and the *Maximus and Balbinus*—we can call the intermediate lives. They discuss multiple lives within a single book. All three focus on the events of the year 238 from different perspectives, and all three mix real information taken from Herodian with fiction. The intermediate lives are followed by a gap between 244 and 260, and the *Historia Augusta* picks up partway into the *Two Valerians*. Four lives attributed to Trebellius Pollio are followed by five of Flavius Vopiscus. All nine of these final lives offer only a minimal outline of factual material filled out with vast amounts of invention. These final lives, like the intermediate lives, include group biographies. The *Two Valerians* is followed by the *Two Gallieni*, and the final biography of the collection collects Carus and his two sons, Carinus and Numerian. There are also two group portraits of usurpers. The biographies of Firmus, Saturninus, Proculus, and Bonosus are often referred to collectively as the *Quadrigae Tyrannorum*, or "four-horse chariot of usurpers," from a phrase at the end of the *Probus* (24.8). The extreme case of group portraits is found in the *Thirty Tyrants*, short accounts of thirty-two different usurpers. The final lives also include some single biographies: the short *Claudius* and *Tacitus*, the more substantial *Probus*, and the lengthy *Aurelian*. The *HA*-author offers his most elaborate webs of allusion in these last lives.

The Lacuna between the *Three Gordians* and the *Two Valerians* Is a Fiction of the Author

The *Three Gordians* concludes with the death of Gordian III in 244. The next section of the text in all surviving manuscripts begins with comments from the very end of the reign of Valerian, after his capture by the Persians in 260. We are thus missing the reigns of Philip and his son (249-51), of Trebonianus Gallus and Volusianus (251-53), of Aemilianus (253), and most of the life of Valerian (253-60).[24] It is a triumph of modern scholarship on the *Historia Augusta* to have demonstrated that this lacuna is not just the unexceptional result of textual dislocations common in ancient manuscripts but is actually the purposeful construction of our creative author.[25] A variety of arguments converge on this conclusion. First, because of a scarcity of sources, the *HA*-author appears to have known only a few actual facts about Philip, which, in line with his regular approach to the later lives, he would likely have deployed in the life itself, had one existed. But most of this small collection of facts about Philip that would appropriately be found in the life itself can be found outside it in extant parts of the *Historia Augusta*, such as Philip's attacks on male-male sex (*Elag.* 32.6; *Alex.* 24.4) and his Secular Games (*Gord.* 33.1-4). The *HA*-author has even placed a Scythian invasion that properly belongs

9

to the time of Philip in the reign of Gordian III (*Gord.* 31.1).[26] In addition, the list of the Thirty Tyrants, described by the author as usurpers who arose during the reigns of Valerian and Gallienus, in fact includes numerous invented personages and figures from other periods of time, as early as the reign of Maximinus, in order to fill it out, but does not include any of the usurpers who would naturally have been described in the lacuna: Jotapianus, Marinus Pacatianus, Lucius Priscus, and Uranius Antoninus.[27]

The lacuna marks more than just a break between lives. It also occurs at the very point where Herodian, one of the author's sources, leaves off. The two pseudo-authors Trebellius Pollio and Flavius Vopiscus, who are credited between them with all nine of the lives after the lacuna, do not appear before the lacuna.[28] This marks the break as otherwise formally significant to the *HA*-author. These last lives are the most inventive and allusive. In addition, the lacuna does not present the "frayed edges" we often see in authentic cases of damaged texts.[29] Birley argues that the *HA*-author is teasing his readers with his own references to the missing books. When making a list of bad emperors, he adds, "although I ought to leave out the Decii" ("tametsi Decios excerpere debeam," *Aur.* 42.6), perhaps an allusion to his omission of their lives. A similar double meaning can be read at *Carus* 3.5. In a survey of the vicissitudes of the Roman state, the *HA*-author makes his way slowly to Alexander Severus, at which point he leaps to Gallienus with the following transition: "It would take too long to compose all the things that followed, for [the Roman state] was not able to experience the emperor Valerian" ("longum est quae sequuntur universa conectere: uti enim principe Valeriano non potuit"). And the *HA*-author offers a flurry of remarks about books and scrolls before and after the fragmentary *Valerian* (*Max. et Balb.* 1.1–2; *Gord.* 1.1–5; *Valer.* 8.5).

Scholars have seen a religious motive for the creation of a false lacuna, since Philip was said by fourth-century writers to have been a Christian, while Decius and Valerian were prominent persecutors of Christians who met with untimely ends. Birley argues that it would have been more difficult for the pagan *HA*-author to celebrate the greatness of Valerian and mourn his capture by the Persians if his persecutions were detailed, since Christians saw his misfortunes as his just deserts.[30] More recently den Hengst has suggested that the death of Valerian would remind readers of the ignoble death of Julian, an emperor whom the *HA*-author appears to favor in other contexts.[31] But the *HA*-author is generally inventive enough to avoid discussing matters that he would prefer to avoid, and Valerian is certainly praised highly in the extant part of his life. The lacuna should better be seen as part of the author's creative play, a witty challenge to readers in a scholarly milieu familiar with truly lacunose texts.[32]

Introduction

The Historical Sources of the *Historia Augusta* Are Few and Are Freely Manipulated

The *HA*-author draws heavily from both literary and historiographical texts to weave his fictions. The historiographical texts are of particular interest because they often provided the framework for individual lives, and of course because they are the sources from which the author drew his potentially true information. The task of source criticism is more complicated for the *Historia Augusta* than for true historiographical texts, since historical accuracy was not a primary concern of the author, and he was happy to alter the texts that he did follow. Our author did not carefully sift and compare various sources as a conscientious biographer might but instead used his few historiographical sources as points of departure for his fictive purposes. The study of the sources reveals that the author did not, as is sometimes assumed, use all of the material at his disposal first and only then, out of desperation, turn to fabrication. The *HA*-author was not the passive victim of his sources but rather the willing and able manipulator of them.

I have treated the question of sources in considerable detail elsewhere and will provide only the essential information here.[33] The *HA*-author relied on the lost work known as the *Kaisergeschichte* and the *breviaria* dependent upon it, by Eutropius and Aurelius Victor, as a framework for the whole work. He relied on the biographer Marius Maximus for the early lives through Elagabalus, on Herodian for the year 238, on Dexippus's *Chronicle* until 270, and finally on a source with affinities to the sources of later Greek authors like Zosimus.

The lost work known as Enmann's *Kaisergeschichte* (abbreviated *KG* in the English-language literature and *EKG* in European works) is used throughout the *Historia Augusta*.[34] The *KG* presented short sketches of each emperor from Augustus up to Constantius II. Although it was short and not especially reliable, the paucity of Latin sources for the second and third centuries led many later historians to turn to it for information. The use of the *KG* can be most easily detected in the *Historia Augusta* by finding parallels in language or in content with the brief histories of Aurelius Victor and of Eutropius, who relied on the *KG* alone for their accounts of the imperial period. The *HA*-author uses not only the *KG* itself, however, but also makes direct use of Victor and Eutropius.[35] Sometimes, of course, it is difficult to know which of these works he is using.

The *KG* and the breviaries that derive from it served as a guide or framework for the author. In some of the later lives of the *Historia Augusta*, virtually the only true information derives from the paragraph-long description of the emperor in the *KG*, embellished by the *HA*-author's invented material. The *KG* tradition often served as a starting point for more elaborate invention. For example, the *KG* described the death of the usurper Aureolus at a place known still to contemporaries as *pons Aureoli*; the *HA*-author follows his account of the death by quoting a short, invented verse inscription, supposedly translated from Greek, that marks Aureolus's tomb and bridge (*Tyr. Trig.* 11.4–5). The *HA*-author also enjoys using the *KG* in a kind of scholarship-theater, where he contrasts his base source with information from the *KG*, referred to as "other historians" or "Latin writers." For example, the *HA*-author purports to be sometimes unsure whether the "Maximus" he finds in Herodian and Dexippus and the "Pupienus" he finds in the *KG* (Victor 26–27; Eutropius 9.2) are the same person (they are: the emperor Marcus Clodius Pupienus Maximus). At one point he contrasts the views of Herodian and Dexippus with those of "Latin writers" in expressing this quandary (*Max. et Balb.* 33.2).

The first group of primary lives—from the *Hadrian* to the first half of the *Elagabalus*—are by far the most factual and likely derive from the work of the lost biographer Marius Maximus, cited twenty-nine times by the *HA*-author, and once by an ancient commentator on the text of Juvenal 4.53.[36] Like Suetonius, Maximus offered extensive genealogical information on the emperors (*Marc.* 1.6), and he is probably the source of this information in all of the early lives of the *Historia Augusta*. He was an innovator in including many primary sources in his biographies: letters, documents, acclamations, and orations (e.g., *Marc.* 25.10; *Comm.* 15.4, 18.2; *Pert.* 2.8, 15.8). The *Historia Augusta* provides citations to lives by Maximus of eight emperors, and the scholiast to Juvenal implies a life of Nerva; it is natural, then, to assume that Marius Maximus has followed Suetonius with lives of the second twelve emperors, and natural as well to identify Marius Maximus with the senator L. Marius Maximus Perpetuus Aurelianus, the general and holder of high offices who was consul for the second time in 223.

The *HA*-author used Maximus for historical material in the early lives but also adapted and parodied many of his characteristic features in the later fictionalized lives. Maximus's use of documents and speeches, for example, may have inspired the numerous exchanges of fake letters that round out the last books. Maximus's careful but exhausting prosopographical studies may also have inspired the *HA*-author to create similar lists of absurd and bizarre names in the later lives. Maximus offers extensive material about the emperors prior to their coronations, at one point in the *Pertinax* quoting from a speech that Marcus Aurelius had made in praise of him. The later lives of the *Historia Augusta* make it seem as if the archives are overflowing with letters written by previous emperors to their eventual successors.

The primary lives of the emperors, which rely on some truthful material from Marius Maximus, contrast sharply with the secondary lives: the lives of usurpers and Caesars. Each secondary life is associated with a particular primary life: Aelius with Hadrian, Avidius Cassius with Marcus, Pescennius Niger, Clodius Albinus, and Geta with Septimius Severus, Macrinus and Diadumenianus with Elagabalus. Material in a secondary life that is true almost always comes from the primary life with which it is associated, and occasionally from another primary life. Otherwise, the secondary lives are mostly the products of invention.

The imperial bureaucrat Herodian is the main source for the account of the years 235–38 in the *Historia Augusta*, encompassing the lives collected under the *Two Maximini*, the *Three Gordians*, and the *Maximus and Balbinus*. Herodian's history, which has been preserved in its entirety, covers the period from the death of Marcus Aurelius in 180 to the accession of Gordian III in 238. Herodian was also used in an unsystematic way in several other lives; some of the ten citations of Herodian by name in the *Historia Augusta* are found in the *Clodius Albinus* and the *Alexander Severus*, for example, and he is used without citation in the *Elagabalus*.[37] The *HA*-author did not use Herodian as much as he might have for the *Alexander Severus*.[38] Instead, when Marius Maximus ran out, the *HA*-author chose to use the *KG* for the chronological structure of the *Alexander Severus*, which is otherwise an elaborate and fantastic invention.

Because we actually possess the text of Herodian, we can watch the *HA*-author as he works with his source. In his comprehensive studies of the use of Herodian by the *Historia Augusta*, Kolb has classified the different approaches of our author to Herodian into several categories: word-for-word translation, abbreviation, supplementation, and the wholesale transformation or transposition of details or entire scenes.[39] In many places, the *HA*-author has supplemented Herodian with false details, invented letters, and fake scholarly digressions. We must expect that he has acted similarly in using other sources that are now lost to us.

For the period from 238 to 270, scholars largely agree that the source of the main historical narrative, in addition to the *KG*, is the third-century Athenian historian Dexippus.[40] Dexippus's *Chronicle* covered about a thousand years, so even if it became more dense toward its conclusion, it was not nearly as rich a source as Marius Maximus or Herodian. Syme mentions in passing that "it cannot be taken as certain that the *HA* is accurate in reporting Dexippus," and Paschoud's detailed study demonstrates the correctness of Syme's intuition.[41] For example, an anecdote found in Caesar, Frontinus, and Servius *auctus* is attributed implausibly to Dexippus.[42]

The last lives of the *Historia Augusta*, from Claudius to Carinus, are largely fiction after the end of Dexippus's history in 270. The author continued to use the *KG*, as we can see by continuing parallels with works derived from the *KG* like Eutropius and Victor. Yet it has long been recognized that some details of the later lives find parallels in certain later Greek works, such as the fifth-century historian Zosimus and the twelfth-century historian Zonaras. A variety of historians have been proposed as the common source, in particular the fourth-century Greek historian Eunapius and the fourth-century Latin historian Nicomachus Flavianus, though it is also possible that we have lost the name along with the work that lies behind these passages.[43] We can say little of the source, and thus little of the use of the source by the *HA*-author, but we can guess that he has freely distorted and adapted it for his own purposes.

Conclusion

The *Historia Augusta* looks like a collection of imperial biographies in the style of Suetonius, but it is fictional, not only in much of its content but even in much of its form. The imperial addresses imply a date for the work that it cannot have, just as the title pages claim multiple authors for a work by a single man. Structural features like the lacunae are inventions as well. Although the *HA*-author uses authentic historical and biographical sources, they serve only as a starting point for his playful alterations and augmentations.

Scholars have struggled to understand the *Historia Augusta* with the tools an ancient historian brings to a historiographical text. This book aims, instead, to situate the work in a literary and scholarly context by studying its most pronounced literary element, the extensive use of allusion, and to explore where such allusions would have been produced and appreciated. The *Historia Augusta* is a biographical collection in appearance alone, for it does not have biography's normal goal of instructing its readers about the lives of its subjects. It must be studied as literary fiction, not as history.

The plan of attack is as follows. In chapter 1, I survey the evidence for allusion in late Latin literature and then provide a representative sample of allusions to authors such as Cicero and Vergil in the *Historia Augusta*. The extravagance of allusion in the *Historia Augusta* makes interpretation challenging. In chapter 2 I explore what sort of audience would be able to appreciate this extravagance. I suggest that the audience would be familiar with debates over the boundaries between history, biography, and fiction that the *Historia Augusta* regularly transgresses. Drawing on recent work on the sociology of reading in the Roman empire, I argue that situating the *Historia Augusta* within an active circle of readers and interpreters helps explain the unusual use of allusion in the work. In chapter 3 I turn to the question of Christianity in the *Historia Augusta*. While many interpreters have seen anti-Christian polemic as an important, or even the most important, purpose of the work, I show that the *Historia Augusta* is, on the whole, neutral toward Christianity. It does, however, include numerous allusions to Jerome, which typically mock his radical views on food, drink, and sex. In chapter 4 I argue that

Introduction

many passages that scholars have seen as evidence for the *HA*-author's political and cultural views are in fact allusions to the historian Ammianus Marcellinus. Recognizing that its author engages with a text, not with his contemporary reality, allows for a reconsideration of the date of the *Historia Augusta*, which I tentatively set in 409. In a short afterword, I show how medieval and modern readings of the *Historia Augusta* have tried to overlook or explain away the allusive fantasies of the author. I conclude, however, that to understand the *Historia Augusta* on its own terms, we must not suppress the allusive fictions as unwelcome intrusions into a biographical work but foreground them as central to the project of author and audience.

 1   Allusion in the *Historia Augusta*

Much of the *Historia Augusta* is not based on historiographical sources. In fact, for the secondary and later lives that together make up almost half of the work, the author had very few historiographical sources to use, had he wanted to. And it is not clear that he did want to. He composed freely instead of following Marius Maximus in writing the second half of the *Elagabalus*, and he similarly composed freely instead of following Herodian in writing the *Alexander Severus*. He wrote lives of the Caesars and usurpers for whom he knew there were no reliable sources, and in the *Thirty Tyrants* and *Quadrigae Tyrannorum* he not only wrote about figures who were not usurpers as if they were usurpers but even invented usurpers who never existed and then wrote about them.

The *HA*-author has, therefore, purposefully devoted considerable amounts of his work to invention. The most striking, and perhaps most surprising, feature of this invented material is how much of it consists of allusions to literary texts. In a traditional text, an allusion, by inviting the reader to interpret the source text in light of the intertext, can have a wide variety of effects, intensifying, undermining, or recasting the original. It is natural to expect that the interpretation of allusions in the *Historia Augusta* should help clarify the author's intentions and purposes, but these interpretations have been largely unsatisfying. It has been argued, for example, that allusions to Jerome in the *Historia Augusta* should be read as anti-Christian polemic (an argument I reject in chapter 3) and, similarly, it has been argued that allusions to Ammianus in the *Historia Augusta* should be read as commentary on contemporary politics (an argument I reject in chapter 4). Allusion in the *Historia Augusta*, it turns out, goes beyond the traditional literary function of clarifying or complicating the meaning of the text through juxtaposition with a source text. The narrative of the *Historia Augusta* is often the product of such free invention that, rather than the source text commenting on the *HA*-text, the *HA*-text exists only as a commentary on the source text.

Although the *Historia Augusta* uses allusion in unusual ways, the mere presence of allusion in the work comes as no surprise. The pervasiveness of allusion in ancient literature is unquestioned. The identification and interpretation of allusion in Augustan and imperial Latin poetry is one of the most common pursuits of the modern classical philologist.[1] There is no shortage of works demonstrating a similar dynamic at play with literary prose. Tacitus alludes to Sallust, Pliny to Cicero, and Apuleius to Vergil and Ovid.[2] Ancient writers used allusion often, and ancient audiences expected it.

Certain aspects of classical reading made a great degree of allusiveness possible. Cicero and Quintilian are only two of the many ancient authorities who stress the importance of memorization.[3] Extremely close reading is depicted in a variety of contexts in antiquity. The community of readers brought to life by Aulus Gellius, for example, put a premium on memorizing and retaining a vast amount of obscure literature. The traditional process of presenting the first stages of a literary work to a sympathetic community with shared tastes and backgrounds would have increased the likelihood of successful allusion to texts known in common.[4]

The use of allusion seems to have grown more important in the literature of the later empire. One reason might be technological. Christians were early adopters of the codex form of book, using codices regularly in the second and third centuries when pagan texts were typically written on rolls. It is not until the fourth century that codices become the predominant medium for all sorts of texts. The superior nature of the codex for cross-referencing made it more valuable for readers of scripture, who would seek parallel passages and proof texts.[5] The writings of the church fathers often appear to be little more than a pastiche of biblical phrases. Since the triumph of the codex form made cross-referencing easier for Christian and non-Christian works alike, we are not surprised to find more rather than less of it.

The Bible and biblical allusion may be dismissed as a special case, but scholars have assiduously demonstrated that the major late Roman poets, such as Ausonius and Claudian, are also highly allusive.[6] In discussing the nature of late antique poetics, Roberts describes how "fragments of earlier poets, invested with brilliance and color by their original contexts, are manipulated and juxtaposed in striking new combinations, often exploiting the contrast with the previous text in sense, situation, or setting."[7] This growth in allusive complexity implies an audience ready and eager to appreciate it. Ware describes the audience of Claudian as "people who are steeped in the classics and proud of their knowledge, who are practiced in playing wordgames and who would welcome the challenge of a complicated network of intertextual allusion."[8]

The trend toward increasing allusiveness in late antique poetry reaches its apogee with the development of the *cento*, a patchwork of half-lines from Vergil or another canonical author that creates new meaning from the poetry of the past. McGill has shown how *centones* are not only *tours de force*, but, like other poetry, can be appreciated artistically by careful attention to the sources of the "allusions" that make up the whole text.[9] Irenaeus notes that an ill-informed reader of a *cento* might not understand that the poetry he sees (or hears) is a patchwork; this suggests that the more sophisticated reader or auditor of a *cento* would recognize the source text and presumably be able to appreciate the piquancy of the juxtaposition between the original context and the new context of at least some of the lines.[10] In the letter introducing his *Cento Nuptialis*, Ausonius claims to have composed the work in a day and a night, and even if we do not take this declaration literally, it must have seemed plausible that a late antique poet could have a substantial percentage of the work of Vergil memorized and at his disposal.[11]

Allusion is central to pagan prose works written in the grand style as well. In *Ammianus Marcellinus: The Allusive Historian*, Gavin Kelly has examined in detail the historian's extensive, complex levels of allusions, which encompass not just the traditional historiographical use of *exempla* or the standard allusions to canonical works but also the intricate blending of material from more than one author and the purposeful alteration of phraseology for meaningful effect.[12] Kelly rejects the dismissive approach of earlier scholars who saw the extensive use of allusion in Ammianus as affected, rote, and the product of his insufficient grasp of the Latin language. He provides many examples of allusions that illuminate their context and are sophisticated in relation to their source texts. His examples suggest that Ammianus's allusiveness is at least as extensive and skillful as what we see in Latin historians of previous generations, and I would argue considerably more so.

One particularly complex example of allusion in Ammianus, first noted by Salemme and treated in detail by Kelly, will serve to demonstrate what Ammianus could expect from his best readers in terms of recognizing and appreciating allusion.[13] Ammianus draws on the following two passages of Gellius, which concern the philosopher Favorinus:

> vocisque et *vultus gravitate composita* tamquam *interpres* et arbiter *Sibyllae oraculorum* (Gell. 4.1.1)

> *With the seriousness of his* voice and *face carefully arranged*, as if he was the *translator* and master *of the Sibyl's oracles*

> Favorinus philosophus adulescenti veterum verborum cupidissimo et
> plerasque voces nimis priscas et ignotas in cotidianis communibusque
> sermonibus expromenti: 'Curius' inquit 'et Fabricius et Coruncianus, anti-
> quiores Horatii illi trigemini plane ac dilucide cum suis fabulati sunt neque
> *Auruncorum* aut *Sicanorum* aut Pelasgorum, qui primi colisse Italiam dicun-
> tur, sed aetatis suae verbis locuti sunt; tu autem, proinde quasi *cum matre
> Evandri* nunc loquare, sermone *abhinc multis annis* iam desito uteris, quod
> scire atque intellegere neminem vis, quae dicis.' (Gell. 1.10.1–2)

> Favorinus the philosopher addressed a young man who was very fond of
> old words and used to uncork many excessively hoary and unknown phrases
> in everyday commonplace conversations: "Curius and Fabricius and Corun-
> canius, the most ancient of men, and those three Horatii, yet more ancient
> than these, would discourse simply and pellucidly with their own contem-
> poraries; they didn't speak with the words of the *Auruncians* or *Sicanians* or
> Pelasgians, who are said to have been the first inhabitants of Italy, but with
> those of their own time. You, however, since you are now speaking as if *with
> Evander's mother*, are using language that was outmoded *many years ago*
> because you want nobody to know and to understand what you are saying."

From material in these two passages of Gellius, the second of which mocks a man obsessed with antiquarianism, Ammianus creates a passage that criticizes those lawyers who specialize in arcane and ancient law:

> hi velut fata natalicia praemonstrantes, aut *Sibyllae oraculorum interpretes,
> vultus gravitate* ad habitum *composita* tristiorem, ipsum quoque venditant,
> quod oscitantur. hi ut altius videantur iura callere, *Trebatium* loquuntur et
> *Cascellium* et *Alfenum* et *Auruncorum Sicanorumque* iam diu leges ignotas,
> cum Evandri matre abhinc saeculis multis. (Amm. 30.4.11–12)

> These men, as though revealing fatal horoscopes, or the *translators of the
> Sibyl's oracles, carefully arrange their serious faces* into a gloomy expression
> and even sell the very fact that they yawn. In order to seem experts on the
> law, they talk *Trebatius* and *Cascellius* and *Alfenus* and legislation of the
> *Auruncians* and *Sicanians*, long-lost and buried *with Evander's mother many
> centuries ago*.

As Kelly notes, Ammianus has changed the "many years" of Gellius to "many centuries" to fit his subject. He needed also to replace Gellius's third-century political figures with archaic legal figures. His replacements, Trebatius, Cascellius, and Alfenus, are lawyers found in Horace (*Sat.* 2.1.4; *Ars P.* 371; *Sat.* 2.3.230). Kelly explains that in Gellius, the three names are followed by "et his antiquiores Horatii illi trigemini" ("and yet more ancient than these, those three Horatii"). Ammianus has decided on an "elaborate and jocular misreading" of the word *Horatii* as a genitive, "and older than/preferable to these, those triplets of Horace's." The three lawyers are then, naturally, taken from various works of Horace.[14] To properly appreciate this allusion, the reader must have Gellius firmly enough in mind not only to recognize the repetition of some words and phrases from two different places in the work, and to note the ways in which the words and phrases are adapted for Ammianus's new context, but even to recognize a joke that depends upon a potentially ambiguous grammatical ending. He must also be familiar enough with the works of Horace to recognize that they are the source of the names in Ammianus.

Ammianus has intensified his criticism of contemporary legalism by alluding to parallels in a predecessor, but he has done so in an extraordinarily complex way. We see that the best readers, at least, could be expected to undercover and appreciate surprisingly intricate webs of allusion.

To accept that a passage contains an authentic allusion will always remain at some level a matter of judgment. There are some general principles to consider, however, when weighing the likelihood of a passage in the *Historia Augusta* being allusive. First, a reader must consider the broad outlines of source criticism. Material in the *Hadrian* or *Marcus Aurelius*, for example, carries a presumption not so much of historical validity but of authentic dependence upon an older historical source. By contrast, the details in the secondary and late lives are usually invented, and therefore a fertile ground for the use of allusion. Second, the *HA*-author puts particular emphasis on certain authors and texts, and an accumulation of circumstantial evidence of allusions to such authors must gradually encourage acceptance.[15] The demonstration that the *Historia Augusta* certainly makes use of a few works of Jerome makes suggestions of further allusion to these and, to a lesser degree, other works of Jerome more likely. Because the work of den Hengst and Birley has definitively demonstrated the use of Ammianus by the *HA*-author, we should certainly be more open to accepting circumstantial references to Ammianus elsewhere in the text. In addition, the *HA*-author not only focuses on specific works but also tends to dwell on a discrete segment of text within each work, such as, for example, book 31 of Ammianus, which should encourage us to accept clustered allusions more easily. Third, while not an infallible method, the use of very rare words or phrases can be used as evidence of knowledge of a text and thus the possibility of allusion. Paschoud, for example, points to a few words that appear only in the works of Pliny the Elder and in the *Historia Augusta*, which must make us more open to finding allusions from Pliny there.[16]

McGill sets forth a standard technique for identifying allusion. The best approach "is to pursue readings that are plausible in terms of the textual strategies of the poems in question and the culture and moment in literary history that produced the text."[17] The difficulty of following traditional methods is exacerbated in the case of the *Historia Augusta* because while readers tend to have some shared understanding of the purpose and nature of most texts under consideration, modern consensus on the purpose and nature of the *Historia Augusta* is unsettled. As a result, readers will certainly not agree that every allusion I discuss is really an allusion, rather than a coincidence. But I hope to demonstrate here, and in the rest of the book, the general method and patterns of the *HA*-author, which depend not on the acceptance of individual claimed allusions but on the plausibility and power of the overall picture.

The rest of this chapter provides a representative selection of literary allusions in the *Historia Augusta*. They range from simple to very complex. Sometimes they offer a humorous commentary on their immediate context; at other times, the allusion itself overwhelms the putative context and becomes the focus of the reader's attention. When taken together, the allusions fail to provide any sustained or systematic tendency beyond a kind of comic anarchy.

Invented Names

The mostly fictional sections of the *Historia Augusta* are populated by scores of fictitious names. Scholars who would have preferred to avoid the problems of the *Historia Augusta* have been forced, in the compilation of prosopographical collections, to develop criteria to judge their reliability.[18] The anachronistic appearance of some names was adduced as evidence in Dessau's first article on the *Historia Augusta*, and Domaszewski wrote an early, eccentric monograph on the question.[19] There are many conceivable ways in which a writer might invent false names, so it is surely significant how often literary allusion appears to be the *HA*-author's starting point.

Among the invented names, the names of the six authors, which must certainly be false, are of particular interest. Not all can be easily interpreted, but they present some provocative possibilities. Peter and Honoré agreed that Trebellius Pollio was particularly associated with usurpers, given his authorship of the *Thirty Tyrants*, although both had explanations that were not especially compelling. Peter connected the name to one of the Thirty Tyrants, Trebellianus,[20] and Honoré, tentatively, pointed to the rare word *rebellio*.[21] Allusion to Cicero and Juvenal provides a more interesting explanation. A certain Trebellius was a partisan of Mark Antony mentioned in Cicero's *Philippics* and in a letter to Cicero from D. Brutus (*Fam.* 11.13).[22] In this letter Brutus states that he managed to arrive with his army in the town of Pollentia an hour before Trebellius did. Domaszewski suggests that the word Pollentia made the author think of Asinius Pollio, another partisan of Antony's. The *HA*-author thereby, he argues, celebrates two rebels of the end of the republic in the name of the biographer of imperial rebels. Den Hengst added two more elements to the consideration of the name Pollio.[23] He points to Juvenal, *Satires* 6.385–88:

> quaedam de numero Lamiarum ac nominis Appi
> et farre et uino Ianum Vestamque rogabat,
> an Capitolinam deberet Pollio quercum
> sperare

> A certain woman from the family of the Lamiae, with an Appian name,
> was asking Janus and Vesta, with wine and grain,
> whether Pollio ought to hope to win
> the Capitoline oak

The poet portrays a woman wondering whether a certain Pollio will win the "Capitoline oak," a reference to the prize for victory in the Capitoline games, a crown made of oak leaves. But for the *HA*-author, den Hengst suggests, the meaning is that Pollio will succeed Julius Capitolinus, the author of the previous sequence of lives. Den Hengst also furthers the connection with Asinius Pollio. In the preface to the life of Firmus, Vopiscus praises Trebellius Pollio for his diligence, while in the preface to the *Aurelian* he reports criticism of Trebellius Pollio for his lack of diligence. In both cases, the language mirrors Asinius Pollio's criticism, reported by Suetonius (*Iul.* 56), of the *Commentaries* of Julius Caesar. Birley has taken the analysis of the name one step further.[24] The Trebellius from the *Philippics* whom Domaszewski had adduced had assumed the cognomen Fides for political purposes, and is denounced by Cicero for the presumption (*Phil.* 6.11). Birley argues that the theme of historical faithfulness is particularly emphasized after the introduction of Trebellius Pollio. He adds that L. Trebellius Fides had an important political ally when he was tribune, namely, Asinius Pollio. We need not settle on a particular "correct" answer for the source of the name. It evokes multiple authors and figures, and the themes of faithfulness and diligence with which both historical Pollios were associated in different ways.

Flavius Vopiscus may also owe his name to a literary allusion. Hohl noted in 1912 that *vopiscus* is a rare Latin word with a striking meaning.[25] According to Pliny the Elder (*HN* 7.47), it refers to the twin who survives and is born when his sibling dies in the womb. Thus Vopiscus should be understood as the last to survive out of the "sextuplets" who make up the author of the *Historia Augusta*.[26] The name is found in Cicero in a passage in the *Philippics* (11.11) where Bestia is referred to as "alter Caesar Vopiscus."[27] Caesar Vopiscus plays a major part in Cicero's dialogue *De Oratore* (2.217–97).[28] In that dialogue, Vopiscus discusses at length the use of jokes and witticisms in speech, and Cicero praises his wit in other contexts, as well. It is certainly appropriate for the author of the last and most inventive lives to be associated with a notorious joker. There is more: when Vopiscus begins to speak about jokes, he claims that the Sicilians, first of all, have distinguished themselves in wit, which, presumably, explains the cognomen Syracusius (*De or.* 2.217).

Julius Capitolinus is, appropriately enough, the narrator, in the *Maximus and Balbinus*, of the events of 238 that unfolded on the Capitol. This life alludes in several places to speeches of Cicero, including the *Philippics* and the *De domo sua*.[29] In the latter, Cicero complains that his rival Clodius had called him "hostem Capitolinum"—the "enemy of the Capitoline" (*Dom.* 7). He claims that he should rather be known as the defender of the Capitoline and its temples, implicitly likening himself to the M. Manlius Capitolinus who had defended the citadel during the Gallic siege. Chastagnol suggests that Cicero's discussion of the pseudonym Capitolinus inspired the *HA*-author to create not only the author "Julius Capitolinus" but also the entire idea of pseudonymous group history.

Vulcacius (also spelled Volcacius or Vulcatius) Gallicanus is granted authorship of only a single life, the *Avidius Cassius*. There are several figures of interest with this first name. A historian Vulcatius is cited in the *Origo Gentis Romanae* (10.2), a text of the later fourth century.[30] Another Vulcatius is mentioned as a commentator on Cicero in a letter of Jerome dating to 397 or 398 (*Ep.* 70.2; also *Apologia adversus libros Rufini* 1.16). The *HA*-author seems to be versed both in Cicero and in the commentary-culture. The most compelling identification, however, is with Vulcatius Sedigitus, a republican scholar who created a canon of Roman comic playwrights. Fragments of his work are quoted in Suetonius's life of Terence (see also Gell. 3.3.1). The existence of a fake historian named, significantly, Vulcatius Terentianus at *Three Gordians* 21.5 suggests that the *HA*-author was familiar with Vulcatius Sedigitus, perhaps through his own reading of Suetonius. As with Vopiscus, then, Vulcacius may also allude to a figure associated with humor. The meaning of the rest of the name is obscure. The cognomen Gallicanus simply means "from Gaul," a form similar to Syracusius, but no exceptional explanation has been offered. Domaszewski pointed to *Gallicanus* at *Pro Cluentio* 23, but there seems to be nothing compelling about this identification.[31] The *v.c.* that follows his name represents the noble title of *clarissimus*, which is not attributed to any other of the authors. This suggested to Baldwin an affiliation with the fourth-century senator Vulcacius Rufinus, who was the uncle of Julian's half-brother Gallus.[32] The resemblance of "Gallus" and "Gallicanus" perhaps strengthens this suggestion, for, as Baldwin notes, *V. C.* "from the ocular point of view" bears a close similarity to *V.G.*, the abbreviation of the name Vulcacius Gallicanus. But neither Gallicanus nor *v.c.* has been adequately explained.

The surnames Spartianus and Lampridius have also proven resistant to interpretation. The author invents the name Lampridia for the mother of Pescennius Niger (1.3), as a kind of joke: *Niger* has a father, Annius *Fuscus* ("dusky"),[33] and a mother whose name seems related to *lampas*, a light or torch, in a life that is filled with color puns. Even less can be said about Spartianus, a name that is obviously reminiscent of Sparta, although the Latin for Spartan is actually *Spartanus*.[34] Aulus Gellius describes a scene where a young man denies the equivalence of the Latin *spartum* and the Homeric *sparta* (*Il.* 2.135), producing mocking laughter that is silenced by the authority of a text of Varro (17.3). Perhaps this scene of laughter was recalled by the *HA*-author, with "Aelius" derived from "Aulus."

The *HA*-author discusses, criticizes, and claims as sources about thirty-four fake historians and biographers, Syme's so-called bogus authors.[35] The author has not typically relied on the sort of bland name for these sources that we would expect from an author who seeks to trick his reader into readily accepting their authenticity. Instead, the names themselves are often contrived from literary allusions that challenge the reader's interpretative ability.

Details about the daily routine of the emperor Tacitus are attributed by the *HA*-author to a biographer with the suggestive name of Suetonius Optatianus (11.7). The name Suetonius is very rare, and the likelihood of another biographer sharing his name is remote.[36] While some of the allusions in the *Historia Augusta* demand considerable knowledge to unravel, the use of the name Suetonius would be clearly identifiable as a kind of joke, and would encourage a reader to approach other elements of the work with great suspicion. The name Optatianus recalls the Constantinian-era poet Publilius Optatianus Porphyrius, who wrote poetry of the sort now referred to as *technopaegnia*.[37] Some of his poems were written as shapes, such as an altar, a water-organ, or a syrinx. Others, when read properly, can be found to contain hidden, patterned verses within the poem proper. Levitan refers to the "gaudy triviality" of Optatianus's verse, and sums up his project as "a modest endeavor to be sure, but one on a preposterous scale." Suetonius Optatianus is therefore the perfect name for a writer who specializes in extravagant biographies with secrets hidden within, a type for the *HA*-author himself.[38]

The *HA*-author mentions two similarly named biographers: Valerius Marcellinus, who is praised at *Maximus and Balbinus* 4.5, and Fabius Marcellinus, who pops up at *Alexander Severus* 48.6 and then again at *Probus* 2.7. These are surely meant to evoke the historian Ammianus Marcellinus, whom the *HA*-author knew well. It may be that other sources of the *Historia Augusta* are lightly camouflaged in the work. In particular, "Aurelius Victor with the cognomen Pinius" is cited as a source in *Macrinus* 4.2, and a few lines below a character has the suggestive name of Festus, which he shares with a fourth-century Latin historian.[39]

Palfurius Sura is credited with maintaining an *ephemeris* of the life of Gallienus (*Gall*.18.3). The word should mean an account book or calendar, and so it may be that Sura is not a historian but an imperial official who recorded the extravagant expenses of the emperor. In any case, his name is identical with that of a senator, poet, and orator who had been banished by Vespasian but eventually recalled by Domitian.[40] The Juvenal scholiast lets slip some colorful details of his life (he participated in a public wrestling match with a Spartan woman) derived from the Marius Maximus life of Nerva (*Scholia ad Iuvenalem* 4.53). Such a character would be the ideal chronicler of the dissolute Gallienus.

The *HA*-author feigns outrage at the historian Gallus Antipater for obsequiously praising the usurper Aureolus (*Claud.* 5.4). The origin of his name is particularly complex. Antipater is described as "ancilla honorum et historicorum dehonestamentum" ("the slave girl and dishonor of all honors and historians").[41] This is an allusion to Sallust's description of a crony of Sulla's: "Fufidius, ancilla turpis, honorum omnium dehonestamentum" ("Fufidius, foul handmaiden and dishonor of all honors," *Hist.* 1.55.21). Ammianus had alluded to the same Sallustian passage in discussing the usurper Procopius: "ad hoc igitur dehonestamentum honorum omnium ludibriose sublatus, et ancillari adulatione, beneficii allocutus auctores" ("Raised in a laughable manner to this dishonor of all honors, he addressed his supporters with servile flattery," 26.6.16). The *HA*-author has echoed Ammianus by using the Sallustian tag in the context of usurpation but has transferred the attack to the historian rather than the usurper. The Sallust passage and the *Historia Augusta* imitation represent the only two times in Latin literature that *ancilla*, a female slave, is used to describe a man. Konrad suggests that in the Sallustian context the point of the word is that Fufidius, a man of low social origin, had obtained power under Sulla by serving the dictator sexually.[42] From where did the *HA*-author derive the name Gallus Antipater? In the *Hadrian* we find the claim, presumably from Marius Maximus, that the emperor preferred a number of archaic

Latin authors to their classical epigones, in particular "Cato to Cicero, Ennius to Vergil, and Coelius to Sallust" (16.3). This Coelius is Coelius Antipater, a historian contemporary with the Gracchi and praised by Cicero. Thus, ironically, despite Hadrian's preference for Antipater over Sallust, the new Antipater is characterized by a Sallustian allusion. And perhaps the fact that this allusion involves a man charged with allowing himself to be used sexually by a superior is particularly appropriate in a Hadrianic context, given the notorious relationship between the emperor and his favorite, Antinous (*Hadr.* 14.6).

The author Gargilius Martialis, twice cited by the *Historia Augusta*, appears to be a medical writer pressed into service as a biographer. While the *HA*-author often invents names, there are no precedents for his decision to convert a real person into a false authority. The name itself, with its potential for allusion, may explain the anomaly. Gargilius Martialis is first described as an author contemporary with Alexander Severus who provided a detailed enumeration of the foods that made up the emperor's diet (*Alex.* 37.9). Later he appears in *Probus* 2.7 in a list of "truthful but inelegant" biographers that begins with a couple of real biographers but continues with several fraudulent ones. Gargilius Martialis is the name of a real writer, an African who wrote, probably in the third century, several treatises on the medicinal uses of plants that survive today only in fragments.[43] Given Gargilius's pairing with "Fabius Marcellinus" in the *Probus*, we cannot follow those scholars who suggest that he might be an actual biographer of Alexander Severus. In the first mention of Gargilius, he is not credited with a biography but with a list of foodstuffs, a topic that befits his botanical and medicinal interests. The *HA*-author is thus likely referring to a real work, probably at second hand via Marius Maximus.[44] This mention of Gargilius Martialis in his source inspired the *HA*-author to think of his namesake, the first-century poet Martial, whom he quotes in the immediately following section of the *Alexander* (38.2; cf. Mart. 5.29). The Martial poem that he cites derives its humor from the belief that eating a hare would result in seven days of beauty, intended ostensibly as commentary on Alexander's habit of eating a hare each day (37.7). But this must reverse the actual order of invention—first the name Martialis leads the author to the poet Martial, and then the chapter is primed with subject matter appropriate for a poem by Martial to comment on. Beyond the reference to hares, there are several other topics in the paragraph that recall favorite subjects of Martial, such as appropriate etiquette at banquets or in gift giving. The sentence immediately after the hare discussion is particularly interesting: "nec divitibus quicquam talium munerum misit, sed ab his semper accepit" ("For he never gave any of these gifts to the rich, though he was always ready to receive presents from them," *Alex.* 37.8). This feels almost like a response to Martial's *Epigram* 4.56, where the poet criticizes his addressee for giving lavish gifts to the rich with the expectation of a legacy. Of course, this is hardly an obscure theme, except that the poem is one of five that Martial addresses to a certain Gargilianus. The *HA*-author seems to have found enough amusement in combining the name of a risqué poet with one of the poet's creations that he made him one of the "truthful" biographers whom our author took as a model.

We find a similar pattern in considering Fabius Ceryllianus, who is cited as the author of a "very careful" history of the times of Carus, Carinus, and Numerian, and as a participant in the debate over the true birthplace of Carus (*Car.* 4.3). This pseudo-debate, discussed further in chapter 4, is based on a passage of Suetonius (*Gaius* 8) in which the biographer offers contested sources for the birthplace of Caligula. The *HA*-author follows Suetonius in portraying himself as sorting through the testimony of several historians and some pieces of documentary evidence to get at the truth. The parody of Suetonius primes us to find a source for the name Ceryllianus in the earlier biographer. Sure enough, the life of Vespasian discusses a certain Cerylus, a freedman who changed his name to imply free birth in order to avoid a higher estate tax upon his death (Suet. *Vesp.* 23.1). Cerylus is mocked by Vespasian with a quotation from Menander in a chapter that would appeal to our author, since it retails the sexual and scatological jokes attributed to the emperor. Cerylus in addition was famous for his name change, as we can see in Martial's *Epigram* 1.67 and Vergil's *Catalepton* 10.7.[45] It is appropriate that he suffer, at the hands of the *HA*-author, another name change, and likewise a change of profession.

To the alert reader the *HA*-author makes it perfectly clear that he is inventing or manipulating names. The son of Gallienus, for example, was named Saloninus. The reason he was given this name is clear and is stated in the biography a few lines after he is introduced: he was named after his mother, Salonina (*Gall.* 21.3), whom Gallienus deeply loved. But the *HA*-author creates a fictitious controversy over the source of the name, claiming that some thought the name derived from his birth in the city of Salonae in Dalmatia (19.3). There is, indeed, a controversy in antiquity over a certain Saloninus, but it is found in the scholarly commentaries on Vergil rather than imperial nomenclature. Many participants in the ancient commentary tradition claim that the mystery child in the fourth eclogue of Vergil was the son of Asinius Pollio, Saloninus, named in honor of Pollio's conquest of Salonae (Servius on *Ecl.* 4.1), or perhaps just because he was born there.[46]

The historian Acholius appears three times in the *Alexander Severus* as a "historian of his times," and then reemerges in the *Aurelian* holding the office of *magister admissionum* under Valerian.[47] Paschoud points to the Acholius who was *vicarius Asiae* around 400, but Domaszewksi is probably correct in arguing that the *HA*-author had in mind Acholius, also called Ascholius, the bishop of

Thessalonica who baptized Theodosius.⁴⁸ Domaszewski's suggestion has been dismissed because, in keeping with his belief that the *HA* was written in the sixth century, he argued that the *HA*-author derived the name Acholius from the *Getica* of Jordanes, written in 551. An easier source, however, lay at hand for the author. Acholius is eulogized by Ambrose in two letters, *Epistles* 15 and 16, written in 383. The letters themselves are unremarkable, but in the two that follow (17 and 18), Ambrose beseeches Valentinian to reject attempts by pagans to reintroduce the Altar of Victory into the senate house. The *HA*-author elsewhere demonstrates his familiarity with these letters and this controversy. In particular, Paschoud shows that the debate in the senate described in chapters 19 and 20 of the *Aurelian*, only a few chapters after the reemergence of Acholius in chapter 12, is a tissue of allusions to these letters.⁴⁹ The Altar of Victory makes an appearance just a few lines before the first introduction of Acholius (*Aur.* 14.2 and 14.6). In his plea for the return of the Altar of Victory, Symmachus asks, "Since all reason is concealed, from where can knowledge of the divine come more rightly than from memory and evidence of favorable events?" ("Nam cum ratio omnis in operto sit, unde rectius quam de *memoria* atque documentis *rerum* secundarum cognitio venit numinum?," Symm. *Relat.* 3.8). At Acholius's first introduction, Alexander is said to have an exceptional memory for things ("*rerum memoria* singularis"), though Acholius used to say, the *HA*-author claims, that he used a mnemonic device (*mnemonicum*), a word otherwise absent from classical Latin. The "thing that inspires memory" perhaps evokes the Altar. In addition, both of Ambrose's earlier letters, 15 and 16, in eulogizing the deceased Acholius, praise in particular his wide-ranging travels; perhaps this is why Acholius is said to have written specifically about the travels of Alexander Severus (*Alex.* 64.5).

Two of the more extravagant names will round out this section. First, Syme rightly calls the name of the historian Maeonius Astyanax, with its doubled Homericisms evoking Troy, a "romantic fantasy" (*Tyr. Trig.* 12.3).⁵⁰ Both Maeonius Astyanax and his namesake, the cousin of Odenathus named Maeonius (*Tyr. Trig.*15.5), appear, appropriately, in eastern contexts. Second, the exotic names of the parents of the emperor Maximinus, Micca and Hababa (*Maximin.* 1.5), derive from a creative interpretation of Herodian (6.8.1):

ἦν δέ τις ἐν τῷ στρατῷ Μαχιμῖνος ὄνομα, τὸ μὲν γένος τῶν ἐνδοτάτω Θρακῶν καὶ μιξοβαρβάρων.

In the army there was a certain man, Maximinus by name, whose ancestry was from one of the semibarbarians in the depths of Thrace.

The *HA*-author takes τὸ γένος not as "race" or "stock," as Herodian intended it, but as "offspring," making him the child of "semibarbarians," μιξοβαρβάρων. Then μιξο- and -βαρβάρων were decomposed into the name of a father and mother, Micca and Hababa![51]

Cicero

Cicero was the most important prose writer for the late Roman period. The name of Cicero occurs nineteen times in the *Historia Augusta*, and six of these mentions include citations, from six different works. Allusions to his work, sometimes quite elaborate, are scattered throughout the *Historia Augusta*. They serve to test the literary knowledge and ingenuity of the reader, and sometimes they are more amusing when their immediate context in the *Historia Augusta* is considered. Overall, however, they mirror other allusions in the *Historia Augusta* in evincing no single purpose or agenda.

The *HA*-author enlivens, by means of a Ciceronian allusion, a dramatic scene in the *Aurelian*. The emperor, at war with the eastern usurper Zenobia of Palmyra, laid siege to the city of Tyana in Asia Minor. Our author claims that Tyana fell when a certain Heraclammon betrayed his native city and allowed the Roman army to enter. Despite Heraclammon's service to Rome, Aurelian, out of disgust at his treachery, sentenced him to death. Reflecting upon this fable, the *HA*-author praises Aurelian for his mixture of severity (*severitas*) and leniency (*lenitas*), the one for allowing the execution of Heraclammon, the other for refusing to indulge the desire of the soldiers to thoroughly sack and loot the city (*Aur.* 23.1). Elaborating on this theme, the author conjures up a letter supposedly written by the emperor himself to an otherwise-unknown Mallius Chilo, in which he explains that he is unable to love traitors, and that he could not trust anyone who would betray his native land (23.4). As Paschoud points out, this name must evoke the name Q. Manlius Chilo, which is found in the manuscripts of Cicero's third Catilinarian (3.14) in a list of members of the Catilinarian conspiracy.[52] The real name of this man was Q. Annius Chilo, as we see in Sallust (*Cat.* 17.3; 50.4), so we can be certain that the *HA*-author is using the text of Cicero, which suffered early corruption, and is not depending on his own general knowledge of late republican history. The name was not chosen at random. At this point in the speech, Cicero is telling the Roman people that upon recognition of the vast conspiracy, the Senate acted with leniency (*lenitas*, 15) in arresting only nine men, Chilo among them, in the hope that punishing them would turn the other traitors away from madness. Aurelian's correspondent, then, has a kind of personal knowledge about the benefits of punishing only a small number of miscreants. The *HA*-author is not making a more general statement about clemency or its opposite, only playing with the idea inherent in Aurelian's sparing of the city and challenging his reader to recognize the game.

Knowledge of Cicero is also essential for understanding an amusing discussion of the genealogy of the emperor Balbinus. Balbinus's ancestry, according to the sources at the disposal of the *Historia Augusta*, was contested: Herodian states that Balbinus was of aristocratic origin (7.10.4; 8.8.4), while Eutropius and so probably the *KG* say that he was ignoble (9.2.1). The *HA*-author has Balbinus "respond" to the controversy by asserting that he could trace his genealogy to republican times (*Max. et Balb.* 7.3):

> familiae vetustissimae, ut ipse dicebat, a Balbo Cornelio Theofane originem ducens, qui per Gnaeum Pompeium civitatem meruerat, cum esset suae patriae nobilissimus idemque historiae scriptor.

> He came of a very ancient family, so he himself used to claim, tracing his descent from Balbus Cornelius Theophanes, who had won citizenship through the agency of Gnaeus Pompey, since he was most noble in his own country and likewise a writer of history.

This is garbled history. The historian Pompeius Theophanes took Cornelius Balbus as his son by adoption, as we know from Cicero (*Balb.* 57; *Att.* 7.7.6).[53] Balbinus's self-asserted and inaccurate claim to nobility represents the *HA*-author's response to the contradiction in his sources. The best reader will then know of divergent accounts of Balbinus's ancestry and will recognize that his inaccurate genealogical information, disproved thanks to knowledge of Cicero, shows him in fact to be ignoble, despite his claim. Of course, there is no reason to believe that the author, or his audience, either knew or cared what the actual background of Balbinus was.

We see a more complicated engagement with Cicero in the case of a double allusion in the *Elagabalus* and the *Alexander Severus* to a passage in the oration *Pro Roscio*.[54] The lives of Elagabalus and Alexander Severus create a diptych in which the author presents an extreme, fictionalized vision of the very worst and then the very best of emperors. In the *Pro Roscio*, Cicero argues that his client is the victim of Chrysogonus, a corrupt henchman of Sulla who has enriched himself unjustly. The description of Chrysogonus's luxurious lifestyle includes the following (*Rosc. Am.* 46.133):

> domus referta vasis Corinthiis et *Deliacis*, in quibus est *authepsa* illa quam tanto pretio nuper mercatus est ut qui praetereuntes praeconem numerare audiebant fundum venire arbitrarentur. quid praeterea *caelati argenti*, quid stragulae vestis, quid pictarum tabularum, quid signorum, quid marmoris apud illum putatis esse?

> a house crammed with *Delian* and Corinthian vessels, among them that *authepsa*, which he recently bought at so high a price that the passers-by, hearing the auctioneer counting out the money, thought that an estate was being sold. In addition, how many items of *embossed silver*, coverlets, pictures, statues, marbles do you think he has at his place?

The word *authepsa*, a kind of "automatic cooker," occurs only once more in Latin literature, in one of the fictional sections of the *Elagabalus* (19.3):

> primus deinde *authepsas* argenteas habuit, primus etiam caccabos, vasa deinde centenaria *argentea* et *scalpta* nonnulla schematibus libidinosissimis inquinata.

> He was the first to use *authepsae* and cooking pots made of *chased silver*, one hundred pounds in weight, some of them defiled by the lewdest designs.

Elagabalus's depravity is proven by the way he outdoes the Ciceronian villain in luxury. He not only possesses multiple examples of the rare *authepsa* but is the first to have them made of silver. Cicero claimed that Chrysogonus possessed embossed silver, and so Elagabalus's silver cookware pieces are also embossed—of course, in his case with perverted sexual images. This is one of many passages in the *Elagabalus* where the emperor is defined in terms of his ability to outdo tyrants of the past in depravity.

The same passage of *Pro Roscio* also left its mark in the *Alexander*. Alexander presented modest gifts to the temples of Isis and Serapis at Rome (26.8):

> Iseum et Serapeum decenter ornavit additis signis et *Deliacis* et omnibus mysticis.

> The shrines of Isis and Serapis he supplied modestly with statues, *Deliaca*, and all the apparatus used in mystic rites.

The adjective *Deliaci*, Delian, is quite rare in Latin literature, and given the proximity to *authepsa*, Dunand convincingly concludes that the same passage in Cicero is the source.[55] The word describes vases in Cicero, so we should understand it here to mean "objects of Delian bronze." Why does the *HA*-author emphasize that Alexander gave gifts of bronze to the sanctuaries? We learn later in the life that Alexander "gave no gold and only a little silver" to temples, relying on the principle expressed in an adapted line of Persius: "in sanctis quid facit aurum" ("what place has gold in sanctuaries?," *Alex.* 44.9; cf. Persius 2.69, with *sanctis* for *sancto*). Bronze gifts, by contrast, are modest (*decenter*), and may seem especially modest when paired with the much more famous Corinthian bronze (cf. Pliny, *HN* 34.9). Cicero also links Corinthian and Delian bronze in his second speech against Verres (2.4.131), so the *HA*-author might think of the word as peculiarly Ciceronian. Thus the luxury of Elagabalus, and the modesty of Alexander, are both emphasized by the same passage in the same speech of Cicero.

Twice the *HA*-author refers to the office of proconsul of Cilicia (*Aur.* 42.4; *Car.* 4.6). Since the office did not exist in the imperial period, the *HA*-author must be inspired by the example of Cicero, the most famous holder of the office (in 51–50 B.C.E.).[56] A closer look at the two passages reveals that the allusion to Cicero is extended in each case. In the *Aurelian*, first, we are told that the emperor had a daughter whose grandson, Aurelianus, was once proconsul of Cilicia. This invented figure followed in the footsteps of Cicero by being widely revered as the best of senators, *senator optimus*. At the time of the purported writing of the *Historia Augusta*, we are told that Aurelianus lives in Sicily. Cicero, of course, served as *quaestor* in Sicily in 75, whence a delegation of Sicilians urged him to undertake the successful prosecution of Verres that lifted him to a new level of fame and influence. And Cicero's desire to serve his exile in Sicily in 58 was thwarted by an amendment to the law of Clodius forbidding him to reside within four hundred miles of Rome (*Planc.* 95–96; *Att.* 3.4). Since the grandson Aurelian is fictitious, the allusion cannot have been contrived to make a biographical evaluation. Instead, the character has been invented to allow for a series of Ciceronian allusions.

A Ciceronian atmosphere also pervades the beginning of the *Carus*, where the *HA*-author offers a number of fictitious sources who differ over whether Carus was born at Rome or not. He cites two (fictitious) documents in which Carus himself claims to be of Roman origin. In the first, Carus is credited with holding the office of proconsul of Cilicia (4.6–7):

> epistula Cari: 'Marcus Aurelius Carus, pro consule Ciliciae, Iunio legato suo. maiores nostri, Romani illi principes, in legatis creandis hac usi sunt

consuetudine, ut morum suorum specimen per eos ostenderent quibus rem publicam delegabant. ego vero, si ita non esset, aliter non fecissem: nec feci aliter si, te iuvante, non fallar; fac igitur, ut maioribus nostris, id est Romanis non discrepemus viris.'

The letter of Carus: "From Marcus Aurelius Carus, proconsul of Cilicia, to his legate Junius. Our ancestors, the chief men of Rome, in choosing their legates observed the following custom, to reveal a sample of their own characters in those to whom they put in charge of the republic. If this were not so, I myself would not have done otherwise, and I have not done otherwise, with your help, if I am not mistaken. Therefore, act so that we may not be different from our ancestors, that is, the Romans."

Junius is not an uncommon name, but perhaps we see a reference in it to C. Junius (*aedile* in 75), the judge whom Cicero defended in the *Pro Cluentio* (89–96). The invocation of *maiores nostri*, "our ancestors," to set out a general principle, is again not the most uncommon trope in Latin literature, but it appears to be particularly Ciceronian. There are four examples in the *Pro Cluentio* alone, for example. In a search of the texts in the Packard Humanities Institute Latin corpus, we find the phrase *maiores nostri* more frequently in Cicero than all other authors combined (67 times in Cicero out of a total of 120 times in all of classical Latin, or 56 percent), and a similar proportion for the two words in all cases (148 out of 247, or 60 percent). *Maiores nostri* is found only one other time in the *Historia Augusta* (at *Thirty Tyrants* 32.5). This passage is also Ciceronian in its suggestion that the fictitious character Calpurnia derives her ancestry from the republican Pisones, since the *HA*-author cites or alludes to Cicero's speech *In Pisonem* on several occasions.[57] The *HA*-author, then, contrived a fake scholarly controversy over the birthplace of Carus in which the emperor claims Roman origins. The Ciceronian phrase *maiores nostri* was natural enough in the context, but for the attentive reader the author embellished the passage with further Ciceronian detail, including the title of *proconsul Ciliciae* itself.

In the second letter cited in the passage, this one supposedly written to the senate, Carus emphasizes the shared bond of *Romanitas* between himself and his audience (*Car.* 5.2–3):

Gaudendum est itaque, patres conscripti, quod unus ex vestro ordine, vestri etiam generis imperator est factus. quare adnitemur ne meliores peregrini quam vestri esse videantur.

> And so, conscript Fathers, you should rejoice that one of your own order and your own nation has been made emperor. We will ensure that no foreigners will seem to be better men than one of yours.

This letter continues the Ciceronian theme through its conclusion with the famous clausula "esse videantur."[58] The trochee-and-third-paeon ending was strongly associated with Cicero, as the third-century grammarian Sacerdos shows: "chorius et paeon tertius facient illam structuram Tullio peculiarem, 'esse videatur'" ("the trochee and third paeon will make that clausula peculiar to Cicero and known as the 'esse videatur,'" Keil, *Gramm. Lat.* 6.494.27–28). The affectation was also noted by Quintilian (10.2.18) and mocked by Tacitus (*Dial.* 22.7).[59] Ironically, the emperor claims Roman origins in the language of Cicero, himself not Roman-born. But again the situation has been contrived in service of the allusions. Carus was probably from Narbo in Gaul; his brief reign as emperor was dedicated to fighting Germans and Persians, and he had no need for or interest in senatorial support.

A Ciceronian allusion probably lies behind an unusual detail in the *Claudius*. The author describes the three honors that he claims the senate had granted to the emperor: a silver shield in the senate house, a golden statue on the Capitol, and a column on the Rostra topped by a silver statue (*Claud.* 3.3–5). These are fairly unremarkable details in the context of the extravagant panegyric that the emperor receives throughout the life, but they raise a question. Eutropius (9.11.2) and the *Epitome* (34.4) both mention the silver shield and the golden statue, so we can assume that the *HA*-author derived them from the *KG*. The column, however, comes as a surprise. A quotation from Ennius that the author offers later in the life, in order to support his equation of Claudius with the republican hero Scipio, provides the key (*Claud.* 7.7).[60] About Scipio, Ennius had written: "quantam statuam faciet populus R., quantam columnam, quae res tuas gestas loquatur?" ("How great a statue will the Roman people make, how great a column, to speak of your deeds?"). This is probably an authentic piece of Ennius, somewhat adapted; Courtney sees clear traces of trochaic rhythm, and Horace seems to have alluded to it in the *Odes* (*Carm.* 4.8.13).[61] The only other evidence of Ennius in the *Historia Augusta* is apparently derived from Cicero, and this phrase too was likely harvested from a lost work of the orator.[62] The very name of Claudius is reminiscent of one of the greatest families of the Roman republic, and Victor (34.2) also evoked the republic in his comparison of Claudius with the Decii, the father and son who sacrificed themselves on behalf of Rome. The combination of the statue and shield found in Eutropius or the *KG*, and the evocation of the republic in Victor or the *KG*, prompted the author to cite the passage from Ennius, the panegyricist of one of the greatest of republican heroes, Scipio Africanus. By adding a column to the list of honors the *KG* had provided, the author makes his citation more "accurate." The attentive reader, familiar with the *KG* and Cicero, could appreciate and enjoy the enhanced honor that Claudius received at the author's hands. The augmentation likewise serves to parody the excessive panegyric of the life by emphasizing the author's willingness to go beyond his historical sources.

Many more examples of Ciceronian allusion can be found in the *Historia Augusta*, but this representative sample reveals a variety of aspects of the author's engagement. Sometimes the allusions are complex. Often they can be recognized by the use of striking names or unusual words. The effect is usually humorous, a humor derived from appreciation of cleverness rather than serving any more pointed or serious purpose. Frequently, allusion comes first—rather than a Ciceronian intertext serving the text by commenting on its meaning, the text itself is invented in order to allow for the intrusion of the Ciceronian intertext.

Pliny, Horace, and More

Particularly bizarre elements of the *Historia Augusta* often raise questions that are best answered by consultation of other texts. Such is the case for an allusion to Pliny the Elder in the life of the usurper Firmus.[63] This usurper is a complete invention of the author, and thus every detail about him is fabricated. The *HA*-author, in trumpeting the wealth of this character, adds an odd detail (*Quad. Tyr.* 3.2): "perhibetur ... tantum habuisse de chartis ut publice saepe diceret exercitum se alere posse papyro et glutine" ("It is said ... that he had so many books that he used often to say in public that he could support an army on the paper and glue"). The meaning of Firmus's boast is not immediately clear. The interpretation of Gibbon has been a common one: "[He] raised an army, which, he vainly boasted, he was capable of maintaining from the sole profits of his paper trade."[64] But for the alert reader of Pliny, there is another, humorous, way to understand Firmus's statement. In his section on the manufacture of paper, Pliny notes that the Egyptians sometimes make a kind of chewing gum out of papyrus (*HN* 13.72), and then a little later in his discussion describes the substance *gluten* as a glue constructed from flour, water, and vinegar, and thus, we must imagine, similarly edible (13.82). The Firmus of the *Historia Augusta* is monstrous, a man known for feats of strength and gluttony and called by the nickname "Cyclops." It is no surprise that such a man's book collection is meant for the belly, not the mind. If a reader should doubt or miss the Pliny allusion, the *HA*-author provides another a few lines later. Firmus is likened to the gladiator "Tritannum ... cuius Varro meminit" ("Tritannus, of whom Varro makes mention," *Quad. Tyr.* 4.2).

The source is probably not direct knowledge of Varro, but rather Pliny (*HN* 7.81), who attributes his information to Varro.

A fairly banal verse of Horace quoted in the *Avidius Cassius* takes on particular resonance if we read each passage in context. The life is a short secondary biography with little factual value. About half of it is dedicated to the reactions among the Roman aristocracy and the imperial family to Avidius's failed attempt at revolution. In response to the uprising, the emperor Marcus was clement and sparing. He treats the vengeful to a history lesson in which he argues that those emperors who were overthrown deserved their fate, while the good emperors, despite attempts on their lives, survived. The *HA*-author claims that although some thought that Marcus's wife, Faustina, was the instigator of the revolt, (fictional) letters reveal that she wanted Avidius's followers punished very severely (*Av. Cass.* 11.2–8):

> cui Antoninus quid rescripserit, subdita epistula perdocebit: 'tu quidem, mea Faustina, religiose pro marito et pro nostris liberis agis. nam relegi epistulam tuam in Formiano, qua me hortaris, ut in Avidii conscios vindicem. ego vero et eius liberis parcam et genero et uxori et ad senatum scribam, ne aut proscriptio gravior sit aut poena crudelior. non enim quicquam est, quod imperatorem Romanum melius commendet gentibus quam clementia. haec Caesarem deum fecit, haec Augustum consecravit, haec patrem tuum specialiter Pii nomine ornavit. denique si ex mea sententia de bello iudicatum esset, nec Avidius esset occisus. esto igitur secura: "di me tuentur, dis pietas mea / cordi est."'

> The following letter will demonstrate what Antoninus wrote back to her: "You are indeed, my Faustina, acting scrupulously on behalf of your husband and our children. For I reread your letter at Formiae in which you urged me to take vengeance on those who conspired with Avidius. But I will spare his children and son-in-law and wife, and I will write to the senate forbidding any excessive confiscation or overly cruel punishment. For there is nothing which commends a Roman emperor to the nations as much as clemency. This made Caesar a god, this deified Augustus, this in particular adorned your father with the name of Pius. Finally, if the war had been settled in accordance with my desires, Avidius would not have been killed. So be free from cares: 'The gods watch over me, my piety is dear to the gods.'" (Hor. *Carm.* 1.17.13–14)

The *Avidius Cassius* is the biography of the first of many usurpers to come, and sets the stage for the prominence of the theme of usurpation in the *Historia Augusta* as a whole with its recurrent interest on the fitting reaction to attempted usurpation. Thus it is appropriate, and it reveals a certain literary sensitivity, to include within this discourse a quotation from the *Odes* of Horace, since the *Odes* are marked by Horace's shifting and evolving reflections on the justice of clemency and punishment in the aftermath of Actium.[65]

For a more elaborate instance of invention through allusion, we can turn to the biography of the usurper Marius, the subject of one of the short biographies in the *Thirty Tyrants*. The *HA*-author found very little to work with, probably no more than a single sentence in the *KG*, in his self-imposed task of writing a biography of this figure. Eutropius describes Marius as *opifex*, a craftsman (9.9.2). Victor says with a bit more precision that he was *ferri quondam opifex*, an ironworker (33.9), and then adds the observation, probably his own, that Marius shared a profession and plebeian status with the republican hero Marius.[66] Both Eutropius and Victor, and therefore presumably their source, the *KG*, also remark on the extreme brevity of Marius's reign, which was either two (Victor) or three (Eutropius) days in length. In reality, the numismatic evidence demonstrates that Marius's reign must have been several months long, which suggests that the *HA*-author, as we would expect, had no additional, reliable sources of information beyond the *breviaria*.[67] These three details—the brevity of the reign, the profession of ironworker, and the coincidence of names—inspire the *HA*-author in various ways as he expands the single sentence of the *KG* into thirteen.

The *HA*-author first expands upon the shortness of Marius's rule. He quotes Cicero joking about a consul who held office for only six hours, and the simple statement that Marius ruled for three days is extended into the observation that he was made emperor on the first day, seemed to rule for the second, and died on the third (*Tyr. Trig.* 8.2):

> Nam ut ille consul qui sex meridianis horis consulatum suffectum tenuit a Marco Tullio tali aspersus est ioco: 'Consulem habuimus tam severum tamque censorium ut in eius magistratu nemo pranderit, nemo cenaverit, nemo dormiverit,' de hoc etiam dici posse videatur, qui una die factus est imperator, alia die visus est imperare, tertia interemptus est.

> For, just as that consul who held the suffect consulship for six hours at midday was mocked by Cicero with the joke, "We have had a consul so severe and censorious that during his magistracy no one has eaten breakfast, no one has eaten dinner, and no one has slept," it would seem also possible to speak in such a way about Marius, who on the first day was made emperor, on the second seemed to rule, and on the third was killed.

The citation of Cicero is marked by the author's "posse videatur," another reference to the orator's signature rhythm. The author's changes to the original text of Cicero (*Fam.* 7.30.1), adding the words "tam severum tamque censorium" and "nemo cenaverit," exacerbate the flaws in the comparison by focusing attention not on the brevity of rule but on the activities undertaken during that brief rule.[68] The problem may simply be an error in the memory of the author or his source text, but the inapposite nature of the comparison might perhaps encourage the reader to return to the source text, and to the other texts that refer to the short consulship of C. Caninius Rebilus, such as Suetonius's *Iulius* 76.2 and *Nero* 15.2.

The author expands Marius's profession from ironworker to "forger of swords and arms," and there follows heavy-handed repetition and wordplay involving the word *ferrum*, iron or sword. In his speech to the troops, he is quoted as saying that he "labors with *ferrum* rather than indulging, as does Gallienus, in wine, flowers, courtesans, and taverns." (The beginning of his speech recalls the words of the republican Marius in Sallust's *Jugurthine War*, 85.1.)[69] "Let men taunt me with working with *ferrum* as long as foreign nations shall know from their losses that I have handled the *ferrum*." He will ensure that barbarians judge the Romans to be "an iron race," and that they especially fear the *ferrum* of the soldiers. In a fantasy about Marius's end, we are told that a fellow soldier who held him in contempt because he had been an employee at the smithy ran him through while proclaiming, "hic est gladius quem ipse fecisti" ("This is a sword that you yourself have forged"). The extraordinary strength imputed to Marius by the *HA*-author is presumably a further development of his profession as ironworker. With a single finger, Marius could reverse oncoming carts or strike strong men so hard that they thought they had been hit by a board, and he was given to crushing all sorts of things between thumb and forefinger. The description of these abilities can also be seen as a parody of Suetonius, who introduced the subject of imperial finger strength into biography with his bizarre claim that Tiberius could bore through a hard apple with his finger, and kill a boy or even a young man with a flick on the head (*Tib.* 68.1). That the *HA*-author found the subject worth parodying is suggested by a recurrence of the theme in the *Claudius*, where we are told that the emperor's fingers were so strong that he often punched out the teeth of a horse or mule (13.5). The *HA*-author then claims that Marius was given the nickname "Mamurius" or "Veturius," a reference to Mamurius Veturius, the forger of the *ancilia*, the sacred shields of Mars. He was the subject of song, dance, and praise at the annual festival of Mars. His source for this piece of learning may have been Ovid (*Fast.* 3.383–84) or Servius (on *Aen.* 8.285). He has thus moved from the worker or ironworker of the *KG*, to the more dramatic manufacturer of weaponry, and finally to the mythical artisan of the most sacred arms of the Roman state. Along the way he has worked in allusions to

Cicero, Suetonius, Sallust, and perhaps Ovid. Although the author, lacking authentic sources of information on Marius, was required to invent if he was to say anything about him, he certainly did not need to invent in this particular way. In fact, if he hoped to fool his readers into thinking he was writing a real biography of Marius, evoking so many intertexts would have been ill advised.

A few sentences from the life of Carus and his sons, Carinus and Numerian, also overflow with allusion and invention. Carinus is treated badly by the *KG*, since it depended upon sources that were probably influenced by the propaganda of Diocletian, who overthrew him. The few words devoted to Numerian in the *KG*, however, make him out to be a good and eloquent man. The *HA*-author will build his fantasy from this thin material. He had already explored the good brother/bad brother theme in the lives of Geta and Caracalla. He may have been particularly inspired by the portrayal in Suetonius of the sons of Vespasian, Titus and Domitian.[70] The author will amplify and extend these themes through a chain of free association.

The *HA*-author suggests that Numerian, like Titus, possessed literary talent (Suet. *Tit.* 3.2), a common marker for excellence more generally in the judgment of the learned historians and biographers of antiquity. He first describes Numerian's talent for declamation, and then claims that Numerian's talents extended into the field of poetry, as well (*Car.* 11.1–2):

> Numerianus, Cari filius, moratus egregie et vere dignus imperio, eloquentia etiam praepollens, adeo ut puer publice declamaverit feranturque illius scripta nobilia, declamationi tamen magis quam Tulliano adcommodiora stilo. versu autem talis fuisse praedicatur ut omnes poetas sui temporis vicerit. nam et cum Olympio Nemesiano contendit, qui Ἁλιευτικὰ, Κυνηγετικὰ et Ναυτικὰ scripsit quique in omnibus coronis inlustratus emicuit, et Aurelium Apollinarem, iamborum scriptorem, qui patris eius gesta in litteras retulit, eisdem quae recitaverat editis, veluti radio solis obtexit.
>
> Numerian, the son of Carus, was extremely civilized and truly worthy to rule; he was also outstanding in eloquence, to such an extent that even as a boy he declaimed in public, and his writings came to be famous, though they were more suitable for a school exercise than they were examples of Ciceronian style. In verse, additionally, he is said to have been so great that he defeated all the poets of his age. He even competed with Olympius Nemesianus, who wrote *On Fishing* (*Halieutica*), *On Hunting* (*Cynegetica*), and *On Sailing* (*Nautica*), and who shone forth, illuminated by all the

crowns; and when he published the things he had recited, like a ray of the sun he outshined Aurelius Apollinaris, who had versified in iambic meter the deeds of Carus.

The poet Nemesianus is the only person mentioned by name in the entire *Life* of Carus, Carinus, and Numerian (with the exception of the emperors themselves) who is not fictional. He can be dated by the dedication in his extant poem *On Hunting* to Carinus and Numerian during the period in which both were emperors after their father's death, between the summer of 283 and the end of 284. In addition to *On Hunting*, Nemesianus has also left us four bucolic poems, his *Eclogues*. The author notably fails to mention those actual poems of Nemesianus while listing other works, on sailing and fishing, that are not extant and are probably invented.[71] Did the *HA*-author not realize that Nemesianus was a bucolic poet, the author of *Eclogues*, through simple unfamiliarity with his work? When reading the *HA*, one should never attribute to ignorance what can be attributed to perversity. Imperial bucolic poetry is evoked in several places in the *Carus*. Several paragraphs earlier, the *HA*-author has attributed a fabricated letter on the death of Carus to an imperial bureaucrat called Julius Calpurnius (8.4). This name was presumably inspired by the other prominent bucolic poet of the imperial period, Calpurnius Siculus. Then there is a detail in the description of the luxurious excesses of Carinus, who the *HA*-author claims wore jewels on his shoes, his clasp, and even his belt ("balteo . . . gemmato," 17.1).[72] A jeweled belt is also an attribute of Diana, according to Nemesianus's *On Hunting*, in the passage that immediately follows the poet's dedication to Carinus and Numerian ("gemmatis balteus," *Cyn.* 92). Calpurnius Siculus has the same collocation, "balteus en gemmis," in his seventh eclogue. Finally there is Aurelius Apollinaris, the other poet with whom the emperor competed, and the subject of some wordplay about light and dark. Long before this life, the *HA*-author had recorded those responsible for the assassination of the emperor Caracalla in a list that appears to be historically accurate, perhaps drawn from Marius Maximus (*Carac.* 6.6). The names include two brothers, one named Apollinaris and the other—Nemesianus![73] The *HA*-author provokes the reader by ostentatiously refusing to mention Nemesianus's bucolic poetry while hiding allusions to it in plain sight.

I detect a joke, too, in the description of Apollinaris as a composer of iambs who wrote the deeds of Carus. It is not uncommon for a historian or biographer to use historical epics like the *De Bello Gildonico* of Claudian or the *Johannis* of Corippus as a source. The church historian Socrates offers a particularly clear discussion of the practice (Soc. 6.6.35–7):

εἰ δέ τῳ φίλον ἀκριβῶς μαθεῖν τὰ ἐν ἐκείνῳ τῷ πολέμῳ γεγενημένα, ἐντυγχανέτω τῇ Γαϊνιάδι τοῦ σχολαστικοῦ Εὐσεβίου, ὃς ἐφοίτα μὲν τηνικαῦτα παρὰ Τρωΐλῳ τῷ σοφιστῇ, αὐτόπτης δὲ τοῦ πολέμου γενόμενος ἐν τέτρασι βιβλίοις ἡρωικῷ μέτρῳ τὰ γενόμενα διηγήσατο· καὶ προσφάτων ὄντων τῶν πραγμάτων σφόδρα ἐπὶ τοῖς ποιήμασιν ἐθαυμάσθη. καὶ νῦν δὲ ὁ ποιητὴς Ἀμμώνιος τὴν αὐτὴν ὑπόθεσιν ῥαψῳδήσας.

If someone wishes to learn more precisely what happened in that war, he should find a copy of the *Gainea* of Eusebius Scholasticus, who was at that time a student of Troilus the sophist. As an eyewitness to the war, he related the events of it in epic meter in four books, and as the events that he discussed had only recently taken place, he became well known. The poet Ammonius has also recently composed another description in verse of the same events.

We would expect a historical epic about the deeds of emperors to be in dactylic hexameter. In the late Roman period, and especially in Greek, iambs were sometimes the meter of didactic poetry, but they are traditionally the meter of abuse.[74] Consider, for example, the definition of iambic given by Diomedes, the grammarian of the late fourth century:

Iambus est carmen maledicum plerumque trimetro versu et epodo sequente conpositum, ut 'mala soluta navis exit alite / ferens olentem Maevium.' appellatum est autem παρὰ τὸ ἰαμβίζειν, quod est maledicere. cuius carminis praecipui scriptores apud Graecos Archilochus et Hipponax, apud Romanos Lucilius et Catullus et Horatius et Bibaculus. (Keil, *Gramm. Lat.* 1.485.11–17)

Iambos is an abusive poem usually composed from a trimeter verse followed by an epode, for example: "the ship sets sail under evil auspices / carrying stinking Maevius" [Hor. *Epod.* 10.1-2]. It derives its name from *iambizein*, that is, to abuse. The most important writers of this sort of poem among the Greeks are Archilochus and Hipponax, and among the Romans, Lucilius, Catullus, Horace, and Bibaculus.

Our author has thus conjured up a grammarian's fantasy, not a heroic epic in praise of an emperor's triumphs but an iambic epic that would presumably be an epic invective on the deeds of Carus. Perhaps we are to imagine that the good son defeated Apollinaris's invective with an epic panegyric on his father's deeds. Having written epic poetry in competition with Apollinaris, and didactic verse in competition with Nemesianus, he falls short of Vergil's generic mastery only in the lack of bucolic poetry, the very genre that has been ostentatiously suppressed by the author.

The description of Numerian's fictional poetic talent poses a challenge to the reader, who should ideally be familiar with imperial bucolic and literary and generic conventions. Like the other allusions we have surveyed so far, they are only very loosely connected to the ostensible subject matter of the biographies themselves, which serve as camouflage by which the author can hide his tricks and games.

Vergil

The most obvious form of allusion is quotation. The *HA*-author prominently features quotations from Vergil in divinatory contexts in a variety of lives. The beginning of the *Hadrian*, for example, contains an unusual phrase: Hadrian is said to have consulted "Vergilian lots" ("Vergilianas sortes"), and the "lot fell out" ("sors excidit") with a quotation from *Aeneid* 8.808–12 (*Hadr.* 2.8). The author immediately follows with alternative scenarios, remarking that the verses may have instead derived from an oracle at the temple of Jupiter at Nicephorium or, again, from the Sibylline verses. The lines, which portray the coming of Numa, reassure Hadrian that he will succeed Trajan. In the *Aelius*, Hadrian's skill at astrology is adduced, and then he is portrayed as quoting *Aeneid* 6.869–70 on the short life of Marcellus, which will parallel that of Aelius (*Ael.* 4.1).

Clodius Albinus received Vergilian verses at the temple of Apollo at Cumae that predicted his coming to the throne (*Aen.* 6.857–58; *Clod. Alb.* 5). This temple is not known for providing oracles (although the cult statue occasionally broke out in a sweat: see Cic. *Div.* 1.98), so it is reasonable to suspect that the author has in mind the famous sibyl of Cumae, who is here imagined as quoting from the epic that features her prominently in the very sixth book that is so frequently quoted by the *HA*-author.

Alexander Severus also receives Vergilian verses from the apostrophe to Marcellus, in his case from the temple of Fortuna at Praeneste (*Aen.* 6.882–83, 4.6), and later is said to have been "celebrated by Vergilian lots" with some of the most famous lines of the *Aeneid* (6.848–54, 14.5). In the republican period, at least, Fortuna at Praeneste gave prophecies by means of a boy drawing from a box of lots written in ancient characters (Cic. *Div.* 2.85), and one would think it surprising for these ancient characters to reproduce lines of Vergil. Claudius also receives Vergilian oracles, both after becoming emperor and once "in the Apennines," an oracular site invented by the *HA*-author (cf. *Quad. Tyr.* 3.4; *Claud.* 10.1–6; *Aen.* 1.265, 1.278, and 6.869).

The most amazing of the Vergilian oracles is delivered when the Delphic oracle is asked who will be the next emperor, who will succeed him, and, finally, how many years the next emperor will rule. The priest responds in Greek, as we are told three separate times, and the author has translated his responses into Latin; his answer to the last question includes the following: "bis denis Italum conscendit navibus aequor / si tamen una ratis transiliet pelagus" (*Pesc. Nig.* 8.6). These lines are adapted from *Aeneid* 1.381, "bis denis Phrygium conscendi navibus aequor," mashed up with Horace, *Odes* 1.3.23–24, "si tamen impiae / non tangenda rates transiliunt vada."[75]

These Vergilian oracles have often been misinterpreted because of the persistent beliefs that divination through the random consultation of sacred texts was common in antiquity, and that the Vergilian oracles in the *Historia Augusta* represent either examples or parodies of the practice.[76] This is in general not correct, and requires a brief digression. A millennium of medieval church bans on so-called *sortes sanctorum* led scholars to overestimate the prevalence of text-sortition in a Christian context; in fact, as Klingshirn has shown, these bans refer not to random consultations of holy books for divinatory purposes (i.e., *sortes biblicae*) but to nonbiblical works specifically designed for divination.[77] In studying the phenomenon, scholars often include Jewish and Christian examples of biblical verses being overheard and then interpreted prophetically, which is not at all the same thing (for example, Antony being inspired to give up his possessions in response to a reading of Matthew).[78] Many commenters on the phenomenon also misrepresent a passage about astrology in Augustine's *Confessions* in a discussion of astrology as a reference to such a practice (*Conf.* 4.3.5). In fact, Augustine describes learning that astrology sometimes seems to work simply by chance, as when a verse of poetry that we happen to be reading appears to address an important concern of ours. No practice of random selection of verses is implied. A passage from Jerome, also often offered as an example of the criticism of biblical lots, is actually aimed against writing *centones*, not prophetic consultation of the Bible (*Ep.* 53.7).[79] In Augustine's famous scene in the garden, he responds to a child's cry of *"Tolle, lege"* ("Take it and read") by picking up the volume of Paul that he had been reading and finding his anxiety dispelled by the verse (*Conf.* 8.12.29; *Rom.* 13:13–14). Augustine's friend Alypius is then similarly moved by reading the next verse of Romans. This is not an example of prophecy through random verse selection either.

Actual evidence for textual divination that parallels Vergilian oracles even somewhat is sparse. There are a few examples of sortition with Homeric verse, not, apparently, through random consultation of a codex or scroll but through the preparation of lots or dice keyed to a list of preselected Homeric verses. Dio describes an oracular site in Apamea that gives Homeric oracles (78.40.4), and a third-century papyrus provides a list of dice results keyed to a series of Homeric verses. The one clear reference to biblical sortition is a discussion in a letter of Augustine in which he has been asked whether it is wrong to "read lots" ("sortes legunt") from the pages of the gospels to predict the future (*Ep.* 55.37).[80] Augustine feels that the Bible should not be used in this way for secular answers but only for spiritual enlightenment. The process imagined may well be similar to that of the Homeric examples, where numbered lots are assigned to preselected verses from the gospels.

Returning to the passages in the *Historia Augusta*, we see that *sortes Vergilianae* appear in a far different context than the modest Homeric or biblical examples. Instead, Vergilian responses issue forth from an indiscriminate selection of the most prominent oracular sites in antiquity, and by means of a wide array of oracular methods, ranging from the drawing of lots to the consultation of astrological books to the pronouncements of inspired priests and prophetesses. The reader familiar with Cicero's *De Divinatione* or a similar book on archaic religion could enjoy the absurdities of this mishmash of rituals. Even the less learned could appreciate the humor of Greek priests at Delphi offering up selections from Vergil.

The absurdity of the Vergilian oracles presented in the *Historia Augusta* is enhanced when we realize that they do not represent a mild exaggeration of an otherwise ubiquitous phenomenon but a purposeful and original invention. Since no learned ancient reader could have failed to recognize the Vergilian lines, even when not attributed to Vergil by name, the citations create a kind of literary fantasy world where Vergil's work surfaces in the most unlikely places. It has been suggested that the frequent recourse to triumphal passages in books 1 and 6 of the *Aeneid* has a polemical, anti-Christian purpose.[81] Such an interpretation ignores the irony inherent in many of the prophecies. The prophecy for Clodius Albinus, for example, announces that he will defeat the Gauls and the Carthaginians. Although he did have success in Gaul, his failure against "the Carthaginian" Septimius Severus demonstrates that the prophecy was actually wrong. Alexander's Vergilian prophecy at Praeneste is also dubious. In response to Elagabalus's plotting against him, he is ominously reminded of the youthful death of Augustus's heir, Marcellus. The Vergilian/Horatian hybrid supposedly translated from Greek is the most intricately constructed. The Vergilian line is spoken by Aeneas to the disguised Venus, explaining that he has lost all but seven ships in his terrible voyage from Troy. The Horatian line is taken from an *Ode* that bemoans the dangers of traveling at sea. The *Ode* is addressed to Vergil himself—although the line from the *Aeneid* with which it is paired suggests that Vergil would not have needed to be reminded of the rigors of the sea!

Vergil, revered in late antiquity by pagans and Christians alike, is presented by the *Historia Augusta* in passages that are clearly fantastical and certain to be recognized as such by a learned audience. The contemporary reader could not have accepted these descriptions as belonging to sober biography. The citations sometimes have a comical aspect, if the reader has sufficient literary and historical knowledge, but cannot be fairly seen to have a religious or political signification. Instead, they present the reader with an interpretative challenge in the form of a playful game.

Conclusion

The late Roman reader could recognize and appreciate surprisingly complex allusions. The *Historia Augusta* stretches the use of allusion to the limits of complexity. Rather than an allusion to a source text being used to comment upon the action of the text itself, often the text itself has been created from the elements of the source text. The practice of Vergilian oracles has been invented in order to offer a new vehicle for allusion. Elagabalus has been given an *authepsa* in order to allude to Cicero. The "historian" Gallus Antipater has been invented, named, and described for the sole purpose of creating a puzzle that links Sallust, Ammianus, and (probably) Marius Maximus writing on Hadrian. The parents of Maximinus, Micca and Hababa, have been called into existence for no other reason than as a play on words for the astute reader of Herodian.

Certainly some of the allusions we have seen are meant to resonate in their immediate contexts. The villainy of Elagabalus, the gluttony of Firmus, and the literary abilities of Numerian are emphasized for those who can detect the allusions lying behind descriptions of their activities. Yet these are the most banal characterizations possible. The reader will be challenged to find any kind of consistent agenda or emphasis in the collected body of allusions in the work, which tend instead to offer a kind of anarchic play with texts and phrases.

For more than a century, scholars have asked what kind of text the *Historia Augusta* is. By focusing on the extravagant and unusual use of allusion in the text, we are prompted to ask a potentially more productive question: what kind of readers did the *Historia Augusta* have? Allusion requires an active, meaning-making reader, what Pucci calls the "full-knowing reader," not in the sense that he knows all, but in recognition of the process whereby "the dissonances of two discrete works are mediated in the give and take of a mental, interpretative dialogue" at the expense of the author's power.[82] The allusions in the *Historia Augusta*, complex yet untethered to a consistent purpose or program, offer an especially large interpretative space in which the reader can and has to work.

In the next chapter, we begin by exploring the playful approach of the *HA*-author to questions of genre, which takes the form of specific textual allusions as well as generic allusions. This prepares us to consider more carefully and fully the question of audience. What kind of readership does the humorous and self-aware, complex but acontextual, use of allusion in the *Historia Augusta* presuppose?

# 2 The *Historia Augusta* and the Ancient Reader

The previous chapter surveys some of the allusions that the HA-author deploys in his work. The allusions present elaborate challenges that test the best readers' abilities to identify and interpret surprising intertexts. This game of allusion is embedded in a context that appears at first glance to be a Suetonian biographical work, but the intensity of allusive play undermines the apparent frame. The appropriation of historiographical or biographical forms for other purposes is not uncommon in ancient literature, however. The best readers of the *Historia Augusta* can recognize and enjoy the ways in which the author represents and exploits the markers of biographical and historiographical forms.

The Genre of Biography

By constructing a biographical frame for his work, the *HA*-author engages with contemporary debates about the definition of biography and its differentiation from historiography. Political biography, in particular, approaches history in many ways, and the closer it comes, the more necessary it becomes for the biographer to differentiate his work.[1] In discussions of ancient biographical genres, it seems to be obligatory to cite a passage from the beginning of Plutarch's life of Alexander (1.1.2–3), where he explains that readers should not complain if some details are left out:

οὔτε γὰρ ἱστορίας γράφομεν, ἀλλὰ βίους, οὔτε ταῖς ἐπιφανεστάταις πράξεσι πάντως ἔνεστι δήλωσις ἀρετῆς ἢ κακίας, ἀλλὰ πρᾶγμα βραχὺ πολλάκις καὶ ῥῆμα καὶ παιδιά τις ἔμφασιν ἤθους ἐποίησε μᾶλλον ἢ μάχαι μυριόνεκροι καὶ παρατάξεις αἱ μέγισται καὶ πολιορκίαι πόλεων. ὥσπερ οὖν οἱ ζωγράφοι τὰς ὁμοιότητας ἀπὸ τοῦ προσώπου καὶ τῶν περὶ τὴν ὄψιν εἰδῶν οἷς ἐμφαίνεται τὸ ἦθος ἀναλαμβαίνουσιν, ἐλάχιστα τῶν λοιπῶν μερῶν φροντίζοντες, οὕτως ἡμῖν δοτέον εἰς τὰ τῆς ψυχῆς σημεῖα μᾶλλον ἐνδύεσθαι καὶ διὰ τούτων εἰδοποιεῖν τὸν ἑκάστου βίον, ἐάσαντας ἑτέροις τὰ μεγέθη καὶ τοὺς ἀγῶνας.

For we are not writing Histories, but Lives, and in the most conspicuous deeds there is not always an example of virtue or wickedness. Instead, a small thing like a phrase or a joke often provides a reflection of character more than battles that kill thousands, or the greatest military formations, or sieges of cities. Therefore, just as painters create likenesses from the face and the details around the eyes, by which the character is revealed, considering least of all the remaining parts, so it is necessary that I attend more to the signs of the soul, and by means of these to portray the life of each, leaving for others great deeds and great strugggles.

As Duff has demonstrated, Plutarch is not offering rules for biography as a genre but addressing concerns specific to the life of Alexander, who had been the subject of so many historical accounts.[2] Only for this reason must Plutarch worry about readers who know more than the biographer can readily include in a life. After all, Plutarch's life of Caesar, which is paired with the *Alexander*, offers a lengthy piece of historical narrative in its recounting of the Gallic Wars, contrasting sharply with Suetonius's own very restrained treatment of Caesar's campaigns. Suetonius, on the other hand, does present a principle that we see in all of his biographies: the discussion of the elements of the subject's life "singillatim neque per tempora sed per species" ("individually, and not in chronological order, but by category," *Aug.* 9). He does not claim that this structure is particular to the genre of biography but simply that it will make his narrative easier to understand.

The imperial biographies of Suetonius represent an innovation, combining elements of biographical portraits in Roman political oratory and Hellenistic portraits of literary figures. It seems clear that there was no stable definition of biography when he wrote.[3] The decisions of Marius Maximus and the *HA*-author to model their work on Suetonius created a subgenre of Suetonian-style biography while leaving many other sorts of biographical writing underdefined. Late Roman thinkers on biography thus faced challenges similar to those of modern scholars in classifying biographies and defining biography as a genre.

Ancient literary theorists could be very prescriptive in their discussions of genre. The firm rules they put forth for dividing genres had not only literary but also cultural and moral dimensions.[4] And this kind of categorization remained important to scholiasts, librarians, and grammarians.[5] Even in antiquity, however, this kind of prescriptivism could be mocked. Lucian's treatise *How to Write History*, often misinterpreted as an actual handbook for practitioners, offers an ironic take on the debates over prescriptive rules for historians, which are portrayed as simplistic and lacking in nuance.[6] Modern scholars are nearly universal in their rejection of strict generic boundaries, preferring to focus on the imitation of models (*imitatio, aemulatio, mimesis*) rather than specific rules.[7] Rosenmeyer goes so far as to question whether genre existed at all in antiquity as a meaningful category, and Edwards more specifically denies that biography is a meaningful ancient genre.[8] Less radical approaches include that of Freyne, who holds that "while it may be possible to speak of particular genres as ideal types, there are as many variations possible as there are authors who wish to convey their experiences," and that of Burridge, who concludes that "genres operate in a middle ground between the two extremes of classical prescriptivism and nineteenth-century descriptivism."[9]

The *Historia Augusta* participates in these generic debates without offering an unambiguous perspective. Sometimes, we will see, the author flaunts his imitation of previous biographers, and at other times he invokes principles or rules of genre. Sometimes he draws lines between history and biography, but at other times he is willing to commingle the two as he works with concepts traditionally associated with historiography. He therefore cannot be said to champion a particular view of biographical genre; rather, he playfully parodies the whole spectrum of approaches found in ancient biographical and historiographical texts. He develops these positions through both specific allusions to his predecessors and what we can call "generic" allusions to tropes and themes that evoke not a specific author but the genre of history or biography.

Suetonius and Marius Maximus as Predecessors

The *HA*-author argues in the preface to the *Probus* (2.7) that biography-writing requires following generic predecessors. Here he particularly draws the traditional distinction between the high style of history and the prosaic devotion to truth of biography:

> Mihi quidem id animi fuit ut non Sallustios, Livios, Tacitos, Trogos atque omnes disertissimos imitarer viros in vita principum et temporibus disserendis, sed Marium Maximum, Suetonium Tranquillum, Fabium Marcellinum, Gargilium Martialem, Iulium Capitolinum, Aelium Lampridium ceterosque, qui haec et talia non tam diserte quam vere memoriae tradiderunt.

> As for me, indeed, it has been my purpose, in relating the lives and times of the emperors, to imitate, not a Sallust, or a Livy, or a Tacitus, or a Trogus, or any other of the most eloquent writers, but rather Marius Maximus, Suetonius Tranquillus, Fabius Marcellinus, Gargilius Martialis, Julius Capitolinus, Aelius Lampridius, and the others who have handed down to memory these and other such details not so much with eloquence as with truthfulness.

The order of biographical writers in this list is significant. The first two names represent real writers of biography, and the last two are pseudonyms for the author himself and thus wholly invented. The middle two are invented in part—Fabius Marcellinus as the biographer-twin of Ammianus Marcellinus, and Gargilius Martialis, the author of agricultural treatises, pressed into service as a biographer. The passage from truth to invention is particularly appropriate in this declaration of dedication to truthfulness. The humor of the passage derives, as often in the *Historia Augusta*, from the juxtaposition of high-minded declarations of truth-telling with allusive, though not particularly elusive, fiction.

The importance of Suetonius as a model, both for the *Historia Augusta* and for would-be biographers in general, is emphasized again in the introduction to the *Quadrigae Tyrannorum*, where Suetonius is praised as a "most accurate and truthful writer" ("emendatissimus et candidissimus scriptor," *Quad. Tyr.* 1.1; cf. *Max. et Balb.* 4.5; *Comm.* 10.2). The praise prepares the reader to expect allusions to the text of Suetonius, much like the allusions we have seen to Cicero or Vergil. The *HA*-author's engagement with Suetonius also reveals how he understands and defines the genre of imperial biography. For example, the *HA*-author several times cites his father or grandfather as a source for particular pieces of information, all of which are fictional (*Tyr. Trig.* 25.3; *Quad. Tyr.* 9.4, 15.5; *Car.* 13.4, 14.1, 15.1, 15.5). It has long been recognized that these passages are inspired by two places in Suetonius where his father (*Otho* 10) and grandfather (*Calig.* 19) are cited as authorities.[10] By appropriating this technique, the *HA*-author defines it as particular to biography. The ability to turn to a privileged insider was an important method of validation in imperial historiography, since decision-making in an autocratic society was performed in secret.[11] At the same time, the *HA*-author through his inventions reminds us that the technique offers the author the unverifiable license to fabricate.

The *Historia Augusta* invites the reader not simply to recall a Suetonian technique but also to compare the Suetonian usages directly with its own examples. Suetonius adduces his grandfather in a much-discussed passage in the life of Caligula concerning the bridging of the Bay of Baiae (*Calig.* 19).[12] He tells us that, having created a road from earth heaped upon ships between Baiae and Puteoli, the emperor rode back and forth for two days, dressed first in triumphal garb and then as a charioteer. Unnamed "others" attribute this action to an attempt to rival Xerxes, or to frighten foreign enemies. Rejecting these interpretations, Suetonius asserts instead that he had heard the real story as a boy from his grandfather, who had heard it from the emperor's men. Tiberius's astrologer, Thrasyllus, had prophesied that Caligula "was no more likely to become emperor than to ride through the gulf of Baiae on horseback" (*Calig.* 19.3).[13] Whether the other ancient explanations for Caligula's actions are correct can be debated, but Suetonius's own explanation is highly unlikely. Caligula had already been emperor for two years, and thus had definitively disproved Thrasyllus's supposed prophecy by the time he constructed the bridge. Suetonius's explanation is noteworthy not only for its illogicality but also for the way that he manipulates his account to excuse Caligula's actions. For Seneca, Josephus, and Dio, the act is explained by madness and hubris. Suetonius, however, has included it among the small number of positive actions of the emperor's reign, purposefully detaching the excessive feasting and violence found in connection with the building of the bridge in other accounts and saving them for much later, in the negative section of the life.[14] To summarize, then, Suetonius's anecdote attempts to whitewash the discreditable behavior of an emperor through an unlikely prophecy known to the grandfather of the author.

The fullest exploitation of the *HA*-author's grandfather is found in repeated mentions in a section of the *Carus* (13.4–15.5). Grandfather was present at the dramatic moment when Diocletian turned on the praetorian prefect Aper at a public meeting and, accusing him of being the murderer of Numerian, ran him through with a sword. The grandfather was close enough to Diocletian, we are told, to have heard the true explanation of this event directly from the emperor. In response to a humorous remark Diocletian made in a tavern while still a simple soldier, a druidess informed him that he would become emperor when he had killed a boar (*aper*). Despite Diocletian's subsequent successful participation in numerous boar hunts, he was repeatedly passed over for the throne, and, as Aurelian, Probus, Tacitus, and Carus successively became emperor, he groused, "I am always killing boars, but the other man enjoys the meat." After the slaying of Aper, Diocletian tells the writer's grandfather that he would have preferred not to be known for such a public act of brutality but was compelled by the need to fulfill the druidess's prophecy. Each emperor, then, had performed an action that was vulnerable to criticism, and each biographer introduced a story from his grandfather that explained the emperor was in fact motivated by a prophecy related to his acquisition of power. The version of the *Historia Augusta*, of course, is more elaborate, and more amusing, than what we find in Suetonius.

The *HA*-grandfather was also present to hear the reluctant usurper Saturninus explain the evil of imperial rule and predict his own imminent death (*Quad. Tyr.* 9.4). This perhaps evokes the association of Suetonius's father with the usurper Otho (Suet. *Otho* 10). He often used to declare, says Suetonius, that Otho loathed civil strife and even preferred suicide to fighting, lest he endanger the lives of his brave soldiers. Evidence for the surprising decency of a usurper is, then, another topic associated with familial knowledge.

Overall, we find that fathers and grandfathers are not just sources in general for the *HA*-author but sources for the same types of information they provided for Suetonius. The references must be recognized first as generic allusions to Suetonian biography but then also as specific allusions to how Suetonius uses the technique.

Another Suetonian technique adapted by the *HA*-author is the scholarly disquisition on the birthplace of an emperor.[15] Suetonius begins his life of Caligula with an encomium of Caligula's father, Germanicus, and then an account of the popular distress over the general's death. There follows an extensive learned digression on a dispute over the emperor's place of birth. Suetonius refutes the theories of two previous writers, Gnaeus Lentulus Gaetulicus and Pliny, by deploying archival, linguistic, and chronological arguments, as well as a passage from a letter written by Augustus. He concludes by settling on the place whose name he had read in the official records, Antium, adding that the emperor spent much time there and, "it is said," planned to transfer the capital of the empire there, as he was sick of Rome. While this show of erudition has been praised by modern scholars ("modèle de discussion historique"),[16] we might suspect that its excesses likely would have seemed eccentric to the ancient reader. The *Carus* similarly begins with a lamentation (for Probus) before claiming that the considerable disagreement about the birthplace of Carus leaves the *HA*-author, in implicit contrast with the Sherlockian Suetonius, unable to determine the truth. We are told that while the biographer Onesimus holds that Carus's parents were Illyrians, but that he was born at Rome, the historian Fabius Ceryllianus holds that he was born not of Illyrian parents but of Carthaginian parents in Illyricum, and the *HA*-author himself had seen evidence that he was born in Milan but registered in Aquileia.[17] As in the Suetonian passage, the *HA*-author is confronted with two authors who disagree as well as a third documentary source. He then quotes an imperial letter, as Suetonius had, and an imperial oration, to the effect that although the actual *patria* of the emperor was unknown, he sought to have contemporaries believe that he was a "Roman born at Rome" ("Romanum, id est Roma oriundum," *Car.* 5.3).[18] When read alongside Suetonius, we find that Carus's invented desire to be Roman despite his foreign birth contrasts pointedly with Caligula's supposed desire to renounce Rome and move away. More generically, the *HA*-author also emphasizes that scholarly research is a feature of biographical writing, though it would be foreign to rhetorical historiography.

The other, less-elaborated, allusion to this Suetonian motif occurs in *Aurelian* 3.1–2:

> divus Aurelianus ortus, ut plures loquuntur, Sirmii familia obscuriore, ut nonnulli, Dacia Ripensi. ego autem legisse me memini auctorem qui eum Moesia genitum praedicaret: et evenit quidem ut de eorum virorum genitali solo nesciatur qui humiliore loco et ipsi plerumque solum genitale confingunt, ut dent posteritati de locorum splendore fulgorem.

> the deified Aurelian was born of a humble family, at Sirmium according to most writers, but in Dacia Ripensis according to some. I remember, moreover, that I read an author who claimed that he was born in Moesia; and, indeed, we happen to be ignorant of the birthplaces of those who, born in a humble position, frequently invent a birthplace for themselves, that they may give their posterity nobility from the cachet of the place.

This passage, viewed retrospectively, prepares the reader for Carus's apparent attempt to claim the glories of Rome for himself in the later passage.

The physiognomic description of the emperor is another feature originating in Suetonian biography that the *HA*-author appropriates and parodies.[19] Suetonius provides a paragraph of quasi-technical description of each emperor's physical features, and similar descriptions of Germanicus and Galba's father.[20] It is likely that Marius Maximus provided similar portraits, since seven of the twelve descriptions found in the *Historia Augusta* are of emperors who were treated by Maximus, and these portraits are generally conventional, resembling those found in Suetonius. The five portraits in the *Historia Augusta* of later emperors, however (*Diad.* 3; *Gord.* 6; Zenobia at *Tyr. Trig.* 30; *Claud.* 13; Firmus at *Quad. Tyr.* 4), are surely inventions of the author, done to emulate and parody their biographical predecessors. On the one hand, the *HA*-author replaces the neutral, "scientific" portraits we see in Suetonius with rhetorical stereotypes. Zenobia is a manly, dark-skinned eastern warrior, Gordian I is an idealized elderly Roman gentleman, and the boy Diadumenianus is an eroticized love object. A weakness for puns is also visible: Clodius Albinus is pale-skinned and Pescennius Niger dark, while the usurper Firmus is a strong and monstrous figure. On the other hand, the *HA*-author also engages with Suetonius on the details of the scientific elements of physiognomy that seek to explain character through outward appearance. The *Historia Augusta* uses unusual diction that parodies that found in the physiognomic treatises, and his remarks on the ways in which emperors sought to alter their appearance can be seen as a comment on the instability of physiognomic investigation.

Although the *HA*-author alludes to Suetonius throughout his collection, the *Elagabalus* offers a particularly fruitful site of allusion. The life divides clearly into two sections. The first part (1.4–18.3) contains elements that must derive from a source nearly contemporary with the emperor, presumably Marius Maximus.[21] Although there are infelicities and errors, we can accept most of it as representative of an authentic historical tradition. The second part, however, a detailed list of the disgraceful and disgusting acts that supposedly marred Elagabalus's rule, is almost entirely fictional, and one source of this fiction is Suetonius. The first words of the *Elagabalus* can be read as encouragement to the reader to turn to Suetonius, the canonical biographer of the first twelve emperors, in interpreting the author's inventions (*Elag.* 1.1):

> Vitam Heliogabali Antonini, qui Varius etiam dictus est, numquam in litteras misissem, ne quis fuisse Romanorum principem sciret, nisi ante Caligulas et Nerones et Vitellios hoc idem habuisset imperium.

> I would never have put the life of Elagabalus Antoninus, who was also called Varius, into writing, so that no one would know that he had been emperor of the Romans, were it not that before him this same imperial office had had Caligulas, Neros, and Vitelliuses.

The *HA*-author reminds the reader again that Suetonian villains served as models for Elagabalus as he makes the transition from history to fantasy (*Elag.* 18.4): "he himself used to say that he imitated Apicius among private citizens and, among emperors, Nero, Otho, and Vitellius" ("cum ipse e privatis diceret se Apicium, imperatorem vero Neronem, Othonem et Vitellium imitari").[22] These Suetonian tyrants, and others, provide models not for the historical Elagabalus but for the *HA*-author's portrayal of a fictional Elagabalus. He creates an Elagabalus who not only partakes in the same disgraceful behavior as previous bad rulers but whose behavior also magnifies or exceeds their actions in striking or humorous ways.

In a programmatic statement, the *HA*-author claims that Elagabalus "invented new types of vice, even going beyond the *spinthrias* of the old emperors, and he was familiar with all the arrangements of Tiberius, Caligula, and Nero" ("libidinum genera quaedam invenit, ut spinthrias veterum imperatorum vinceret, et omnis apparatus Tiberii et Caligulae et Neronis norat," *Elag.* 33.1). The unusual word *spinthrias*, connected with three Suetonian emperors, directs us to two passages in the earlier biographer. First, Tiberius is claimed as the imperial originator of the type (Suet. *Tib.* 43.1):

> Secessu vero Caprensi etiam sellaria excogitavit, sedem arcanarum libidinum, in quam undique conquisiti puellarum et exoletorum greges monstrosique concubitus repertores, quos spintrias appellabat, triplici serie conexi, in vicem incestarent coram ipso, ut aspectu deficientis libidines excitaret.

> At his retreat on Capri he devised small rooms as a site for his secret lusts, in which were selected herds of girls and male prostitutes, inventors of monstrous forms of sex whom he was calling *spintriae*, who in groups of three performed their unchaste acts in turns before his eyes, so that by the sight he could excite his faltering desire.

Later Suetonius claims that Caligula, in the admirable early days of his rule, "banished from the city the *spintriae*, with their monstrous lusts, barely persuaded not to drown them in the sea" ("spintrias monstrosarsum libidinum aegre ne profundo mergeret exoratus, urbe submovit," *Calig.* 16.1). Thus to the alert reader Elagabalus is revealed as a student of Tiberius and Caligula, or at least the Suetonian account of the emperors. But he is a student determined to surpass his teachers.

The claim that Elagabalus outdid the banquets of Vitellius (*Elag.* 24.4) encourages us again to compare Suetonius with the *Historia Augusta* (20.5–21.4). At palace banquets, both Vitellius and Elagabalus served a particularly disgusting mix of foods (Suet. *Vit.* 13.2; *Elag.* 20.6). Vitellius is said to have served pike liver, pheasant brain, peacock brain, flamingo tongue, and lamprey milt, while Elagabalus offered mullet viscera, flamingo brain, thrush brain, partridge eggs, pheasant head, and peacock head. The *HA*-author engages directly with Suetonius to describe an Elagabalus who systematically outdoes Vitellius in a nearly point-by-point fashion. Elagabalus offers six repulsive flavors, Vitellius only five. While Vitellius served a single organ of his fish (the liver), Elagabalus presented all the offal from his fish. Vitellius served the brain of the pheasant and peacock, while Elagabalus served the entire head of those birds. Vitellius served the tongue of the flamingo, and Elagabalus flamingo brain. Vitellius served milt, Elagabalus eggs.[23] We can also consider a passage from the life of Caligula in which flamingoes, peacocks, and pheasants also appear (Suet. *Calig.* 22.3). These birds are not part of a banquet but are among the regular offerings made at the temple that Caligula set up to his own divinity. Bizarre sacrificial meat is also appropriate for Elagabalus to consume personally, given his own religious eccentricities.

The Elagabalus of the *Historia Augusta* likewise rivals and surpasses Suetonian tyrants in luxurious behavior. For example, Caligula is said to have had a slave executed "for stealing a strip of silver from a couch" ("ob detractam lectis argenteam laminam," Suet. *Calig.* 32.2), while Elagabalus has more impressive (and ridiculous) couches "made from solid silver" ("solido argento factos habuit lectos," *Elag.* 20.4).[24] Caligula invented the idea of bathing in perfumed water (Suet. *Calig.* 37.1), and Elagabalus does him one better by refusing to swim in any pool not perfumed with saffron or another noble ingredient (*Elag.* 19.8). While Nero would take a dip in water chilled by snow (Suet. *Ner.* 27.2), Elagabalus once made a mountain of snow in the summer just for fun (*Elag.* 23.8). Nero created a dining room with an ivory ceiling made of rotating panels, which could open up and shower the guests with flowers (Suet. *Ner.* 31.3). In Elagabalus's version of this luxury, so many flowers poured down on his guests that several, unable to crawl free, were smothered to death (*Elag.* 21.5).

Elagabalus also outstrips the bad emperors of Suetonius in outrageous behavior. Nero famously disgraced himself in the eyes of Suetonius by his insistence on performing musical theater (Suet. *Ner.* 20–21, 22.3–24.1). Yet Nero only played the lyre and sang. Elagabalus not only sings and dances but, a regular one-man band, also plays the pipes, horn, pandura, and organ (*Elag.* 32.8). Evidence of Domitian's excessive lustfulness includes the rumor that he depilated his concubines with his own hand (Suet. *Dom.* 22.1). Elagabalus—or rather the *HA*-author, creating an Elagabalus who comically transgresses the limits set by the tyrants of Suetonian biography—takes Domitian's actions several steps further (*Elag.* 31.7):

> in balneis semper cum mulieribus fuit, ita ut eas ipse psilothro curaret, ipse quoque barbam psilothro accurans, quodque pudendum dictum sit, eodem quo mulieres accurabantur et eadem hora; rasit et virilia subactoribus suis adhibens novaclam manu sua, quo postea barbam fecit.

> In the baths he was always with the women, and he himself treated them with a depilatory ointment, applying it also to his own beard, and, shameful to say, to the same place where the women were treated and at the same time. He also shaved the manly parts of the members of his retinue, applying the razor with his own hand, with which he would afterward shave his beard.[25]

Finally, Suetonius may well have influenced not only the content of the *Historia Augusta* but even the structure. Bird suggests that the structure of the end of the *Historia Augusta* was designed in emulation of the end of Suetonius.[26] The

Quadrigae Tyrannorum presents four usurpers whose biographies as narrated are entirely fictional. The very existence of a third-century usurper named Firmus may be doubted. These short lives of usurpers are followed by the lives of Carus and then his two sons, the good Numerian and the depraved Carinus. The invention and placement of the *Quadrigae Tyrannorum* lives parallel the short lives of the usurpers Galba, Otho, and Vitellius in Suetonius, just as the *Carus, Numerian, and Carinus* mirrors the concluding lives of Suetonius: those of Vespasian and his two sons, the good Titus and the wicked Domitian.

The biographies of Marius Maximus are not extant, and it is difficult to know how much weight the Maximus-hypothesis can bear. If the sketch by Birley of Maximus as a second-century general and biographer is accepted, however, we would be remiss if we neglected to consider his influence on the *Historia Augusta* with regard to themes as well as content.[27] A number of unusual features of the *Historia Augusta* may have their origins in emulation of Maximus. For example, the only acclamations in the primary lives are those chanted after the death of Commodus (*Comm.* 18–19), which are explicitly attributed to Maximus. Perhaps the tedious repetition of acclamations in the secondary and late lives represents an allusion to and parody of Maximus. Similarly, we would expect that Maximus, who held many high offices in his career, would have had access to official documents, and he may have reproduced many in his verbose work. In the *Pertinax*, we are told that Maximus included a speech of Marcus in which he nominated Pertinax for the consulship (*Pert.* 2.8, and cf. 15.8); this is reminiscent of the many letters of recommendation by a sitting emperor about a future emperor that litter the later lives. As long as we are blaming Maximus for the most enervating parts of the *Historia Augusta*, let us note the long list of goods for sale after the death of Commodus (*Pert.* 8.2) and compare it to the similar lists in the later lives: a list in the *Claudius*, for example, also includes some of the luxury clothing found in the Pertinax list (*Claud.* 17). Finally, I would note a passage in the *Severus* where the emperor puts many dissidents to death: "damnabantur autem plerique, cur iocati essent, alii, cur tacuissent, alii, cur pleraque figurata dixissent, ut 'ecce imperator vere nominis sui, vere Pertinax, vere Severus'" ("Several were condemned because they had made a joke, others because they had been silent, others again because they had said some things with double meanings, such as 'Behold an emperor with a true name—truly pertinacious, truly severe,'" *Sev.* 14.12–13). Perhaps this was one inspiration, anyway, for the repetitive wordplay on emperors' names that we see in the later and secondary lives.

Allusions to Suetonius (and Maximus) thus present two frames for interpretation. Often the reader benefits from returning to the intertext, which is humorously parodied or exaggerated in the typical manner of the *HA*-author. The author is also making a more general claim about biography in incorporating tropes such as the relative as informant, the scholarly inquiry, or the formal physiognomic study. These features are elevated above the simple eccentricities of Suetonius to become generic features of biography in the world of the *Historia Augusta*.

History versus Biography

The *HA*-author reveals himself to be fully conversant with the generic markers his contemporaries used to differentiate the writing of biography and history. Rather than offering a consistent philosophy of his methodology, such as we see often in the canonical biographers and historians, his haphazard appropriation of biographical and historiographical commonplaces typically provides humor through the contrast between the seriousness of the frame and the triviality or absurdity of the content. These themes are introduced not, typically, as allusions to specific authors but in a way that would evoke for the knowledgeable reader a variety of authors and works. Just as the best reader will recognize and enjoy the author's complex allusions, so too will he appreciate the inconsistent and humorous ways in which the tropes of biography and historiography are deployed and parodied in the *Historia Augusta*.

A central theme in both biography and history is that of truth, which differentiates these genres from fictional genres, and therefore is particularly ripe for abuse by the writer of fiction. The *HA*-author is at his least believable when he speaks of truthfulness. We can probably see an echo of a biographical discussion on truth from Marius Maximus at *Didius Iulianus* 3.8. The author tells us that the people were angry at reports of luxurious feasting by Didius Iulianus, but he rejects these reports with the claim that they were recognized to be false ("quod falsum fuisse constat") and then adds evidence of his abstemiousness. We find that Dio, however, presents these reports as true (73.13.1). The *HA*-author picks up on this technique and deploys it in *Elagabalus* 30.8. After reporting that Elagabalus was said to build baths and palaces, use them once, and then demolish them, he adds: "sed et haec et alia nonnulla fidem transeuntia credo esse ficta ab his, qui in gratiam Alexandri Heliogabalum deformare voluerunt" ("however, these and some other things that are beyond belief, I believe to have been invented by those who wished to smear Elagabalus in order to ingratiate themselves with Alexander"). On the one hand, the *HA*-author uses the language of the biographer who judiciously weighs the evidence before him. On the other hand, the humor derives from the fact that it is the *HA*-author himself who has fabricated many details of the life, not of course to curry favor with Alexander but certainly in order to serve his literary purpose of exaggerating the faults of Elagabalus while exaggerating the virtues of Alexander.

The *HA*-author makes a virtue of the lower stylistic register found in biography and other antiquarian literature, in contrast to historiography, by asserting that he purposefully eschews elegance in favor of truth.[28] "I promise neither power nor eloquence, but the historical facts, which I do not allow to perish" ("neque ego nunc facultatem eloquentiamque polliceor sed res gestas, quas perire non patior," *Prob.* 1.6). This is a theme to which the *HA*-author returns repeatedly. The most striking example occurs in the elaborate set piece that introduces the *Aurelian*. The narrator is speaking with the prefect Junius Tiberianus, who amusingly criticizes the accuracy of Trebellius Pollio, one of the avatars of the *HA*-author (*Aur.* 2.1–2):

> me contra dicente neminem scriptorum, quantum ad historiam pertinet, non aliquid esse mentitum, prodente quin etiam in quo Livius, in quo Sallustius, in quo Cornelius Tacitus, in quo denique Trogus manifestis testibus convincerentur, pedibus in sententiam transitum faciens ac manum porrigens iocando praeterea: 'Scribe,' inquit, 'ut libet; securus, quod velis, dices, habiturus mendaciorum comites, quos historicae eloquentiae miramur auctores.'

> I said in response that there was no writer treating historical material who had not lied about something, and even pointed to places where Livy, Sallust, Cornelius Tacitus, and, finally, Trogus could be refuted by obvious proofs; he came over to my opinion, and, stretching out his hand, he jokingly added: "Write as you please. You will be safe in saying whatever you want, having as fellow liars those authors whom we admire for their historical style."

Atticus in Cicero's *Brutus* has something similar to say about style and lies: "at ille ridens: tuo vero, inquit, arbitratu; quoniam quidem concessum est rhetoribus ementiri in historiis, ut aliquid dicere possint argutius" ("He smiled and said: 'As you like, since rhetoricians are allowed to lie in historical matters to make their argument more clever,'" *Brut.* 11.42). Atticus is discussing the use of history by orators, not historians themselves, but his examples include the Alexander-historian Clitarchus. The close link between rhetoric and history made creative enhancement of the past by historians far from unknown. Seneca, too, states baldly that historians are liars, both by omission and by the purposeful inclusion of untrue material for the sake of popularity (*Q Nat.* 7.16). So the *HA*-author shows Tiberianus engaged in a legitimate ancient controversy about the nature of truth in rhetorical historiography—yet the conversation itself is historically impossible, as is much of the life in which it is embedded.

The *Thirty Tyrants* begins with a sharp repetition of the traditional argument that biography is stylistically unpretentious, in contrast to history or rhetoric: "Scriptis iam pluribus libris non historico nec diserto sed pedestri eloquio, ad eam temporum venimus seriem in qua . . . triginta tyranni . . . exstiterunt" ("After having written many books with neither historical nor oratorical elegance, but only everyday language, we have now reached the times in which the thirty tyrants arose," *Tyr. Trig.* 1.1). The author returns to the theme at the end of the book: "da nunc cuivis libellum non tam diserte quam fideliter scriptum. neque ego eloquentiam mihi videor pollicitus esse, sed rem" ("Now give this book, written not elegantly but truthfully, to whomever you want. It seems to me that I have not promised elegance, but only the facts," 33.8). This concluding passage makes it clear that the contrast in the introduction of the *Thirty Tyrants* is between rhetoric and truth.

The life of Aureolus in the *Thirty Tyrants* presents what can only be understood as a parodic comment on the notion of the conflict between rhetoric and truth. On many occasions, in suspect conditions, the *HA*-author quotes verses in Latin that he claims have been translated from Greek.[29] The quality of these verses ranges from poor to terrible.[30] In this particular case, the translation is attributed to "a certain grammar teacher," perhaps a joke pointing to the actual profession of the *HA*-author, who is also the author of the poem (*Tyr. Trig.* 11.6–7):

> hos ego versus a quodam grammatico translatos ita posui, ut fidem servarem, non quo non melius potuerint transferri, sed ut fidelitas historica servaretur, quam ego prae ceteris custodiendam putavi, qui quod ad eloquentiam pertinet nihil curo. rem enim vobis proposui deferre, non verba.
>
> These verses, translated by a certain teacher of grammar, I have provided to preserve the facts, although they could be translated better; but in order to preserve the historical truth, which I have thought must be guarded above all else, as I care not at all about eloquence. For I have decided to offer you the truth of the matter, not fancy words.

The quality of the verses is so low that they can hardly be construed, so in part this is an ironic apology for incompetence. Further humor arises because poetry is one place in which style really ought to win out over truth or historical accuracy, by the standards of every critic. The *HA*-author champions his devotion to *fidelitas historica*, which is lacking elsewhere in the work, at the least appropriate moment.

The biographer may use the lack of rhetorical elegance to differentiate his genre as more true than historiography, but the historian traditionally distinguishes the truthfulness of his own work from panegyric. Tacitus's claim in the *Annales* to have written "without fear or favor" is the classic example of the concern for bias, in particular toward the powerful, in historiography.[31] Ammianus recognizes this theme when he defensively admits that his celebration of Julian may seem almost like panegyric: "Quidquid autem narrabitur, quod non falsitas arguta concinnat, sed fides integra rerum absolvit documentis evidentibus fulta, ad laudativam paene materiam pertinebit" ("What I will tell you will appear almost to be panegyric, although it is not constructed from clever falsehoods, but from the unaltered truth of the facts based on clear evidence," 16.1.3), and, sure enough, he does include criticism of a variety of Julian's actions and decisions. In the final lines of Ammianus, the historian's claim that future historians must write with a "greater pen" ("maiore stilo") is a regretful warning that political necessity demands that in the future, historical works will have to be panegyrics, in contrast to real and truthful history like his own.[32]

The exuberant praise that the *HA*-author offers the emperor Probus skirts the boundary between history and panegyric. See, for example, *Probus* 22.1:

> Conferenti mihi cum aliis imperatoribus principem Probum, omnibus prope Romanis ducibus, qua fortes, qua clementes, qua prudentes, qua mirabiles exstiterunt, intellego hunc virum aut parem fuisse aut, si non repugnat invidia furiosa, meliorem.
>
> When I compare the emperor Probus with other emperors who stood out as courageous, merciful, wise, or admirable, I think that this man was equal to nearly all, or, if no crazed jealousy stands in the way, better than all.

The author shows that he recognizes the importance of the distinction: "longius amore imperatoris optimi progredior quam pedestris sermo desiderat" ("From love of the best emperor I go beyond what prosaic style demands," 21.1). Similarly, the author addresses forthrightly the charge that he praises the emperor Claudius in order to win the favor of his descendant, Constantius, but appeals to his reader's own knowledge and the author's upright life to deny it: "sed testis est et tua conscientia et vita mea me nihil umquam cogitasse, dixisse, fecisse gratiosum ("but your moral sense and the evidence of my life witness that I have never thought, said, or done anything to flatter," *Claud.* 3.1). The author several times returns to the charge of flattery (6.5, 8.2), in a final instance disproving the charge definitively by including material unflattering to the emperor (11.5). Again, the invented figure Annius Cornicula, who praises Gallienus sycophantically, is presumably meant to be a panegyricist; his name, "little crow," evokes a squawking and deceitful bird

(*Gall.* 17.2).³³ His lies contrast with the truth about Gallienus's character that the *HA*-author provides.

The imperial addresses of the *Historia Augusta* can be seen to reflect concerns about bias and the truth status of history. Marincola notes, "Though comfortably ensconced in the other historical genres—biography, memoirs, epitomes—dedications do not seem to have been a common feature of large-scale or 'Great' historiography."³⁴ Sallust, Livy, Tacitus, and presumably Ammianus (to judge from the generalizing nature of his concluding words) all lack dedications, which would have been thought to compromise their independence. Antiquarian writers, such as biographers, have to balance their purported commitment to the truth with their pride in having knowledgeable inside sources for their material, particularly in the imperial period. Thus Suetonius's (lost) dedication to Hadrian's praetorian prefect Septicius Clarus may have served to emphasize his insider status and his access to imperial records. The invented addresses of the *HA*-author to emperors and other government officials offer an interesting solution to the conflict between knowledge and bias. While his various pseudonymous authors are portrayed as the ultimate insiders, offering up their works to emperors and others with special knowledge of their subjects, their extraordinary freedom to chide or even insult emperors and grandees suggests that they are able to rise above dependence on or danger from even the most powerful in the state.

The *HA*-author admits, in a way, to malfeasance in the question of bias when he admits that he is omitting details of the life of Saloninus Gallienus, lest Saloninus's descendants be offended (*Gall.* 19.8). This may parody the discussion in Ammianus of the opposite scenario, where descendants complain to the historian that their ancestors are insufficiently celebrated for their underwhelming deeds (Amm. 26.1). The *HA*-author appeals to Cicero (the lost dialogue *Hortensius*) in support of his claim, as had Ammianus (a lost letter to Nepos). The suggestion is ridiculous, since the *HA*-author dedicates not only the entire life of Gallienus but also the lives of the Thirty Tyrants to denigrating and slandering the emperor; a few extra criticisms of his son could hardly serve to cross some sort of line for his poor descendants.

Ancient historians further distinguished their works by emphasizing the elevated nature of their subject, implicitly relegating the everyday and trivial to lesser genres such as biography and paradoxography. Given the contrast in the definitions of "trivial" implied by the material included by the founders of history, Herodotus and Thucydides, this was clearly a flexible benchmark. Tacitus recognizes that his material might seem trivial when compared with the great achievements of the republic, and he reassures readers that he will not describe senatorial opinions in detail unless they are particularly good or bad (*Ann.* 4.32.1, 3.65.1–2). Dio is less punctilious: while he recognizes that the majesty of history might be sullied by his reports of the trivial and disgraceful activities of Commodus, he announces his intention to include events simply because he was an eyewitness to them (72.18.3–4).[35]

The question of what material is too trivial for the somber majesty of history comes to the fore particularly for a reader of the prefaces of Ammianus. Two prefaces survive, to book 15 and to book 26, and their arguments are, on the surface at least, contradictory. As Ammianus prepares to discuss the age of Julian, he states that he will ignore critics who feel that he is writing too much (15.1.1). When he turns, nine books later, to the age of Valentinian and Valens, he explains that the task of history is to deal with important events, and not to explore trivial things ("praeceptis historiae . . . discurrere per negotiorum celsitudines assuetae, non humilium minutias indager causarum," 26.1.1). It is true that Ammianus has sophisticated reasons for this shift in emphasis.[36] Nevertheless, the interpretation of these passages has been seen as a challenge by modern scholars, and would presumably have been so for ancient readers as well.

The *HA*-author, perhaps inspired by Ammianus, engages with the question of triviality in a variety of ways. We recall Plutarch's support for the proper minor detail in the introduction to his *Alexander*: "Instead, a slight thing like a phrase or a joke often reveals character more than battles when thousands fall." At *Macrinus* 1.1, this Plutarchan idea of "just the right detail" is put forth, although only in a hesitant manner.

> Vitae illorum principum seu tyrannorum sive Caesarum qui non diu imperarunt, in obscuro latent, idcirco quod neque de privata eorum vita digna sunt quae dicantur, cum omnino ne scirentur quidem, nisi adspirassent ad imperium, et de imperio, quod non diu tenuerunt, non multa dici possunt: nos tamen ex diversis historicis eruta in lucem proferemus, et ea quidem quae memoratu digna erunt. non enim est quisquam, qui in vita non ad diem quodcumque fecerit. sed eius qui vitas aliorum scribere orditur, officium est digna cognitione perscribere. et Iunio quidem Cordo studium fuit eorum imperatorum vitas edere, quos obscuriores videbat; qui non multum profecit. nam et pauca repperit et indigna memoratu adserens se minima quaeque persequuuturum, quasi vel de Traiano aut Pio aut Marco sciendum sit, quotiens processerit, quando cibos variaverit et quando vestem mutaverit et quos quando promoverit. quae ille omnia exsequendo libros mythistoriis replevit talia scribendo, cum omnino rerum vilium aut nulla scribenda sint aut nimis pauca, si tamen ex his mores possint animadverti, qui re vera sciendi sunt, sed ex parte, ut ex ea cetera colligantur.

> The lives of those emperors, usurpers, or Caesars who did not rule for a long time lie hidden in obscurity, because there is nothing worth telling in their private lives, since they would indeed not have been known at all if they had not aspired to power, and not much can be said about their rule, because they did not hold power for long. Nevertheless, we shall bring into the light what we have unearthed in various historical works, and they will be things worthy of memory. For there is no man who has not done something or other each day of his life. But the one who sets out to write the lives of others has the duty to record things worth knowing. Junius Cordus, indeed, was eager to write about the lives of those emperors whom he was considering rather obscure. He did not accomplish much, for he found few things and they were not worth remembering, and he asserted that he would seek out the most trivial things, as if it must be known about Trajan, or Pius, or Marcus, how many times he took a walk, when he varied his diet, when he changed his clothes, whom he promoted and when. By searching out and writing all this sort of material, he filled his books with historical trivia, when in fact either nothing at all should be said about trivial material or only in those few occasions when character is able to be demonstrated by such things. True character must be known, but only from a detail from which the whole can be understood.

After apologizing for the paucity of information to be found about the lives of usurpers and junior emperors, the *HA*-author states that he has managed to uncover some material and pledges that it will be "worthy of memory." He adds as an axiom that the writer of lives should record only those events "worth knowing." In his criticism of Cordus for including trivial details of everyday life, however, he partially rejects the Plutarchan formulation, although he does allow that petty matters, if they must be included, may be discussed when revelatory of character. But the thrust of the passage, despite the nod toward biographical themes of character and revelatory detail, is to present a common topos of grand historiography, the insistence on including only what is *dignum memoratu*.[37]

The *HA*-author elsewhere more actively adapts for his biographies the historiographical theme of the rejection of triviality. In a passage in the *Three Gordians* (21.4), Cordus is again criticized for his trivialities. The author in this passage recognizes that this form of criticism is proper to historiography but embraces the terminology of historiography for himself, commenting on:

> Cordum, qui dicit, et quos servos habuerit unusquisque principum et quos amicos et quot paenulas quotve chlamydes. quorum etiam scientia nulli rei

> prodest, si quidem ea debeant in historia poni ab historiografis, quae aut fugienda sint aut sequenda.
>
> Cordus, who says what slaves every single emperor had and what friends, and how many mantles and how many cloaks. This knowledge offers no benefit. Historians ought to include in their works things that are to be avoided, or sought after.

Also telling is a passage in the *Maximus and Balbinus* where Cordus is once again the example of excess (4.5):

> Sed priusquam de actibus eorum loquar, placet aliqua dici de moribus atque genere, non eo modo quo Iunius Cordus est persecutus omnia, sed illo quo Suetonius Tranquillus et Valerius Marcellinus, quamvis Curius Fortunatianus, qui omnem hanc historiam perscripsit, pauca contigerit, Cordus vero tam multa, ut etiam pleraque et minus honesta perscripserit.
>
> But before I speak of their acts, it is appropriate that some things be said about their characters and birth, not in the way in which Junius Cordus sought to include all things, but rather as Suetonius Tranquillus and Valerius Marcellinus did. For although Curius Fortunatianus, who wrote the history of this whole period, touched upon only a few things, Cordus wrote so many things that he included too much, even some indecent material.

The *HA*-author distinguishes between the great mass of detail that Cordus describes and the more restrained method of revealing character found in "Suetonius Tranquillus and Valerius Marcellinus." By using the name of his most important biographer and the almost-name of his most important historian, the *HA*-author claims for biography this traditionally historiographical rejection of excessive detail. Of course, the contrast between claim and reality provides humor.

The *Maximus and Balbinus* passage also addresses another way in which material can be unsuitable for biography—its indecency (*minus honesta*). This theme recurs at the end of the *Elagabalus* in a humorous way, for the author concludes the life, replete with disgraceful and shameful acts, by saying he had passed over many details, since they were too disgraceful and shameful to include (*Elag.* 34.2–3).

While the details of history for the historian are traditionally garnered through eyewitness and inquiry, biography reveals its antiquarian nature through recourse to documents and archival research. The *Historia Augusta* magnifies its discussion of research and evidence far beyond the Suetonian model, again to parodic effect.

One aspect of the *HA*-author's pseudo-research, his citation, favorable or unfavorable, of a large number of invented historians, biographers, and other sources, is considered in chapter 1. Invented names prompt the reader to think allusively. When the *HA*-author says that four authors wrote a life of Trajan—Marius Maximus, Fabius Marcellinus, Aurelius Verus, and Statius Valens (*Alex.* 48.6)—we note that Trajan's life was in fact the subject of works by Marius Maximus, Ammianus Marcellinus, Aurelius Victor, and, finally, Eutropius, who dedicated his work to Valens.[38] Even more common than false citations, particularly in the later lives, is the ceaseless flaunting of unnamed authorities upon which the *HA*-author relies, often for spurious information. Here are some selections from only one book, the *Thirty Tyrants*: "plerique adserunt" (3.2); "de hoc . . . a multis multa sunt dicta" (6.4); "de hoc plane multa miranda dicuntur" (13.2); "quantum plerique scriptores loquuntur" (15.7); "de hoc, utrum imperavit, scriptores inter se ambigunt. multi enim dicunt . . . alii adserunt . . . multi et . . . dixerunt" (18.1–3); "scriptores temporum . . . dixerunt" (18.13); "plerique loquuntur" (24.1); "plerique loquuntur" (31.4); "alii dicunt" (32.3). The humor provoked by the self-portrait of a falsely punctilious scholar is augmented by the emphasis in the preface on the obscurity of the biographical subjects: "ut non multa de his vel dici possint a doctioribus vel requiri, deinde ab omnibus historicis qui Graece ac Latine scripserunt ita nonnulli praetereantur uti eorum nec nomina frequententur" ("that not much concerning them can be either related by scholars or demanded of them, and since some of them have been omitted by all those historians who have written in Greek or in Latin who don't even mention their names," 1.2). The theme of the obscurity of the subject is found in other prefaces to lives that also cite a blizzard of authors, named and unnamed, as sources (*Aur.* 1.4; *Prob.* 1.3; *Quad. Tyr.* 1.1).

Another source of authority for the *HA*-author that is flaunted to the point of parody is the monument.[39] Ancient historians only occasionally used monuments to support their claims.[40] The *HA*-author may respond in particular to the description of the Egyptian obelisk and its inscription provided by Ammianus (17.4).[41] Just as the excesses of citation become so great that they become a joke, so too do the excesses of other forms of research. The author describes, for example, as evidence for the extravagant games put on by the young Gordian, a spectacular painting, which he claims can still be seen "even now" ("etiam nunc," *Gord.* 3.7). But the painting as described would have, implausibly, contained more than 1,300 discrete animals. Moreover, it can be found, according to the author, in the house of Pompey, which the author states has been an imperial possession since the time of Philip. The house of Pompey, however, is last known to have existed in the era of Tiberius (Suet. *Tib.* 15). On the unlikely chance that it still existed in the late empire, the *HA*-author has carefully made it an imperial property, accessible only to "insiders" like himself. Similarly, a mosaic of Aurelian at the house of the Tetrici, which demonstrates how the Tetrici were reconciled with the emperor, has been viewed by the author because he is, it seems, a friend of the family (*Tyr. Trig.* 25).

Gordian's tombstone is conveniently located in Persian territory, placing its implausible inscription at a distance (*Gord.* 34.2-3):

> Gordiano sepulchrum milites apud Circesium castrum fecerunt in finibus Persidis, titulum huius modi addentes et Graecis et Latinis et Persicis et Iudaicis et Aegyptiacis litteris, ut ab omnibus legeretur: 'divo Gordiano victori Persarum, victori Gothorum, victori Sarmatarum, depulsori Romanarum seditionum, victori Germanorum, sed non victori Philipporum.'

> The soldiers built a tomb for Gordian near the camp at Circesium in the territory of Persia, adding the following inscription in Greek, Latin, Persian, Hebrew, and Egyptian letters, so that it could be read by everyone: "To the deified Gordian, conqueror of the Persians, conqueror of the Goths, conqueror of the Sarmatians, queller of mutinies at Rome, conqueror of the Germans, but no conqueror of Philippi."

This alludes to the passage in Ammianus where Julian and his troops spot the tomb of Gordian on the way east (23.5.7). The Ammianus passage in which the tomb is described is particularly multilingual: the soldiers and tomb are in Persia; the nearby town of Zaitha, we are told, means "olive tree" in Aramaic ("Iudaicae litterae," 23.5.7); examples of Greek oracles are adduced (23.5.9); and Etruscan religious specialists are perhaps reminiscent of Egyptians (23.5.10). The tomb of Valerian junior (*Valer.* 8.3) is to be found "near Milan"; the tombs of the Victorini (*Tyr. Trig.* 7.2) are to be found "near Cologne"; and the tomb of Censorinus can be found "near Bologna" (*Tyr. Trig.* 33.4). Again the inaccessibility of the location undercuts the suggestion of authoritative evidence, as even a minimally observant reader would see.

Sometimes physical evidence is portrayed as inaccessible because it has been destroyed. Maximinus had paintings picturing his military successes posted before the senate house, but of course the senate had them destroyed after his death (*Maximin.* 12.10–11). The fictitious usurper Piso had a chariot dedicated to him, but it was destroyed to make way for the Baths of Diocletian (*Tyr. Trig.* 21.6). Two fantastic statues of Tacitus and Florian, of marble and thirty feet high, "were struck by lightning and so thoroughly broken that they lay scattered in fragments" ("deiectae fulmine ita contritae sunt ut membratim iaceant dissipatae," *Tac.* 15.1). Even that multilingual tombstone inscription to Gordian was destroyed by Licinius, we are told, perhaps to explain its absence from Ammianus's account (*Gord.* 34.5). These are all examples of what could only be ridiculously unnecessary highlighting of fraudulence if perpetrated by an author who sought to deceive his audience.

Other discussions of evidence in the *Historia Augusta* are also best seen as fantastical and humorous. We are told that the material for the *Aurelian*, including a diary by the emperor himself, has been written on linen books ("libri lintei") stored in the Ulpian Library (*Aur.* 1.7). Linen books evoke distant antiquity and are associated with Sibylline oracles in fourth-century texts.[42] The joke relies on the incongruity of using a rare and fanciful medium to preserve banal, everyday material, such as a letter of Valerian that describes the sternness of the young Aurelian (*Aur.* 8.1).[43]

The urban prefect Junius Tiberianus will present our author with these linen books, which appear to be inaccessible to ordinary men. The recourse to privileged information, a recurrent theme in the *Historia Augusta*, is uncommon in ancient historiography, typically deployed only in discussions of foreign lands, as in Herodotus's citation of Egyptian priests in his second book, or Ctesias's claim to have drawn on documents from the Persian archives.[44] We similarly see the citation of sacred texts that only priests can read in Heliodorus's novel *Aithiopika* (2.38). The technique evokes the scholars in Aulus Gellius who deploy their insider library access and knowledge as a way to assert their superior control of a text (e.g., 5.21).[45] A key example in the *Historia Augusta* is in the *Tacitus* (8.1–2):

> Ac ne quis me temere Graecorum alicui Latinorumve aestimet credidisse, habet in bibliotheca Ulpia in armario sexto librum elephantinum in quo hoc senatus consultum perscriptum est cui Tacitus ipse manu sua subscripsit. nam diu haec senatus consulta quae ad principes pertinebant in libris elephantinis scribebantur.

> In order that no one judge that I have blindly trusted a Greek or Latin author, the sixth bookcase in the Ulpian Library has an ivory book, in which this decree of the senate has been written out, which Tacitus himself signed by his own hand. For a long time, decrees of the senate that pertained to the emperors used to be written in ivory books.

Ivory is an exotic material for an ancient book, despite the author's pseudo-antiquarian claim that imperial decrees were always written in ivory volumes. The very specific information of its location is confounded by its presence in a library, the Bibliotheca Ulpia, that probably did not still exist in the fifth century. Together we have a particularly extravagant example of a piece of evidence that disproves its claim through its absurdity. An audience familiar with the basics of history- and biography-writing in antiquity would only be amused, not tricked or outraged, by the exploitation and parody of these details.

Historiography and Ancient Fiction

A particular pleasure of reading the *Historia Augusta* derives from the author's use of the language of sober scholarship to defend his absurdities. In the preface to the *Macrinus*, for example, the author criticizes the invented biographer Cordus for a fixation on trivialities. Cordus is said to have described the details of an emperor's food or clothing when he ought to have selected only those few details that shed light on the whole character of the man (*Macr.* 1.4). Of course, this sort of high-minded criticism (cf. Amm. 26.1) appears ludicrous given the extreme frivolity of the details we find in the secondary and late lives. Of what interest is it that Claudius wrote to the general Regalianus requesting two Sarmatian bows and two cloaks with *fibulae* (*Claud.* 10.13)? Is the fact that Firmus is said to have consumed an entire ostrich in a single day truly a sign of his character (*Quad. Tyr.* 4.2)? Why must we learn that the games of Carus, Carinus, and Numerian included not only a tightrope walker but also a wall climber, whose act consisted of fleeing from a bear (*Car.* 19.2)?

Consider also the epilogue to the *Quadrigae Tyrannorum* (15.9), where the author explains why he has devoted a section of his work to four obscure usurpers: "et potui quidem horum vitam praeterire quos nemo quaerebat; attamen, ne quid fidei deesset, etiam de his quae didiceram intimanda curavi" ("I could indeed have omitted the lives of these men, about whom no one was asking, but, in order that there may be no lack of *fides*, I have worked to make familiar the things that I had learned about these also"). Thus the author asserts that the reason he has written these lives, which are entirely fictional constructions of fantasy and allusion, is in order, amazingly, to prevent a lack of *fides*. Burian points out that this emphasis on *fides historica* is at its peak exactly where the *Historia Augusta* is at its most ludicrous.[46] He sees the claim of *fides* as part of a desperate attempt to convince the reader that his fantasy is reality, and concludes that the *HA*-author is a hypocrite: "Im Grunde machte der *HA*-Verfasser oft eben das, was er bei anderen Autoren kritisierte."[47] Could this appeal to *fides*, and this criticism of invented rivals, really work to convince a reader? (It didn't work for Burian.) If the author truly wished his inventions to be believed, he could have simply made them less ridiculous, rather than insisting that the ridiculous is true.

In fact, just as the ancient reader was attuned to elaborate patterns of allusion, so too was he able to recognize traditional generic markers and to appreciate their use and abuse. Other ancient texts, and the evidence from the *Historia Augusta* itself, show that authors and readers recognized and enjoyed crossing the boundaries of biography, history, and fiction. We should not think of the allusive play in the *Historia Augusta* as part of a trick or surprise for the unwary reader. The ancient reader, familiar with fictionalized history, would recognize that the later lives present something closer to biographical parody than actual biography, and the elaborate use of allusion would not undercut sober biography but rather support a comical travesty.

Ancient fiction often makes use of a wide range of authenticating techniques common to historiography and to other scholarly genres.[48] The ancient novel has clear affinities with historiography, presenting fictionalized versions of historical figures, setting adventures in historical settings, and making use of historiographical techniques to create a kind of mock realism.[49] Chariton, usually considered the most naïve of the novelists, provides extensive evidence of this phenomenon. His historiographical frame and his frequent use of "historical details and devices" is well documented.[50] As Alvares shows, Chariton has created an alternative history—an erotic history—that depends upon the reader's recognition of historiographical tropes deployed in clever and unfamiliar ways.[51] Similarly, Hunter argues that the reader's awareness of the differences between novel and history serves Chariton as a "literary stratagem of considerable sophistication."[52] To offer another example, the very title of Lucian's *True Histories* induces pleasure when the reader recognizes the work's fictional nature in light of the ways in which historians traditionally emphasize their devotion to the truth. Lucian's prologue mocks the claims to experience and autopsy that are common in the historians, and he cites several false inscriptions as "evidence" for his fairy tale, in ways meant to evoke the use of epigraphical evidence by Herodotus and other historians. *True Histories* requires an audience that recognizes and appreciates both the conventions and their parody.[53]

An important element of historiographical parody is the citing of invented texts and authorities, what Ni-Mheallaigh calls "pseudo-documentarism": "Its most basic purpose is to lend the fiction an air of authenticity, veracity, and documentary importance by creating for the fiction an extra-literary referent such as that which is normally attributed to historiography. . . . [These techniques] are converted also into signals to the knowing reader, playfully advertising the fictionality of the text."[54] The *Ephemeris belli Troiani* is a novel of Homeric revisionism with a particularly elaborate frame. It claims to have been written in Phoenician by Dictys of Crete, a participant in the Trojan War, then sealed in a chest and discovered and translated into Greek at the time of the emperor Nero. On the one hand, the frame serves, as Merkle says, as a *Beglaubigungsapparat* "designed to produce in the reader a belief in the text's reliability and genuineness."[55] And yet the frame is so convoluted and absurd that it immediately provokes suspicion as well, and the fact that Dictys is from Crete, notorious home of liars in antiquity, is a joke and a signal to the reader that the prologue is not meant seriously.[56] The *Wonders beyond Thule*, a fragmentary novel by Antonius Diogenes, also had an elaborate framing device: a letter that contained a letter, which discussed writings found on cypress wood tablets, which were transcribed, and so on.[57] It is possible that readers of novels may have occasionally been fooled by pseudo-documentarism. After all, Augustine thought it was at least possible that Apuleius's *Metamorphoses* was autobiographical (*De civ. D.* 18.18). For most readers of Lucian, Dictys, or Antonius Diogenes, however, the frame and the recognition of the frame contribute to the enjoyment of the fiction.

The *Life of Apollonius of Tyana* by the third-century author Philostratus provides more direct parallels to the *Historia Augusta* with its citation of invented sources. This lengthy biography, although based on a historical figure of the first century, is heavily fictionalized. It shares with Dictys and Antonius Diogenes an introduction that offers a romantic source for the information behind the work. Philostratus says that a certain Damis, a disciple of Apollonius, composed a memoir of his travels with the master. These papers were apparently preserved in family archives until they were revealed to Julia Domna, the wife of the emperor and an intimate of Philostratus, who commissioned him to write a more polished version based on Damis's writings. Since the *Life* contains many errors that could not have been committed by a contemporary of Apollonius, and since Damis is otherwise unknown to history, the reality of Damis has long been doubted.[58] Philostratus's familiarity with mock-authenticating framing devices is made clearer by the introduction to another fictional work of his, the *Heroicus*. This work, like that of Dictys, purports to tell the "real" story of the Trojan War through a dialogue between a Phoenician and a mysterious vinedresser who has gained his knowledge through an acquaintance with the hero Protesilaus. In several places the author appears to purposefully contradict the account of Dictys (*Her.* 30.1, 33.1).[59] This comical intertextual relationship with Dictys reveals Philostratus's expectation that his readers were fully aware of this kind of fictional framing. This frame should be understood, of course, not as a lie or a false claim of special knowledge but as a literary technique common to ancient fiction. It provides a literary game for the reader but also places the narrative between history and fiction, the same space where we also find, for example, speeches in traditional ancient historiography.[60]

The *Historia Augusta* is not a novel, and its political biographies are distant from the adventures and philosophical discourses that make up the *Life of Apollonius* or the love and adventure of the Greek romance. The point of overlap lies in our recognition that sophisticated readers and writers in antiquity understood and playfully manipulated historiographical techniques that included invented sources, elaborate prologues with references to hidden information, and claims for truthfulness at the most unlikely moments. Literal-minded historians of the modern era may have failed to interpret and appreciate these games, but we should hesitate before assuming that the intended audience of the *Historia Augusta* was equally insensible.

The Audience of the *Historia Augusta*

There is no solving the problem of the *Historia Augusta*. As Mehl says, the issues are so many and so interconnected that "immer mindestens eine weitere unbekannte bzw. unsichere Grösse mitbetrachtet werden muss."[61] But if we cannot understand a private joke without some unknowable details, we can nevertheless recognize that it is a private joke and perhaps surmise something of the context in which it was told. We can make progress by eliminating the impossible explanations for the work, and by better situating it in the context of imperial Roman reading and scholarship. The allusiveness of the *Historia Augusta*, and the particular nature of that allusiveness, are central to rejecting traditional explanations for its peculiarities and offering new ones.

Early commenters such as Dessau and Hohl imagined profit as an important motive for the fraudulence of the *Historia Augusta*. The prologues addressed to Diocletian and Constantine, for example, were supposedly meant to deceive potential book purchasers into believing that the "authors" were of the highest social standing, and would therefore have access to the most accurate information. The frequent use of variations on contemporary aristocratic names—the Ceionii or Faltonii, for example—sought to flatter and attract aristocrats into acquiring biographies that demonstrated the prominence of their families in the second- and third-century empire. Perhaps, as well, the author inserted the Probus's prophecy about the greatness of the emperor's descendants to attract the support of modern Probi and their circle.

These early scholars relied on the belief that the Roman book market was similar to that of a modern, capitalist society. Birt, for example, imagined that ancient publishers regularly received manuscripts from authors, copies of which they made and sold.[62] Modern research into the book trade in antiquity makes the idea of fraud-for-profit less tenable.[63] A typical work in antiquity was first shared with a wider audience by recitation. A final, revised version of the work would then be copied upon request for friends of the author. Further distribution was mostly through additional copying by and for friends. Booksellers played a comparatively minor role in the circulation of books, and the opportunity for profit would have been limited. Nevertheless, there are some possible examples of this kind of fraud on a much smaller scale. Aulus Gellius found manuscripts at bookshops that provided eccentric readings of Vergil and other classical authors, and works that falsely purported to be written by Galen were offered for sale at some shops. It is possible, as more cynical modern scholars suspect, that these were not errors but frauds perpetrated to make a sale. Such frauds, if that is what they were, required considerably less work than the compilation of the *Historia Augusta*, of course. There would surely have been more economical ways of profiting from aristocratic family pride than this elaborate production.

Whether or not material could be forged and sold for profit in the ancient book market, the allusiveness of the work demonstrates the impossibility of imagining the *Historia Augusta* in particular as a purposeful fraud created to deceive its audience. Any student of ancient biography could invent plausible details of second-century imperial life without creating webs of allusion—especially, as we will see in the next chapters, allusions to contemporary fourth- and fifth-century texts. Using such material could only increase the likelihood that the fraud would be discovered. An author desiring to deceive would also avoid the extreme absurdity found in some of the secondary or later lives, especially when coupled with editorial asides that decry triviality and the treatment of disgraceful material.

Implicit in a lot of more recent thinking about the *Historia Augusta* is Straub's theory of two audiences.[64] For Straub, the ordinary member of the audience reads the *Historia Augusta* simply for information and entertainment, but the more sophisticated audience members are able to understand and interpret the hidden allusions. The model requires both a message that the *HA*-author wants to impart and a reason why he must do so secretly. For Straub and some epigones, the message is one of tolerance for paganism, and the obstacle is an antipagan establishment. The flaws in Straub's specific theory of a plea for Christian tolerance are demonstrated in the next chapter. Here I want merely to point out that the extravagance of allusion could only distract from any serious message that the author intended. Problems of dating render impossible another version of the two-audiences theory, that of Baynes, who argues that the *Historia Augusta* was written as propaganda on behalf of the emperor Julian.[65] But the allusive excess of the *Historia Augusta* would have made Baynes's argument untenable in any event. Playful allusion to Cicero or Suetonius could hardly help to promote the policies of a particular emperor. Similar objections may be made against any positive political program for the work, such as Honoré's argument that the author was providing running commentary on the serious events of the 390s (why include so much silliness?), or

Cameron's suggestion that the praise of the Constantinian dynasty in the *Claudius* was tied to the marriage of Gratian and Constantia (how is praise to be read in the context of subterfuge and nonsense?).[66] The frivolity of the *Historia Augusta* undercuts any serious agenda.

Sustained interpretations like those of Baynes and Straub are much less prominent today. Instead, scholars like Chastagnol and Paschoud speak of tendencies and opinions, without offering global explanations for the work. Particularly influential for all modern scholars has been the work of Syme, especially his description of the author as a "rogue grammarian." "The author is a scholar, devoted to the techniques of research. He likes libraries."[67] "The author's milieu is no mystery. He has the tastes of a scholiast—and the mentality."[68] Syme sees the author as a *littérateur* with no overall purpose or tendency but playfulness. Accepting that the personality of the author is that of a rogue grammarian does not, however, explain why he wrote such a mystifying work. Syme himself offers no sustained argument on the purpose of the *Historia Augusta*, only stray comments strewn throughout his works. At times Syme seems to agree with Dessau in seeing the work as a hoax, a purposeful deception. For example, in discussing the author's fabrication of names, Syme begins, "If a writer wishes to cover up his tracks . . ."[69] And similarly, "If an author is anxious to be plausible, he may try to convey an impression of novelty (and hence of authenticity) by names that look original because different."[70] In other places he offers a variation, perhaps, of Straub's "two-audiences" theory: "And, though he may not have set out to deceive all his readers . . ."[71] "As the *HA* advances toward its termination, the author exhibits a progressive audacity in his inventions. And here and there the deceiver lifts the veil, gently."[72] "But he is patently a rogue scholar, perverse, delighting in deception, and not reluctant to be found out toward the end."[73] For Straub, the dangers of persecution required an evasive presentation. To what end would the *HA*-author camouflage his fraud, with the intent of being properly interpreted by only a few?

Let us consider a modern parallel, a twentieth-century scholar who (some believe) forged an ancient Christian text. In 1958 the American scholar Morton Smith claimed to have discovered in a monastery near Jerusalem an otherwise unknown letter of Clement of Alexandria containing two passages from a version of the gospel of Mark that Smith called "Mystic" or "Secret Mark."[74] The passages suggested that Jesus had personally baptized his followers, naked and at night, into an esoteric version of Christianity that may have included some form of physical contact. Upon publication in 1973, the text was immediately controversial, and many doubts about its authenticity have been raised in the forty years since. Carlson, in a book that charges Smith with fraud, argues that Smith included details in his forgery that were meant as sly jokes. For example, Carlson claims that the reference to "adulterated salt" in the text was not only anachronistic but a clue, because the technology of salt granulation was only developed in the twentieth century—by the Morton Salt company![75] The framing of the gospel fragments is also suspicious. Clement explains in detail why the text was unknown—it was found only in Alexandria, it was carefully guarded, it was read only by initiates—and he enjoins his addressee, "Theodore," to lie and deny its existence, if necessary. Yet this secret is presented in what purports to be a published letter of Clement. And the letter breaks off at a particularly amusing place: it concludes, "and so the true explanation, and the one which comports with true philosophy, is . . ."[76] The potential parallels with the *Historia Augusta* are clear.

If Secret Mark is a forgery by Smith, rather than an authentic document or an earlier forgery, why did he do it? Most suspect that the reason was ideological. Perhaps Smith the lapsed Episcopalian priest meant to attack traditional Christian belief, or perhaps the lifelong bachelor meant to strike a blow for gay liberation. It seems possible to some, however, that Smith may have committed a hoax simply for the fun of it: "I can just see Smith laughing from his grave at having duped so many well-trained scholars with his cleverly composed 'gospel.'"[77] Can this modern model find ancient parallels?

The nature of ancient reading, writing, and scholarship makes the image of a solitary writer weaving chains of allusion for his own amusement unlikely, and perhaps impossible. A suggestive, but ultimately illusory, example comes from a tax roll on papyrus found in Egyptian Karanis. The names of taxpayers on the roll have been rendered informally, sometimes with the Egyptian form of the name or an Egyptian nickname, followed often by Greek translations of the Egyptian name. Some of the Greek words are quite unusual and poetic. At one point the Egyptian nickname *Panpin*, which means "mousetrap," is glossed with an obscure word for mousetrap, *andiktes*, which is found elsewhere only in Callimachus (Pfeiffer *fr.* 177, line 33). This striking word is said by Youtie to help us to

> resurrect an anonymous but well delineated personality. Among the clerks in the tax bureau was one whose role as *érudit manqué* comes through to us even after so long a time. The linguistic facility, the literary culture once so promising and now so pointless, the trivial display for no eyes but his own, the light and barely sarcastic touch—they are all there. And what could be more satisfying to a tax clerk with pretensions to learning than a borrowing from Callimachus furtively inserted into a gigantic money register, where no one would ever notice it?[78]

This language is reminiscent of Syme's description of the *HA*-author, whose "fancy goes to odd facts, peculiar names, rare words (both the archaic and the technical)."[79] "The author (many signs betray it) was himself a *scholasticus* who conceived higher ambitions."[80] We suspect, at first, an ancient analogue to Morton Smith, delighting in allusiveness for his own secret joy.

Yet there is a sequel to this tale of a sarcastic bureaucrat that emphasizes the communal practices of ancient reading and scholarship into which we must situate the *HA*-author. When van Minnen returned to the evidence for Roman Karanis, he was able to put these tax rolls in context.[81] The tax collector was not an anonymous, low-ranking bureaucrat but the chief tax collector, Socrates by name. His house contained abstruse Greek literature, including grammatical papyri, Menander, and the *Acta Alexandrinorum*. More important, there were some fragments of Callimachus at the house next door, suggesting the presence of another intellectual who shared Socrates's interests and would recognize his allusions. Rather than providing an example of a lone, romantic figure, the tax document turns out to make a very different point about the inevitable enmeshing of reading and studying in antiquity within a broader community.

We must, then, turn from the individual and from an excessively modern vision of writing, publication, and reading to look more closely at the community in which a text like the *Historia Augusta* may have arisen.[82] It is a commonplace to note that reading in antiquity was typically done aloud. Although silent reading was not uncommon, reading was often considered a social and participatory act. Thus Gavrilov demonstrated, for example, that Augustine was not puzzled or amazed by the fact that Ambrose read the Bible silently, as has often been claimed. Instead, he was surprised and disappointed that Ambrose did not read aloud in a manner that would allow auditors to participate in questioning and debating the meaning of the text.[83] Whether a text was read in a symposium, in a classroom, or in a synagogue, it would normally be subject to challenge and interrogation.

In the ancient classroom, students and teachers engaged in the study of a philosophical or religious text discussed and debated it. Epictetus, for example, or a designated student read aloud from a selected Stoic text. Terms were discussed and defined, arguments were logically dissected, and hypotheses were proposed, with a give-and-take between teacher and student.[84] In some cases, such as the classroom of Plotinus as described by Porphyry, questions to the teacher could lead to digressions in the middle of the reading (*Plot.* 13.10–17). Gellius's teacher, the Platonist L. Calvisius Taurus, reserved questions for the end of the exposition (*NA* 1.26).[85] Similar discussions and exchanges were typical in Jewish circles in Alexandria, from the evidence of Philo, and in Jerusalem, from the evidence of Luke.[86]

These habits of exposition and questioning were found far from the classroom. Plutarch teaches the young to be active listeners to poetry, and to engage with poetry as it was being recited at a symposium: "One must not tremble and bow down before everything like a coward, or superstitiously as in a temple, but rather be habituated to shouting out boldly, 'wrong!' and 'badly done!' just as much as 'right!' and 'well done!'"[87] When Trimalchio interrupts the rhetorician Agamemnon, who is recounting an oration he had pronounced earlier in the day, he is not rude for interrupting; the problem is simply that his comments are witless (Petron. *Sat.* 48). In the sympotic context, "education turns out to be teamwork."[88] One might suppose that the formal recitation would be more decorous than a symposium, but at Pliny's recitations of his oratory or poetry, he "welcomes, even demands, active intervention by his audience."[89] He is indignant on behalf of a friend who recited an outstanding work to an audience that refused to speak, sitting motionless like deaf-mutes (*Ep.* 6.17).

Outside the classroom, where the hierarchy of learnedness was less clear, scholars engaged with texts and the public in an agonistic manner. Aulus Gellius provides our best evidence for scholarly debate in the empire.[90] Gellius and his literary/scholarly group read aloud and debated in a variety of settings. Although reading and study could be pursued in private, it was in public that reputations were made. Activities that seem dry and scholastic to modern audiences, such as a close reading and comparison of the bucolic poetry of Theocritus and Vergil, took place as part of dinner entertainment (*NA.* 9.9). The rhetor Favorinus, taking a walk, spies a copy of Sallust's *Catiline*, which he orders to be read aloud. He interrupts the reading to ask Gellius a question about the text, which inspires general conversation and debate; the passage in question is reread, and Favorinus has the final word (*NA.* 3.1). Quite often Gellius presents us with a scenario where the man learned in texts, particularly obscure and archaic ones, soundly demolishes an upstart's pretensions to learning. As Johnson summarizes: "It is fundamental that this text-centered community negotiates what is correct and what is incorrect, who is right and who is wrong, within the context of their closed society."[91]

The intellectual world of Galen, as revealed in his works, provides further evidence for contentious public scholarship in the second century. Once at a public lecture a passage was selected at random from the work of Erasistratus, *On Bringing Up Blood*, and Galen spoke on it *ex tempore* (*On His Own Books* 1, 19.14K). On another occasion Galen improvised at length on the flaws of a rival physician, Julianus (*Against Julianus* 2.2, 18A.253K).[92] Public disputation over scripture was common in early imperial debates between Jews and Christians and by rival sects within each group, and continued into late antiquity.[93] Disputes between Christians and Manicheans took place before crowds and relied on the sacred texts of each religion.[94]

The importance of the audience is the focus of a recent study of the *New* (or *Strange*) *History* by Ptolemy the Quail. This work, in six books, is known through excerpts quoted by the Byzantine patriarch Photius and by some expanded versions of specific passages in the works of Byzantine scholars. It appears at first to be a work of scholarship that offers alternative or expanded versions of familiar stories from Greek legend and history. Ptolemy's stories are typically ridiculous—he claims that Heracles was the lover of Nestor, for example, and that Odysseus was called *Outis* as a child because he had big ears. Ptolemy cites a wide variety of sources for his claims, some of which are known (such as Herodotus) but many of which are found only in Ptolemy, and are thus suspect. The study of Hercher in the nineteenth century demonstrated the fictitious nature of the work and its "sources," and despite attempts at rehabilitation by Chatzis and Tomberg, the recent treatment by Cameron reaffirms that it was entirely the product of invention.[95] Cameron offers two contrasting approaches to evaluating Ptolemy and his use of fake sources; he is either the perpetrator of a "deliberate, bare-faced forgery" or he is an especially egregious participant in a tendency common to paradoxographers more generally: "citing sources they had not seen and knew no one would check."[96] We should rather agree with Hose in finding an explanation beyond the choices of liar or fool.[97] The work of Ptolemy represents both a joke and a challenge for an audience, perhaps symposiastic, fully aware of its fictionality. For those who are immersed in the culture of literary arguments and scholarship, Ptolemy's stories present amusing puzzles. For example, Herodotus tells us several times that Xerxes personally witnessed the battle of Salamis (e.g., 8.88.3). In the reading culture of antiquity, such a claim, when read aloud, might easily provoke a question: "How was the Persian emperor able to see so clearly and so far away?" Ptolemy offers the answer (at Photius *Bibl.* 190):

> τούτου τοῦ Εὐπόμπου παῖδα δράκοντα τοὔνομα ὀξυωπέστατον γενέσθαι φασίν, ὡς διὰ σταδίων κ΄ θεωρεῖμ ῥᾳδίως· ὃν καὶ Ξέρξη ἐπὶ χιλίοις συγγενόμενον ταλάντοις καὶ συγκαθεζόμενον ὑπὸ τῇ χρυσῇ πλατάνῳ διηγεῖσθαι βλέποντα τὴν Ἑλλήνων καὶ βαρβάρων ναυμαχίαν καὶ τὴν Ἀρτεμισίας ἀνδρείαν.

> They say that this Eupompus had a son named Drako who was so sharp-sighted that he could easily see twenty stades. He placed him in service to Xerxes for a thousand talents, and sitting with the king under the golden plane tree he described the sea battle of the Greeks and Persians and the courage of Artemisia.

Ptolemy again provides his listeners with a humorous test when he answers a question with which, Suetonius tells us, the emperor Tiberius used to torment grammarians: what was the name Achilles used when he was disguised as a girl at

Scyros (Suet. *Tib.* 70)? Ptolemy provides five different answers to this presumably canonical question.[98] As Cameron shows, some of the answers Ptolemy gives make a kind of logical sense for a reader with sufficient Homeric knowledge.[99] For example, because Achilles was worshiped under the name "Aspetos" at Epirus, to suggest that he held that name at Scyros challenges the reader/listener to explain the reference. On the other hand, only a simple and obvious joke explains the name "Kerkusera" for the transvestite Achilles, a feminine name formed from the noun *kerkos*, slang for the penis. The invented scholar credited with the coquettish name Kerkusera, Aristonicus of Tarentum, would fit easily into the *Historia Augusta*. He shares the given name of the first-century Homeric scholar Aristonicus of Alexandria, but rather than hailing from the scholars' city of Alexandria, he comes from the luxury-loving city of Tarentum.[100]

It is worth dwelling for a moment on Cameron's dissection of an invention by Ptolemy derived from a passage of Lycophron.[101] Ptolemy attributes to a variety of Homeric figures a counselor or adviser whom he calls a *mnemon*. At one point he attributes his information about Noemon the Carthaginian, whom he claims as the *mnemon* of Achilles, to the Hellenistic poet Lycophron. Ancient scholars on a passage of Lycophron (*Alex.* 240–41), Cameron shows, interpreted the adjective *mnemon* as a proper name and associated this Mnemon with a messenger sent by Thetis to Achilles according to an extra-Homeric tradition. Ptolemy, instead, seems to have taken *mnemon* as a title for a minor official, as it was commonly used in Greek cities in the early imperial period, and multiplied its use to apply to other heroes in addition to Achilles. Cameron must be right to say that this cannot be a case where Ptolemy has blindly followed an ignorant or deceptive source. The invention must be his own. Ptolemy, however, is not like the deceptive teacher in the Lucianic dialogue *The Teacher of Rhetoric*, who advises his protégé to create interesting words and, if challenged, to invent poets or historians who can serve as obscure and uncheckable authorities for his fraud (*Teacher of Rhetoric* 17). Ptolemy has instead provided the very information that Cameron, and presumably others, can use to demonstrate his invention. Should we not better understand, instead, that the translation of *mnemon* was a disputed point in scholarly circles—or just in Ptolemy's circle—and the attentive audience member, perhaps with the help of other auditors and with reference to the text of Lycophron, could recognize and appreciate the game that Ptolemy is playing? The work was designed for symposiastic discussion and debate, and for an audience well aware of its tricks and jokes.

The anonymous *Collection of Greek and Roman Parallel Stories* included in the corpus of Plutarch is even more interesting as an example of historiographical rather than literary parody. Cameron denounces this work, too, complaining that for "sheer triviality, gross ignorance, and irresponsible fabrication no other ancient work I can think of (not even the *Historia Augusta*) comes even close."[102] The collection consists of forty-one brief accounts of events from, typically, Greek history, followed by events from Roman history that parallel them. Despite the valiant efforts of Schlereth, accepted by Boulogne, we must accept Jacoby's arguments, augmented by Cameron's, that the work and its scholarly apparatus are fictitious.[103] What kind of fiction? Again, the evidence suggests that we see here not an incompetent and purposeless attempt at deception but a parody or game for a witting audience.

The brief prologue to the work begins with the claim that "the majority of people think that tales of ancient events are inventions and myths because of the incredible elements they contain" (305a). This is an appropriate preview, reminiscent of a novel, for a work of historical myth and invention. The work is a parody of historiography in general, and more specifically of the pairing of Greek and Roman lives that we see in Plutarch, and of the ancient literature that seeks to show Greek origins for Roman practices.[104] It is impossible to determine the original context in which the work was produced, but it is hard to imagine that the absurdities would not have been obvious to a contemporary. For example, consider the perfect parallel in every detail of the following invented story with the canonical story of the Horatii and Curiatii (309d–e):

> Τεγεάταις καὶ φενεάταις χρονίου πολέμου γενομένου, ἔδοξε τριδύμους ἀδελφοὺς πέμψαι τοὺς μαχησομένους περὶ τῆς νίκης. καὶ Τεγεᾶται μὲν οὖν τοὺς Ῥηξιμάχου παῖδας, Φενεᾶται δὲ τοὺς Δημοστράτου προὐβάλλοντο. Συμβληθείσης δὲ τῆς μάχης, ἐφονεύθησαν τῶν Ῥηξιμάχου δύο· ὁ δὲ τρίτος τοὔνομα Κριτόλαος στρατηγήματι περιεγένετο τῶν Δημοστράτου· προσποιητὴν γὰρ φυγὴν σκηψάμενος καθ' ἕνα τῶν διωκόντων ἀνεῖλε. Καὶ ἐλθόντος οἱ μὲν ἄλλοι συνεχάρησαν, μόνη δ' οὐκ ἐχάρη ἡ ἀδελφὴ Δημοδίκη· πεφονεύκει γὰρ αὐτῆς τὸν κατηγγυημένον ἄνδρα Δημόδικον. Ἀναξιοπαθήσας δὲ ὁ Κριτόλαος ἀνεῖλεν αὐτήν. Φόνου δ' ἀγόμενος ὑπὸ τῆς μητρὸς ἀπελύθη τοῦ ἐγκλήματος.

> When a war between the Tegeans and the Pheneans had continued for a long time, it was agreed to send triplet brothers to fight for the victory. The Tegeans put forth on their behalf the sons of Rheximachus, the Pheneans the sons of Demostratus. When battle began, two of Rheximachus's sons were killed. But the third, Kritolaus by name, by a trick he outlived the other two sons of Demostratus. He pretended to run away and killed his pursuers one at a time. And when he came home all the rest rejoiced with him; but his sister Demodice alone did not rejoice, for he had killed her

betrothed, Demodicus. Kritolaus, angered at the unworthy treatment, killed her. Prosecuted for murder by his mother, he was acquitted of the charge.

Making up historical narratives was a standard part of rhetorical education.[105] The *Parallela Minora* seem custom-made for the kind of analysis that Quintilian suggests is appropriate for historical narratives in an educational setting (*Inst.* 2.4.18):

> Narrationibus non inutiliter subiungitur opus destruendi confirmandique eas, quod ἀνασκευή et κατασκευή uocatur. Id porro non tantum in fabulosis et carmine traditis fieri potest, uerum etiam in ipsis annalium monumentis: ut, si quaeratur 'an sit credibile super caput Valeri pugnantis sedisse coruum, qui os oculosque hostis Galli rostro atque alis euerberaret,' sit in utramque partem ingens ad dicendum materia: aut de serpente, quo Scipio traditur genitus, et lupa Romuli et Egeria Numae; nam Graecis historiis plerumque poeticae similis licentia est. Saepe etiam quaeri solet de tempore, de loco, quo gesta res dicitur, nonnumquam de persona quoque, sicut Liuius frequentissime dubitat et alii ab aliis historici dissentiunt.

> Narratives, advantageously, offer the exercise of refuting and confirming them, which is called *anaskeue* and *kataskeue*. This is able to be done not only with traditional stories and poems, but even with historical records. If it should be asked whether it is believable that a raven sat on the head of Valerius when he was in battle, and with its wings and beak attacked the face and eyes of the enemy Gaul, much material for debate exists on either side; or we might argue about the snake from which it is said that Scipio was engendered, and the wolf of Romulus, and the Egeria of Numa. For many Greek historians are as free as poets. Often we can ask the time and place where events are said to occur, and sometimes even the person who did them is unknown. Livy, for instance, is frequently in doubt, and historians often disagree.

Compilers of ancient historical fragments have been forced to confront the many authorities that Pseudo-Plutarch cites for his ridiculous parallels. Cameron calculates eighty citations to thirty-eight authors and fifty-seven works in the short compilation.[106] These excesses must be part of the joke, an over-the-top demonstration of scholarly punctiliousness in the service of silliness. Cameron, however, thinks that "perhaps the most intriguing thing" about this blizzard of fake citations "is that many readers not only did not question them but apparently looked on them as a key part of his stories."[107] The imputation of this view to "many" readers seems out of line with the evidence. Eighteen extracts of the work appear in the anthology of Stobaeus (probably fifth century) and six in John Lydus (sixth century). These late compilers should not get to represent "many readers." Clement of Alexandria (died around 215) is the only other author to quote the work and its false sources, three times in the *Protrepticus*. The *Protrepticus* is a frontal assault on pagan mythology in which material from mythographic handbooks is compiled to be mocked and ridiculed. Clement's aim was not to assure scholarly accuracy but to shock the conscience of the reader with so much pagan wickedness attributed to so many different authors. He does not provide good evidence for how a contemporary reader approaching the work with an open mind would have interpreted it.

These examples of pseudo-scholarship, in which an author hides jokes and allusions for an informed audience, can serve as a starting point for understanding the *Historia Augusta*. We should think not only of a particular author but of the audience, perhaps a small, scholarly circle for which the work was composed and read. Rather than a circle of *literati* as in Gellius's case, this circle would have a particular interest in biographical writing, and the *Historia Augusta*, rather than an attempt to fool its audience, would be presented as a challenge, and as a starting point for learned discourse.

While the literary scholarship that survives from antiquity is mostly focused on poetry, there is evidence for interest in historiography and biography in works such as Aristarchus's commentary on Herodotus or Lucian's parody of historiographical commonplaces in *How to Write History*. Gellius mentions a dinner with the philosopher Favorinus at which history was recited in both Greek and Latin (*NA* 2.22). While most of our evidence for scholarly circles in antiquity is found in the idealized, literary portraits we see in Gellius or Macrobius, a document from Oxyrhynchus provides unmediated evidence for such a circle at work. A papyrus letter with three or four different hands reveals the search by a group for some obscure volumes on ancient drama, books 6 and 7 of Hypsicrates's *Characters in Comedy* and prose epitomes of Thersagoras's *Myths of Tragedy*.[108]

Two passages in the *Historia Augusta* describe scholarly groups with an interest in historiography, the very kinds of groups within which I propose we place the composition, recitation, and discussion of the work itself. In the introduction to the *Quadrigae Tyrannorum*, the author describes for us a scholarly circle arguing over the legitimacy of the usurper Firmus (2.1–2):

> Scis enim, mi Basse, quanta nobis contentio proxime fuerit cum amatore historiarum Marco Fonteio, cum ille diceret Firmum, qui Aureliani temporibus Aegyptum occupaverat, latrunculum fuisse, non principem, contra ego mecumque Rufius Celsus et Ceionius Iulianus et Fabius Sossianus

> contenderent, dicentes illum et purpura usum et, percussa moneta, Augustum esse vocitatum, cum etiam nummos eius Severus Archontius protulit, de Graecis autem Aegyptiisque libris convicit illum αὐτοκράτορα in edictis suis esse vocatum. et illi quidem adversum nos contendenti haec sola ratio fuit quod dicebat Aurelianum in edicto suo non scripsisse quod tyrannum occidisset, sed quod latrunculum quemdam a re publica removisset, proinde quasi digne tanti princeps nominis debuerit tyrannum appellare hominem tenebrarium, aut non semper latrones vocitaverint magni principes eos quos invadentes purpuras necaverunt. ipse ego in Aureliani vita, priusquam de Firmo cuncta cognoscerem, Firmum non inter purpuratos habui, sed quasi quendam latronem; quod idcirco dixi ne quis me oblitum aestimaret mei. sed ne volumini quod brevissimum promisi multa conectam, veniamus ad Firmum.

> For you know, my Bassus, how great an argument we had recently with Marcus Fonteius, the lover of history, when he said that Firmus, who had occupied Egypt in the time of Aurelian, had been a robber, not an emperor, but I, and together with me Rufius Celsus and Ceionius Julianus and Fabius Sossianus, argued against him, saying that Firmus had both worn the purple and was called Augustus on the coins that he struck, and Severus Archontius even brought out coins of Firmus and proved, moreover, from Greek and Egyptian books that he had been called *autocrat* in his edicts. Fonteius, on the other hand, against us, had only the argument that Aurelian had written in his edict not that he had killed a usurper, but that he had removed a robber from the state, as if a renowned emperor must call such a shadowy figure a usurper, or as if great emperors did not always call "robbers" those whom they kill when attempting to seize the purple. I myself, in my *Life of Aurelian*, before I knew everything about Firmus, thought that he was not among those who had worn the purple, but was only an ordinary criminal, which I have repeated so that no one may think that I have forgotten what I said. So as not to add too much, however, to a book which I promised to make very short, let us now turn to Firmus.

Here seven men, at least one of whom is an *amator historiarum*, debate whether Firmus should be considered an actual *imperator* or merely a robber (*latrunculus*). This debate over terminology has been claimed as a parody of Christian quarreling over heresy and orthodoxy, but it is common in all types of secular scholarship as well.[109] The participants appeal to the evidence of coins, to official edicts promulgated by Firmus and by Aurelian, and to Greek and even Egyptian books to make their case. The scene is evidently parodic. Marcus Fonteius, who thinks Firmus was merely a criminal, knows something of criminality himself, as he shares his name with the praetor whose looting of Gaul was defended by Cicero, and the use of Egyptian evidence is reminiscent of the appeal to Phrygian inscriptions in ancient novels. It nevertheless presupposes the reasonableness of a gathering and a debate by *amatores historiarum* over historical definitions and historical facts.

Another passage in the *Thirty Tyrants* also presupposes groups of history devotees (31.7–10).

> Studiose in medio feminas posui ad ludibrium Gallieni, quo nihil prodigiosius passa est Romana res publica, duos etiam nunc tyrannos quasi extra numerum, quod alieni essent temporis, additurus, unum qui fuit Maximini temporibus, alterum qui Claudii, ut triginta viri hoc tyrannorum volumine tenerentur. quaeso, qui expletum iam librum acceperas, boni consulas atque hos volumini tuo volens addas, quos ego, quem ad modum Valentem superiorem huic volumini, sic post Claudium et Aurelianum his qui inter Tacitum et Diocletianum fuerunt, addere destinaveram. sed errorem meum memor historiae diligentia tuae eruditionis avertit. habeo igitur gratiam, quod titulum meum prudentiae tuae benignitas implevit. nemo in templo Pacis dicturus est me feminas inter tyrannos, tyrannas videlicet vel tyrannides, ut ipsi de me solent cum risu et ioco iactitare, posuisse.

> I carefully included women to mock Gallienus, more monstrous than any whom the Roman state has suffered under; now I will add two more usurpers, supernumeraries, so to speak, who were from different periods, one who lived in the time of Maximinus, the other from the time of Claudius, so that thirty men will be included in this book of usurpers. I ask you who have received this now-completed book to think well of me and, just as I included the elder Valens in this book, to willingly add to your volume these men, whom I had planned to include after Claudius and Aurelian to those who lived between Tacitus and Diocletian. But the accuracy of your learning, mindful of history, prevented my error. And so I am thankful that the kindness of your wisdom has fulfilled my title. No one in the temple of Peace will say that I included women among the usurpers, female usurpers or, rather, "usurpresses," as they are accustomed to mock me in laughter and jokes.

First, the author has had his work read by another scholar, who has offered valuable corrections. Second, the temple of Peace in the forum of Vespasian, which was adjacent to a library, is represented as a gathering place for intellectuals who share the scholarly interest in defining usurpers. At the temple, which a modern scholar describes as "a popular venue for public intellectual debate" in the second century, the author is subject to the kind of jokes and jeers that we associate with ancient scholarship in the works of Gellius and Galen.[110]

Conclusion

The *Historia Augusta* belongs within the kind of group described above, perhaps a small circle of scholars with a particular interest in biography. The existence of such a group might help explain the surprising fact that the author had not only the *KG* in front of him but also Eutropius and Aurelius Victor.[111] Who but a scholar, or group of scholars, would possess and use all three of these *breviaria*, the latter two of which were almost entirely dependent upon the former? A circle familiar with the *KG* and its offspring might have had a particular interest in epitomes. The primary lives, I would suggest, represent the author offering his epitome of Marius Maximus. In reading these lives together, the author and his audience could have discussed their content as well as the quality of the epitomization. Even in the primary lives, the author seems to have included some of his own inventions, such as the Vergil oracles in the *Hadrian*, as a test or puzzle. In other lives, the author's inventions were more elaborate, and required more knowledge and more cleverness for the audience to recognize and unravel. In the nonprimary lives, although allusion and parody were paramount, recognition of the material derived from source texts such as the *KG* or Herodian may still have been part of the game. Thus there need be no sharp distinction between historical and nonhistorical sources; both were intended to be altered, and to be recognized.

In Pucci's study of allusion, cited at the end of chapter 1, he shows how ancient authors had feared the allusion as a moment when the reader is freed from authorial control to pursue meaning on his own.[112] In reader-response criticism, the idea of "interpretative communities" helps alleviate this authorial anxiety by ensuring that similar preoccupations, understandings, and values would be shared "in-house."[113] Group reading represents in some ways the ultimate in interpretative communities. Interpretations that threaten to diverge too far from authorial intent could be disqualified by the intervention of the author himself, and the author could also alert readers to overlooked allusions and intertexts.

In the chapters that follow, I look particularly at allusions in the *Historia Augusta* to Jerome and to Ammianus Marcellinus. Some scholars have interpreted the engagement of the *Historia Augusta* with these authors and their subjects as offering substantive commentary on contemporary religious and political affairs.

The evidence shows instead that the *HA*-author holds no consistent opinion on these subjects, which his complex allusions could not in any case support. Yet we should not see our allusive author as a solitary madman weaving his allusions for his own perverse reasons, a figure unprecedented in the ancient world. The social and agonistic nature of ancient reading allows us to understand these allusions instead as authorial inventions designed for a participating audience with a shared collection of interests and intertexts.

 Religion in the *Historia Augusta*

From a modern perspective, the period in which the *Historia Augusta* was written is primarily notable for the final conversion of the Roman elite from paganism to Christianity. At the beginning of the fourth century, Christianity had been a forbidden religion, persecuted at the direction of the emperor himself; by the turn of the fifth century, Christian emperors had ruled for a nearly unbroken three-quarters of a century, and the administrative apparatus of the church had permeated society across the empire. By the late fourth century, even the majority of the senatorial aristocracy had become Christian.[1] Therefore it is not surprising that scholars of the *Historia Augusta* have sought to connect the work to the religious developments of its time.

A first-time reader of the *Historia Augusta*, however, would be unlikely to consider religion a central focus of the work. In its explicit treatment of religion, the *Historia Augusta* is roughly comparable to Suetonius or to Ammianus, with occasional but not deeply substantive discussions of traditional cult, Christianity, and Judaism. A large number of the religious references in the *Historia Augusta*, for example, are the presentations of omens, typically of the birth or death of an emperor. This is a common topic in the biographies of Suetonius and, one would imagine, Marius Maximus, and it allowed for the kind of absurdity and allusiveness that the *HA*-author enjoys, but it can hardly be taken as any sort of statement on religion. Some of these omens, for example, are derived directly or indirectly from Livy.[2] So when the *HA*-author has Clodius Albinus place the purple horns of a white bull in the temple of Apollo (*Clod. Alb.* 5.3–4), he directs the reader not to think deeply about traditional methods of priestly prediction but to recognize his literary variations on Livy's description (1.45.4) of a similar omen associated with attempted usurpation, by a Sabine in earliest Rome.

The opinions of the *HA*-author on religious matters are wholly conventional, free from the fervent Christian or pagan beliefs expressed by some of his contemporaries. His engagement with religion comes mostly in the form of allusion to texts that deal with religion. As we have seen in previous examples of allusion in the *Historia Augusta*, these allusions often pose a challenge to readers because of their complexity. They are often humorous because of incongruous juxtapositions between the past and the present, or the earnest and profane. Since the text of the *Historia Augusta* is often invented or distorted in order to include allusion, the focus remains on the intertext rather than the context.

Christianity in the *Historia Augusta*

The *HA*-author mentions Christ or Christians explicitly only twelve times, mostly without obvious attempts at denigration or celebration.[3] Thus it is understandable why Syme would conclude that "Christianity . . . does not engage any serious or sustained interest in the HA."[4] With a work like the *Historia Augusta*, of course, overt mentions are hardly the only source for interpretation. We know that the *HA*-author is frequently allusive, and of necessity his references to contemporary Christianity would have to be veiled in order to perpetuate his fictional date of publication. To detect and interpret allusions to Christianity in the *Historia Augusta*, however, the reader must have a proper understanding of the context in which the *HA*-author wrote.

Certain key claims about religious struggle in the period have been accepted by almost all modern historians of the late fourth century. According to the standard narrative, conflict between Christian emperors and pagan aristocrats escalated in the 380s, when the emperor Gratian, under the influence of the hardline Christian bishop of Milan, Ambrose, renounced the pagan title of pontifex maximus, withdrew state funding for pagan cults, and removed the Altar of Victory from the senate house.[5] A flurry of antipagan legislation from Theodosius in 391 and 392 outlawed animal sacrifice, resulting in a desperate last stand by pagan aristocrats. When a figurehead named Eugenius was raised to the purple, Nicomachus Flavianus and other staunch traditionalists seized their opportunity, and sacrifice was reinstated. The pagan cause was lost forever when Theodosius defeated Eugenius at the Frigidus River in September 394, and Nicomachus Flavianus committed suicide in despair. Moderns have often been sympathetic toward the defeated pagans, in part because they were considered true lovers of classical literature, the texts of which they reverently copied and edited. In this light, scholars have often understood hidden references to Christianity in the *Historia Augusta* to be the work of a fearful and angry pagan, surreptitiously denigrating a victorious opponent and hoping for the tables to turn.

All historians of the period must now confront the arguments of Alan Cameron's *The Last Pagans of Ancient Rome*. This monumental work has challenged almost every *idée reçue* of the standard narrative of the period. He demonstrates that, except for Gratian's removal of state funding from public cult, the actions and legislation of Gratian and Theodosius were not particularly different in kind or efficacy from those of earlier Christian emperors, that the battle of the Frigidus did not represent a clash between pagan and Christian in reality or in the general perception of contemporaries, and that Nicomachus Flavianus, Symmachus, and other senatorial aristocrats were not ideological or intellectual pagans, nor were they particularly learned in the classics by the standards of their day.

It is easy to see how Cameron's work renders untenable the theories of scholars who made this romantic story of religious strife central to the very genesis and nature of the *Historia Augusta*. The work of Johannes Straub presents the most systematic example of this approach. In a book, *Heidnische Geschichtsapologetik in der christlichen Spätantike* (1963), and in a further series of articles, he argues that the *Historia Augusta* was a work of anti-Christian apologetics, inspired by the *Historia contra paganos* of the Christian writer Orosius.[6] He claims that the best readers could identify allusions in the *Historia Augusta* to contemporary Christian practice, to patristic literature, and to the Bible, which together constituted a plea for tolerance and respect for ancestral paganism. Straub's approach did not find many followers, as its problems were evident even in the 1960s. Some of Straub's examples of hidden allusions were far-fetched but, more important, even if all were accepted as valid, they would still make up only a tiny fraction of the work as a whole. These few allusions could hardly represent the purpose of the work, which could not be further from the seven books of Orosius. The Christian writer systematically subordinates all of world history to his theological agenda. In addition, the need for secrecy and care in the expression of anti-Christian opinions is often assumed but never demonstrated. In fact, ferociously anti-Christian works, such as the history of Eunapius, are closely contemporary to the *Historia Augusta*. Speyer's comprehensive survey shows that although Christians actively banned and destroyed books that were considered heretical, pagan literary works were hardly ever targeted.[7] The works of astrologers were ordered destroyed in 409, but this is merely an extension of the standard imperial prohibition against magical texts more generally (*Cod. Theod.* 9.16.12; cf. Amm. 29.1, Paulus *Sent.* 5.23.18). Although Speyer blames ecclesiastical "Bücherzensur," with the support of imperial edicts, for the loss of much anti-Christian literature, he fails to provide evidence for such a sweeping claim.[8] He offers, instead, evidence that ritual books and oracles were destroyed in the course of temple destruction in the fourth and fifth centuries.

It is unsurprising that Christians did not, for the most part, choose to copy anti-Christian treatises (although works of Plotinus and Julian, among others, do survive), but Speyer offers no evidence for the active suppression or punishment of anti-Christian literature, with the single exception of Porphyry. Porphyry's anti-Christian works, although they were apparently suppressed in some way by Constantine (Socrates, *Hist. eccl.* 1.9), were nevertheless continuously engaged with in detail by the church fathers of the fourth and fifth centuries, and then were (again?) ordered destroyed in 448 by Theodosius II and Valentinian III.[9] Thus, even a treatise specifically designed to refute the truth of the Christian religion found wide circulation during the period in which the *Historia Augusta* was written. Straub's theory fails both in imputing a message to the *Historia Augusta* and in providing a reason to camouflage the message.

Callu and Festy offer a complex theory of the origin and nature of the *Historia Augusta*, but it too cannot withstand Cameron's arguments.[10] They begin with the importance of the *Annales* of Nicomachus Flavianus, a work that they claim was condemned and removed from public libraries at the behest of Theodosius after the Frigidus. They see the origins of the *Historia Augusta* in the combined efforts of friends and family of Nicomachus to perpetuate his memory by writing about the imperial past, but in the biographical rather than historical mode in order to safely differentiate their efforts from his. Finally, in a third stage of writing, they imagine the younger Flavianus, angered by his inability to rehabilitate his father in the years between 394 and 399, defacing this previously straightforward biographical collection with the perversities and prejudices that it now contains. This series of hypotheses must first be judged unproven because of an almost complete lack of evidence for an impressively complex sequence of events. But it must also be judged extremely implausible in light of what Cameron shows us about the Nicomachi and their role in the events of the end of the fourth century.[11] There is no good evidence that Nicomachus Flavianus the Elder was a staunch pagan traditionalist or that his suicide was anything other than the act of a senator who had chosen the wrong side in a civil war. No precedent exists for the banning of a work because of pagan sentiments. If the work had in fact been condemned, it would have been the last thing that Nicomachus junior would have wanted to mention on the inscription that announced his own rehabilitation in 431.[12] Because the death of Nicomachus and the battle of the Frigidus in general were unrelated to paganism in the eyes of contemporaries, the incorporation of anti-Christian elements into the final redaction of the *Historia Augusta* would be inexplicable, especially because there is no reason to think that Nicomachus junior was a committed pagan of any kind.

Cameron's challenges to the standard narrative also have implications even for those scholars of the *Historia Augusta* who had not made pagan-Christian conflict central to their interpretation. Chastagnol's approach to religion in the *Historia Augusta*, for example, is more typical of the current scholarly consensus. He argues that while the *Historia Augusta* as a whole does not present a coherent religious program, it does often present the points of view associated with the aristocratic Roman pagan of the standard narrative.[13] He describes the period in which the *Historia Augusta* was composed as "une époque pendant laquelle le christianisme est triumphant ou triomphaliste et le paganisme nettement sur la défensive."[14] Chastagnol sees the hidden messages about Christianity that he detects in the *Historia Augusta* as "irreverent" or "mocking" rather than aiming for a more serious reaction. Although Chastagnol recognizes that in general pagans were free to write as they pleased, he suggests that official tolerance might wax and wane, and believes that at his proposed time of publication of the *Historia Augusta*, 399 or 400, criticism of Christianity might have been particularly unwise, given the very recent conflict with paganism that culminated with the Frigidus. But Cameron has shown that the aristocratic Roman pagan whom Chastagnol evokes never existed, and therefore the idea that fear drove the *HA*-author to write in code in the years after the Frigidus is also no longer tenable.

In the next section I support Cameron's rejection of the imputation of anti-Christian polemic to the *HA*-author through an examination of explicit and implicit references to Christianity that scholars have claimed for the work. Some of the purported implicit comments should be rejected as implausible. Others, both implicit and explicit, are either positive or neutral toward Christianity or, if negative, tend to criticize asceticism and other features of early fifth-century Christianity that many Romans, Christians or non-Christians, rejected. As a group, these references are unremarkable.

Explicit References to Christianity

The first mention of Christianity in the *Historia Augusta* is in the *Severus*, where it is claimed that the emperor instituted a ban on conversions to Christianity or to Judaism (17.1). Modern historians agree that this is untrue, and Barnes notes that considering Judaism and Christianity together is both typical of the *Historia Augusta* and very atypical of the approach of the Roman state.[15] The chronology of the *Historia Augusta* is confused at this point, but it may be that the author's claim in some way reflects a war between Jews and Samaritans that Jerome mentions in his *Chronicle* (293d). I think it is best to suppose that the *HA*-author or his source has made a mistake here. The context and the nature of the simple sentence do not suggest that the emperor's decision is either blameworthy or praiseworthy, and so it should not be taken as a commentary on Christianity or imperial policy toward Christians more generally.

We are told that Elagabalus threatened to transfer the Jewish, Samaritan, and Christian gods to the temple of his own god (*Elag.* 3.5). Since Elagabalus is a bad emperor, his threats against Christianity would seem to reflect positively on the religion. His threat may be contrasted with Alexander's construction of a *lararium* for worship that included images of Christ, along with deified emperors and ancestors, Orpheus, Abraham, and Apollonius (*Alex.* 29.2). Rather than subjugate other gods to one, as Elagabalus did, Alexander will keep them on a common footing. A similar idea is found in the suggestion that Alexander planned to build a temple to Christ (43.6–7):

> Christo templum facere voluit eumque inter deos recipere . . . sed prohibitus est ab his, qui consulentes sacra reppererant omnes Christianos futuros, si id fecisset, et templa reliqua deserenda.
>
> He wished to build a temple to Christ and receive him among the gods . . . but he was kept from this because those who examined the sacred victims reported that if he did, all men would become Christians and the other temples would be abandoned.

The humor here is derived from the *HA*-author's ability to tell the future retrospectively. The passage is anti-Christian only if one presupposes that the author is anti-Christian and therefore finds the prospect of temple abandonment abhorrent. Note that Alexander did not change his mind on principled grounds but rather was prevented from carrying out his design by the professional sacrificers, who obviously had a vested interest in the perpetuation of sacrifice—a joke against pagans, not Christians.

Alexander, represented throughout his biography as an ideal emperor, explicitly refuses to punish or persecute Christians (22.4). His tolerance of Christianity should surely be seen as a positive statement about the religion. When Christians took over a piece of public property to which a tavern claimed the rights, "rescripsit melius esse, ut quemadmodumcumque illic deus colatur, quam popinariis dedatur" ("Alexander decreed that it was better that a god of some sort be worshiped there than for it to be handed over to innkeepers," *Alex.* 49.6). Claiming that a church was more respectable than a tavern does not represent the highest possible praise for Christianity, but it again reveals the emperor's genial tolerance toward the faith.

Alexander went beyond toleration to emulation in adopting a Christian practice for the selection of officials (*Alex.* 45.6):[16]

> Ubi aliquos voluisset vel rectores provinciis dare vel praepositos facere vel procuratores, id est rationales, ordinare, nomina eorum proponebat, hortans populum, ut si quis quid haberet criminis, probaret manifestis rebus, si non probasset, subiret poenam capitis; dicebatque grave esse, cum id Christiani et Iudaei facerent in praedicandis sacerdotibus, qui ordinandi sunt, non fieri in provinciarum rectoribus, quibus et fortunae hominum committerentur et capita.

> Whenever Alexander desired to give someone the governorship of a province, or make him an army officer, or appoint him a procurator, that is, a tax collector, he was putting forward their names and encouraging the people to prove, with clear evidence, any accusation that anyone wanted to bring against him; and if it were not proven, the accuser would be put to death. He used to say that it was unfortunate that this was not standard procedure for provincial governors, to whom fortunes and lives were entrusted, since the Christians and Jews did it for those who were to be ordained as priests.

Once more, the association of Christianity with the good emperor Alexander, and his endorsement of its customs, can only reflect well upon the faith.

Finally we turn to the lengthy letter of Hadrian, which expostulates at length on Christians, Jews, and Samaritans, including claims that appear anti-Christian: the Christian bishop, the letter-writer claims, worships Serapis; every Christian is an astrologer or magician; and the Christian's only god is money (*Quad. Tyr.* 8). The critical focus of the author here, however, is the Egyptians, not the Christians.[17]

Here are some excerpts:

> 7.4-5: sunt enim Aegyptii, ut satis nosti, vani, ventosi, furibundi, iactantes, iniuriosi, atque adeo varii, liberi, novarum rerum usque ad cantilenas publicas cupientes, versificatores, epigrammatarii, mathematici, haruspices, medici. nam in eis Christiani, Samaritae, et quibus praesentia semper tempora cum enormi libertate displiceant.

> For the Egyptians, as you know well, are vain, windy, mad, boastful, noxious, and, in addition, fickle, unrestrained, desirous of novelty even in popular

song, versifiers, epigram-writers, astrologers, soothsayers, and quacks. For among them are Christians, Samaritans, and those for whom present circumstances are always displeasing, despite their excessive freedom.

8.2–4: illic qui Serapim colunt Christiani sunt, et devoti sunt Serapi qui se Christi episcopos dicunt. nemo illic archisynagogus Iudaeorum, nemo Samarites, nemo Christianorum presbyter non mathematicus, non haruspex, non aliptes. ipse ille patriarcha cum Aegyptum venerit, ab aliis Serapidem adorare, ab aliis cogitur Christum.

Those who worship Serapis there are Christians, and those who say they are bishops of Christ are devoted to Serapis. There is no synagogue head of the Jews there, no Samaritan, no Christian priest, who is not an astrologer, a soothsayer, or an anointer. Even the Patriarch himself, when he comes to Egypt, is forced by some to worship Serapis, by others to worship Christ.

8.7: unus illis deus nummus est: hunc Christiani, hunc Iudaei, hunc omnes venerantur et gentes.

Their one god is money, and this the Christians, this the Jews, this all the nations worship.

Saturninus, a Moor, is called a Gaul by the *HA*-author in order to create a kind of super-usurper, combining the fractious nature of the Gauls (cf. Amm. 15.12.1) with the stereotypically revolutionary nature of the Egyptians (cf. Amm. 22.6.1, 22.11.4, 22.16.23).[18] Perhaps Paschoud is also correct that a learned joke is intended on the revolt of Cornelius Gallus in Egypt in the reign of Augustus.[19] Thus the rambunctious nature of the Egyptians is the focus. The religious diversity of Egypt was a regular cause of violence, in actual fact and as portrayed in Ammianus (15.7).

The *HA*-author, rather than focusing his criticism on Christianity, has diffused it by including the Jews and Samaritans, a trio we also find in *Elagabalus* 3.5. The emphasis is on the absurd, intensified by the use of weird words like *patriarcha* and *archsynagogus*. It is obviously not flattering to state that Christians are astrologers and obsessed with money, but the logic of the passage would argue that these criticisms are not true of Christians in general but only those in Egypt.

Implicit References to Christianity

Many scholars who claim to have discovered hidden references to Christianity start with the presumption that Christianity must be a preoccupation of the author. For example, numerous scholars have argued (or assumed) that the *HA*-author intended his portrait of the emperor Elagabalus, a depraved champion of eastern cult and a rejecter of traditional religion, to be interpreted as a Christian *avant la lettre*. Many have seen in elements of the *Elagabalus* criticisms of the practices of Constantine in particular.[20] Turcan provides the most elaborated argument for understanding it as an extended, satirical attack on Constantine's life and character, but ultimately his case does not convince.[21] While there are a few passages that might conceivably evoke some features of the first Christian emperor, many of the purported parallels that Turcan provides are standard elements of the historical tradition that can be seen to connect with Constantine only in the most general of ways.[22]

Turcan finds it "drôle" that the *Elagabalus* is addressed to Constantine and claims to have been written at the emperor's request, but of course many lives are addressed to Constantine, and the language of the *HA*-author about and to Constantine is deferential. The dedication would be a missed opportunity for the author if he had intended to make the parallels apparent. Turcan argues that we should compare the wickedness of Elagabalus's mother, Julia, with the purported saintliness of the mother of Constantine, Helena, and also finds it significant that Julia, like Helena, was said to be originally of low birth. But these details appear to be true, or at least are found in other sources. Elagabalus is denounced for luxury, for gluttony, and for the appointment of men of low social standing to government offices, accusations that are indeed paralleled by those found in *KG*-sources on Constantine but are also stock accusations against the figure of the tyrant.[23] Elagabalus attributed his success over Macrinus to the intervention of his god, as did Constantine in explaining the defeat of Maxentius, another parallel between the two historical figures that says nothing of the approach of the *HA*-author. Turcan notes that Constantine, like Elagabalus, worshiped the sun for a long time, a true and unremarkable fact that would not fit an anti-Christian agenda if any reader of the *Elagabalus* should be reminded of it. The claim that Elagabalus sought to subordinate all other cults in Rome to his own is judged by Barnes to be at least plausible, and is not necessarily a comment on Christianity, especially not the Christianity of Constantine.[24] The accounts of Elagabalus plundering other sanctuaries to adorn his own ("cleptomanie cultuelle," 3.4, 6.7–8, 7.5–7), which Turcan sees as evoking Constantine's transfer of temple statuary to adorn his new capital,

Constantinople, may be an elaboration of an anecdote in Herodian (5.6.3) or may otherwise derive from a factual source.

Two of Turcan's arguments require particular attention. First, the refusal of Elagabalus to take vows on the Capitol (15.7) appears to parallel a similar story told by Christian detractors about Constantine (Zos. 2.29.5).[25] Zosimus, the fifth-century pagan historian who reports this story, would have learned it from Eunapius (or Nicomachus Flavianus, for adherents to that theory), and thus our author could have been familiar with it. But it seems natural that an emperor like Constantine or Elagabalus, each of whom was notorious for promoting a nontraditional and exclusive god, would have refrained from traditional religious practice (or would have been slanderously accused of having done so). The *HA*-author may be reflecting his original source here, or he may have adapted this one detail from his knowledge of Constantine's action, but this does not seem like enough encouragement for the reader to understand all of Elagabalus's actions in the light of Constantine's. Second, Turcan interprets the claim that Elagabalus heedlessly drove a chariot drawn by four elephants around the Vatican, destroying tombs (*Elag.* 23.1), as a jab at Constantine, who had a large pagan cemetery destroyed when he converted the small shrine of St. Peter to a basilica. This is ingenious but unlikely. We know of the destruction of the cemetery only through modern archaeological excavation, and no extant ancient source mentions it.[26] There is no reason to think that the *HA*-author or his audience even knew it had existed. Tacitus (*Ann.* 14.4.4) does describe Nero racing chariots on a private track on the Vatican, however, and Pliny refers to the racetrack as the circus of Nero and Caligula (*HN* 36.74), so Elagabalus's behavior can easily be interpreted as an exaggerated form of the behavior of his degraded predecessor. The sentence in the *Historia Augusta* describing Elagabalus driving an elephant continues with the claim that he also harnessed four camels to a chariot, in emulation, no doubt, of Nero as described by Suetonius (*Nero* 11.1).

The two references to Apollonius of Tyana himself in the *Historia Augusta* have been understood as evidence for the author's partisan, pro-pagan sentiments, but they are, rather, parodic allusions. In the first mention in the *Historia Augusta* of Apollonius, we are told that his bust was included in the crowded sanctuary of Alexander Severus for worship along with the best previous emperors, Jesus, Abraham, Orpheus, and Alexander's own ancestors (*Alex.* 29.2). Dio claims that Caracalla built a shrine to Apollonius (presumably without any anti-Christian purpose, 77.18.4), and it is possible that the *HA*-author found this information in Marius Maximus and has creatively expanded upon it in the *Alexander Severus*. The second mention of Apollonius in the *Historia Augusta* is more significant (*Aur.* 24.3–9):

fertur enim Aurelianum de Tyanae civitatis eversione vere dixisse, vere cogitasse; verum Apollonium Tyanaeum, celeberrimae famae auctoritatisque sapientem, veterem philosophum, amicum vere deorum, ipsum etiam pro numine frequentandum, recipienti se in tentorium ea forma, qua videtur, subito adstitisse, atque haec Latine, ut homo Pannonius intellegeret, verba dixisse: 'Aureliane, si vis vincere, nihil est quod de civium meorum nece cogites; Aureliane, si vis imperare, a cruore innocentium abstine; Aureliane, clementer te age, si vis vivere.' norat vultum philosophi venerabilis Aurelianus atque in multis eius imaginem viderat templis. denique statim adtonitus et imaginem et statuas et templum eidem promisit atque in meliorem redit mentem. haec ego et a gravibus viris comperi et in Ulpiae bibliothecae libris relegi et pro maiestate Apollonii magis credidi. quid enim viro illo sanctius, venerabilius, antiquius diviniusque inter homines fuit? ille mortuis reddidit vitam, ille multa ultra homines et fecit et dixit; quae qui velit nosse, Graecos legat libros qui de eius vita conscripti sunt. ipse autem, si vita suppetet atque ipsius viri favor visque iuverit, breviter saltem tanti viri facta in litteras mittam, non quo illius viri gesta munere mei sermonis indigeant, sed ut ea quae miranda sunt omnium voce praedicentur.

It is reported that Aurelian truly thought and spoke about destroying the city of Tyana, but Apollonius of Tyana, the wise man with the most celebrated reputation and authority, a philosopher of old, truly a friend of the gods, a man often taken as a divine being, suddenly appeared, in his usual form, before Aurelian, when the emperor was returning to his tent. He spoke to him in Latin, so that the Pannonian could understand: "Aurelian, if you wish to conquer, you should not think about the slaughter of my fellow citizens. Aurelian, if you wish to rule, abstain from the blood of innocents. Aurelian, act mercifully, if you wish to live." Aurelian recognized the face of the venerable philosopher, as he had seen his image in many temples. Immediately stunned, he promised him an image and statues and a temple, and was restored to normality. I myself learned these things from serious men, and read them again in books in the Ulpian Library, and believed it the more because of Apollonius's greatness. For what was more holy, more venerable, more ancient, and more divine among men than that man? That man restored life to the dead, and he said and did many supernatural things. Whoever wants to know these things, let him read the Greek books that have been written about his life. In fact, I myself, if my life is long enough and the favor and power of the man himself help out, will write a brief account of his life, not because the deeds of that man require the gift of my words, but so that those amazing deeds are pronounced in the voice of all.

For Paschoud, this anecdote is derived from Nicomachus Flavianus and depicts Apollonius as the "Christ païen"; for Brandt, the vision of Apollonius is meant to evoke the vision of the cross seen by Constantine, although the context and substance of the visions seem on the face of it quite different.[27] But Apollonius belonged to Christians as well as pagans in late antiquity. It is true that he could be put forward as a rival of Christ, as seen most explicitly in the treatise of Hierocles, published in 305, which we know thanks to a rebuttal by Eusebius. Christian writers are therefore careful to characterize Apollonius as a magician (Arnobius, *Adversus gentes* 1.52; Lactantius, *Div. inst.* 5.3.7–21, for example). Even Eusebius, however, is willing to admit that Apollonius was a wise man.[28] Augustine approved of his chastity (*Ep.* 138.18) and Jerome of his learnedness (*Ep.* 53.1.2–4). The Gallic bishop Sidonius praises him extravagantly a century later (*Ep.* 8.3.4–6). Apollonius is, therefore, not a representative of aggressive paganism but of the philosophical traditionalism praised by Christians and pagans alike.[29]

The humor in the passage would undercut any attempt to strike a blow against Christianity on behalf of militant paganism. First there is the author's amusing explanation that the Greek Apollonius spoke in Latin to allow the Pannonian emperor to understand him. This recalls other places in the work where the author claims to have translated from the Greek texts, often verses, that would logically not have been in Latin. Second, the suggestion that the emperor recognized Apollonius from his portrait in many temples anticipates the skeptical reader's question about how the emperor could have recognized the philosopher in the first place. There is no reason to think that Apollonius's portrait really was found in many ancient temples. Instead the *HA*-author continues to expand upon the nugget of information that lies behind the passage about sanctuaries in the *Alexander Severus*. In addition, the *HA*-author's claim to have gotten his information from "trustworthy men" and from "works in the Ulpian Library" represents his equivalent of the notebooks of Damis or the tablets of Dictys. The author concludes with the surprising suggestion that he himself plans to write a life of Apollonius, thereby drawing attention to the way in which he resembles Philostratus in his construction of a fictional work based on a historical framework. The *HA*-author apparently plans to be even more sensationalistic than Philostratus was: whereas Philostratus prudently hedges on whether the girl Apollonius is said to have resurrected was dead or merely close to it, the *HA*-author categorically claims that Apollonius raised people from the dead.[30]

The treatment of the emperors Valerian and Gallienus in the *Historia Augusta* has often been claimed as another piece of evidence for the author's anti-Christian slant. The Christian tradition portrays Valerian as a great persecutor of Christians and his son Gallienus as a tolerator of them, while the *HA*-author clearly favors Valerian and dislikes Gallienus.[31] In this case, however, the opposite of the Christian tradition is not anti-Christian but simply "secular" or "standard." Aurelius Victor (32–33) and Eutropius (9.7–8), working from the *KG* to create short, religiously neutral histories, are the model for the *HA*-author. They emphasize military disaster and Gallienus's personally dissolute behavior as much as the *HA*-author does.

Several attempts have been made to link legal matters discussed in the *Historia Augusta* to specifically Christian legislation. Straub argues that the decisions of Alexander Severus first to forbid senators to lend money at interest, and then to cap the interest rate at 6 percent, is meant to evoke, for the contemporary reader, the law of Arcadius in 397 that forbade usury and the law of Theodosius II in 405 to limit interest to 6 percent.[32] Cameron argues that the parallels are simple coincidences, and he is probably right.[33] In any case, the link to Christianity that Straub suggests is tenuous. He suggests that Christians particularly opposed usury, and that the depiction of a pagan emperor legislating against it would strike a blow for religious tolerance. If any reader did draw a religious lesson from this detail of secular legislation, which is doubtful, it would presumably be favorable toward Christianity for continuing to pursue a practice attributed to a good emperor of the past.

Chastagnol suggests, reasonably enough, that two references to the "seventh day" in the *HA* can be connected with Christianity and perhaps with Christian legislation enforcing rest on Sunday (*Cod. Theod.* 2.8.1, 321).[34] When Avidius Cassius took over as commander of the Syrian legions, he proved his toughness by holding inspections and requiring weapons training "on the seventh day" (*Av. Cass.* 6.2–3). Perhaps the joke is that the soldiers would otherwise anachronistically be at rest on the seventh day. Alexander Severus went up to the temple on the Capitol "on the seventh day," and in the next sentence is seen considering establishing a temple to Christ (*Alex.* 43.5–6). Thus it appears that Alexander, who is in other respects a kind of Christian fellow traveler, treats Jupiter Optimus Maximus like Christ, as a god to be worshiped every Sunday. If an attitude toward Christianity is to be derived from these passages, it must be somewhere between neutral and mildly favorable. But the jokes, such as they are, seem to be about anachronism, not ideology. For the audience of the *Historia Augusta*, Christianity is a regular part of their contemporary existence, whether or not they professed it. The retrojection of the present into the past has no profound ideological weight in this case. Chastagnol also argues that the discussions of the taxation of prostitutes and pimps and other matters of taxation in *Alexander Severus* 24.3–5 evoke unpopular tax policies instigated by Constantine. Even if we accept that the *HA*-author has this intention, there is no reason to see in this a religious message.[35]

Syme sensed a "Christian odour" in some names mentioned in *Gordian* 25.3—Gaudianus, Reverendus, and Montanus—and Birley went further in claiming, "More straightforward is the anti-Christian sneer in the three evil counselors of Gordian's mother."[36] This is problematic for several reasons. First, the invented name "Gaudiosus," which would seem to carry the same import as "Gaudianus," is included in a list of outstanding generals trained by Probus (*Prob.* 22.3); is this to be interpreted as a pro-Christian argument? Second, the context of the *Gordian* passage needs to be more fully appreciated. Timesitheus writes a letter to his son-in-law, Gordian (III), celebrating the fact that Gordian has successfully prevented eunuchs from running the government. Gordian responds favorably, while admitting that eunuchs had been excessively influential in the past (*Gord.* 25.1–3):

> Imperator Gordianus Augustus Misitheo patri et praefecto. nisi dii omnipotentes Romanum tuerentur imperium, etiam nunc per emptos spadones velut in hasta positi venderemur. denique nunc demum intellego, neque Feliciones praetorianis cohortibus praeponi debuisse, neque Serapammoni quartam legionem credendam fuisse, et, ut omnia dinumerare mittam, multa non esse facienda quae feci; sed diis gratias, quod te insinuante, qui nihil vendis, didici ea, quae inclusus scire non poteram. quid enim facerem, quod et mater nos venderet et consilio cum Gaudiano et Reverendo et Montano habito vel laudaret aliquos vel vituperaret, et illorum consensu quasi testium, quod dixerat, adprobaret?

> From the Emperor Gordian Augustus to Timesitheus, his father-in-law and prefect. If the omnipotent gods did not watch over the Roman empire, even now we would be sold by purchased eunuchs as if under the spear. Now I know that Felicio ought not to have been placed in charge of the praetorian guard, and Serapammon ought not to have been entrusted with the fourth legion, and, to avoid enumerating every single thing, I should not have done many things which I did. But thanks to the gods, I have come to know the things that I was unable to learn myself from you, who are not corrupt. For what was I to do, since even my mother was selling me out, getting advice from Gaudianus and Reverendus and Montanus and praising or

blaming others accordingly, and she was approving what she had said with the consensus of these men as witnesses.

While "Felicio" might also be construed as a Christian name, "Serapammon," of course, could not be.[37] Of the three eunuch counselors, the name "Montanus" stands out. This is not a Christian name at all, but it is the name of a famous Christian, the second-century Phrygian heretic. It is presumably because Montanus associated with women and was from Phrygia, known to the ancients as the home of the castrated devotees of the mother goddess Cybele, that Jerome abuses Montanus in a letter as "abscisum et semivirum ... Montanum" ("Montanus, the castrated half-man," 41.4). The *HA*-author, having read the Jerome passage, appropriated the name of a man he probably believed to be an actual eunuch. This is an allusion to Jerome, and not an anti-Christian statement. Syme claims that "Reverendus" was a Christian name without being able to find any Christians with the name.[38] Better is Chastagnol's explanation, from the description of a huge eunuch leading a chorus of worshipers of Cybele in Juvenal (6.512–13), "ingens / semiuir, obsceno facies *reuerenda* minori" ("a huge eunuch, with an appearance revered by perverted youth").[39] Chastagnol thinks that the third name, "Gaudianus," is a reference to the poet Claudian, the tormentor of the eunuch Eutropius, which is unlikely, but possible. I have no more compelling explanation for the name of Gaudianus, but it seems clear that eunuchs, not Christians, are the target of the *HA*-author in this passage.[40]

Chastagnol argues that two diatribes—one in the *Aurelian* (15.4–6) and one at the very end of the *Carus* (20.4–21.1)—are indirect critiques of Christianity.[41] The narrator concludes his work with complaints directed toward a certain Messalla, whom he accuses of wasting his patrimony, giving away his riches to actors and buffoons. In the *Aurelian* he had also regretted the waste of a patrimony. Chastagnol suspects that these complaints would be heard by contemporaries as directed against radical ascetics such as Jerome who encouraged the dissipation of the patrimonies of senatorial aristocrats to support monks and other discreditable causes. If we accept Chastagnol's arguments, we must see that this is not a critique of Christianity more generally but of the sort of Christianity represented by Jerome, an object of disgust for many contemporaries, Christians as well as non-Christians.

Allusions to Jerome

Jerome of Stridon was a provincial of middling birth who had to force his way into the circles of aristocrats and power to which he aspired. Recent scholarship on Jerome has emphasized his mixture of radicalism and shameless self-promotion.⁴² Cain has recently demonstrated how he carefully crafted the letters that make up his first collection to portray himself as both Christian intellectual and monastic hero.⁴³ Some letters in this first collection recount how, because of his sinfulness, he originally feared entering the monastic life but soon immersed himself fully in its squalor and terror. Other letters are crafted to demonstrate his literary and biblical knowledge and his orthodoxy. He thus presented himself to the aristocratic patrons he hoped for as a man who had matched the superhuman and romantic exploits of the eastern monks, but who was also imbued with the Christian and classical culture appropriate for the grandees of Rome. In reality, as Rebenich points out, Jerome did not live in a desert cave but rather on the estate of a wealthy friend, where he had access to books and companions.⁴⁴

The asceticism and monasticism that Jerome championed were abhorrent to fourth-century pagans, as a famous passage of Eunapius on monks (*VS* 472) makes clear: ἀνθρώπους μὲν κατὰ τὸ εἶδος, ὁ δὲ βίος αὐτοῖς συώδης ("they were men in appearance, but lived the life of swine"); ὀστέα γὰρ καὶ κεφαλὰς τῶν ἐπὶ πολλοῖς ἁμαρτήμασιν ἑαλωκότων συναλίζοντες ("they collect the bones and skulls of criminals who had been put to death for numerous crimes").⁴⁵ Libanius (*Or.* 30.8-10) complains that monks, eating and drinking to excess, destroy rural shrines with abandon. Two passages in Rutilius Namatianus (*De reditu* 1.439-52 and 515-26) express particular horror at monks who have exiled themselves to the isolation of islands, like Jerome's friend Bonosus (Jer. *Ep.* 3).⁴⁶

Monasticism was viewed with suspicion, however, by a broad spectrum of Roman society, not only pagans but also many Christians. Ascetics rejected their political and social responsibilities, and their failure to provide heirs put patrimonies at risk. More generally, the antinomianism central to the monastic ideal in its formative period suggested an anarchism particularly unappealing to aristocrats and other elites. Christian emperors promulgated several laws seeking to lessen the power and influence of monks, who were prone to interfere with the normal functioning of society.⁴⁷ Regular clergy also resented the monks, who boasted that their more rigorous way of life made them morally superior. The works of Jerome in particular offer an unending stream of abuse of the clergy, who are charged with luxury, hypocrisy, gluttony, and greed.⁴⁸ The anonymous so-called Ambrosiaster, for example, probably a presbyter, rejected the utopian and radical ideas of Jerome and instead "provided scriptural, logical, and spiritual support for existing social hierarchies and norms."⁴⁹ Jerome in turn sought to marginalize him by, among other things, failing to include him in his *De viris illustribus* and sniping at him in his letters.⁵⁰

Thus Jerome, in the early fifth century, although he had supporters, had no shortage of enemies. His former friend Rufinus complained that his extreme views had embarrassed true Christians and had been eagerly publicized by, among others, pagans: "When he was living at Rome he wrote a treatise on the preservation of virginity [Jer. *Ep.* 22 to Eustochium], which all the pagans and enemies of God, all apostates and persecutors, and whoever else hated the Christian name, competed among themselves to publicize" ("libellum quondam de conservanda virginitate Romae positus scripsit, quem libellum omnes pagani et inimici Dei, apostatae persecutores et quicumque sunt, qui Christianum nomen odio habent, certatim sibi describebant," *Apol.* 2.5).[51] One need not have been a pagan to find Jerome's views abhorrent and his personality obnoxious. Mockery of Jerome, the expert mocker of his day, would have been seen as deserved by Romans across the religious spectrum.

Although Cameron's rewriting of the history of paganism and Christianity renders impossible many previous interpretations of the *Historia Augusta*, he is wrong to dismiss the many allusions to Jerome. Cameron denies that the *HA*-author alludes to Jerome because he rejects the idea that the *Historia Augusta* encodes a secret message against Christianity,[52] but I contend that the allusions are not meant to be secret, nor are they meant to comment seriously on Christianity. Cameron argues that the *HA*-author would have to be incompetent to include anachronisms and allusions to contemporary texts that would reveal his deception.[53] In the absence of any intended deception, however, the basis for Cameron's objection disappears.

Allusions to Jerome in the *Historia Augusta* can typically be characterized as mocking and irreverent toward a figure who was widely disliked during his lifetime for his temperament and his extreme views. From the massive oeuvre of Jerome, I have identified a limited selection of works that the audience would need to be familiar with to appreciate the *HA*-author's allusions: a handful of letters, the two commentaries on Matthew and Isaiah, and the *Life of Hilarion*. Although scholars have identified a variety of places where the *Historia Augusta* seems to allude to the Bible, I contend that the substantive allusions to the Bible that can be found in the *Historia Augusta* derive from Jerome's letters or the books of Matthew or Isaiah; Jerome's commentaries on these two biblical books had already been independently identified as sources for allusion. Therefore, I conclude that allusions to the Bible in the *Historia Augusta* are really just further allusions to Jerome. To this discussion of Jerome I append some comments on the use of Ambrose by the *Historia Augusta*. Ambrose, like Jerome, was what Cameron calls a "strong" Christian, a radical by contemporary standards. These sometimes complex, often-humorous allusions function in the *Historia Augusta* much as allusions to Cicero do. They test the ingenuity of the reader rather than proclaim ideological loyalties.

The *Life of Hilarion*

Jerome wrote lives of three saints: Paul, Hilarion, and Malchus. These were the first hagiographical works in Latin and proved to be immensely popular.[54] He appropriated themes from novel-writing in his attempt to compete with contemporary Greek hagiography, especially the *Life of Antony*. His first work in this genre, the *Life of Paul*, was composed between 375 and 380. There is no external evidence for this Paul, presented as the founder of Egyptian monasticism and thus a model for Antony, and he may have been entirely Jerome's invention. In any case he is presented in a mythical and literary form: he meets a hippocentaur and a satyr in the desert, for example, and when Paul meets Antony, Jerome marks the occasion with a pair of Vergilian quotations. The biography of Malchus the Captive Monk describes, with details Jerome claims to have heard from Malchus himself, the story of an ascetic who is enslaved by nomads but manages to maintain his chastity and eventually to escape. It contains some fantastic elements and was likely written in 388. The *Life of Hilarion*, written before 393, has a more certain historical basis, since Hilarion is known through Sozomen and Epiphanius, but, as Weingarten shows, Jerome drew extensively on the *Metamorphoses* of Apuleius in composing it.[55] The monk Hilarion undergoes tribulations similar to those of the ass Lucius, but Jerome transforms the themes and images of the bawdy novel into Christian and ascetic ones. If we imagine our author and his circle as having a particular interest in biography, this new style of biography might have attracted their attention, and through this text they may have been led to other writings of Jerome.

In 1927 Schmeidler noted the parallels between the preface to Jerome's hagiographic *Life of Hilarion* and the preface to the *Probus* attributed to Vopiscus. First, the *Historia Augusta* (*Prob*. 1.1–6):[56]

> Certum est quod Sallustius Crispus quodque Marcus Cato et Gellius historici sententiae modo in litteras retulerunt, omnes omnium virtutes tantas esse quantas videri eas voluerint eorum ingenia qui unius cuiusque facta descripserint. inde est quod Alexander Magnus Macedo, cum ad Achillis sepulchrum venisset, graviter ingemescens: 'felicem te,' inquit, 'iuvenis, qui talem praeconem tuarum virtutum repperisti,' Homerum intellegi volens qui Achillem tantum in virtutum studio fecit quantum ipse valebat ingenio. Quorsum haec pertinent, mi Celsine, fortassis requiris. Probum principem, cuius imperio Oriens, Occidens, Meridies, Septentrio omnesque orbis partes in totam securitatem redactae sunt, scriptorum inopia iam paene nescimus. occidit, pro pudor, tanti viri et talis historia, qualem non habent bella

Punica, non terror Gallicus, non motus Pontici, non Hispaniensis astutia. sed non patiar ego ille, a quo dudum solus Aurelianus est expetitus, cuius vitam quantum potui persecutus, Tacito Florianoque iam scriptis, non me ad Probi facta conscendere, si vita suppetet, omnes qui supersunt usque ad Maximianum Diocletianumque dicturus. neque ego nunc facultatem eloquentiamque polliceor, sed res gestas, quas perire non patior.

It is true what Sallust and the historians Marcus Cato and Gellius have recounted in their works as a maxim, that all the virtues of all men are as great as they have been made to appear by the genius of those who described the deeds of each one. Thus did Alexander the Great of Macedon, when he had come to the tomb of Achilles, groan deeply, "Young man, you are fortunate, who found so great a herald of your virtues," meaning Homer, who made Achilles as great in his eagerness for virtue as he himself was great in genius. Perhaps you are wondering, my Celsinus, what this refers to? Because of a lack of writers, we know almost nothing of the emperor Probus, in whose rule east, west, south, and north, and all parts of the world, were restored to perfect security. The history of so great a man, such a man as neither the Punic Wars had, nor the Gallic terror, nor the disturbances at Pontus, nor the clever Spaniards, has shamefully perished. But I, who once sought to write the life of Aurelian alone as well as I could, and who now have also written lives of Tacitus and Florian, will not allow the deeds of Probus to evade me, and if my life is long enough, I will tell of all the emperors who remain up to the time of Maximian and Diocletian. I promise neither power nor eloquence, but the historical facts, which I do not allow to perish.

Here is Jerome (*Vit. Hilar.* 1.1–8):

Scripturus vitam beati Hilarionis habitatorem eius invoco Spiritum sanctum, ut qui illi virtutes largitus est, mihi ad narrandas eas sermonem tribuat, ut facta dictis exaequerentur. 'Eorum enim qui fecere virtus, ut ait Crispus, tanta habetur quantum eam verbis potuere extollere praeclara ingenia.' Alexander Magnus Macedo, quem vel aes vel pardum vel hircum caprarum Daniel vocat, cum ad Achillis tumulum pervenisset: 'Felicem te, ait, o iuvenis, qui magno frueris praecone meritorum,' Homerum videlicet significans. Porro mihi tanti ac talis viri conversatio vitaque dicenda est, ut Homerus quoque, si adesset, vel invideret materiae vel succumberet. Quamquam enim sanctus Epiphanius, Salaminae Cypri episcopus, qui cum Hilarione plurimum versatus est, laudem eius brevi epistula scripserit quae vulgo legitur, tamen aliud est locis communibus laudare defunctum, aliud defuncti proprias narrare virtutes. Unde et nos favore magis illius quam iniuria coeptum ab eo opus aggredientes maledicorum voces contemnimus, qui olim detrahentes Paulo meo nunc forsitam detrahent et Hilarioni, illum solitudinis calumniati, huic obicientes frequentiam; ut qui semper latuit, non fuisse, qui a multis visus est, vilis extimetur. Fecerunt hoc et maiores eorum quondam Pharisaei, quibus nec Iohannis eremus ac ieiunium nec Domini Salvatoris turbae, cibi potusque placuerunt. Verum destinato operi imponam manum et Scyllaeos canes obturata aure transibo.

Before I write the life of blessed Hilarion, I invoke the Holy Spirit who dwelled in him, so that the one who lavished virtues on him should provide me with the words for narrating his story, that my words might be equal to his deeds. For the virtue of those who have acted, as Sallust says, is appreciated just as much as outstanding geniuses are able to praise them. Alexander the Great of Macedon, whom Daniel calls either the ram, or the panther, or the male goat, when he had arrived at the tomb of Achilles said, "You are fortunate, young man, who enjoy a great herald of your virtues," obviously meaning Homer. But I must tell of the deeds and life of so great a man that if Homer were present, he would either be jealous of my material or be inadequate for it. Although holy Epiphanius, bishop of Salamis in Cyprus, who spent a lot of time with Hilarion, wrote a tribute to him in a short letter which is read by many, yet it is one thing to praise a dead man with commonplaces, another to speak of the virtues specific to the dead man. We set forth on the work begun by him with favor rather than harm, dismissing the voices of the slanderers who previously disparaged my Paul, and now, perhaps, will also disparage my Hilarion. They attacked Paul with condemnation of his solitude, and blame Hilarion for his worldly engagement, saying that the one who always hid did not exist, and the one who was seen by many was worthless. The ancestors of these men, the Pharisees, did the same thing. Neither the desert fasting of John, nor the Lord and Savior in the crowd, eating and drinking, was pleasing to them. But I will set my hand to the work I have resolved to do, and I will pass by the dogs of Scylla with my ears stuffed with wax.

The passages combine two commonplaces. First, they include material from the introduction to the monograph on the Catilinarian conspiracy by Sallust, who is cited by name by both authors, claiming that the merit of those who have performed deeds is rated only as high as the eloquence of those who praise the deeds allows (*Cat.* 8.4). Jerome combines a reference to an earlier part of the Sallustian work (*Cat.* 3.2) with a verbatim citation of this passage, while the *HA*-author offers a vague paraphrase of it. There follows another much-cited anecdote with a similar message, this one derived from the Cicero's *Pro Archia* 24: Alexander, standing at the tomb of Achilles, called him fortunate for having Homer as his bard. Both Jerome and the *HA*-author alter the Cicero passage in ways that are similar enough to make it clear that they have not independently combined these anecdotes. The similarity of the phrases that follow the anecdotes—"tanti ac talis viri conversatio vitaque" in Jerome and "tanti viri et talis historia" in the *Historia Augusta*—makes it very unlikely that they draw from a shared, lost source.[57]

For almost a century, scholars have compared the two passages for the specific purpose of determining who copied whom, which would be of great importance for dating the *Historia Augusta*. Jerome's *Life of Hilarion* was written certainly after 385 and before 392, perhaps in 390, according to its latest editor. The Sallust passage is presented verbatim by Jerome but is paraphrased by the *HA*-author; the Cicero passage, on the other hand, is closer to the original in the *HA*-version than in Jerome. Because both authors are likely familiar with the original sources, it has proven difficult to find consensus through philological means on which is the imitator and which the source.[58] Most recently Cameron has devoted eleven full pages out of thirty-nine in his entire chapter on the *Historia Augusta* to an attempt to prove that the *Historia Augusta* came first.

Rather than once again considering the question of priority on narrow philological grounds, let us instead consider the broader context of the two prologues. What purpose does this allusion serve for the *HA*-author? Both Jerome and the *HA*-author are writing biographies of historical figures that have been elaborated and expanded with literary flourishes and outright invention. Just as Jerome boasts of his earlier *Life of Paul*, so the *HA*-author "Vopiscus" lists his previous biographies. We learn from the rest of Jerome's defensive prologue that critics had doubted the veracity of his most recent biography, and we know that these critics had good reason to doubt, since the *Life of Paul* is likely a complete fiction from beginning to end. The biographer of Probus is abusing the truth openly for an audience that appreciates the joke. There is irony, then, when he alludes to the prologue of Jerome, which introduces a work in which the same abuse of the truth is carried out in the hope of deceiving the audience. Paschoud's suggestion that Jerome was seen as a "rival" is too strong, if we take him to mean that the *HA*-author sought to promote a "pagan" heroism that would compete with the Christian version of Jerome.[59] Allusion to a liar would undercut this purported goal in the eyes of anyone who could recognize and interpret the allusion. Instead, we should understand the *HA*-author to be contrasting his own knowing and playful deception with the brazenness of Jerome's deception on behalf of radical monasticism, which the *HA*-author saw as a degraded and foolish way of life.

Strangely, Cameron suggests that the fact that Jerome is the author of more than a hundred similar prefaces "crammed with classical allusions" is an argument in favor of the priority of the *Historia Augusta*.[60] Why, in all of his voluminous writings, would Jerome have borrowed this generic passage, and this one alone, out of all the rich material offered by the *Historia Augusta*? In fact, no author at all has been convincingly shown to have borrowed from the *Historia Augusta* throughout most of the fifth century. On the other hand, the *HA*-author is an inveterate practitioner of allusion to a broad array of intertexts. The works of Jerome provide additional material for his allusive play.

Cameron focuses only on one passage of Jerome, although there are others that may be equally convincing. Another reference that should be attributed to the influence of Jerome's *Hilarion* is the brief mention of the god Marnas in *Alexander Severus* 17.4. Marnas was the principal god of Gaza, a version of Baal associated with Zeus.[61] Hilarion's activity in Gaza includes a pair of miracles designed to demonstrate the impotence of Marnas in the face of Christ. First, he cured the three children of a prominent woman, who begged him for help with the claim that Marnas would be demeaned by a successful healing in the name of the Christian god (*Vit. Hilar.* 8.1–7). The second miracle was granted to a certain Gazan Christian, Italicus (11.3–4):

> Sed Italicus, eiusdem oppidi municeps christianus, adversus Gazensem duumvirum, Marnae idolo deditum, circenses equos nutriebat. Hoc siquidem in Romanis urbibus iam exinde servatur a Romulo, ut propter felicem Sabinarum raptum Conso, quasi consiliorum deo, quadrigae septeno currant circuitu, et equos parties adversae fregisse victoria sit.

> Italicus was a Christian citizen of the same town who raised racehorses to compete against the duumvir of Gaza, who followed the false god Marnas. This custom [i.e., chariot-racing on the feast of Consualia, 21 August] has been maintained in Roman cities since the time of Romulus, to celebrate the fortunate seizure of the Sabine women. The chariots raced seven times around the circus in honor of Consus, the god of counsel, and exhausting the horses on the other team meant victory.

Italicus's opponent was aided by demonic magic, but Italicus was able to persuade Hilarion to counter it with his own God-derived power to ensure Italicus's safety and triumph, which duly occurs (11.11–13):

> Clamor fit vulgi nimius, ita ut ethnici quoque ipsi concreparent: 'Marnas victus est a Christo.' Porro furentes adversarii Hilarionem 'maleficum christianorum' ad supplicium poposcerunt. Indubitata ergo victoria et illis et multis dehinc circensibus plurimis fidei occasio fuit.
>
> The noise of the crowd increased, as the pagans themselves shouted together, "Marnas has been conquered by Christ." The frenzied opponents demanded that Hilarion be punished as an evildoing Christian. This undeniable victory was an occasion for conversion for them and many later circus audiences.

This is a striking story with an antiquarian touch that might provoke interesting discussion in a scholarly milieu.

The same passage is subtly evoked in the *Alexander Severus*, chapters 16 and 17:

> Leges de iure populi et fisci moderatas et infinitas sanxit neque ullam constitutionem sacravit sine viginti iuris peritis et doctissimis ac sapientibus viris isdemque disertissimis non minus quinquaginta, ut non minus in consilio essent sententiae, quam senatus consultum conficerent, et id quidem ita ut iretur per sententias singulorum ac scriberetur, quid quisque dixisset, dato tamen spatio ad disquirendum cogitandumque, priusquam dicerent, ne incogitati dicere cogerentur de rebus ingentibus. fuit praeterea illi consuetudo, ut, si de iure aut de negotiis tractaret, solos doctos et disertos adhiberet, si vero de re militari, militares veteres et senes bene meritos et locorum peritos ac bellorum et castrorum et omnes litteratos et maxime eos, qui historiam norant, requirens, quid in talibus causis, quales in disceptatione versabantur, veteres imperatores vel Romani vel exterarum gentium fecissent.
>
> Referebat Encolpius, quo ille familiarissimo usus est, illum, si umquam furem iudicem vidisset, paratum habuisse digitum, ut illi oculum erueret: tantum odium eum tenebat eorum, de quibus apud se probatum, quod fures fuissent. addit Septiminus, qui vitam eius non mediocriter exsequutus est, tanti stomachi fuisse Alexandrum in eos iudices, qui furtorum fama laborassent, etiamsi damnati non essent, ut, si eos casu aliquo videret, commotione animi stomachi choleram evomeret toto vultu inardescente, ita ut nihil loqui posset. nam cum quidam Septimius Arabianus, famosus crimine furtorum et sub Heliogabalo iam liberatus, inter senatores principem salutatum venisset, exclamavit: 'O Marna, O Iuppiter, O di inmortales, Arabianus non solum vivit, verum etiam in senatum venit, fortassis etiam de me sperat; tam fatuum, tam stultum esse me iudicat.'

He established many just laws about the rights of the people and the treasury, and he did not issue any law without twenty most learned jurists and no less than fifty most eloquent men, so there would be no fewer opinions in his council than would issue a senate decree. He solicited the opinions of individuals and what each had said was recorded, yet time was provided before they spoke for questioning and introspection, so that they might not be compelled to speak unreflectively about important matters. It was his custom, in addition, if he was dealing with law or public business, to summon only the learned and eloquent, but if he was dealing with military affairs, he would summon veterans and distinguished old men who were knowledgeable about geography and wars and camps, and he would also ask authors, especially those who knew history, what had been done in cases similar to those under debate, by former rulers of Rome or of foreign nations.

Encolpius, who was very close to the emperor, used to report that if he ever saw a judge who was a thief, he had a finger prepared to pluck out his eye, so great was his hatred for those whom he judged corrupt. Septimius, who has written up a pretty good biography of the emperor, adds that Alexander had such anger against those judges who suffered from the reputation of corruption, even if they had not been condemned, that if he should see such a judge by chance, with a burning expression and a convulsion of anger he would pour forth so much bile that he was unable to speak. When a certain Septimius Arabianus, infamous for accusations of corruption, and recently set free during the reign of Elagabalus, had come with the senators to pay his respects to the emperor, Alexander exclaimed: "O Marnas, O Jupiter, O immortal gods, Arabianus not only lives, but he even comes into the senate; perhaps he even hopes for some favor from me, judging that I am so empty-headed and foolish."

Although Weingarten remarks that "the cult of Marnas at Gaza appears to have been widely known," her only evidence is the *Life of Hilarion* and the *Historia Augusta*. Otherwise the god is unknown to Latin literature.[62] It is Jerome alone who returns to him frequently, not only in the *Hilarion* but also in a letter (107.2.3) celebrating the destruction of the sanctuary: "iam et Aegyptius Serapis factus est Christianus, Marnas Gazae luget inclusus et eversionem templi iugiter pertimescit" ("Now Egyptian Serapis has become Christian, now at Gaza Marnas, imprisoned, mourns, and fears the overturning of his temple"). He returns to him yet again in his *Commentary* on Isaiah 17: "Hoc et nostris temporibus videmus esse completum: Serapeum Alexandriae, et Marnae templum Gazae in ecclesias Domini surrexerunt" ("We see that this has been fulfilled in our time: the Serapeum at Alexandria and the temple of Marnas at Gaza have been rebuilt as churches of the Lord"). The *HA*-author and his audience, with their love of the outlandish, mock Jerome's obsession with this otherwise-unknown eastern god and create a pastiche of sections from the beginning of Cicero's first oration against Catiline (1.2 and 1.9), with the unexpected addition of Marnas to the apostrophe *di immortales*. The god of Gaza was presumably also the inspiration for the near eastern name of the supposed miscreant, Septimius Arabianus.

Nothing in the *HA*-author's use of Marnas implies any particular attitude toward the destruction of his temple. An ordinary westerner, even a pagan, would presumably feel little attachment to an obscure eastern god on any account, and the placement of the god's name in an exclamation in the midst of a parody of Cicero would be a most incongruous way to express any religious position at all. Why, then, did the *HA*-author choose to mention Marnas at this place in particular? Chapter 16 of the *Alexander Severus* explains in elaborate detail the absurd lengths to which Alexander supposedly went in order to make good decisions in concert with good advisers, a topos of historiography and biography taken to an extreme. Huge councils of lawyers, statesmen, soldiers, and *litterateurs* are regularly summoned to help Alexander choose wisely. When we reexamine the circumstances of the chariot race at Gaza at which Marnas was defeated, we find that it took place during the celebration of the Consualia, "in honor of Consus" in his character as god of counsel. The celebration was, further, in honor of the "stealing" of the Sabine Women. Chapter 17 of the *Alexander* focuses on theft and Alexander's outrage against a thief.

Letters

In his autobiographical entry in *De viris illustribus*, Jerome included a bibliography of his own work up to the time of its publication in 393. The longer letters 14, 18, 20, 21, 22, 36, 39 are listed with individual titles, as are two letter collections: *To a Variety of Friends* and *To Marcella*. Cain identifies the former collection as comprising letters 2–13 and 15–17, and the second as comprising the letters to Marcella written at Rome in 384 and 385, which are 23–29, 32, 34, 37, 38, 40–44. The letters to Pope Damasus (19, 20, 21, 35, 36) seem to have circulated together as well.[63]

Jerome's third epistle is the subject of a particularly extravagant intertextual relationship with the life of Bonosus from the *Historia Augusta*. Bonosus was the fourth of the usurpers gathered together between *Probus* and *Carus* in the section moderns call the *Quadrigae Tyrannorum*, "the four-horse chariot of usurpers," after a (probably Hieronymian) phrase that the *HA*-author uses in passing. Little is known about any of the usurpers whom the *Historia Augusta* collects in this chapter, Bonosus included. The *KG* had reported that Probus defeated Bonosus after the latter rose in revolt in Cologne; every other detail that the *HA*-author provides is fictitious.[64] This provides fertile ground for allusive play.

Wine drinking is a focus in several of the lives of the *Quadrigae Tyrannorum*. Bonosus, for his part, "drank as much as no other man had; Aurelian used to say that he was born not to live, but to drink" (a play on words: "non ut vivat natus est, sed ut bibat," *Quad. Tyr.* 14.3). But "no matter how much he drank, he was always calm and sober, and, as Onesimus, the writer of a life of Probus, relates, he was even wiser after drinking" ("ipse quantumlibet bibisset, semper securus et sobrius et, ut Onesimus dicit, scriptor vitae Probi, adhuc in vino prudentior," 14.4). "He had a miraculous quality, in addition: he pissed out however much he drank, without damage to his chest, stomach, or bladder" ("habuit praeterea rem mirabilem, ut quantum bibisset tantum mingeret, neque umquam eius aut pectus aut venter aut vesica gravaretur," 14.5).

This Onesimus, the supposed biographer of Probus who is cited as the source for the *HA*-author's knowledge of Bonosus's alcoholic wisdom, is quoted five more times in the later books of the *Historia Augusta*: once more in the *Quad. Tyr.* (13.1) and four times in the *Carus* (4.2, 7.3, 16.1, 17.3). None of the citations offers information that has any claim to authenticity. In this passage in the *Quadrigae Tyrannorum*, Onesimus is described as a biographer of Probus, but he goes unmentioned in the *Probus* itself. In fact, the *HA*-author claims in the preface to the *Probus* that the emperor is almost unknown because writers about him are scarce. Nevertheless, there is a persistent temptation among modern historians to connect this Onesimus with the similarly named Onasimus discussed by the *Suda* (O 327). In addition to the difference in name, the *Suda* entry is not about our Onesimus. The *Suda*'s Onesimus is described as active during the reign of Constantine as a "historian and orator"; no specific historical, and certainly no biographical, works are attributed to him, although he is credited with a considerable number of oratorical works. The modern literature on Onasimus/Onesimus must be seen as a historical relic of the attempts to justify, at least partly or indirectly, the false claim of the *Historia Augusta* to be a product of the Constantinian era.[65]

Chastagnol discovered the true origin of the name Onesimus in the third letter of Jerome.[66] Jerome wrote this letter from Antioch to his friend Rufinus in Egypt around 375. The letter celebrates a mutual friend who has fully embraced the extreme monastic life that Jerome has been contemplating. The friend has forsaken his wealth, his position, and his family to live in squalor on a desert island—the very scenario that so angered and disgusted Rutilius Namatianus. After abandoning his mother, sister, and brother, this monk took the final step and separated from his dearest friend to live in utter solitude, Jerome tells Rufinus. This brave monk is named Bonosus, just like the poorly known usurper. And the name of the friend whom he has abandoned is Onesimus, just like the fictitious biographer.

The simple juxtaposition of these two uncommon names in two nearly contemporary authors is striking. Details about the "biographer" Onesimus that frame the passage serve to deepen the connection with Jerome and underscore the parodic nature of the allusion. The first mention of Onesimus occurs in the Proculus section of the *Quadrigae Tyrannorum*, where he is claimed as an authority for the story that Proculus was raised to the purple by a banquet game that got out of hand (*Quad. Tyr.* 13.1): "in imperium vocitatus est, ludo paene ac ioco, ut Onesimus dicit (quod quidem apud nullum alium reperisse me scio)" ("[Proculus] was called to take up the imperial power almost by a game and joke, as Onesimus says—something that I have certainly not found in any other author"). Although "game and joke" ostensibly describes the manner in which Proculus was called to the throne, we should also connect the phrase more closely with "Onesimus dicit": Onesimus speaks in jokes and in fun. And the emphasis on the claim that the *HA*-author has not found his material in any other source is a metatextual suggestion to the reader to do the opposite and expect some other source to undergird the playfulness that follows. In a passage toward the beginning of the *Carus* (4.5), Onesimus is brought forth as an expert on Carus's birthplace. Although all of our historical sources agree that Carus was born in Gaul, Onesimus is said to have concluded that he was born in Aquileia, which is not coincidentally the home of Rufinus, to whom Jerome's letter was addressed. And in the last appearance of Onesimus, later in the *Carus*, the pseudo-biographer is credited with the false claim that Constantius I was governor of Dalmatia (17.6), the probable homeland of Jerome himself.

Bonosus the usurper is a parody of the Bonosus of *Epistle* 3.4–5 in various ways. Jerome tells us that his friend was highly educated, while the usurper, we are told, learned nothing of literature (*Quad. Tyr.* 14.1). The monk is a metaphorical soldier, a fighter who seeks victory wearing the armor of the apostles; the usurper is of course an actual soldier (*Quad. Tyr.* 14.2). The monk Bonosus, Jerome tells Rufinus, lacks creature comforts but is closer to God (*Ep.* 3.4.3): "nulla euriporum amoenitate perfruitur, sed de latere domini aquam vitae bibit" ("he does not enjoy the pleasure of decorative water ponds, but he drinks the water of life from the side of the Lord"). The claim of Aurelian that Bonosus was born "not to live, but to drink" scrambles the words of the monk who "drinks the water of life" (*Quad. Tyr.* 14.3). The more the usurper Bonosus drank, the more sober (*securus*) he became (14.4); the same adjective is used of the monk. Jerome, considering the struggles that Bonosus will face on his desert island, worries that the devil will come to him when he is weak with fasting and disease, but knows that ultimately the power of Christ will protect him. The equivalent miracle ("rem mirabilem," 14.5) for the usurper is bodily and base: despite his heavy drinking, he enjoys easy urination without problems in the belly or bladder. In the next sentence of the *Historia Augusta*, we are told that Bonosus seized imperial power after the Germans burned Roman galleys on the Rhine ("hic idem, cum quodam tempore in Rheno Romanas lusorias Germani incendissent . . . sumpsit imperium," 15.1). The *KG* preserves the information that Bonosus attempted to seize the throne in Cologne, and so the claim of usurpation on the Rhine may be conceivably be derived from the *KG*. It is more likely, though, that the *HA*-author is continuing to work from the letter in which Jerome recalls that he knew Bonosus from infancy and, after school at Rome, that they lived together and shared the same food ("cum post Romana studia ad Rheni semibarbaras ripas eodem cibo, pari frueremur hospitio," *Ep.* 3.5.2). In these short phrases, we see repeated the words "Roman" and "Rhine," and Jerome's *semibarbaras* is the equivalent of *Germani*. The *HA*-author may have wandered from *studia* to *ludus* to *lusoria*.

Chastagnol has shown further evidence of the use of *Epistle* 3 elsewhere in the *Historia Augusta*.[67] The following passage describes the drinking habits of the emperor Elagabalus (*Elag.* 21.6):

> Condito piscinas et solia temperavit et rosato atque absinthiato. vulgum ad bibendum invitavit et ipse cum populo tantum bibit, ut in piscina eum bibisse intellegeretur, viso quod unus bibisset.
>
> He mixed rose and wormwood seasonings into his fish ponds and bathtubs. He invited the common people to a drinking party, and he himself drank so much with the people that it was understood, when they saw what one man had drunk, that he had been drinking from a fish pond.

The *Elagabalus* cites the gourmand and cookbook author Apicius several times.[68] In this passage, the description of his baths and pools as "seasoned" (*condito*) with rose (*rosato*) and wormwood (*absinthiato*) evokes the first recipes of the first book of Apicius: seasoned wine (1.1), wormwood-flavored wine (1.3), and rose-flavored wine (1.4). The monk Bonosus, alone on the island, did not possess fish ponds, but he drank water from the side of the Lord. The emperor drinks from one of his ponds, in which he had mixed his own cocktail, and he is not alone but in a crowd. Further, the *HA*-author uses the word *piscina* for "fish pond" in six other places (in addition to the two instances in the quotation above). The letter of Jerome, however, had used another word: *euripus*. *Euripus* appears only once in the *Historia Augusta*: five or six sentences after this passage in the *Elagabalus*, in a similarly invented passage.

The *HA*-author's play with Jerome's portrayal of Bonosus can be seen as a response, in a way, to the words of Jerome that introduce his narration: "Let the marvels invented by the lies of Greek and Roman writers give way to the following story, which is true" (cedant huic veritati tam Graeco quam Romano stilo mendaciis ficta miracula," *Ep.* 3.4.1). The *Historia Augusta* is proud to offer fiction that, like the parody of the preface to the *Life of Hilarion*, draws attention to the dubiousness of Jerome's own claims to veracity. We can also see that the *HA*-author has chosen to turn Jerome's purposefully shocking story of renunciation into a celebration of consumption.

Another passage in the *Elagabalus* also reveals the use of Jerome's letters by the *HA*-author.[69] Elagabalus was a teenager when he became emperor, and his mother and grandmother wielded considerable influence during his reign; the historical tradition looks upon this female-dominated period with distaste. The *HA*-author uses the criticisms of his sources as jumping-off points for further fantastic elaboration. In chapter 4 he claims that, in an act unprecedented in Roman history, a woman, Elagabalus's mother, Symiamira, entered the senate house and participated in senate business. A fictional claim follows (*Elag.* 4.3–4):

> Fecit et in colle Quirinali senaculum, id est mulierum senatum, in quo ante fuerat conventus matronalis, solemnibus dumtaxat diebus et si umquam aliqua matrona consularis coniugii ornamentis esset donata, quod veteres imperatores adfinibus detulerunt et his maxime, quae nobilitatos maritos non habuerant, ne innobilitatae remanerent. sub Symiamira facta sunt senatus consulta ridicula de legibus matronalibus: quae quo vestitu incederet, quae cui cederet, quae ad cuius osculum veniret, quae pilento, quae equo, quae sagmario, quae asino veheretur, quae carpento mulari, quae bovum, quae sella veheretur et utrum pellicia an ossea an eborata an argentata, et quae aurum vel gemmas in calciamentis haberent.

> He created a *senaculum*, that is, a senate of women, on the Quirinal Hill, in a place where matrons had met before, but only on holidays, or when some matron had been granted the insignia of consular marriage, which the old emperors used to provide for their relatives, especially those who had not married aristocrats, so that they would not lose their nobility. Under the influence of Symiamira, absurd senatorial decrees on laws for matrons were passed: who could leave the house in what clothing, who must yield to whom, who must offer a kiss to whom, who might ride on a chariot, a

horse, a pack-animal, or an ass, who might be borne in a carriage pulled by mules or oxen, who might be borne in a litter, and whether the litter should be leather or bone or ivory or silver, and who could have gold or gems on their shoes.

The idea of the *senaculum* as a senate of women is a fantasy of the *HA*-author. The word *senaculum* is normally used for the antechamber of the senate house (cf. Varro, *Ling.* 5.166; Val. Max. 2.2.6), but the *HA*-author has made a kind of grammatical joke by treating the locative-*ulum* ending as a diminutive. Straub was the first to interpret the joke in the phrases *mulierum senatum* and *conventus matronalis* by pointing to similar language in two passages of Jerome. Jerome was notorious for his leadership of aristocratic widows and virgins in Rome, which he brashly celebrated, referring to a "matronarum . . . senatus" in a letter to the widow Marcella (*Ep.* 43.4) and to a "conventu feminarum" in the treatise *Against Jovinian* (1.47). Straub points out that the term *conventus matronarum* is found in an innocuous context in Suetonius (*Galb.* 5.1), where it simply refers to a gathering of aristocratic women, but that the term *conventus* can have a different meaning in later antiquity, as our word "convent" reveals: a monastic community of women. Jerome is thus criticized for excessive entanglement with aristocratic women, just as Elagabalus was. Perhaps the placement of this *senaculum* on the Quirinal, as Chastagnol suggests, provides a kind of counterpart to the circle of Jerome, which was famously centered on the Aventine.[70]

Individually the textual parallels *conventus* and *senatus* are not, perhaps, decisive, and some scholars, such as Turcan, deny that they provide evidence of the connection between Jerome and the *Historia Augusta*.[71] But Turcan is incorrect in claiming that the feminine legislation of *Elagabalus* 4.4 finds no place in the works of Jerome. On the contrary, Chastagnol's investigation of Jerome's letter to Eustochium (*Ep.* 22), the very letter that Rufinus claims has been read by all of Rome, even pagans (*Apology* 2.5), makes the connection certain.[72] In this letter, which Jerome had given the title *On Virginity*, he implores Eustochium to follow the monastic life and urges her not to have contact with *consortia matronarum* who boast of their important spouses. The activities that Jerome decries are paralleled by those that are the subject of the legislation by the women's senate in the *Historia Augusta*. For example, inappropriate clothing is condemned in 22.13 and throughout the letter. The question of precedence is discussed in 22.15, where Jerome argues that Blesilla may be older than Eustochium but is inferior to her in holiness, having once been married. In 22.16 we see members of the clergy kissing women who are rich but undeserving, and a discussion of litters, both featured in the *senaculum* passage. In addition to the criticism of rich women borne in litters, Jerome refers to other modes of transport that appear in the *Historia Augusta*: he condemns rich and dandified men for their horses (22.28), celebrates a horse for throwing his rider (22.41), and twice evokes Jesus on an ass (22.24, 22.41). One other word used for a vehicle, the *sagmarius*, a kind of chariot, is late and very rare, occurring one other time in the *Historia Augusta*, once in Servius, and once, perhaps significantly, in Jerome's *Life of Hilarion*. The final decree of the feminine senate determines who might wear gold or jewels on her shoes. The *HA*-author has a particular interest in jeweled shoes, which recur at *Elagabalus* 23.4, *Alexander Severus* 4.2, and *Carus* 17.1. He probably got the idea from the *KG*, which claimed that Diocletian had begun the practice of wearing them (Victor 39.3; Eutropius 9.26). But he may have been inspired to insert his *idée fixe* in this passage because of two references in *Epistle* 22: the introductory suggestion that Eustochium walks "laden with gold" (22.3), and the celebration of the shoelessness of Moses, Joshua, and Jesus himself (22.19). Overall we see a traditional, satirical approach to women. Female busybodies in the age of Elagabalus were empowered to legislate on trivialities, just as Jerome indulges his unmanly obsession with the proper nature of women's clothing in his own "senate of women."

Epistle 22 received additional attention from the *HA*-author.[73] Jerome refers to Samson as "leone fortior, saxo durior" ("braver than a lion and harder than a rock," *Ep.* 22.12.1). In the biography of Proculus (*Quad. Tyr.* 12.4), the *HA*-author attributes to the usurper a masculine wife with the name of Samso. In the next section (22.13.1), Jerome laments, "Piget dicere, quot cotidie virgines ruant, quantas de suo gremio mater perdat ecclesia" ("It is shameful to speak of how many virgins fall each day, how many are lost from the bosom of the church, their mother"). The *HA*-author is prepared with the answer to the implied rhetorical question—how many virgins do in fact "fall" each day?—in a (fake, of course) letter of Proculus (*Quad. Tyr.* 12.7):

> Proculus Maeciano adfini salutem dicit. centum ex Sarmatia virgines cepi, ex his una nocte decem inii, omnes tamen, quod in me erat, mulieres intra dies quindecim reddidi.

> From Proculus to his relative Maecianus, greeting. I have taken a hundred virgins from Sarmatia. I slept with ten of these in a single night; all of them, however, I made into women, as far as was in my power, in the space of fifteen days.

Instead of virgins lost from their "mother," the church, these virgins are made into mothers. Jerome asks for, and receives, not only a number but a rate, expressed in terms of fallen virgins per day. Proculus's letter is addressed to a fictitious kinsman named Maecianus because Eustochium, the addressee of Jerome's *Epistle* 22, was a member of the family of the Furii Maecii. Chastagnol would also argue for the influence of this letter later in the *Quadrigae Tyrannorum*, where the wife of Bonosus, Hunila, is described as "a woman of unequaled excellence and also of noble family, though by race a Goth" ("femina singularis exempli et familiae nobilis, gentis tamen Gothicae," *Quad. Tyr.* 15.4), which perhaps evokes the description of Eustochium as "nobili stirpe generatam" (*Ep.* 22.11.1) and especially as "Romanae urbis virgo nobilis" (22.15.1). Paschoud sees the *tamen* of the *HA*-author as offering the same kind of responsiveness to Jerome that we saw in his answer to Jerome's rhetorical question: Eustochium is a noblewoman of Rome; Hunila is noble *although* she is of Gothic extraction.[74]

The proper behavior of women is also the subject of a series of allusions in the last pages of the *Thirty Tyrants*. After he describes thirty usurpers, many of whom are invented or provided with invented details, the *HA*-author apologizes for the inclusion of two women in the group (31.7–12). He proposes to add two more men, although they are chronologically out of place: Titus, who rose under Maximinus, and Censorinus, whom he places under Claudius. Titus (*Tyr. Trig.* 32) appears to be a version of the man called Quartinus by Herodian (7.1.9–10). He is embellished with fictitious details and in particular an invented and ideal traditional wife, Calpurnia. Censorinus (*Tyr. Trig.* 33) is entirely a creation of the author; his name also evokes the traditional Roman values that he represents: he is "a true soldier and a man of old-fashioned dignity in the senate house" ("vir plane militaris et antiquae in curia dignitatis," 33.1). These idealized Roman figures, male and female, contrast with the Christian ideals of virgin and monk in Jerome's letters. To further emphasize the contrast, the portraits are framed with language derived from Jerome's biblical commentaries (32.5–6):

> Huius uxor Calpurnia fuit, sancta et venerabilis femina de genere Caesoninorum, id est Pisonum, quam maiores nostri univiriam sacerdotem inter sacratissimas feminas adoarunt, cuius statuam in templo Veneris adhuc vidimus acrolitham sed auratam. Haec uniones Cleopatranos habuisse perhibetur, haec lancem centum librarum argenti, cuius plerique poetae meminerunt, in qua maiorum eius expressa ostenderetur historia.

> His wife was Calpurnia, a holy and venerated woman from the family of the Caesonini, that is, the Pisones, whom our ancestors revered among the most holy of women, a priestess married only once. We still see her statue, golden with marble limbs, in the temple of Venus. She is said to have had

the pearls of Cleopatra, and a platter formed from a hundred pounds of silver, which many poets have recalled, on which the history of her ancestors was carved.

On the surface, Calpurnia typifies the traditional Roman aristocrat. She shares her name with the wife of Julius Caesar and evokes the republican aristocratic family of the Pisones. She is devoted to traditional Roman religion, and she is wealthy. Further evidence of her traditional *Romanitas* is provided by describing her as supplanting Cleopatra, the foreign temptress of Caesar, for her gilded statue is said to have been placed in the temple of Venus Genetrix where, in reality, Caesar had placed a statue of Cleopatra (Dio 51.22.2). She also is said, in a more direct link, to have possessed the pearls of Cleopatra. The impossibility of such possession would be clear to the learned reader, for Pliny tells us that Cleopatra possessed the two largest pearls ever seen, one of which she dissolved in vinegar and drank down to demonstrate her extravagance to Antony, and the second of which was made into earrings for the statue of Venus in the same temple in which her statue was mounted (*HN* 9.119–21). (The familiarity of the *HA*-author with this pearl story is revealed earlier, when Alexander Severus dedicates two large pearls to Venus [*Alex.* 51.3].)

Straub focused particularly on the description of Calpurnia as a "holy and venerated woman" ("sancta et venerabilis femina") and a "priestess married only once" ("univiriam sacerdotem").[75] The "once-married woman" is regularly praised in pagan and Jewish epitaphs, but the concept has a particular resonance for Christians, who forbade remarriage, and for Jerome in particular, who extravagantly praised his circle of widows who refused to remarry. The collocation "sancta et venerabilis" is appropriate to Vestal Virgins, as we see, for example, in Livy (1.20.3), although Vestals, who became priestesses as girls, could marry after their thirty-year term of service. The idea of a once-married priestess is reminiscent, then, not of a Vestal but of another female cult, the priestesses of Juno. Calpurnia, therefore, considered among the most holy of women, revered and honored, is described as a mixture of Vestal and priestess of Juno. These themes are highlighted in *Epistle* 49, to Pammachius.[76] In this letter, Jerome defends his views on celibacy against critics, arguing that they are mistaken in accusing him of thinking that celibacy was the only thing that mattered. On the contrary, he states, faith and works are essential, for "on such terms as these the virgins of Vesta or of Juno, who was constant to one husband (*univira*), might claim to be numbered among the saints." Thus the *HA*-author offers a counterexample to Jerome's assertion, for his Calpurnia is a devotee of Vesta and Juno who does indeed merit recognition as a saint. The allusion mocks Jerome's promotion of celibacy rather than celebrating the caricature of Roman virtue that the author has created.

Schwartz points to a linguistic parallel that further supports the use of *Epistle* 49 by the *HA*-author.[77] Jerome reports that Paul allowed men to pray if they had not had sex with their wives (49.15, "si non cum uxore cubuisset"). This same scruple was self-imposed upon Alexander Severus in the passage where he prepares to pray to his odd collection of gods, who included the deified emperors, Apollonius of Tyana, Abraham, Orpheus, and Christ himself, and is expressed with the same language: "si non cum uxore cubuisset" (*Alex.* 29.2).

One part of the description of Calpurnia remains insufficiently explained: the silver *lanx*, or platter, that presented the *historia maiorum*, literally "the history of ancestors," and "which many poets have recalled." Straub likens the platter to the Kaiseraugst plate that depicts scenes from the life of Achilles.[78] But we may see here another sly joke by the *HA*-author, alerting us to the satirical approach he is taking with Jerome's work. The grammarian Diomedes, who wrote in the late fourth century, offers a possible derivation of the word "satire" from the *lanx satura*, a dish filled with various foods and offered to the gods. The *Historia Augusta* is the history of the ancestral emperors but in a satirical form more appropriate to poets than real historians.

Chastagnol argues that the discussion in Jerome's *Epistle* 29.5.3 of the priestly vestments of Aaron (Ex. 28:4 and 39:1-2) is echoed by the *HA*-author in both the *Clodius Albinus* and the *Alexander Severus*.[79] Jerome notes that the garments of gold, purple, and scarlet were reserved for the chief priest alone, while the other priests wore the purest linen, which was entirely white. A letter in *Clodius Albinus* 2.5 combines the colors gold, purple, and scarlet with the idea that only the emperor could wear certain colors, while a passage in *Alexander* 40.6-11 again discusses the three colors. Alexander reserves the fancy dress for times when he is acting as consul or, more significantly, pontifex maximus, and he argues in favor of wearing at other times linen unadorned by purple, scarlet, or gold.

The curious discussion of Moses in the preface to the *Claudius* can also be interpreted as an intertextual engagement with the letters of Jerome. The author, apologizing for the shortness of the reign of the emperor, digresses somewhat awkwardly to address the question of the maximum lifespan of a human being (*Claud.* 2.4-5):

> Doctissimi mathematicorum centum viginti annos homini ad vivendum datos iudicant neque amplius cuiquam iactitant esse concessos, etiam illud addentes, Mosen solum, dei, ut Iudaeorum libri loquuntur, familiarem, centum viginti quinque annos vixisse; qui cum quereretur quod iuvenis interiret, responsum ei ab incerto ferunt numine neminem plus esse victurum. quare, etiamsi centum et viginti quinque annos Claudius vixisset,

ne necessariam quidem mortem eius exspectandam fuisse, ut Tullius de Scipione loquitur, stupenda et mirabilis docet vita.

The most learned astrologers agree that humans are granted one hundred and twenty years of life, and no one has been given more, even adding the fact that Moses alone, the friend of God according to the books of the Jews, lived to be one hundred and twenty-five; when he complained that he was dying young, they say that the response from the unknown god was that no one would live longer. But even if Claudius had lived one hundred and twenty-five years, his amazing and miraculous life, as Tully says of Scipio, shows us that we must not have expected him to die a natural death.

This preface provides evidence of the use of Jerome's *Epistle* 10, addressed to a centenarian named Paul.[80] Jerome speaks of "doctissimi quique Graecorum" and follows with a quotation from Cicero. Despite Paul's advanced age, his righteousness has preserved him as if he were an adolescent, in contrast to Moses's complaint that he is dying despite being a youth. Finally, Jerome's most learned Greeks are said to have been rewarded for praising their kings or emperors; the *HA*-author is engaged in this same task of panegyric, in this preface and throughout the *Claudius*.

The *HA*-author seems aware that the Bible claims that 120 years is the maximum age allotted to a human life (Gen. 6:3) and that Moses is said to have reached this age (Deut. 34:7), which he could have learned from *Epistle* 52.2. But then how to explain his claim that Moses was actually 125 when he died? The outward limit of human life was a source of debate in both pagan and Christian sources. For example, Pliny (*HN* 7.153–59) provides a list of men who attained exceptional ages, some as old as 800, and Censorinus (*DN* 17) reports that Epigenes thought the maximum age for a person was 112, Berosus 116, and others 120 or more. One hundred and twenty was a common answer to the question, perhaps, as Syme suggests, deriving from Varro; we find this number in various authors (Tac. *Dial.* 17.4; Manilius 3.560–80; Arnob. *Adversus Gentes* 2.71; Lactant. *Div. inst.* 2.13; Serv. on *Aen.* 4.653). Syme asks, "In the matter of Moses, why did he choose 125, not 120?" and answers, "This too may be play: he likes to create wilful variants, parading science or scholarly dubitation."[81] I would imagine the author not only paraded scholarly dubitation, but also invited it, by raising a contentious and interesting subject for debate and discussion. Perhaps a participant would be well versed in the works of Jerome and able to point to his early commentary *Hebrew Questions on Genesis*, where he is forced (at Gen. 6:3) to confront the contradiction between the claim that human life is limited to 120 years and the numerous biblical figures who are said to have lived well beyond that limit.

The passage from the letter of Hadrian, which I noted previously for its criticism of Egyptian Christians, Jews, and Samaritans, might actually represent an allusion in part to *Epistle* 107 of Jerome: "iam et Aegyptius Serapis factus est Christianus, Marnas Gazae luget inclusus et eversionem templi iugiter pertimescit." ("Now Egyptian Serapis has become Christian, now at Gaza Marnas, imprisoned, mourns, and fears the overturning of his temple," 107.2.3). Not only does this passage show a devotee of Serapis worshiping Christ but it also mentions Marnas, in whom the *HA*-author showed interest earlier. Several other obsessions of the *HA*-author appear early in the letter: the name Toxotius (107.1.2, cf. *Maximin.* 27.6) and the alleged Gracchan ancestry of the family (107.2.2, cf. *Gord.* 2.2).[82] And the letter itself offers some ethnographic detail that could have stimulated the *HA*-author; just as Christians, pagans, Jews, and Samaritans act similarly, so, too, in dietary matters, do the Jews, Brahman Indians, and Gymnosophists in Egypt (*Ep.* 107.8).

Equally Hieronymian in origin may be the metaphorical use in the *Historia Augusta* of the term *quadrigae*, properly a four-horse chariot, to describe the four usurpers Firmus, Saturninus, Bonosus, and Proculus. The word appears often in Jerome.[83] The *HA*-author concludes the *Probus* thus (24.6–8):

> Haec sunt quae de Probi vita cognovimus, vel quae digna memoratu aestimavimus. nunc in alio libro, et quidem brevi, de Firmo et Saturnino et Bonoso et Proculo dicemus. non enim dignum fuit ut *quadrigae tyrannorum* bono principi miscerentur. post deinde si vita suppetet, Carum incipiemus propagare cum liberis.

> These are things we have learned about the life of Probus, or rather the things we have judged worthy to commemorate. Now in another book, indeed a short one, we will speak about Firmus, Saturninus, Bonosus, and Proculus. For it was not appropriate to mix a *four-horse chariot* of usurpers with a good emperor. Afterward, if our life is long enough, we will begin to pass on the story of Carus and his children.

The use of *quadriga* is common in Jerome, especially in the biblical commentaries, and three examples are representative. In *Epistle* 52.13.3, the four virtues—prudence, justice, temperance, fortitude—are called a *quadriga*; in *Epistle* 53.9.2, the four evangelists are called *quadriga domini*; and in *Epistle* 66.2.2 he refers to his disciples Paula, Paulina, and Eustochium, along with their companion Pammachius, as a *quadriga* of holiness. Thus the *HA*-author takes an unusual term used repeatedly for praise by Jerome and attaches it to his group of depraved usurpers, whose lives will be constructed in part from the travesty of Jerome.

Commentaries

Jerome was best known to later ages as a biblical exegete, having composed commentaries on about two dozen books of the Bible. Patristic exegesis shares much in common with the secular scholarship of the age, which often also takes the form of lemmata from the source text—Vergil or some other classical writer—followed by grammatical, historical, and allegorical information and interpretation. Schlumberger was the first to show that the exegetical works of Jerome were also used by the *Historia Augusta*, which alludes to the prologues of two of Jerome's biblical commentaries, those on Isaiah and Matthew.[84] The *Thirty Tyrants* concludes as follows (*Tyr. Trig.* 33.7–8):

> Habes integrum triginta numerum tyrannorum, qui cum malevolis quidem sed bono animo causabaris. Da nunc cuivis libellum non tam diserte quam fideliter scriptum. Neque ego eloquentiam mihi videor pollicitus esse, sed rem, qui hos libellos quod de vita principum edidi non scribo sed dicto, et dicto cum ea festinatione quam, si quid vel ipse promisero vel tu petieris, sic perurges ut respirandi non habeam facultatem.

> You have the complete number of the thirty usurpers, you who used to argue with spiteful men although your intentions remained good. Now give this book, written not elegantly but truthfully, to whomever you want. It seems to me that I have not promised elegance, but only the facts. I do not write, but dictate, those books which I have published about the lives of the emperors, and I dictate with such speed, that whether it is something I promise or you demand, you urge me on so much that I do not have a chance to breathe.

This passage is a second-person apologetic address to a recipient who had demanded that the book be written with haste. It contrasts oddly with the introduction, in which the *HA*-author addresses a general readership and simply explains that he has collected, with difficulty, what information he could about these obscure figures. This should encourage us to look beyond the text to understand what the *HA*-author is doing here.

This passage follows the two final lives of the *Thirty Tyrants*, both of which had drawn heavily upon Jerome's *Epistle* 49. This primes the reader to search for further Hieronymian influence. Schlumberger points to phrases in the prologue to the commentary on Isaiah, particularly Jerome's claim to be dictating ("dictamus haec, non scribimus": compare "non scribo sed dicto" in the *Historia Augusta*) and his claim to be seeking "not eloquence, but knowledge of the scriptures" ("nec iactamus eloquentiam, sed scientiam quaerimus Scripturarum"; the *HA*-author has also refused to promise *eloquentiam*). These are commonplaces, to be sure, but the coincidence of commonplaces is multiplied when Schlumberger introduces the preface to another of Jerome's prologues, from the commentary on Matthew. This passage contains numerous points of contact with the *Historia Augusta*; it is also a second-person address that emphasizes the speedy dictation of the work as an excuse for a lack of eloquence.

These two minor allusions could be dismissed as simply a curiosity were it not for more connections between the *Historia Augusta* and precisely these two books of the Bible, Isaiah and Matthew. Previous scholars have noted the biblical allusions and sometimes even suggested that the *HA*-author was familiar with both the biblical texts and the tradition of commentary on them. But I would argue that we can explain all of the connections that scholars have offered between the Bible and the *Historia Augusta* by understanding the source text in each case to be Jerome's commentary on either Isaiah or Matthew.

Jerome's commentary on Matthew was published in 398. The commentary on Isaiah has a more complicated publishing history. In *Epistle* 71.7, Jerome states that he has recently published a commentary on the dream vision of Isaiah, books 13–23. This independent work does not survive, as it was incorporated into the full commentary on the whole book of Isaiah that Jerome published in 409. The prologue to the shorter and earlier work is preserved as the prologue to the fifth book of the full commentary. Schlumberger, who accepts the traditional earlier dating of around 400, seems to have thought that the *HA*-author had read only the shorter work, but if we accept a later date for the *Historia Augusta*, the author could have had access to the whole of the commentary.

Medieval manuscripts of patristic commentaries differ in the amount of the original biblical text that is reproduced. It appears that for his commentary on Matthew, at least, Jerome originally wrote out only the parts of the gospel upon which he wanted to comment.[85] Eighth-and ninth-century copies of the commentary, however, derive from a common source of indeterminate age that has added additional pieces of the gospel beyond Jerome's own lemmata, and in general we might expect the commentary either to be supplemented with the biblical text or to accompany it. The commentaries on the books of the Hebrew Bible, by contrast, seem originally to have included most or all of the text under consideration, since Jerome needed to demonstrate the differences between his Hebrew translations and the translations of the Septuagint, so a reader of the commentary on Isaiah would also be a reader of Isaiah itself.[86]

The *Probus* contains a particularly striking passage that may engage with the commentary on Isaiah (*Prob.* 20.1–6):

> Quibus peractis, bellum Persicum parans, cum per Illyricum iter faceret, a militibus suis per insidias interemptus est. causae occidendi eius haec fuerunt: primum quod numquam militem otiosum esse perpessus est, si quidem multa opera militari manu perfecit, dicens annonam gratuitam militem comedere non debere. his addidit dictum eis grave, si umquam eveniat, salutare rei publicae, brevi milites necessarios non futuros. quid ille conceperat animo qui hoc dicebat? nonne omnes barbaras gentes subiecerat penitusque totumque mundum fecerat iam Romanum? 'Brevi,' inquit, 'milites necessarios non habebimus.' quid est aliud dicere: Romanus iam miles erit nullus? ubique regnabit, omnia possidebit mox secura res publica. orbis terrarum non arma fabricabitur, non annonam praebebit, boves habebuntur aratro, equus nascetur ad pacem, nulla erunt bella, nulla captivitas, ubique pax, ubique Romanae leges, ubique iudices nostri.

After these things were completed, Probus, preparing for war with Persia, was traveling through Illyricum and was killed in an ambush by his own soldiers. These were the reasons given for his assassination: first, because he never allowed a soldier to be idle, and indeed built many things with military manpower, saying that a soldier ought not eat free rations. He added a claim that would be serious for the soldiers if it ever came to pass, although beneficial to the state, that soon soldiers would not be needed. What was he thinking when he used to say this? Had he not subjected all the barbarian nations, and made the world entirely and fully Roman? "In a short time," he said, "we will not need soldiers." This is another way of saying, "There will no longer be Roman soldiers. Unthreatened Rome will rule everywhere, and possess all things. The world will not build arms, nor will it furnish rations, oxen will be kept for the plow and horses bred for peace, there will be no wars, no captivity, peace everywhere, Roman laws everywhere, our judges everywhere."

The question-and-response style, foreign to classical biography, is standard in the commentary tradition. The utopian vision is reminiscent of Isaiah. In particular "orbis terrarum non arma fabricabitur ... boves habebuntur aratro, equus nascetur ad pacem" evokes Isaiah 2.4: "et conflabunt gladios suos in vomeres, et lanceas suas in falces." The utopias of the *Historia Augusta* and of Isaiah differ, for the peace of Probus is not the Christian ideal of nonviolent unity but is imposed by force.[87] In his *Commentary* on Isaiah 2.4, Jerome connects both sorts of utopias by claiming that the conquest of the Mediterranean by Augustus prepared the world for the more significant peace of Christ. The *Probus* combines in this passage both

Augustus and Christ, the military conquest followed by the transformation of weapons into farm implements. The reader is invited to compare and contrast these Christian and imperial versions of utopia.

The *Tacitus* raises the theme of "boy emperors," which may also derive from the book of Isaiah (*Tac.* 6.5):

> dii avertant principes pueros, et patres patriae dici impuberes, et quibus ad subscribendum magistri litterarii manus teneant, quos ad consulatus dandos dulcia et circuli et quaecumque voluptas puerilis invitet.

> May the gods protect us from boys being named emperor, and from immature children being called Father of the Country—boys whose hands are guided by a schoolteacher to affix names to an official document, who grant consulships in return for candy and cakes and whatever their childish pleasure demands.

The phrase *pueri principes* is biblical, the words of the Lord who will destroy Jerusalem (Isa. 3:4): "et dabo pueros principes eorum, et effeminati dominabuntur eis" ("I will give children to be their rulers; the effeminate will rule over them"). The august Roman figure of Nicomachus, in a speech in the senate addressed to the emperor, borrows some language, comically, from the Bible.[88]

Schlumberger considers the prologue to the commentary on Matthew an even more important source for the passage in the epilogue to the *Thirty Tyrants* than the commentary on Isaiah. We find suggestive support for the use of the commentary on Matthew in several allusions that Straub had attributed to the direct use of the gospel of Matthew. The most complicated involves the adoption and promulgation by Alexander Severus of the Golden Rule (*Alex.* 51.6-8):[89]

> Si quis de via in alicuius possessionem deflexisset, pro qualitate loci aut fustibus subiciebatur in conspectu eius aut virgis aut condemnationi aut, si haec omnia transiret dignitas hominis, gravissimis contumeliis, cum diceret: 'visne hoc in agro tuo fieri quod alteri facis?' clamabatque saepius, quod a quibusdam sive Iudaeis sive Christianis audierat et tenebat, idque per praeconem, cum aliquem emendaret, dici iubebat: 'Quod tibi fieri non vis, alteri ne feceris.' quam sententiam usque adeo dilexit ut et in Palatio et in publicis operibus praescribi iuberet.

> If anyone left the road and trespassed on the property of another, he was punished before the emperor in accordance with his rank, either with clubs or rods or death, or, if his rank put him above all these, by the

harshest condemnations, saying, "Do you want this to be done by another in your field?" He was quite often exclaiming a thing that he had heard from some Jews or Christians, and he was remembering it, and ordering that it be spoken by a herald when he was correcting someone: "What you do not wish to be done to you, do not do to another." He esteemed this maxim so much that he ordered it to be inscribed in the palace and on public buildings.

Straub's analysis of this passage leads to a difficult and ultimately unlikely result. He notes that versions of the "Golden Rule" can be found not only in Christian scriptures but in pagan and Jewish texts as well. The *HA*-author has chosen to highlight its Christian origin, Straub points out, despite the fact that even Christians tend to recognize it as an element of the natural law shared by pagans and Christians alike (for example, Augustine describes it as a "common saying," *vulgare proverbium*). Straub argues that the *HA*-author, by presenting a good pagan emperor taking an idea that could rightfully be considered pagan but respectfully embracing it as Christian, means to suggest that contemporary Christian emperors ought also to be tolerant and to embrace non-Christian ideas, while recognizing the pagan ideas at the heart of many Christian ones. This approach takes the *HA*-author too seriously. We should understand this passage instead as a complex allusion to a Christian text that is anachronistically placed in the life of a non-Christian emperor. No message, pro-or anti-Christian, need be implied.

The claim that Alexander heard the Golden Rule, an idea that can indeed be pagan, from "some Christian or Jew" focuses our attention specifically on Jerome, the Christian who is the source for most of the Christian material in the *Historia Augusta*. The uncertainty over whether Jerome is Christian or Jewish is perhaps a joke implying criticism of his close association with Jews and with the Hebrew language. The Golden Rule appears in three places in the gospels, in the following forms: Luke 6:31, "prout vultis ut faciant vobis homines et vos facite illis similiter" ("Do to others as you would have them do to you"); Luke 10:27, "ille respondens dixit diliges Dominum Deum tuum ex toto corde tuo et ex tota anima tua et ex omnibus viribus tuis et ex omni mente tua et proximum tuum sicut te ipsum" ("He answered, 'You shall love the Lord your God with all your heart, and with all your soul, and with all your strength, and with all your mind; and your neighbor as yourself'"); and Matthew 7:12: "omnia ergo quaecumque vultis ut faciant vobis homines, et vos facite illis. haec est enim lex et prophetae" ("In everything do to others as you would have them do to you; for this is the law and the prophets"). While on first glance there is no particular reason to prefer one over the other as the source of the *Historia Augusta* text, the broader context of the *Historia Augusta* passage argues for Matthew as the source.

In Matthew, the most Jewish of the gospels, Jesus explains that the Golden Rule sums up the most significant of the Hebrew scriptures, the Law (*lex*), or five books of Moses, and the Prophets (*prophetae*). Jesus may be alluding to a teaching of the Rabbi Hillel, "What is hateful to you, do not to your neighbor: this is the whole Law; the rest is mere commentary" (Babylonian Talmud, Tractate Shabbat 31a).[90] The Alexander Severus of the *Historia Augusta* is portrayed as unfamiliar with the religious texts to which the terms "Law" and "Prophets" refer. The first context in which the Golden Rule arises is a legal one concerning the question of trespass by soldiers: "Si quis de via in alicuius possessionem deflexisset." The general sense of this legal question can be found at *Codex Theodosianus* 7.1.12 (384): "tribuni vel milites nullam evagandi per possessiones habeant facultatem."[91] Alexander's remedy for those who violate the law of trespass is to quote the Golden Rule at them—his understanding of Jesus's claim that the Golden Rule is the "Law." In addition, Alexander had the Golden Rule proclaimed regularly by his *praeco*, or herald, *praeco* being the classical or secular Latin word for *propheta*, "one who speaks forth."[92] Alexander understands *Prophetae* not as a nominative plural but as a genitive or dative singular, "this is a task for the herald." Such, then, is Alexander's faulty understanding of Jesus's reference to the "Prophets." The readers of the *Historia Augusta*, living in a Christian milieu, would presumably understand what the Law and the Prophets refer to, but they are able to appreciate the humor in a third-century emperor's attempt at an interpretation.

An unusual passage in the *Alexander Severus* may derive from the gospel of Matthew (14.3–4):[93]

> Ipse cum vatem consuleret de futuris, hos accepisse dicitur versus adhuc parvulus et primum quidem sortibus: 'te manet imperium caeli terraeque' intellectum est, quod inter divos etiam referetur.
>
> And when Alexander himself consulted a prophet about the future, being still a small boy, it is said that he received the following verses from the lots: "Empire awaits you on earth and in heaven." It was understood that he would be included even among the gods.

The phrase "imperium caeli terraeque" occurs nowhere else in extant Latin literature, so it seems not unreasonable to compare it with Matthew 28:18: "data mihi est omnis potestas in caelo et in terra."[94] The words are spoken by Christ after the resurrection, as Alexander is predicted to enjoy *imperium caeli* after his own death.

There are two other possible references to the book of Matthew that again may be attributed to Jerome's commentary rather than directly to the Bible. Among the omens announcing the birth of Alexander Severus was the appearance of a bright star in the east above his birthplace: "It is said that on the day after his birth a star of the first magnitude was seen for the whole day at Arca Caesarea, and also that near the house of his father, the sun was encircled with a gleaming ring" ("fertur die prima natalis toto die apud Arcam Caesaream stella primae magnitudinis visa et sol circa domum patris eius fulgido ambitu coronatus," *Alex.* 13.5). Star omens of this sort are not uncommon in classical literature, but it is not impossible that the *HA*-author, in a life that is particularly influenced by Christian themes, and in an effort to make Alexander seem particularly saintly, has borrowed the omen from Matthew 2 (the only gospel to report it).[95] Paschoud has suggested that *Alexander Severus* 36.2 is also meant to evoke the Bible.[96] "Selling smoke" is a standard late antique term for offering bribes, and the upright nature of the emperor Alexander is demonstrated when he has the villainous Verconius Turninus suffocated by a fire of wet logs, with a herald pronouncing the quip: "He is punished by smoke, who sold smoke" ("fumo punitur, qui vendidit fumum," 36.2). This may be a reference to the words of Jesus: "All who draw the sword will die by the sword" ("omnes enim, qui acceperint gladium, gladio peribunt," Matt. 26:52). The (invented) name Turninus evokes incense, so it is appropriate that he die by smoking. It might be thought humorous that a character with a particularly pagan name dies hearing words that are associated with Christ.

The *HA*-author most likely engages with the Bible through the commentaries of Jerome. We might at first be surprised to find that a secular work would engage with biblical commentaries. But our author, having read the biographical *Life of Hilarion* by Jerome, might easily move on to a commentary by Jerome on another biographical work, the gospel of Matthew. More generally, we have situated the *HA*-author and his audience within a scholarly milieu, and the prologues to Matthew and Isaiah include many sentiments common to all forms of ancient scholarship: references to the effort involved in composition, the numerous sources consulted, and the pressures of time. We should not be surprised to see the *HA*-author mockingly appropriate these sincerely meant commonplaces from Jerome for his own comic inventions in the *Thirty Tyrants*. The allusive engagements of the *HA*-author with utopianism in Isaiah and the Golden Rule in Matthew cannot be seen as particularly critical of Christian doctrine, or even of Jerome. The author has served up for his audience the complex and challenging task of unraveling allusions to unexpected texts.

Ambrose

Paschoud argues for the *HA*-author's knowledge of Ambrose's *Epistle* 18, urging the removal of the Altar of Victory from the senate house in 383, along with Symmachus's speech (*Relat.* 3) to which Ambrose was responding.[97]

The removal of the altar by Gratian was indeed a pivotal moment in the history of traditional Roman religion, and the paired arguments quickly passed into legend and literature, as evidenced, for example, by Prudentius's versifying of the conflict in his *Contra Symmachum* of around 402.[98] The use of Ambrose by the *Historia Augusta* should not be seen as evidence of deep devotion to ancient cult and of longing for the restoration of the Altar, however. Instead, the allusions represent the conflict over the Altar as another quaint and vaguely absurd episode in the religion of the past. This controversy is no longer a live one for the audience.

In a passage based on pure fantasy (*Aur.* 18.4–20.8), we are told that a *senatus consultum* or decree of the senate was passed to urge the consultation of the Sibylline Books in response to military danger.[99] The Sibylline Books were in reality consulted only in response to prodigies, not military threats. The concern over a military threat would be more appropriate to the struggle over the Altar of Victory and its role in protecting the state. The senator "Ulpius Silanus" is the first to speak. He claims that he has always favored requesting the help of the gods but that others had sought to curry favor with Aurelian by claiming that he was so great that he did not need divine help. This perhaps mirrors and rejects the Christian arguments in favor of removing the Altar (Ambr. *Ep.* 18.7; Symm. *Relat.* 3.3 and 3.9). Silanus then calls upon the *pontifices* to ascend to the temple of Apollo on steps wreathed in laurel and to read the Sibylline Books with veiled hands, to the accompaniment of a chorus of orphaned (and therefore religiously appropriate) boys. In reality the pontifices never had a role in the consultation of the Sibylline Books, and Paschoud suggests that their involvement here makes the conflict more clearly mirror the one over the Altar of Victory and the disestablishment of traditional priesthoods. The senate favors this decree by a jumble of methods, voting with hands, feet, and voice. There follows the consultation, the purification of the city, the chanting of hymns, and the celebration of the ancient rites of the Amburbium and Ambervalia.

In the letter of Aurelian that follows, the emperor proclaims his support for the consultation and for the performance of rites that have supported the Roman state since its earliest days. He expresses surprise that the senate was so hesitant to approve, "just as though you were consulting in a gathering of Christians and not in the temple of all the gods" ("quasi in Christianorum ecclesia, non in templo deorum omnium tractaretis," *Aur.* 20.5). Both the speech of Silanus and Aurelian's words imply an atmosphere where pagans are a hesitant minority rather than the obvious majority they would have been in the time of Aurelian. The reference to the senate house as a temple is perhaps an ironic reference to Ambrose's complaint that the presence of the Altar had turned the senate house into a temple (*Ep.* 18.10).

The involvement of the senate and the pontifices, the issue of military victory, the repeated mention of the ready availability of funds for sacrifice, and the suggestion of paganism under siege all reflect aspects of the debate over the Altar of Victory. The question of the Altar is considered here, however, as just another quaint religious relic of "the old days," embedded as it is amid the purifications, veilings, and sacrificial rituals that, as Paschoud admits, were "purement livresque, accumulant par association d'idées des cérémonies qui s'excluent, et qu'on ne peut célébrer n'importe quand durant l'année." Such a garbled mess could not be meant to convey devotion to pagan ritual. Instead, the Altar is subsumed in a parody of the kind of learned antiquarianism that focused on the religious activities of decades past.

The mishmash of three different kinds of voting in *Aurelian* 20.2 represents a parody of political antiquarianism that parallels the religious examples. In the dialogue that opens the *Aurelian*, our author tells his interlocutor Junius Tiberianus that all the historians were guilty of falsehood, and points out lies that he had uncovered in Sallust, Tacitus, Livy, and Trogus. Tiberianus responds (2.1-2): "pedibus in sententiam transitum faciens ac manum porrigens iocando praeterea: 'Scribe,' inquit, 'ut libet; secures, quod velis, dices, habiturus mendaciorum comites quos historicae eloquentiae miramur auctores'" ("He came over to my opinion, and, stretching out his hand, he jokingly added: 'Write as you please. You will be safe in saying whatever you want, having as fellow liars those authors whom we admire for their historical style'"). The first phrase in the passage, "pedibus in sententiam transitum faciens," corresponds to *Aurelian* 20.2: "pedibus in sententias euntibus," a method of voting by moving to a particular part of the senate.[100] The second phrase, "manum porrigens," corresponding to "manus porrigentibus" (20.2), rarely refers to voting, but two passages in which it does, Cicero's *Pro Flacco* 15 and 17, are striking. In them, Cicero decries the moblike behavior of the ignorant Greeks who vote with outstretched arms. The final method of voting in *Aurelian* 20.2 is "plerisque verbo consentientibus" ("with very many expressing their consent in words"). In the context of *Aurelian* 2.1, the consensus reached was that all historians are liars. Thus the *HA*-author provides us with three methods of voting: one a traditional Roman method, one associated with demagogic Greeks, and a third associated intratextually with deceit. A decision to resort to traditional cult practices that has been achieved by such dubious methods can hardly be seen as a celebration of paganism in the face of Christianity. Instead we have a challenge for an audience prepared to discuss and debate ancient sources on republican political procedures.

In an excessively laudatory celebration of the new emperor Probus, a member of the senate is portrayed as praying first to the Capitoline trio of Jupiter, Juno, and Minerva, then to the goddess Concordia, and finally to Romana Victoria, the very Victory whose Altar was removed under Gratian (*Prob.* 12.7). Paschoud writes that "ce passage est évidemment l'un de ceux où la dévotion païenne de l'auteur de l'HA se manifeste d'une manière très frappante."[101] It is striking in how not-striking it is. A conventional detail in a sea of conventional details, the passage demonstrates that the *HA*-author seeks to convey no particular feelings in any direction toward the Altar and the goddess of Victory.

In addition to Jerome and Ambrose, it has been argued that the *HA*-author was familiar with other Christian writers, including Lactantius, Tertullian, and Arnobius of Sicca, but the arguments are generally too generic to be convincing.[102] Paschoud suggests two more potential biblical allusions that again seem too tenuous to accept.[103] The *HA*-author does not have a particularly broad or deep knowledge of Christianity and Christian literature; rather, he has specific knowledge of a few texts by Jerome and Ambrose. Although he is unsympathetic toward the style of Christianity championed by Jerome, his allusions encourage mockery rather than anger or fear. He is consumed neither by Christianity nor by traditional cult but by the use of intertexts that themselves sometimes engage with religion.

Conclusion

The *Historia Augusta* does not shy away from discussion of pagan cult or Christian religion, both openly and in allusions, although it refers to them infrequently enough that it is impossible to see religion as a central focus. The *HA*-author has little to say about Christianity or paganism themselves, but he does make use of the Christian authors Jerome and Ambrose. It is easy to say that the author disapproved of Jerome, since just about every contemporary of the bishop did, but this disapproval says little about the author's religious feelings. He could even have been a Christian, or certainly his audience could include Christians. As we would expect from someone writing long after the heyday of Roman paganism, he knows little about pagan religious practice, which he treats in an antiquarian manner. Cameron's revisionist portrait of Christianity and paganism at the turn of the fourth century is wholly congruent with the evidence of the *Historia Augusta*.

The *HA*-author's engagement with Christian authors is limited. Given the biographical focus of his circle, it seems reasonable to assume that he came to be interested in Jerome through his pioneering hagiographic biographies. Having discovered that a charlatan and radical was inventing fake biographies, why not adorn his own fake biographies with the raw material of the charlatan and radical? Jerome's apologetic and defensive prologue to the *Life of Hilarion*, itself parodied by the *HA*-author, suggests that not only pagans but also ordinary Christians rejected Jerome's fantastical *Life of Paul*. The letters and commentaries of Jerome that were known and exploited by the author and his audience are themselves often biographical, historical, or scholarly in form. The only other Christian author he read, Ambrose, had been engaged in a high-profile debate about state policy, and there is no good evidence for his knowledge of Ambrose outside of his contribution to that debate. Allusions to Jerome are like allusions to Cicero—opportunities for the author to cleverly engage a source text in the guise of providing biographical information.

The *HA*-author primarily engages with specific aspects of Christianity: the ascetic renunciation of food and sex and the proper behavior of women. Food, sex, and women are standard elements of the biographical genre and of satirical material more generally. Jerome and radical Christianity serve as objects of fun because of their perceived obsession with these vulgar topics. The idea that the *HA*-author is anti-Christian because of such mockery substitutes the values of the early middle ages for the values of the late Roman period.

 4   Imperial History Reimagined

Scholars writing about imperial historians and biographers have frequently explored their authors' views on the traditional subjects of politics, administration, and society. The pages of the *Historia Augusta Colloquium* are filled with inquiries of these sorts, often quite skillfully done; for example, we find careful studies of the portrayal in the *Historia Augusta* of the consulship, of the Roman people, of the Arabs, and of imperial ideology.[1] These studies have been pursued with particular diligence for the *Historia Augusta*, since the author's views on these subjects, it was hoped, might provide evidence for dating the work more precisely, and might also offer some insight into the nature and purpose of his deceptions. The cumulative result of a century of studies of this kind, however, has proved far less useful than one would have hoped. The opinions of the *HA*-author are boringly conventional. We learn, for example, that the author supports the senate, condemns emperors who kill senators, worries over the problem of the imperial succession, supports traditional culture and military conquest, and disdains foreigners, soldiers, and provincials.[2] The *Historia Augusta* has many eccentricities, yet its views are surprisingly commonplace.

The opinions expressed in the *Historia Augusta* are bland because the work is fundamentally concerned with literature, not life. Although scholars have often sought to understand the author's views on events of his own day through his portrayal of the second and third centuries, these attempts have been less than successful because when the author is freely inventing, his attention most often turns to other texts, not to contemporary events. A particularly important source for the author was the *Res Gestae* of Ammianus Marcellinus. What some have considered the views of the *Historia Augusta* are often, upon further examination, reflections and manipulations of the work of Ammianus. The author's use of Ammianus is consistent with his use of other literary texts. He does not deeply engage with the historian but challenges his reader to recognize specific passages and general themes as part of his playful game.

Ammianus as a Source for the *Historia Augusta*

Ammianus Marcellinus was the author of a history in the moralizing and classicizing style covering events from the accession of Nerva in 96 to the death of Valens at Adrianople in 378. Evidence from within the work makes it clear that it was published in the last decade of the fourth century.[3] The *HA*-author could not, of course, keep up the pretense of Constantinian-era authorship and openly allude to Ammianus, but his use of the historian is frequent and often complex.

The *HA*-author specializes in allusions that test the reader's ability to recognize complex connections in the absence of context. A good example of this method can be found in a long passage from the *Aurelian*, where an apparently meaningless section of a fictitious letter turns out to be constructed from a number of names and details found in sections 31.7 and 31.11 of Ammianus (*Aur.* 10.3–11.6):[4]

> tunc cum Ulpius Crinitus publice apud Byzantium sedenti Valeriano in thermis egit gratias, dicens magnum de se iudicium habitum quod eidem vicarium Aurelianum dedisset; quare eum statuit adrogare. Interest epistulas nosse de Aureliano scriptas et ipsam adrogationem. epistula Valeriani ad Aurelianum: 'Si esset alius, Aureliane iucundissime, qui Ulpii Criniti vicem posset implere, tecum de eius virtute ac sedulitate conferrem; nunc te cum requirere potuissem, suscipe bellum a parte Nicopolis, ne nobis aegritudo Criniti obsit. fac quicquid potes; multa non dico: in tua erit potestate militiae magisterium. habes sagittarios Ityraeos trecentos, Armenios sescentos, Arabas centum quinquaginta, Saracenos ducentos, Mesopotamenos auxiliares quadringentos. habes legionem tertiam Felicem et equites catafractarios octingentos; tecum erit Hariomundus, Haldagates, Hildomundus, Carioviscus. commeatus a praefectis necessarius in omnibus castris est constitutus. tuum est pro virtutibus tuis atque sollertia illic hiemalia et aestiva disponere ubi tibi nihil deerit, quaerere praeterea ubi carrago sit hostium, et vere scire, quanti qualesque sint, ut non in vanum aut annona consumatur aut tela iaciantur, in quibus res bellica constituta est.'

When Ulpius Crinitus publicly thanked Valerian as he sat in the baths at Byzantium, he said that the emperor's appointment of Aurelian to be his vicar was evidence of the emperor's high opinion of him. Therefore, the emperor decided to adopt him. It is of interest to know about the letters written about Aurelian, and the adoption itself. The letter of Valerian to Aurelian: "If there were another man, dearest Aurelian, who was able to fill in for Ulpius Crinitus, I would confer with you about his virtues and diligence, but now I should wish to ask you to undertake combat operations around Nicopolis, so that Crinitus's illness will not harm our campaign. Do whatever you can! In short: the control of the soldiers will be in your power. You will have three hundred Ituraean archers, six hundred Armenians, one hundred and fifty Arabs, two hundred Saracens, and four hundred auxiliary troops from Mesopotamia. You will have the Third Legion, known as "Lucky," and eight hundred armored cavalrymen. You will also have with you Hariomundus, Haldagates, Hildomundus, and Carioviscus. Necessary supplies have been stored in all the camps by the prefects. Your job will be, using your virtue and wisdom, to establish winter and summer camps in places where no supplies will be lacking, and in addition to find where the baggage train of the enemy is, and to know with certainty how many and what sort of troops there are, so that supplies are not consumed, nor weapons wasted, in vain—principles on which military science has been established."

The following passages from Ammianus's final book concern events leading up to the disastrous battle at Adrianople:

> Haec ex Thraciis magno maerore accepta Valentem principem in sollicitudines varias distraxerunt. et confestim Victore magistro equitum misso ad Persas, ut super Armeniae statu pro captu rerum componeret inpendentium, ipse Antiochia protinus egressurus, ut Constantinopolim interim peteret, Profuturum praemisit et Traianum, ambo rectores, anhelantes quidem altius, sed inbelles. qui cum ad loca venissent, ubi particulatim perque furta magis et latrocinia multitudo minui deberet hostilis, ad id, quod erat perniciosum, intempestive conversi legiones ab Armenia ductas opposuere vesanum adhuc spirantibus barbaris opere quidem Martio saepe recte conpertas, sed inpares plebi immensae, quae celsorum iuga montium occuparat et campos. (31.7.1–2) . . . verum articulorum dolore Frigerido praepedito vel certe, ut obtrectatores finxere malivoli, morbum causante, ne ferventibus proeliis interesset, universos regens ex communi sententia Richomeres Profuturo sociatur et Traiano tendentibus prope oppidum Salices; unde haud longo spatio separatum vulgus inaestimabile barbarorum ad orbis rotundi figuram multitudine digesta plaustrorum tamquam intramuranis cohibitum spatiis otio fruebatur et ubertate praedarum. Praevia igitur spe meliorum Romani duces, si fors copiam attulisset, ausuri aliquid gloriosum Gothos, quidquid molirentur, sagaciter observabant id scilicet praestruentes, ut, si aliorsum castra movissent, quod fecere creberrime, terga ultimorum adorti plures perfoderent contis magnamque spoliorum averterent partem. hoc intellecto

hostes vel transfugarum indiciis docti, per quos nihil latebat incognitum, in eodem loco diu manserunt; sed oppositi exercitus metu praestricti aliorumque militum, quos affluere iam sperabant, tessera data gentili per diversa prope diffusas accivere vastatorias manus, quae optimatum acceptis . . . statimque incensi malleoli, ad carraginem, quam ita ipsi appellant, aliti velocitate regressae incentivum audendi maiora popularibus addiderunt. (31.7.5–7) . . . His forte diebus Valens tandem excitus Antiochia, longitudine viarum emensa venit Constantinopolim, ubi moratus paucissimos dies seditioneque popularium levi pulsatus, Sebastiano paulo ante ab Italia, ut petierat, misso, vigilantiae notae ductori pedestris exercitus cura commissa, quem regebat antea Traianus: ipse ad Melanthiada villam Caesarianam profectus, militem stipendio fovebat et alimentis et blanda crebritate sermonum. Unde cum itinere edicto per tesseram Nicen venisset, quae statio ita cognominatur: relatione speculatorum didicit refertos opima barbaros praeda a Rhodopeis tractibus prope Hadrianopolim revertisse: qui motu imperatoris cum abundanti milite cognito, popularibus iungere festinant, circa Beroeam et Nicopolim agentibus praesidiis fixis: atque ilico ut oblatae occasionis maturitas postulabat, cum trecentenis militibus per singulos numeros lectis Sebastianus properare dispositus est, conducens rebus publicis aliquid, ut promittebat, acturus. (31.11.1–2)

When this information was received from Thrace with great sorrow, the emperor Valens was distracted by many concerns. And at once he sent Victor, commander of the cavalry, to Persia, to set in order the situation in Armenia in the face of the looming threats. He himself, intending to leave Antioch at once, and set out for Constantinople, sent ahead Profuturus and Trajanus, both commanders who were eager to advance but were unskilled in war. When they had arrived in places where it was necessary to harass the enemy piecemeal and sneakily, as if leading a gang of bandits, in a most dangerous and inappropriate fashion they sent the legions brought from Armenia against the barbarians, who were still breathing madness. While the Armenian troops were indeed experienced in the work of Mars, they were no match for the immense mob that had occupied the tops of tall mountains as well as the plains. . . . But when Frigeridus was hindered by joint pain, or, as his slanderous enemies claimed, was pretending to be sick to avoid the heated battles, Richomeres became top commander by common consent, and joined with Profuturus and Trajanus, who were headed for a place near the town of Salices. Not far from there, a huge mob of barbarians had arranged their many wagons in a circle, and enjoyed their peace and the richness of their booty as if surrounded by city walls. Therefore the Roman generals, led by hope of better things, intending to dare something glorious against the Goths if chance offered the opportunity, were watching whatever they did carefully. They were of course preparing for this—if they should move their camp elsewhere, which they did very frequently, by launching an attack in the rear they could kill many with spears and recapture a great part of their spoils. When the enemy recognized this, or learned it from the evidence of deserters through whom nothing was left unknown, they remained in the same place for a long time. But gripped by fear of the opposing army, and of the other soldiers whom they were expecting soon to increase it, they sent a message in the manner that Goths do to summon predatory bands from all over, who at once, like fire darts, returned to their wagon-train, as they themselves call it, and with winged speed they encouraged their compatriots to greater acts of daring. . . . In those days Valens, having finally left Antioch, came by a long journey to Constantinople, where he delayed for only a few days, and was shaken by a mild revolt of the people. To Sebastian, a leader of well-known vigilance, he entrusted the leadership of the infantry, the position that Trajanus had held before. Sebastian had recently been sent from Italy as he requested. He went himself to the imperial villa near Melanthias and tried to win over the soldiers with money, rations, and frequent supplicating speeches. Having received orders for a journey, he arrived at Nice, as the military post was called. The report of the scouts told him that barbarians with the best spoils had returned to the area around Adrianople from the lands around Rhodope. When they learned that the emperor was coming with many troops, they hastened to join up with their fellow Goths who were in fortified camps around Beroea and Nicopolis. And at once, as the timeliness of the opportunity offered demanded, with three hundred soldiers selected from each legion, Sebastian was directed to rush to the place, with the intention of doing—so he promised—something advantageous to the state.

The word *carrago*, found at Ammianus 31.7.7, occurs only here outside the *Historia Augusta* in all of Latin literature. Ammianus felt the need to define this technical term for a kind of "wagon-train" used by Gothic troops, but the word is used multiple times in the *Historia Augusta* (*Gall.* 13.9; *Claud.* 6.6, 8.2, 8.6; *Aur.* 11.6) in inconsistent ways and in passages of dubious reliability, without the author's feeling compelled to offer a definition.[5] *Catafractarii*, or armored troops, is another word found in technical contexts, such as papyri and the *Notitia Dignitatum*, but among literary texts only in Ammianus and the *Historia Augusta* (Amm. 16.2.5,

16.12.7, 16.12.63; *Alex.* 56.5, *Claud.* 16.2, *Aur.* 11.4, 34.4). *Catafractarii* are also known by the term *clibinarii*. Ammianus and the *HA*-author use similar language to convey the relationship between the two terms: "catafractarios, quos illi clibanarios vocant" (*Alex.* 56.5); "catafracti equites, quos clibanarios dictitant" (Amm. 16.10.8). The definition and discussion of unusual words is a frequent activity in the world of Aulus Gellius, and the recognition that an unusual word in the *Historia Augusta* had been used in Ammianus may have served readers as a point of entry to the other elements borrowed from the historian.

Valerian's mention of the emperor Trajan (10.2) is inspired by Ammianus's presentation of the general Trajanus, and the mention of Trajan has also inspired the name of a general in the letter, Ulpius Crinitus, derived from the emperor Trajan's full imperial name: Marcus Ulpius Nerva Traianus. Ulpius Crinitus gave public thanks to Valerian for appointing Aurelian his deputy while in Byzantium (*Aur.* 10.3), the city (under the name of Constantinople, of course) to which the general Trajanus was sent by Valens (Amm. 31.7.1). The city of Nicopolis appears in both places: *Aurelian* 11.1, Ammianus 31.11.1. The illness of the general Crinitus parallels the illness of the general Frigeridus in Ammianus (31.7.5). Ammianus 31.7.2 describes legions drawn from Armenia, as does the *Historia Augusta* (*Aur.* 11.3).

In addition, the letter as a whole takes on a layer of irony when considered in the light of the Ammianus passage. Valerian is particularly concerned that the necessary supplies be stockpiled, since success in war depends upon provisioning (*Aur.* 11.5–7), while book 31 of Ammianus details the failure of the Roman generals to provide for the starving Goths and the destructive warfare that followed (31.4.8–11). The reference to the Third Legion, the Lucky ("legionem tertiam Felicem," *Aur.* 11.4), is perhaps a reference to the grim statement by Ammianus after the defeat at Adrianople that only a third of the army survived (31.13.18). This defeat was recognized as a disaster by contemporaries.[6] The ability of the *HA*-author to indulge in intertextual play reveals his distance from the actual events at Adrianople, and his audience's interest in Ammianus's account rather than the disaster itself.

Chapter 8 of the *Claudius* also draws material from book 31 of Ammianus. The term *carrago* from Ammianus 31.7.7 is found at *Claudius* 8.2 and 8.5, and the words "campi ossibus latent tecti" evoke Ammianus's famous description of the battlefield at Ad Salices (31.7.16): "albentes ossibus campi."[7] Book 31 also provides the key to the name of Hunila, who, according to the *HA*-author, was the Gothic wife of the usurper Bonosus (*Quad. Tyr.* 15.3–7). A fictitious letter of the emperor Aurelian claims that in a previous letter he had established Gothic noblewomen, including Hunila, and given them stipends, at Perinthus in Thrace. Two passages from Ammianus 31.6 should be consulted. In Ammianus 31.6.3 we learn that Fritigern had settled a mixed group of Goths, Huns, and Alans ("Gothi Hunis

Halanisque permixti") at Perinthus. The *HA*-author has mixed together (*permixti*) the words *Huni* and *Halani* in order to form the name of his Goth, Hunila.[8] In 31.6.8 the general Julius sends letters to assemble the Goths who had been established throughout Thrace under the guise of paying them stipends. The echoes in the *Historia Augusta* are clear.[9] By constructing the *Claudius* from pieces of the final book of Ammianus, the *HA*-author implicitly contrasts the great Roman victories he attributes to Claudius with the disaster at Adrianople under Valens. The humor in this comparison is made clear by the way in which the *HA*-author manipulates the two thousand barbarian ships he found in Ammianus 31.5.15. In *Claudius* 8.1, the two thousand ships that Claudius defeated are compared to the two thousand ships of the Trojan expedition, although the *HA*-author explains that "the pen of a poet contrived that number, truthful history includes this one" ("sed illud poeticus stilus fingit, hoc vera continet historia"). The *HA*-author portrays his own fiction as true history, and Ammianus's history as if it were fiction.

There is similar acontextual use of Ammianus in the *Claudius* and at the beginning of the *Aurelian*.[10] The princess of the house of Constantine, who was affianced to Gratian, was nearly kidnapped while she stopped to eat, but the governor Messalla placed her in a state carriage ("eam iudiciali carpento inpositam," Amm. 29.6.7) and hurried her to Sirmium. The princess Constantina appears at *Claudius* 13.3, and the invented governor Messalla at *Claudius* 16.1. At the end of the Ammianus passage (29.6.17), the historian describes conditions at Rome under the prefect of the city, whose name was Claudius. The *HA*-author, who, in the *Claudius*, tediously restates the claim that Claudius was the progenitor of the Constantinian house, can thus be seen retrojecting elements from an adventure of the last member of the family into the life of the first. At the beginning of the *Aurelian*, which immediately follows the *Claudius*, the author describes a ride in a state carriage ("iudicali carpento," *Aur.* 1.1) and presents a debate over the birthplace of Aurelian that concludes, falsely, that he was born at Sirmium (3.1). The invented scholarly controversy over the birthplace contrived by the *HA*-author encourages readers to consider other texts and intertexts. While Paschoud notes that the claim that Aurelian was born at Sirmium is "une pure invention," the invention should not be seen as entirely "pure" but instead as an allusion to Ammianus.[11] The Ammianus passage continues by describing the deeds of the young Theodosius in fighting the Sarmatians, who are restrained by a garrison installed in Illyricum (Amm. 29.6.15-16); the young Aurelian is said to have defeated Sarmatians in Illyricum (*Aur.* 6.3) in a campaign invented by the *HA*-author.[12] Aurelian is presented as a good emperor in the *Historia Augusta*, and his success as a general is here enhanced by his assimilation to Theodosius, whom Ammianus describes as "afterward a most glorious emperor" ("princeps postea perspectissimus,"

29.6.15). This allusion undercuts those who would argue that the anti-Christian author of the *Historia Augusta* particularly hated or feared Theodosius. Instead, the purpose of these allusions is the challenge of identification, not the secret insinuation of political points.

Book 15 of Ammianus is another frequent source for the *HA*-author in contriving allusions.[13] Ammianus himself was part of the delegation sent to betray and kill Silvanus, a Frankish general who was forced into usurpation during the reign of Constantius. In this emotionally heightened and memorable part of the work, Ammianus tells us that Silvanus considered appealing to his fellow Franks' ethnic solidarity ("barbarica fides," 15.5.15) but was told that he would surely be betrayed and killed by them. The scene finds an echo in the fictitious discussion of the usurper Proculus in the *Historia Augusta*, who is originally credited with an Italian ancestry (*Quad. Tyr.* 12.1; see also 13.5). When Proculus's revolt against Probus fails, the *HA*-author suddenly claims that Proculus was actually of Frankish origin, and was betrayed and killed by Franks, who are described as accustomed to break an oath with a laugh. Frankish faithlessness is not a fourth-century cliché but rather an allusion by the *HA*-author to a striking scene in Ammianus.

In Ammianus's discussion of the Gauls, he paints a vivid image of Gallic women as large, fierce, and violent (Amm. 15.12.1). Proculus's wife, we are told, was a masculine woman who bore the name Samso, although she was originally named Vituriga (*Quad. Tyr.* 12.3). "Vituriga," Syme points out, evokes a Gallic tribe, the Bituriges, and the biblical "Samso" underscores her nature.[14] Proculus's son "Herennianus" (12.4) may also evoke Ammianus; Chastagnol suggests that the name derives from a friend of the historian's, Verennianus, who also appears in book 15 (Amm. 15.5.22, 18.8.11).[15] Central to the tragedy of Silvanus was the forging of letters by a certain Dynamius, who framed the Frank with the connivance of powerful allies at court. Proculus's brief biography is also centered on a letter explaining that he has deflowered ten women in a single night, and one hundred in fifteen days (*Quad. Tyr.* 12.7, discussed in chapter 3). The *HA*-author states that he must quote Proculus's letter, "since the slightest things are pleasurable and bring some charm when they are read" ("quoniam minima quaeque iucunda sunt atque habent aliquid gratiae cum leguntur," 12.6). This methodological principle is the opposite of what we expect from the author, who elsewhere decries the inclusion of *minima* (*Macr.* 1.4).[16] The letters of Dynamius destroyed an innocent man ("vitam pulsaturum insontis," Amm. 15.5.5), while the actions of Proculus ruin innocent maidens; both letters are fictitious and slanderous constructions of their authors ("ad arbitrium figmenti conpositum," 15.5.5). The *HA*-author undercuts the gravity and terror of the destruction of Silvanus in Ammianus with a trivial and comical parallel.

The fictitious letter of Hadrian, which the *HA*-author cites in the life of Firmus (*Quad. Tyr.* 8) as evidence for the disgraceful character of the Egyptians, also alludes to Ammianus's book 15.[17] The first nine sentences of the letter criticize the Egyptians in a variety of ways. The last line of the letter abruptly shifts to the discussion of special drinking cups, and the unexpected warning that a certain Africanus, not otherwise mentioned, might drink too much from them (*Quad. Tyr.* 8.10):

> Calices tibi allassontes, id est diversi coloris, transmisi, quos mihi sacerdos templi obtulit, tibi et sorori meae specialiter dedicatos, quos tu velim festis diebus conviviis adhibeas. caveas tamen ne his Africanus noster indulgenter utatur.

> I have sent you cups that are *allassontes*, that is, multicolored, which a priest of the temple gave to me, and which are now to be presented to you and to my sister. I would like you to use them at banquets on holidays. Yet make sure that our Africanus does not use them indulgently.

The reference must be to a party described by Ammianus, presided over by a provincial governor named Africanus, at which excessive drunkenness led to treasonous complaints and then attempts at usurpation by the guests (Amm. 15.3.7):

> In convivio Africani Pannoniae secundae rectoris apud Sirmium poculis amplioribus madefacti quidam arbitrum adesse nullum existimantes licenter imperium praesens ut molestissimum incusabant. quibus alii optatam permutationem temporum adventare veluti e praesagiis affirmabant, nonnulli maiorum augurio sibi portendi incogitabili dementia promittebant.

> At a dinner party of Africanus, the governor of Pannonia Secunda, at Sirmium, certain men, tipsy from too much to drink and thinking that there were no officials present, were openly attacking the current rule as most oppressive. Some were claiming, as if from prophecies, that the hoped-for change of circumstances was coming, and others were promising, with witless madness, that the prophecies of their ancestors predicted it.

This passage in Ammianus, which the *HA*-author has incorporated into his Egyptian narrative, immediately follows a discussion of Mercurius, known as the Count of Dreams for his wicked practice of taking the dreams mentioned by dinner party guests, interpreting them in the most damning fashion, and reporting them to the emperor. His informing was so injurious that "certain learned men were grieving that they had not been born near the Atlas mountains, where it is said that dreams are not seen" ("maerebantque docti quidam, quod apud Atlanteos nati non essent, ubi memorantur somnia non videri," 15.3.6). This piece of knowledge Ammianus drew from the historian most associated with Egypt, Herodotus (6.184). Egyptian knowledge in Ammianus, linked with oppression and tyranny, is juxtaposed with the riotous and trivial behavior of the Egyptians in Hadrian's letter.

An exchange of letters in the *Two Valerians* (1.1–4) can be read as a response to a similar exchange in Ammianus. A series of letters from subject kings to the Persian king Sapor warn him against triumphalism over the capture of Valerian because of the resilience and might of the Romans. There are some pointed similarities between these letters and the exchange of letters between Constantius and a different Sapor in Ammianus (17.5.3–14).[18] The names of the authors of the first two letters in the *Historia Augusta*, Velsolus and Velenus, have inspired flurries of emendation and exasperation, with Syme concluding that "'Velsolus' and 'Velenus' elude investigation."[19] It seems merely to be a case of simple wordplay: the names are derived from the title of Sapor in Ammianus, "brother of Sun and Moon" ("frater Solis et Lunae," 17.5.3). "Velsolus" evokes the sun (*sol*), and "Velenus" the moon (*selene*). In Ammianus, Sapor claims that the ancestors of the Romans had stolen Armenia and Mesopotamia from the Persians by guile (*fraude*); in the *Historia Augusta*, Velsolus warns Sapor that the kidnapping of Valerian by guile (*fraude*) may prove dangerous for his descendants. Constantius resists the arrogance of Sapor with the claim that the Roman empire had stumbled occasionally but had never been defeated in battle. Velsolus makes the same argument but then offers the specific examples of Roman defeats at the hands of the Gauls, the Carthaginians, and Mithridates.[20] The *HA*-author humorously allows the third-century letter-writer to predict the future, and to enhance the *exempla* of the fourth-century letter-writer.

The *HA*-author takes hyperbolic passages in Ammianus and applies them with a straight face to his emperors. For example, Ammianus describes the absurd lengths to which Constantius went in prosecuting cases of magic as treason; in particular, he claims, men were condemned to death for the innocuous act of wearing an amulet to protect against disease ("si qui remedia quartanae vel doloris alterius collo gestaret," Amm. 19.12.14). In the *Caracalla* we find very similar language describing this unlikely imperial prohibition, claiming that Caracalla condemned those "qui remedia quartanis tertianisque collo adnexa gestarunt" (5.7). The language and the scenario are too close for coincidence.[21] The bodyguards of Caracalla are twice referred to as *protectores* in passages close to this one (5.8, 7.1). The title is anachronistic for Caracalla's day, but common in the *Res Gestae*— it is the title that Ammianus himself held.[22] The author has provided a clue to lead alert readers toward the intertext. The effect is to undermine the mood of tyrannical claustrophobia that Ammianus evokes, by taking a mordantly exaggerated idea seriously.

Similarly the *HA*-author takes an odd detail from Ammianus's portrayal of Constantius and turns it into a comical method for evaluating many of his imperial subjects. Von Haehling collects a number of passages in the *Historia Augusta* that mention the emperors' fruit-and vegetable-eating habits.[23] At *Severus* 4.6, for example, Septimius Severus rebukes Caracalla, then five years old, for too lavish a distribution of fruit to his friends. Later Severus is described as abstemious and desirous only of his native beans (*Sev.* 19.8). Pertinax ate lettuce (*Pert.* 12.2), like Tacitus (*Tac.* 11.2), while Maximinus Thrax abstained from vegetables (*Maximin.* 4.2). Clodius Albinus is described as a fruit maniac, consuming huge amounts of melons, peaches, grapes, and figs (*Clod. Alb.* 11.2). The wicked Carinus liked to swim amid bobbing melons and apples (*Car.* 17.3). Von Haehling argues that fruit-eating was a symbol of luxury in the ancient world, supporting this assertion with selected examples, one of which is a passage in Ammianus in which the historian claims that the emperor Constantius refrained from eating fruit as long as he lived (Amm. 21.16.7). Von Haehling concludes by claiming that the *HA*-author draws a distinction between emperors who eat fruit, and are therefore excessively given to luxury, and emperors who eat beans, and are therefore virtuous. In my own investigation of this question, I found that the ancients did not condemn excess fruit consumption any more than excess food consumption in general.[24] I argue instead that Ammianus's comments are specific to Constantius and reflect criticism of the emperor's religious views. I agree, therefore, with von Haehling's suggestion that the *HA*-author contrasts the fruit-eaters with the non-fruit-eaters, but I would explain this not as the product of some general ancient sentiment toward fruit but entirely as allusion to and parody of the passage in Ammianus. The good emperor Gordian II, for example, is the perfect anti-Constantius (*Gord.* 21.1): "pomorum et olerum avidissimus fuit, in reliquo ciborum genere parcissimus, ut semper pomorum aliquid recentium devoraret" ("He was most desirous of fruits and greens and most sparing toward other types of food, so that he was continually devouring fresh fruit"). The barbarous Maximinus Thrax, by contrast, ate nothing but huge quantities of meat (*Maximin.* 4.1).

Paschoud offers a striking example of the complexity with which the *HA*-author engages with Ammianus.[25] In a fictitious scene, Valerian is said to have enumerated various rewards granted to the young Aurelian in return for his success against the Goths (*Aur.* 13.3). Among the rewards is an absurd assortment of medals: four mural crowns, five rampart crowns, two naval crowns, and two civic crowns. Julian, we learn from Ammianus, had restored the practice of bestowing such crowns, and he hands out naval, civic, and camp crowns after a victory against the Persians (Amm. 22.6.16). In a second passage, Ammianus states that the soldiers who fought gallantly were rewarded with siege crowns, in accordance with ancient custom (24.4.24). "Rampart crown" appears to be an alternative term for the camp crown, which we can determine by studying the chapter of Aulus Gellius where the antiquarian describes the camp crown as decorated with a picture of a rampart (*NA* 5.6.17). Therefore, Valerian presents three of the crowns found in the book 24 of Ammianus, but for the fourth the *Historia Augusta* has the naval crown, not the siege crown. Gellius provides a disquisition on the varieties of crowns (5.6.8), stating in particular that the siege crown is properly bestowed not on the soldiers who storm a city, as we see in Ammianus, but on the general who lifts a siege. Either Ammianus or Julian was mistaken in believing that bestowing the siege crown on soldiers followed ancient usage; the *HA*-author is happy to issue a roundabout correction. The topic is ripe for discussion and debate by an audience interested in antiquarian literature.

Many passages in the *Historia Augusta* that interpreters have found puzzling or unusual are best understood as allusions to Ammianus, even if the interpretation of the allusion is not always easy. In the course of an unnecessary digression in the *Elagabalus*, for example, we are told of the founding of the city of Oresta, later known as Adrianopolis (*Elag.* 6.6). The claim that this city was "often" stained with human blood ("saepe cruentari hominum sanguine") requires the author to know not only about the defeat of Maximinus by Licinius in 313 but also about the death of Valens in 378, the culmination of Ammianus's history.[26] Elagabalus's plan to import a column of stone from Thebes (*Elag.* 24.7) inevitably brings to mind Ammianus's extensive discussion of Thebes and obelisks (Amm. 17.4), in which he claims that the obelisk that Constantius brought to Rome was sacred to the sun god and emphasizes the hubris involved in its transport.[27] We find that the *HA*-author falsely claims that Claudius assumed power in late March, and then portrays the senate, having abandoned the rites of the Magna Mater, assembling in the temple of Apollo (*Claud.* 4.2). Ammianus relates how, in late March, after a fire at the temple of Apollo (Amm. 23.3.3), Julian celebrated the rites of the Magna Mater (Amm. 23.3.7). For one more example, consider the *HA*-author's ruminations over whether Diocletian, at the moment in which he seized power, could really have shouted a line of Vergil, "Aeneae magni dextra cadis" ("by the hand of the mighty Aeneas you perish," *Aen.* 10.830): "Quod ego miror de homine militari, quamvis plurimos plane sciam militares vel Graece vel Latine vel comicorum usurpare dicta vel talium poetarum" ("I am amazed at this quotation from a military man, although I know, of course, that very many soldiers borrow phrases in both Greek and Latin, taken from the writers of comedy and other such poets," *Car.*

13.4). The best evidence as to whether an emperor, upon taking power, can quote epic poetry is found in Ammianus 15.8.17, where Julian mordantly quotes Homer as he is installed as Caesar: ἔλλαβε πορφύρεος θάνατος καὶ μοῖρα κραταιή ("purple death and strong fate seized him"; cf. Hom. *Il.* 5.83, 16.334, 20.477). Whereas Diocletian takes power by the sword, Julian is passively lifted into the emperor's carriage. Diocletian shouts his triumphant quotation; Julian, by contrast, whispers his fatalistic verse: "susceptus denique ad consessum vehiculi receptusque in regiam hunc versum ex Homerico carmine susurrabat" ("Finally, he was taken up to sit with the emperor in his carriage and taken to the palace, whispering this verse from the Homeric poem").

Ammianus and the Good Emperor

In an article written in 1924 that was expanded into his monograph of 1926, Norman Baynes offered an intriguing solution to the problem of the *Historia Augusta*. He argued that the *Historia Augusta* should be dated to the reign of the emperor Julian, and that it was written to "further the constitutional and religious programme of the Apostate."[28] It is "propaganda directed to a popular audience."[29] Baynes's theory responded to the German scholarship of previous decades. Dessau had dated the *Historia Augusta* to the Theodosian era, based in part on the soothsayers in the *Probus* (24.2-3) who predicted fame for generations of Probi, a prophecy that could be read as a reference to the joint consulship of the sons of the prominent Petronius Probus in 395.[30] But Mommsen had asked what purpose the extravagant praise of the house of Constantine in the *Claudius* would have served in the Theodosian era.[31] Baynes claimed that the praise of Constantine stemmed from Julian's claim to the throne through hereditary title from the Claudian/Constantinian house, while the skepticism about Christianity and the celebration of senatorial power that he saw elsewhere in the *Historia Augusta* reflected other aspects of Julian's program. Baynes further interpreted the Probus oracle as a "real" prophecy, representing the hope that some of the prominent Probi of the Julianic period would go on to exercise great power; he suggested that the head of the family may have been the patron of the work itself.[32]

Baynes's overall theory cannot be true, for even if we accept his argument that the *HA*-author uses the *KG*, not Eutropius, in the *Marcus*, the extensive use of Ammianus and Jerome requires him to be writing in the 390s at the earliest. Baynes was charmingly modest when describing his personal insistence upon the rightness of his theory: "In the present paper I have tried to give a reasoned statement of my case; if my suggestion will not withstand criticism, let it be, once and for all, scotched and buried; I have no wish to add to the number of moribund theories which cumber the battle-field of *Historia-Augusta-Forschung*."³³ In fact he was perhaps too modest, because although he was incorrect about the date of the *Historia Augusta* and therefore necessarily wrong about its purpose, he rightly recognized parallels between the *Historia Augusta* and the career of the emperor Julian. These parallels should not be understood as commentary, serious or otherwise, on Julianic policies by a contemporary observer. Instead, we should understand the *HA*-author to be engaging intertextually with Ammianus, who makes Julian the central hero of his history.

Baynes's general argument fails as do all theories of the *Historia Augusta* that posit a political or religious purpose. There is too much material in the *Historia Augusta* that would shed no light on any aspect of the regime of Julian, and too much playful allusion that would detract from any serious message. Baynes's attention, however, to the *Alexander Severus*, much of which is fantasy designed to portray Alexander as the perfect emperor, remains compelling. Where Baynes saw propaganda on behalf of the new emperor Julian reflected in this fantasy, we will see Ammianus's literary Julian adapted and refracted.

There are stereotypical traits applied to good emperors in imperial Roman historiography and biography that one would expect to find in both Ammianus's Julian and the Alexander Severus of the *Historia Augusta*, but the parallels between the two are more specific and more pointed than mere stereotypes. In a section of the *Res Gestae* devoted to an elaborate encomium of the young Julian, Ammianus tells us that Julian lived abstemiously, prayed secretly (*occulte*) to Mercury, and, perhaps aided by this prayer to the "swifter consciousness of the universe" ("mundi velociorem sensum") was able to tend to public business ("rei publicae munera") most diligently (16.5.5). Ammianus's Julian was impressively learned, most of all in philosophy, but also in history, poetry, and rhetoric. His outstanding ability in rhetoric is demonstrated, Ammianus tells us, by the purity of style of his letters and speeches. "In addition to these things, he had adequate fluency also in Latin conversation" ("super his aderat latine quoque disserendi sufficiens sermo," 16.5.7). A philosopher at heart, Julian found military instruction necessary because of his position in the state (15.5.9). All of these themes recur in chapter 3 of the *Historia Augusta* life. Alexander was trained in both literature and the military arts. In Latin he was not very proficient, however, as the mediocre quality of his speeches before the senate and the soldiers made clear. Here the *HA*-author plays with the different roles of Latin in the second and fourth centuries. Julian was eloquent in Greek but only adequate in Latin. For Alexander, being "adequate" in Latin could only mean a lack of eloquence in his speeches before a Latin-speaking senate. While Alexander did not love the Latin language, he loved those who wrote in the language ("litteratos homines") very much. He was eager to make sure that the writers whom he thought worthwhile were informed of all he did, publicly or privately ("publice et privatim"), so that they could include it in their books. This parallels the Ammianus passage on a metatextual level. Given Ammianus's expressed knowledge of Julian's secret pagan devotions in addition to his public activities, the *HA*-author jokes that Julian, despite his own failings at Latin, must have favored one Latin historian, Ammianus himself, with detailed information.

The praise of Julian in Ammianus includes the claim that his learning, even as a young man, was immense, the product of an extraordinary memory; Ammianus tells us that if it were true, "as different authors report," that Cyrus, Simonides, and Hippias had powerful memories thanks to the consumption of certain potions, then Julian must have drained "the entire cask of memory" ("totum memoriae dolium," 16.5.8). A good memory is not a clichéd quality attributed to good emperors or even good philosophers, but Alexander's is also reported to be excellent (*Alex*.14.6)—although the invented author Acholius is said to have claimed that Alexander made use of a mnemonic device of some sort. Thus the metaphor of artificially enhanced memory in Ammianus is transformed into a reality in the *Historia Augusta*. The same passage of the *Historia Augusta* extends and exaggerates Ammianus's description of Julian's eyes: "venustate oculorum micantium flagrans, qui mentis eius argutias indicabant" ("burning with the charm of shining eyes, which revealed the acuteness of his mind," 25.4.22). Alexander's eyes are so excessively fiery that they are hard to look at for long, and the acuity of his mind is so intense that he can very frequently read the minds of others: "nimius ardor oculorum et diutius intuentibus gravis, divinatio mentis frequentissima" ("His eyes were very brilliant and hard to look at for a long time. He was very often able to read thoughts," *Alex*. 14.6). The *HA*-author repeatedly takes a detail from Ammianus and playfully extends or distorts it.

Alexander's activities upon becoming emperor mirror and then supersede similar activities that Ammianus attributes to Julian. Ammianus 22.3 offers a decidedly mixed judgment of Julian's purge of officials of the previous regime. Although some officials deserved their sentences of death or exile, others were unfairly swept up in the net. Next Julian dismissed all of the palace attendants (*palatinos*, 22.4.1-2). In particular he sent away the barbers and cooks who had become rich off of palace work, as they were not necessary to him ("ut parum sibi necessarios," 22.4.10). Ammianus has mixed feelings about these actions as well: a true philosopher would have been more discriminating and kept those few attendants who were modest and virtuous. Alexander also institutes a purge when he takes office, but he "responds" to the criticism of Ammianus by being more careful. He purges only those who were both "among the most foul sort" ("ex genere hominum turpissimo") and had been appointed by Elagabalus, "that disgraceful man" ("impurus ille," *Alex.* 15.1), thereby avoiding injustices. He follows the precepts of Ammianus by retaining those who were indeed necessary ("nec quemquam passus est esse in Palatinis nisi necessarium hominem," 15.2).

Alexander also learned from Ammianus's critiques of Julian's actions in legal matters. Julian recognized that he was often hasty and excitable when serving as a judge, and so permitted his advisers to openly correct him when necessary (Amm. 22.10.3). Alexander surpasses Julian by playing the role of sober adviser himself. He encouraged his massive retinue of advisers to write down their counsels and meditate upon them for a while before speaking, so that no one would offer opinions in haste (*Alex.* 16.3). More generally, Alexander's exaggerated attention to laws and jurists (15.6–17.4) perhaps reflects a recognition that Ammianus's sharpest criticisms of Julian derive from his opposition to laws on Christian teachers and city councilors (Amm. 22.10.7, 25.4.19–21).

Ammianus's Julian is wise to the ways of flatterers, and when those in search of favors showered him with the greatest praises ("plausibus maximis") and claimed that he possessed perfect reason, he had a sharp and sarcastic response: "I would rejoice and exalt myself, if I were praised by those whom I know are able to blame me if I did or said something wrong" ("gaudebam plane praeque me ferebam, si ab his laudarer, quos et vituperare posse adverterem, si quid factum sit secus aut dictum," 22.10.4). Alexander goes further when confronted by flattery, expelling flatterers of low rank or ridiculing the high-ranked flatterer with a huge burst of laughter ("ingenti cachinno," *Alex.* 18.1). Again we have not only a stock theme—the philosopher-emperor's immunity to flattery—but a similar setting in which Alexander exaggerates the response that the *HA*-author had read in Ammianus.

Ammianus the soldier lets us know that Julian was loved by the troops, and the *HA*-author creates an Alexander who surpasses Julian in solicitousness to a ridiculous degree. Although Constantius had allowed the young Julian, as Caesar in Gaul, to eat lavishly, Julian rejected elegant food and contented himself with the rations of a soldier (Amm. 16.5.3). Alexander, too, eats like a soldier and does so with his tent open, so all can see (*Alex.* 51.5; cf. also *Hadr.* 10.2, *Pesc. Nig.* 11.1). Julian may have personally known and been able to greet by name many soldiers (Amm. 20.4.12), but Alexander knows their names, ranks, pay rates, and lengths of service, the product of late-night poring over military records (*Alex.* 21.6–8). When a soldier was sick, he could expect a visit from the emperor, and when a soldier was very sick the emperor would have him quartered in the home of a local grandee (47.2). It would be a mistake to imagine that the *HA*-author is sharing his opinions about proper military organization or the role of the emperor in relation to the army. The allusion is a comment on how emperors are portrayed in literature, not how they behave in life.

Julian's refusal to follow in the footsteps of the paranoid Constantius and to obsess over the threat of usurpation is also adopted and exaggerated by Alexander. A certain man accused his enemy of having royal robes made to further a treasonous plan. Julian, in disgust at this charge, ordered royal shoes to be sent to the accuser, to convey the message that "without great power, cheap rags are nothing" ("sine viribus maximis quid pannuli proficient leves," Amm. 22.9.11). Alexander takes this approach to a potential usurper a step further, not only presenting him with imperial accoutrements but also introducing him to the senate and having him join in a military campaign, until he withdraws in terror (*Alex.* 48). The *HA*-author concludes the anecdote with a veiled joke. He claims that some have thought that this event occurred during the reign of Trajan, but it is not to be found in the various accounts of Trajan's life, including the one by the (apocryphal) author named Fabius Marcellinus. It is to be found in other (apocryphal) authors on Alexander, however, and the *HA*-author claims that he has chosen to report their account to ensure that his reader gets real history, rather than rumor. An important source for the life of Alexander turns out, however, to be a Marcellinus after all.

History versus Textuality

Scholars have often gone astray in interpreting and contextualizing the *Historia Augusta* because they have wrongly assumed that the author is revealing his own circumstances and interests when he is, instead, revealing those of the sources on which he relies. Several of the themes that scholars have explored—the author's contempt for eunuchs at court, his interest in the office of *praefectus urbi*, and his knowledge of the law—are better understood as preoccupations not of our author but of Ammianus. The *HA*-author does not always allude directly to the text of Ammianus, but his discussions of these themes are colored by the historian's concerns.

Stroheker was the first to discuss the theme of the *princeps clausus*, the secluded emperor, who is condemned in *Alexander Severus* 66 and *Aurelian* 43.[34] Both passages warn of the danger to the state when the emperor is kept isolated and dependent exclusively on his advisers for information and advice. The concern is a logical one and has antecedents in historiographical literature. For example, Herodotus associates monarchical cloistering with the east in his claim that the Mede Deioces was the first to sequester himself (Hdt. 1.99), and Pliny contrasts Trajan's willingness to mingle with his subjects with Domitian's seclusion (*Panegyricus* 49.1). The secession of Tiberius to Capri, discussed and decried by Suetonius, represents another example. At the beginning of the fifth century, the historian Sulpicius Alexander complained of Valentinian II's being closed up in the palace in Gaul ("clauso . . . principe," at Gregory of Tours *Hist.* 2.9), and in his panegyric to the emperor Majorian in 458, Sidonius laments (perhaps alluding to Sulpicius) that Honorius and Valentinian III were shut away ("principe clauso," 5.358) while powerful advisers ran things. Thus, while the concern makes more sense in the later fourth and fifth centuries, when emperors are more prone to isolation or are simply reduced to figureheads, it had also been raised in earlier centuries.

One particular aspect of the emperor's inaccessibility that was especially distasteful to the ancients and that is highlighted in each of the *princeps clausus* passages was the power of eunuchs. A cloistered emperor was more dependent on his household staff, which in later antiquity typically included eunuchs.[35] Zawadzki notes a series of passages in the *Historia Augusta* sharply critical of the power of eunuchs (*Alex.* 23.4-7, 45.4-5, 66.3-67.1; *Gord.* 23.7-25.3; *Aur.* 43.1-4) and claims that they would be anachronistic if dated to the reigns of Diocletian and Constantine. The criticism made sense only, he said, during the reigns of Constantius II or Arcadius, periods when eunuchs held powerful positions in the state. Zawadzki went so far as to claim that the aggressive criticism of eunuchs at court required the *HA*-author to remain anonymous.[36] Chastagnol favored the reign of Arcadius and a date around 399 for the *Historia Augusta*, while Stern earlier had argued for a date in the reign of Constantius II.[37] In fact, eunuchs were prevalent in imperial circles at least as early as the reign of Diocletian, and were present in aristocratic households throughout the imperial period.[38] Criticism of eunuchs in government would have been appropriate at any time in the fourth or fifth century, and thus cannot serve as a reliable measure for dating the work.

Still, it is worth following up on the suggestion that the eunuchs who infested the government of Constantius II, according to the hostile account of Ammianus, have something to do with the negative portrayal of eunuch power in the *Historia Augusta*. Tougher finds that Ammianus paid disproportionate attention to eunuchs, and that this concentration on eunuchs only during the reign of Constantius is a literary device meant to blacken his reign with the vices of his subordinates.[39] Since the *HA*-author contrasts the good Alexander Severus and the bad Elagabalus by allusion to Ammianus's Julian and Constantius, it is unsurprising that he portrays Alexander as removing eunuchs from government positions that they held under Elagabalus (*Alex.* 23.4-7), just as Julian expelled the courtiers of Constantius. Criticism of the greed of eunuchs is found in both authors (*Alex.* 45.4-5; Amm. 14.11.3, 18.5.4). The *HA*-author warns that eunuchs will keep the emperor from receiving true information, an admonition that he may have learned from Ammianus (*Alex.* 66.3-67.1; Amm. 15.2.10, 18.4.2-4). Finally, the sentiment with which Ammianus introduces the good eunuch Eutherius is paralleled by the language with which the *HA*-author introduces the bad emperor Elagabalus. The

HA-author reminds his reader that not all of the emperors are as terrible as Elagabalus: "sed cum eadem terra et venena ferat et frumentum atque alia salutaria, eadem serpentes et cicures" ("but the same earth bears poisons as well as grain and other helpful things, not only serpents but also domesticated beasts," *Elag.* 1.2). Ammianus tells his readers that there is a single eunuch, at least, who is admirable: "sed inter vepres rosae nascuntur et inter feras nonnullae mitescunt" ("but among thorns roses are born, and among wild beasts some are tamed," Amm. 16.7.4).[40] The emphasis on eunuchs in the *Historia Augusta* is a response to Ammianus's own emphasis on eunuchs in his history, rather than a reaction to current events.

A similar analysis applies to Johne's argument that the *HA*-author devotes special attention to the office of *praefectus urbi*, or prefect of the city, a position associated with the exaltation of Rome and of the senatorial aristocrats who held it.[41] This appears to be another instance where the author is working from his sources rather than revealing a personal interest. According to Johne's data, fifteen actual holders of the office are mentioned in the *Historia Augusta*. Twelve are from the parts of the history for which Marius Maximus was a source. Two other *praefecti* are derived from Herodian and/or the *KG*.[42] Finally, there is the set piece at the beginning of the *Aurelian*, where our author converses with a certain Junius Tiberianus in his carriage. While a real man of this name served as prefect, this scene is fictitious. Beyond the actual prefects who derive from legitimate sources, the *HA*-author's inventive nature did not produce many fake ones. The jurist Salvius Iulianus is falsely given a prefecture (*Did. Iul.* 1), an invented prefect Ceionius Albinus is the recipient of a letter of Valerian (*Aur.* 9.2), and an invented Aelius Cesettianus introduces Tacitus to the army and people (*Tac.* 7.2). The invented usurper Censorinus was three times prefect, but he also held an absurdly long list of other offices as well (*Tyr. Trig.* 33.1).[43] Does this list of prefects, real and imagined, suggest a particular fixation on the position? The lack of comparative evidence makes it difficult to say. Even if we are inclined to say that the *HA*-author devotes inordinate attention to the urban prefecture, before we attribute this to a social or political predilection we should consider the literary environment in which he writes. First, Marius Maximus, the author probably behind most of the mentions of the office, himself served as urban prefect, and thus would naturally have noted and celebrated previous holders of the office. Second, Ammianus devotes considerable attention to urban prefects, even though the city of Rome otherwise plays little part in his grand narrative. The *HA*-author thus follows two of his models in highlighting holders of the office, rather than having an independent interest in the position.

Honoré argues, building on the work of Straub and Liebs, that the *HA*-author is particularly knowledgeable about the law, but once again the legal knowledge of the author does not reveal his own personal interests but those of his literary sources.⁴⁴ While the *HA*-author mentions a lot of legal experts and writers, and is favorable toward them, the favor rarely rises beyond the cliché that a man skilled at law is a good adviser for an emperor. The large majority of the lawyers mentioned are from the parts of the *Historia Augusta* that derive from Marius Maximus. The one exception is the presence of (Herennius) Modestinus, included on a list of otherwise invented teachers of the son of Maximinus. Modestinus was in fact prominent during the reign of Maximinus's predecessor Alexander Severus, so it is unlikely that he was the tutor of Maximinus's son. For Honoré, the explanation of this transposition is that the author felt that "a prominent legal author should be given some role in imperial history"; because the *HA*-author had already exaggerated the role of Ulpian under Alexander, Modestinus had to be included in the next reign. But Maximinus and his son are both portrayed as boorish barbarians. Modestinus's inclusion in the life in no way speaks well for him or for the law. After Modestinus, we note that authentic legal figures never appear in the later books of the *Historia Augusta*, when the author was most freely inventing and expressing his own interests. The rest of Honoré's case is more ingenious than convincing. His demonstration that a reference to the Lex Fufia Caninia on the manumission of slaves is incorrect (*Tac.* 10.7) is turned into a demonstration of the author's subtle legal learning, as is the absurd attempt by Didius Julianus to compel Pescennius Niger not to revolt by issuing a legal proclamation (*Pesc. Nig.* 2.7).⁴⁵ There is no reason to conclude that the *HA*-author was deeply knowledgeable about the law, or a lawyer himself. In at least one passage, we find that his flawed legal knowledge is the result of his reliance on Ammianus instead of the legal codes. In a discussion of Alexander's skill at provisioning his army, the author notes that soldiers were not compelled to carry rations for the usual ("ut solent") period of seventeen days (*Alex.* 47.1). In Gaul, Ammianus tells us, Julian had taken part of the seventeen days' worth of supplies from each man and stored the provisions in forts (Amm. 17.9.2). The actual law of Constantius preserved in the *Codex Theodosianus* (7.4.5) specifies twenty days, not seventeen, and Ammianus's reference to seventeen days is particularly striking because he has himself only just mentioned twenty days (Amm. 17.8.2).⁴⁶ The *HA*-author is interested in the number of days Ammianus cited, not the actual legal requirements.

The Traditional Date of the *Historia Augusta*

As we have seen, many fourth-century themes or ideas in the *Historia Augusta* are the product of the author's engagement not with the world around him but with the text of Ammianus or another author. This has implications for determining when the work was written. In his final consideration of the problem, Dessau concluded that the *Historia Augusta* should be dated to the last decade of the fourth century, and this has remained the general view of most scholars into the twenty-first century.[47] A reexamination of the arguments will reveal the weakness of this consensus. In the next section, I propose a new and later date.

Scholars have often suggested that allusions to events surrounding the battle at the Frigidus River (6 September 394) suggest a contemporaneous date. Hartke's interpretation of the wind in *Gordian* 16.2 as a reference to the miraculous wind that is said to have led to the defeat of Eugenius in that battle has often been accepted:[48]

> Fertur autem tanta multitudo Gordiani partium in bello cecidisse, ut, cum diu quaesitum sit corpus Gordiani iunioris, non potuerit inveniri. fuit praeterea ingens, quae raro in Africa est, tempestas, quae Gordiani exercitum ante bellum ita dissipavit, ut minus idonei milites proelio fierent, atque ita facilis esset Capeliani victoria.

> It is said that so many on Gordian's side died in the war that although the body of Gordian II was sought after for a long time, it could not be found. There was in addition a huge storm, which is unusual in Africa, and which dispersed the army of Gordian before the battle to such an extent that the soldiers were less ready for battle, and the victory of Capelianus was easy.

Syme supports Hartke by noting that the *HA*-author derived his information about the loss of the younger Gordian's body from Herodian, whom he followed up to this point, but then diverged from his source to add the detail about the storm. That suggests, Syme thinks, that the author has inserted a piece of contemporary news into his historical account.[49] This interpretation cannot be correct.[50] Ratti shows that the evidence of Zosimus 1.16.1 demonstrates that Dexippus, Zosimus's source and also a source for the *Historia Augusta*, is the ultimate source of the storm. Thus the storm is not a hidden allusion to the events at the Frigidus but just an account of an actual third-century storm.

Syme suggests that the invented name Eugamius is another allusion to Eugenius and his defeat in 394, but this is unconvincing. Among the fictions in the life of the younger Maximinus are lists of his purported teachers (*Maximin.* 27). Interspersed among names such as Modestinus and Titianus, who appear to be real authors, are Fabillus and Philemon and Eugamius, who are likely not.[51] Eugamius is said to be responsible for teaching the young Maximinus rhetoric (27.5). The name, it has been claimed, evokes the usurper Eugenius, originally a teacher.[52] Eugenius was described as a rhetor in some sources (Zos. 4.54.1) but as a mere grammarian in others (Soz. 5.25.1), perhaps a controversy alluded to in our author's discussion of the father of the usurper Bonosus. Bonosus used to claim that his father was a rhetor, but the *HA*-author has learned in the course of his research that he was merely a grammarian (*Quad. Tyr.* 14.1). While this sort of allusion is not foreign to the *Historia Augusta*, the names are not so similar, nor the professions so unusual, as to encourage us to accept these connections without further evidence.

The claim that the emperor Decius was sending young Claudius to garrison Thermopylae (*Claud.* 16) has been interpreted as evoking the activities of Alaric in late 395 and 396.[53] Alaric's desperate army headed south through the pass at Thermopylae without being contested by the local commander, Gerontius, and again negotiated the Corinthian isthmus and was able to lay waste to the Peloponnesus until Stilicho's army arrived in 397. Contemporaries suspected treason. Claudius's appointment, it has been suggested, may underscore the need for a more trustworthy (*devotior*) leader to protect Greece. This is an unnecessary interpretation. The last sections of the *Claudius* are strongly panegyrical and entirely fictional. The emperor is credited with a variety of offices and commands that he never held. In keeping with this context, we should see the *HA*-author simply granting Claudius the opportunity to successfully defend Thermopylae, thus outdoing Leonidas and the Spartans, who suffered the most famous defeat in ancient history.

Paschoud argues that the fictitious consultation of the Sibylline oracle in the *Aurelian* (18.5–21.4) is an important piece of evidence for a date around 400.[54] The *HA*-author attributes Roman military success to the consultation of the oracle, which Paschoud argues would be impossible after Stilicho burned the Sibylline Books, an event that must have taken place before his death in August 408 (Rut. Namat. 2.41–60). In addition, Paschoud suggests, the celebration of the power of pagan ritual to defeat German enemies would have been problematic after the pagan Radagaisus was defeated by Christians in 406.

Paschoud is incorrect in his reading of both the tone and the content of the passage. If the *HA*-author were making a sincere point about the power of pagan ritual to achieve military success, he would not have included a comical mishmash of different pagan rituals that have nothing to do with the Sibylline Books.[55] The passage is better understood as a parody of antiquarian learning. In Ammianus 18.1.7, Julian is said to have consulted the books before his Persian campaign, which he launched despite the response urging him not to leave the borders of the Roman empire. The *Historia Augusta* passage should be read as an elaborate expansion of the Ammianus notice. In addition, the Sibylline Books that Stilicho is said to have destroyed are not the ancient books that we see, for example, in Livy, which likely no longer existed at the end of the fourth century. The *Historia Augusta* refers to the versified prophecies attributed to the Sibyl, many with Jewish or Christian origins, which were regularly rewritten to provide contemporary political commentary in a veiled manner.[56] Stilicho did not destroy official senatorial books of the distant pagan past but a hostile contemporary "prophecy" that he found politically dangerous.

Paschoud also champions the argument of Johne, who has studied the attitude of the *HA*-author toward the various imperial residences of the emperors in the fourth century.[57] All of these (Byzantium/Constantinople, Nicomedia, Antioch, Sirmium, Trier, and Milan) are compared, Johne claims, unfavorably to Rome, but Ravenna, the residence of Honorius after 404, is not. Therefore, Johne concludes, the *HA*-author, who is a partisan of Rome and resents the fact that emperors reside elsewhere, must be writing before 404. Otherwise he would have included some negative elements in his references to Ravenna also. Although we can accept that the *HA*-author favors Rome, the rest of this argument falls apart upon close examination of the details. The more historically significant cities in this list—Byzantium, Antioch, and Milan—are mentioned frequently in the *Historia Augusta* in positive as well as negative ways, although most often neutrally. Here, for example, is a list of the passages in which the *HA*-author mentions Milan: the grandfather of Didius Julianus was from Milan (*Did. Iul.* 1.2); Geta was probably born at Milan (*Geta* 3.1); Valerian Junior was buried at Milan (*Val.* 8.3); Gallienus may have been killed at Milan (*Gall.* 14.9); the wicked Aureolus was killed at Milan (*Claud.* 5.3); the Marcomanni devastated Milan during the reign of Aurelian (*Aur.* 18.3); Milan was one of many cities to which the senate wrote after the accession of Tacitus (*Tac.* 18.6); Milan is one of many cities Carus may have come from (*Car.* 4.4); Carinus indulged in luxury by strewing his dining rooms and bedrooms with roses from Milan (*Car.* 17.3). It is impossible to look at this list and conclude that the *HA*-author is attempting to make Milan look bad in the interest of Roman partisanship. The less frequently mentioned cities also fail to support this theory. Trier is mentioned twice in the *Historia Augusta*. First, it is the recipient of a letter from the senate celebrating its freedom upon the accession of Tacitus (*Tac.* 18.5). Second, we are told that coins of the usurper Victoria still circulate at Trier (*Tyr. Trig.* 31.8). No readers would be roused to anti-Treviran sentiments by these claims. Nicomedia is also mentioned twice by the *Historia Augusta*. It was plundered by Scythians during the reign of Gallienus (*Gall.* 4.8), and Elagabalus lived there in a depraved manner while wintering at Nicomedia (*Elag.* 5.1). Before we put too much weight on the last fact, it should be noted that it is not an invention of our author but was part of the historical record (Dio Cass. 80.7), and the *HA*-author immediately goes on to point out that even upon his return to Rome, Elagabalus's misbehavior continued, as he did nothing but send out agents in search of well-endowed men to be brought to the palace for his enjoyment (*Elag.* 5.3). Again, Nicomedia could hardly be the target of this passage or of the *HA*-author more generally. The author's attitude toward the various cities is too varied to provide any indication of the date of the work.

Much of the historical evidence that scholars have offered, therefore, provides little guidance for determining the date of publication of the *Historia Augusta*. We should turn, instead, to the evidence from literary allusion, which provides a more solid basis on which to determine the *terminus post quem* of the work. The date of the *Res Gestae* of Ammianus Marcellinus is obviously of great importance.[58] Ammianus notes that the historian Aurelius Victor served as urban prefect, an office that he held in 389/90 (21.10.6). He mentions the death of Petronius Probus, which probably happened in 390 (27.11). He compares the Serapeum in Egypt with the eternal Capitol at Rome, which would be a discordant comparison once monks destroyed the Serapeum in the summer of 391 (22.16.12). And, finally, a letter of Libanius that can be dated to 392 and refers to events a bit earlier praises a certain Marcellinus who is reciting extracts from a prose work at Rome (*Ep.* 1063). On the other hand, elements of the description in Ammianus's last book of the Huns, a people previously unknown to ethnography, seem to have been echoed in several works of Jerome that date as early as 393.[59] The preface to Jerome's *Life of Malchus*, which appeared in 392, also appears to have been influenced by Ammianus.[60] It is true that some scholars have argued for a later date for the *Res Gestae*, but these arguments tend to be based on assumptions about the constraints of historical writing under Theodosius or Eugenius that are speculative at best.[61]

Some of the allusions to Jerome that I claimed in chapter 3 move the date beyond the end of the *Res Gestae*. Jerome's early letters and *Life of Hilarion* are both mentioned in his *De viris illustribus* (135), which was published in 392 or 393. *Epistles* 52 and 53 have been dated to 394, *Epistle* 66 and the *Commentary on Matthew* have been dated to 398, and *Epistle* 107 is dated to 401 or 402.[62] The outlier is the *Commentary on Isaiah*, which was completed before the sack of Rome in August 410, although parts of it were separately published.

The use of other literary texts has not proven helpful for narrowing the date of the *Historia Augusta*. Chastagnol argues for the *HA*-author's extensive use of certain poems of Claudian.[63] In fact, he narrows the date of publication to 399–400 by these allusions.[64] These parallels have not, however, been universally accepted.[65] The suggested allusions lack sophisticated connections to their source texts; instead the passages merely rework traditional themes or conventional expressions.[66] Chastagnol also argues for the use by the *HA*-author of the *Epitome rei militaris* of Vegetius.[67] Some of the parallels he offers are striking (especially Veg. *Mil.* 2.24 as a source for *Av. Cass.* 6.4), but most seem to reflect just the stereotyped language of armor, provisioning, and recruiting. As a result, his argument has not found many supporters. If we accept Vegetian influence for the sake of argument, we must confront the problem of the date of Vegetius. Chastagnol is one of many who support a Theodosian date for Vegetius, which, if correct, does not advance the *terminus post quem* beyond what Ammianus and Jerome have already done. On the other hand, Charles is the most recent scholar to argue for a date in the reign of Valentinian III, and thus after 425.[68]

Historical and literary evidence for the date have different implications. Historical evidence generally implies a nearly contemporaneous date with the events alluded to, so those scholars who see allusions to the Eugenius and the battle of the Frigidus argue for a date not long after 395. Allusions to literary texts, however, provide *termini post quem* without providing *termini ante quem*. Cicero, Suetonius, Ammianus, and Jerome were potentially available to our author for decades and centuries after they were published. We should agree with den Hengst, then, that "the problem of the *terminus ante quem* remains open," and with Syme that "nobody can disprove a later date [than 394–98] should some valid arguments emerge."[69]

Probus and the *Principes Pueri*

Since the case for dating the *Historia Augusta* to 399–400 is not certain, we can reexamine the evidence that remains without preconceptions and seek an alternative context for the work. While I reject the idea that the *HA*-author is commenting extensively and seriously on contemporary political events, he can still be seen to derive humor from the anachronistic retrojection of contemporary events into the second-or third-century world of his work.

An exceptional passage that does seem to engage with contemporary events concerns the oracle at the end of the *Probus* (24.2–3):

> sane quod praeterire non potui, cum imago Probi in Veronensi sita fulmine icta esset ita ut eius praetexta colores mutaret, haruspices responderunt huius familiae posteros tantae in senatu claritudinis fore ut omnes summis honoribus fungerentur. sed adhuc neminem vidimus, posteri autem aeternitatem videntur habere, non modum.

> I am unable, indeed, to leave out that when a statue of Probus near Verona was struck by lightning and the colors of the statue's robe were changed, the soothsayers reported that his descendants would be of such eminence in the

senate that they would all hold the highest offices. But so far we have seen none, and moreover "descendants" can refer not to a limited number of generations, but to eternity.

The prophecy makes no sense in the context of the Constantinian empire, but the consulship of Petronius Probus in 371 and his sons' joint consulship in 395 make the prediction of multiple generations of the highest officeholders immediately understandable. We must, then, place the composition of the *Historia Augusta* after 395, or, technically, 394, as Ratti points out, since the consulships would be known in advance of their tenancy.[70] The oracle is even more pointed if the *Historia Augusta* was written after 406, when Flavius Anicius Petronius Probus held the consulship. Cameron argues that the oracle must refer to Probus alone, not his sons.[71] This seems contradicted by the plain text of the oracle, which applies to "descendants" in the plural. The fact that the sons are Anicii, not Probi, which Cameron believes is decisive, seems likewise irrelevant to the oracle, which does not specify the names of the future generations. Cameron has framed the problem incorrectly when he discusses the fake oracle with the assumption that the *HA*-author included it with the goal of winning the favor of either the father or the sons. The *Historia Augusta* would be a most bizarre vehicle for the flattery of a contemporary politician. In an atmosphere of allusions, jokes, and parody, what reader would feel glorified by this kind of mention? The oracle itself is a joke, not a blandishment, as the second sentence makes clear.

A passage in the *Tacitus* has long been recognized as important for determining the date and the broader nature of the *Historia Augusta*. After the death of the emperor Aurelian, the *Historia Augusta* (falsely) claims that there followed an interregnum of six months. Contrary to much recent precedent, the narrative continues, the army asked the senators to choose a new emperor, and the senate selected the elderly Tacitus from their number. A certain senator, Maecius Faltonius Nicomachus, encouraged the reluctant Tacitus to accept the position with the following words (*Tac.* 5.3–7.1):

> Interrogatus praeterea qui post Tacitum sedebat senator consularis Maecius Faltonius Nicomachus in haec verba disseruit: 'Semper quidem, patres conscripti, recte atque prudenter rei publicae magnificus hic ordo consuluit, neque a quoquam orbis terrae populo solidior umquam exspectata sapientia est, attamen nulla umquam neque gravior neque prudentior in hoc sacrario dicta sententia est. seniorem principem fecimus et virum qui omnibus quasi pater consulat: nihil ab hoc inmaturum, nihil praeproperum, nihil asperum formidandum est; omnia seria, cuncta gravia et quasi ipsa res

publica iubeat auguranda sunt. scit enim qualem sibi principem semper optaverit, nec potest aliud nobis exhibere quam ipse desideravit et voluit. enimvero si recolere velitis vetusta illa prodigia, Nerones dico et Heliogabalos et Commodos, seu potius semper Incommodos, certe non hominum magis vitia illa quam aetatum fuerunt. dii avertant principes pueros, et patres patriae dici impuberes, et quibus ad subscribendum magistri litterarii manus teneant, quos ad consulatus dandos dulcia et circuli et quaecumque voluptas puerilis invitet. quae malum ratio est habere imperatorem qui famam curare non noverit, qui quid sit res publica nesciat, nutritorem timeat, respiciat ad nutricem, virgarum magistralium ictibus terrorique subiaceat, faciat eos consules, duces, iudices quorum vitam, merita, aetates, familias, gesta non norit. sed quo diutius, patres conscripti, protrahor? magis gratulemur quod habemus principem senem quam illa iteremus quae plus quam lacrimanda tolerantibus extiterunt. gratias igitur diis inmortalibus ago atque habeo, et quidem pro universa re publica, teque, Tacite Auguste, convenio petens, obsecrans ac libere pro communi patria, legibus deposcens ne parvulos tuos, si te citius fata praevenerint, facias Romani heredes imperii, ne sic rem publicam patresque conscriptos populumque Romanum ut villulam tuam, ut colonos tuos, ut servos tuos relinquas. quare circumspice, imitare Nervas, Traianos, Hadrianos: ingens est gloria morientis principis rem publicam magis amare quam filios.' Hac oratione et Tacitus ipse vehementer est motus et totus senatorius ordo concussus, statimque adclamatum est: 'Omnes, omnes.'

Having been asked his opinion, Maecius Faltonius Nicomachus, the consular senator who sat beside Tacitus, spoke the following words: "Always, indeed, conscript Fathers, has this magnificent order worked prudently and correctly for the state, nor has more reliable wisdom ever been expected from another nation in the entire world, and yet, no decision more serious or prudent has ever been given in this sacred place. We have made emperor an older man, who will consider the interests of all like a father. From this man we must predict that we need not fear anything untimely, hasty, or harsh. All things will be serious, all things sober, and just as the state itself would order. For he knows what sort of emperor he has always desired for himself, and is not able to act differently for us than he himself has desired and wished for. For if you wish to recollect those old monsters, I mean the Neros and Elagabaluses and Commoduses, or rather always Incommodious ones, certainly their vices were more the product of their ages than the men themselves. May the gods protect us from boys being named emperor, and from immature children being called Father of the Country—boys whose hands are guided by a schoolteacher to affix names to an official document, who grant consulships in return for candy and cakes and whatever their childish pleasure demands. What is the reason—it is evil!—to have an emperor who does not know how to protect his reputation, who does not know what the common good is, who fears his guardian and looks to his nurse, who is subject to the fear and blows of the rod of the schoolmaster, who makes consuls, generals, and judges men whose life, merits, age, families, and deeds he does not know. But how much longer, conscript Fathers, should I drag it out? Let us rejoice that we have an old man for an emperor, rather than repeat things that were lamentable to those who suffered them. Therefore, I have and give thanks to the immortal gods on behalf of the entire state, and I implore you, Tacitus Augustus, requesting, begging, and demanding on behalf of our common homeland and the laws, that if the fates should overtake you too quickly, you not make your little boys heirs to the empire, nor that you abandon the state, the senate, and the Roman people, as if they were your personal estate, your tenants, your slaves. So look around, imitate the Nervas, Trajans, and Hadrians: it is the great glory of a dying emperor to love the state more than his sons." Tacitus himself was deeply moved by this speech, and the whole senatorial order was struck by it, and at once they shouted, "All, all are in agreement."

"May the gods protect us from boys being named emperor!" Faltonius prays. The prayer is inappropriate in the mouth of a third-century senator, because it is not until the later fourth century that emperors began to be proclaimed before the age of majority.

In Hartke's exhaustive study of the questions this passage evokes, he recognizes that there were several child emperors in the fourth century, including Constans (fourteen years old in 337), Gratian (sixteen in 375), and Valentinian II (twelve in 383), but he concludes that this speech made the most sense in the period after the death of Theodosius on 17 January 395.[72] Theodosius's older son, Arcadius, seventeen years old, became emperor in the east, and his younger son, Honorius, aged ten, became emperor in the west. The half-barbarian general Stilicho, whose relationship with the senatorial aristocracy was rocky at best, was effectively the western emperor, given Honorius's youth. Paschoud follows Hartke in identifying Arcadius and Honorius as the boy princes to be decried, arguing that the rise of powerful enemies such as Gildo and Alaric in the later 390s would have inspired particular alarm among elites who hoped for strong leadership.[73] This identification fits well with interpretations of the *Historia Augusta* that emphasize pagan–Christian conflict. For Hartke and Paschoud, Maecius Faltonius Nicomachus is meant to evoke Nicomachus Flavianus, described in Christian sources as a militant pagan, whom the orthodox Christian Theodosius defeated in the course of putting down the usurper Eugenius in 394. Eugenius was a civilian, not a soldier, which fits well with another theme of the *Tacitus*. Thus the scorn for child emperors has been seen not only as a comment upon contemporary political administration but as a covert pagan attack on Christian rulers.

Cameron, arguing that the *Historia Augusta* was written before 385, must reject the arguments for allusion to events after 395. He argues that concern about boy emperors was as appropriate in the 370s as in the 390s.[74] He notes that Gratian was only nineteen, a year older than Arcadius, when he became sole ruling emperor in 378, and that even after the proclamation of Theodosius in the east in 379, the west was ruled by the nineteen-year-old Gratian with a seven-year-old colleague, Valentinian II. Moreover, he adds evidence from Symmachus and Ambrose, among others, showing that contemporaries had concerns about youthful emperors falling under the sway of bad advisers.[75] The use of Ammianus and Jerome by the *HA*-author renders Cameron's arguments for the date of the *Historia Augusta* impossible, but he does succeed in demonstrating that concern for child emperors need not be placed only in the Theodosian epoch.

The 370s and the 390s are not the only periods in which complaints about child emperors could have had contemporary resonance. In 1912 Seeck made a case for the year 409, but his argument was quickly dismissed.[76] He constructed an unconvincing allegorical interpretation of the *Historia Augusta* out of scraps of various lives, without considering the work as a whole. Seeck's dating has been revived recently, however, in a less prescriptive fashion by Neri, who would date the *Historia Augusta* to after 408.[77] Neri's proposal, with some supplements and alterations, makes good sense of the passage and is consistent with other source-critical questions as well.

The period from 408 to 410 marked the culmination of a series of challenges to Stilicho's effective rule in Honorius's name, which he had undertaken in 400. In early 408, the Gothic leader Alaric, whom Stilicho hoped would be his ally in an attempt to win the province of Illyricum for the west, demanded a large cash payment.[78] Stilicho's attempt to persuade the Roman senate to accept his terms was resisted at first, and although his conciliatory policy was ultimately accepted, both the senators and some courtiers began to grow cool toward him. By the end of the year, following a massacre of Stilicho's supporters, Stilicho himself was executed and his policies reversed. Alaric, denied funds, laid siege to Rome in the winter of 408–9, which was only lifted after payment of a massive ransom. Negotiations between Honorius and Alaric in 409 having fallen apart, Alaric seized the granaries of Rome and announced a new Roman emperor, Priscus Attalus. Attalus was a prominent senator who had corresponded with Symmachus in the 390s. More recently, during the first siege of Alaric, he took part in a failed senatorial embassy to Honorius begging for relief (Zos. 5.44.1). He was serving as prefect of the city when he became emperor. His brief reign ended in the summer of 410, when Alaric reconciled briefly with Honorius. The events of this period seem to be echoed in several passages of the *Historia Augusta*.

The fictionalized portrayal of the emperor Tacitus in the *Historia Augusta* highlights a number of features that could apply to Priscus Attalus as well. Attalus, like Tacitus, must have been fairly old by the time he became emperor, and he was also a leading member of the senate (Olympiodorus 3, *fr.* 6 Blockley). Tacitus is described as *litteratus*, and Attalus's literary pretensions are clear from Symmachus's correspondence with him (*Ep.* 7.18). Tacitus is said to be pleased at the senate's choice for consul, even though it meant that his brother could not hold the office, and Zosimus reports that the Romans were particularly pleased with the selection of a certain Tertullus as consul. Most of all, Attalus was a rare civilian emperor at a time when few were to be found. Even the civilian Eugenius led troops in the battle of the Frigidus. Although the real Tacitus was probably a soldier-emperor like the others of the later third century, the *HA*-author has him express concern about his ability to perform his duties as emperor, since he is old and unable to fight. The senate expresses in return adamant support for a civilian leader in repeated acclamations (*Tac.* 5.1–2):

> 'Imperatorem te, non militem facimus'; dixerunt vicies. 'Tu iube, milites pugnent'; dixerunt tricies . . . 'Severus dixit caput imperare, non pedes'; dixerunt tricies. 'Animum tuum, non corpus eligimus'; dixerunt vicies.
>
> "We are making you an emperor, not a soldier," they said twenty times. "You give the orders, let the soldiers fight," they said thirty times. . . . "Severus said that the head rules, not the feet," they said thirty times. "We choose your mind, not your body," they said twenty times.

This colloquy can be seen as an optimistic (or ironic) spin on a situation where Alaric had total control over the army and Attalus was limited to the role of civilian representative of the aristocracy.

The *Tacitus* provides a fictional but elaborate description of the interplay between army and senate that led up to the emperor's appointment, which can also be interpreted in the context of Attalus's proclamation. The *HA*-author states that the army first asked the senate to appoint an emperor but that the senate felt that it was not up to the task and requested that the army offer its own candidate. The army rejected the senate's demurral and again demanded that the senate make the choice. We have two accounts of how Attalus became emperor. Olympiodorus was the ultimate source for Socrates, Sozomen, and Zosimus, all of whom agree that Alaric compelled the Romans to accept Attalus as their emperor.[79] By contrast, the church historian Philostorgius claims that the senate was allowed to choose (12.3): καὶ ψηφισαμένων τῶν Ῥωμαίων (τοῦτο γὰρ αὐτοῖς Ἀλλάριχος ἐνεδίδου), Ἄτταλον αὐτοῖς ἀναγορεύει Βασιλέα ("After the Romans voted [Alaric granted them this], he proclaimed Attalus their emperor"). It is not impossible, as Neri argues, that Philostorgius is correct. Given Attalus's position as prefect of the city, he would be a reasonable and easy choice for the senate to make. Sozomen tells us (presumably drawing upon Olympiodorus) that after his proclamation, Attalus συγκαλέσας δὲ τὴν γερουσίαν Ἄτταλος λόγον διῆλθε μακρὸν καὶ λαμπρῶς μάλα πεπονημένον, ὑπισχνούμενος τὰ πάτρια τῇ συγκλήτῳ φυλάξειν ("assembled the senators, and addressed them in a long and very splendidly wrought speech, in which he promised to preserve the ancestral rights of the senate," 9.8.2). Such a speech would have been grotesque without at least the illusion of senatorial support for him. But perhaps it was indeed perceived as grotesque. Neri assumes that the *HA*-author must be a sincere supporter of Attalus and his regime. It may be instead that we are meant to read the *Tacitus* ironically, as a parody of the heavy-handed propaganda with which Alaric and Attalus sought to camouflage their seizure of power.

Maecius Faltonius Nicomachus, the name given to the leading man of the senate, appears to be an amalgam of three holders of the rank of prefect of the city (*praefectus urbi*) in the late fourth and early fifth centuries: Furius Maecius Gracchus (376), Faltonius Probus Alypius (391), and Nicomachus Flavianus the Younger (399–400, 408). Chastagnol argues that the *HA*-author's support for the ideology of this passage is emphasized by the allusion to a leading senator in office at the very time of writing: "Le nom même du sénateur influent qui, dans l'H.A., ose formuler une telle critique, un Nicomaque, suffit à démontrer que celle-ci est d'actualité au moment où l'auteur rédige son oeuvre."[80] Chastagnol refers to Flavianus's first term in 399–400, when he believes the *Historia Augusta* was written, but his comment would also, of course, apply to his second term in 408.

The argument of Faltonius is not wholly coherent. First the senator celebrates Tacitus's advanced age, which ensures that he will be thoughtful and dignified. Youth, Faltonius claims, shares the responsibility for the depraved behavior of previous emperors such as Nero, Elagabalus, and Commodus, who were, although young, still old enough to rule as adults (aged seventeen, fifteen, and nineteen upon their respective assumptions of power). He then proceeds to decry emperors who were not *adulescentes* like his examples, but rather *pueri*, prepubescent boys, who are beaten by schoolmasters, have not yet learned to write, and can be bribed with candy. *Puer* can be used to describe a ten-year-old like Honorius, a puppet of Stilicho, or the seven-year-old Valentinian II, who did the bidding of his mother and his eunuch advisers. Neither Arcadius, seventeen in 395, or Gratian, nineteen in 378, could be called *puer*. They were quite old enough in Roman terms to rule, and were certainly not the schoolboys of Faltonius's speech.

Neri shows that the period after 408 allowed for a better pair of *pueri*. The first would be Theodosius II, aged seven, who became eastern Augustus upon the death of Aracadius in May 408. The second was Honorius, a boy at his accession in 393, who, despite having reached the age of majority in the intervening period, had been Stilicho's puppet for more than fifteen years. I would add a third *puer* into the mix. Many sources report the rumor, current in 408, that Stilicho would seek to nudge aside Theodosius II and install his own son Eucherius, twelve years old, as emperor.[81]

The curious millenarian prophecy at the end of the *Tacitus*, toward which the author exhibits an urbane irony, can also be interpreted as a comment on the brief reign of Attalus (*Tac.* 15.1–5):

> Horum statuae fuerunt Interamnae duae, pedum tricenum, e marmore, quod illic eorum cenotafia constituta sunt in solo proprio; sed deiectae fulmine ita contritae sunt ut membratim iaceant dissipatae. quo tempore responsum est ab haruspicibus quandocumque ex eorum familia imperatorem Romanum futurum seu per feminam, seu per virum, qui det iudices Parthis ac Persis, qui Francos et Alamannos sub Romanis legibus habeat, qui per omnem Africam barbarum non relinquat, qui Taprobanis praesidem imponat, qui ad Iuvernam insulam proconsulem mittat, qui Sarmatis omnibus iudicet, qui terram omnem qua Oceano ambitur, captis omnibus gentibus, suam faciat, postea tamen senatui reddat imperium et antiquis legibus vivat, ipse victurus annis centum viginti et sine herede moriturus. futurum autem eum dixerunt a die fulminis praecipitati statuisque confractis post annos mille. non magna haec urbanitas haruspicum fuit qui principem talem post mille annos futurum esse dixerunt, quia, si post centum annos praedicerent, forte possent eorum deprehendi mendacia pollicentes, cum vix remanere talis possit historia. ego tamen haec idcirco inserenda volumini credidi ne quis me legens legisse non crederet.

Their two statues, thirty feet tall and made of marble, were set up at Interamna, where their cenotaphs had been set up on their own soil. Struck by lightning, they were so thoroughly destroyed that they lay in pieces scattered about. When this happened, the soothsayers claimed that there would be a Roman emperor someday from their family, either through the female or the male line, who would give judges to the Parthians and Persians, who would place the Franks and Alamanni under Roman jurisdiction, who would not leave a barbarian in all of Africa, who would impose a governor on Taprobane, who would send a proconsul to the island of Iuverna, who would be judge to all the Sarmatians, who would make his own all the land that borders Ocean, having subdued all the nations; and yet afterward he would restore power to the senate and live by the laws of old, destined to live for a hundred and twenty years and to die without an heir. They said that it would come to pass a thousand years from the day when the lightning struck and the statues were smashed. Was this not evidence of the great cleverness of the soothsayers, who said that such an emperor would arise after a thousand years, because, if they had predicted it after a hundred years, they might have been caught in a lie while such a story could still barely be remembered. Nevertheless, I felt that this should be included in my volume, lest my readers believe I had not read it.

The prophecy is referred to again, humorously, in the next section (*Tac.* 16.4): "et Floriani liberi et Taciti multi extiterunt, quorum sunt posteri, credo, millesimum annum exspectantes" ("Both Florian and Tacitus left many children, whose descendants, I suppose, are awaiting the coming of the thousandth year")

While Sozomen describes the speech of Attalus as a celebration of the restoration of ancient senatorial rights and privileges, Zosimus claims that Attalus arrogantly insisted that he would conquer the entire world for the Romans (6.7.3). The dismissal of a prediction of universal rule is perhaps a commentary on Attalus's words, from an author and for an audience who saw his grandiose plans collapse in a matter of months.

If we interpret commentary on utopianism in the *Historia Augusta* as an ironic reaction to the contrast between the idealized hopes and the depressing reality of the short reign of Attalus, we can reconsider the interpretation of the *Probus* offered by Paschoud.[82] He argues that the portrayal of Probus as an outstanding general and emperor who died too young, preventing a period of peace and prosperity for the empire, is meant to evoke Julian. Probus's successor Carus, religiously neutral and successful in battle, represents Valentinian I, and his wicked son Carinus represents the antipagan Gratian. This allegory is a hopeful one for its intended pagan reactionary audience, Paschoud says, for it opens the possibility that a new Diocletian, a new fierce pagan champion, will soon arise. Thus, Paschoud concludes, the final books of the *Historia Augusta* are "une sorte de conte philosophico-historique qui transmet, peu après 395, à un cercle de lecteurs bien précis une vision alternative, politiquement incorrecte, de l'histoire."[83] This allegory does not hold together. The portrayal of Probus in the *Historia Augusta* is derived from a striking passage from the *KG*: the emperor stated that once he had conquered the world, there would be no need for soldiers.[84] The depiction of Probus as a military genius and the extended utopian speculations all have their origins in this claim. The characters of Carus and Carinus in the *Historia Augusta* are much as they appeared in the *KG*, and the disappearance from the allegory of Jovian and Theodosius on the one hand, and Numerian on the other, makes it hard for a reader to make the connections that Paschoud sees. It is not impossible, however, to imagine that Probus evokes Julian not in a serious and nostalgic way but in a parodic way, remembering the exaggerated praise and overblown hopes for Julian that contemporary propagandists and even Ammianus preserve. This parody of utopian ideals would have had a special resonance after Attalus's short-lived pledge to restore republican government.

Pottier attempts in a lengthy article to interpret the *Two Maximini*, the *Three Gordians*, and the *Maximus and Balbinus* as an extended roman à clef directed against Stilicho as represented by Maximinus Thrax, with his son Maximinus the Younger as Eucherius and Alexander Severus as Honorius.[85] Although the overall argument is often strained or unconvincing, some potential allusions to the later career of Stilicho in the *Maximini* also support a late date for the *Historia Augusta*. The characterization of Maximinus as a bandit or public enemy is striking. He is "latro improbus" (*Max. et Balb.* 17.1), "nefarius latro" (*Max. et Balb.* 17.2), "sceleratus latro" (*Max. et Balb.* 17.6), and "hostis publicus" (*Maximin.* 15.9, 16.5, 18.2, 20.8, 26.2; *Gord.* 11.7, 11.9, 11.10; *Max. et Balb.* 1.4, 2.11). This kind of language is applied elsewhere in the *Historia Augusta* only to usurpers, not legitimate emperors. It is particularly common, however, in late fourth-century and early fifth-century contexts, and Claudian deploys it against the enemies of Stilicho.[86] Perhaps it was seen as poetic justice that the first laws to describe a usurper as *praedo publicus* were directed against Stilicho, in an imperial constitution of 22 November 408 (*Cod. Theod.* 9.42.22), followed by another law in which Stilicho is described as *hostis publicus* (*Cod. Theod.* 7.16.1, 10 December 408). The *HA*-author claims that Alexander Severus was perhaps assassinated by soldiers angry because he planned to abandon the German invasions in the west and turn his attention to the east (*Maximin.* 7.5), a scenario unmentioned by Herodian. It does parallel, however, the charge laid by Olympius against Stilicho, in the ear of Honorius, that Stilicho had abandoned the west to Alaric in order to pursue intrigues in the east and establish Eucherius on the throne (Zos. 5.31.3, 5.32). In addition, Maximinus is described as *semibarbarus*, or half-barbarian, a word that occurs only two other times in extant Latin literature: once in Lactantius (*De mort. pers.* 18.13) and once in Jerome, in a letter of 408 specifically in reference to Stilicho (*Ep.* 123.16.2). The *HA*-author may have found the language in Jerome, or the term may have been prevalent in contemporary polemic against the general.

The effusive praise of Constantine in the *Claudius* was seen as problematic by Mommsen when paired with a Theodosian date. He asked, *cui bono?*[87] In whose interest was the praise of the long-dead house of Constantine? Cameron's Gratianic date is in part offered as an answer to Mommsen's question.[88] Cameron notes that Gratian married a granddaughter of Constantine in 374 (she died in 382/83), marking the last time that the blood of Constantine would have figured in contemporary political discourse.[89] Although there is praise for Constantine in the *Claudius*, there is also criticism of the emperor elsewhere, of a sort that would be highly inappropriate to true panegyric, as Dessau saw.[90] How would a partisan of the house of Constantine feel about the claim that Constantine had been a slave to his eunuchs (*Alex.* 67.1)? The *Historia Augusta* would be a bizarre vehicle for praise (or for the hope of patronage), in any case, from Constantine, or Petronius Probus, or Theodosius, or the family of the Nicomachi, or any other group. No public person would wish to be associated with a work consisting of puns and parodies, and a reader could not be expected to differentiate between ironic and nonironic sections of the work.

As I mentioned at the beginning of this chapter, the *Historia Augusta* alludes to Ammianus's account of the attempted kidnapping of Flavia Maxima Constantia, the granddaughter of Constantine who married Gratian. Ammianus emphasizes how disastrous her capture would have been (29.6.7): "evenisset profecto tunc inexpiabile scelus, numerandum inter probrosas rei Romanae iacturas; paulo enim afuit quin filia caperetur Constanti" ("Surely at that time an irreparable crime would have been committed, to be numbered among the shameful disasters of Roman history, for the daughter of Constantius was very nearly captured"). Birley suggests that the "vivid vignette" would leave "a deep impression on its auditors or readers."[91] It might have been particularly vivid around 409 or 410, when the imperial princess Galla Placidia was in fact captured by Alaric.

Baynes had felt that only a date in the reign of Julian would allow for praise of the hereditary principle and of the house of Constantine, but also for the celebration of merit in the selection of emperors and the rejection of automatic heirs. There is a later date, however, when praise for Constantine and praise for Julian were combined, and when blind obedience to the hereditary principle was rejected.[92] The usurper Flavius Claudius Constantinus, whose name so aggressively links him to earlier dynasties, and who renamed his children Constans and Julian to make the connection even stronger, was raised to the purple in Britain in 407, was briefly recognized by Honorius in 409, and was deposed and murdered in 411. No one need suppose that the *HA*-author was a particular supporter (or opponent) of Constantine III, nor that he sought his patronage or support. But Constantine's attempt to legitimize his rule by his connection to Claudius in the early fourth century would have been of particular interest in the face of another British usurper undertaking the same task of legitimization.[93]

Conclusion

Ammianus provided a particularly important intertext for the author of the *Historia Augusta*. The allusions rely often on specific knowledge of the text of the historian, not just his subject matter. We do not find in these allusions serious commentary on Ammianus and his times but instead playful distortions of the often grim and portentous historian. Even when creating a good emperor, Alexander, from elements of Ammianus's Julian, the author's focus is not so much on the consideration of what makes an emperor good as on the ways in which Ammianus describes a good emperor.

The *HA*-author was not interested in Ammianus as a source of historical information. Ammianus had written perhaps twenty years before the composition of the *Historia Augusta*, about events another twenty years and more in the past. The *HA*-author and his audience saw Ammianus as an antiquarian text, as a model for grand history, in contrast to biography, and as a source of curiosities. His use of Ammianus focuses on trivialities: unusual words, the dietary habits of the emperors, eunuchs, and military medals. The destruction of the innocent Silvanus in Ammianus is invoked in the comical sexual exploits of the usurper Proculus. The *HA*-author reduces Ammianus's account of the massacre at Adrianople—the culmination of his epic history—into bits and pieces of a meaningless fictional letter.

Once the *HA*-author is revealed as fundamentally a commenter on texts, not events, the date of publication of the work is less anchored. The conflict between paganism and Christianity can no longer be seen as a live controversy by the 390s, so there is no compelling reason to follow the traditional dating of the *Historia Augusta* to that period. The *Historia Augusta* does not seem to have engaged deeply with contemporary politics, but certain passages take on particular humor or piquancy when read in the context of events at Rome between 408 and the fall of the city in August 410. Like the frequent allusions to literary texts that populate the *Historia Augusta*, these allusions to contemporary events do not provide a serious or sustained critique but depend on the humor and surprise that come from retrojecting contemporary events into a past context.

# Afterword

The *Historia Augusta* is densely allusive, as is much of the Latin literature of the fourth and fifth centuries. Allusion in the *Historia Augusta*, however, does not serve the traditional purposes of informing and complicating the narrative of the work itself. Instead, the source texts are often the target of the allusions. The solemnity of Ammianus or the radicalism of Jerome are undercut or parodied by fictitious material presented in a biographical frame. The frame itself is then also manipulated and mocked for an audience familiar with biographical and historiographical conventions and debates. The *Historia Augusta* itself offers no consistent arguments or positions on contemporary affairs. It is the starting point for discussion, not the discussion itself.

I argue in chapter 2 that the allusiveness and pretense of the *Historia Augusta* is best understood by situating the work within a scholarly circle of readers and debaters. While this is not a theory that admits of definitive proof, many unusual features of the *Historia Augusta* make more sense if we imagine such a group. For example, an ancient work of literature, even a scholarly work that aimed for more general circulation and popularity, benefited from limiting its allusiveness to well-known authors and texts, but the author of a text meant for internal consumption by a small group would know well the shared literary culture of the group. With the *Historia Augusta*, the notion of "interpretative communities" championed by reader-response critics is taken to its logical endpoint. The background knowledge, and the interpretative strategies, of group members could be known, negotiated, and discussed.

The surprising intertexts of the *Historia Augusta* are more readily explained if we posit a small, scholarly audience. The use of not only the *KG* but also Eutropius and Victor has already been mentioned. Ammianus's dense, rhetorically elaborate history "in the grand style" did not find many readers; the learned grammarian Priscian at Constantinople was one of the few we know. Jerome, I have argued, may be for us primarily a Christian author, but he can also be categorized as a scholarly author with a particular interest in biography. The manipulative play of

Afterword

language and genre that typifies the *Historia Augusta* evokes the world of Aulus Gellius rather than the world of Augustine.

A group with a shared and limited reading list also makes more elaborate allusion possible. The allusions to Ammianus that I have argued for in the *Alexander Severus*, for example, make more sense in a context where listeners ask questions, draw comparisons, and consult the text of Ammianus directly. A reference to an unusual word or concept can trigger a comment, a question, or a consultation: the appearance of Marnas in the *Historia Augusta* and in Jerome might be one example. Some of the recurring themes of the *Historia Augusta*, such as the nature of legitimacy and usurpation, or the nature and purpose of biography itself, are illuminated by comparison with passages in Suetonius and Ammianus, among others.

Many of the author's inventions are likely too specific to a particular time, place, and group for us to understand, but we can easily imagine ways in which the text could provoke discussion and argument. What is the meaning of the many unusual and technical words, and in what other texts are they found? What is anachronistic about the discussions of ancient oracles and cult practices in the Vergilian *sortes* or in the *Aurelian*? What examples can we advance to support the speaker's claim that all of the canonical historians have lied? How is biography to be differentiated from history, or *historiae* from *annales*? How do Ammianus's Julian and Alexander Severus, or Elagabalus and Suetonius's Nero, compare? Where in Ammianus or Jerome do these words, phrases, or themes recur?

The *HA*-author cannot have seriously sought to deceive his audience. The allusions and the pseudo-authenticating devices are frequent and obtrusive, and they evoke a tradition of imposture common in classical literature. The author has frequently chosen to invent when there was no need to do so. For example, the *HA*-author could have offered a life of Elagabalus based on Marius Maximus that would have been the equivalent of a primary life. Instead he wrote a second half of the life that was not only fantasy but was, as we have seen, particularly focused on Suetonian allusion. The *Alexander*, too, could have been based, like the intermediate lives, on Herodian. Instead, it is wholly invention, with its own particular focus, I have argued, on manipulating Ammianus and his Julian. The decision to include full-scale lives of usurpers and Caesars would have been an unnecessary innovation for an author seeking to deceive. If we recognize, instead, that the author positively sought out opportunities for his inventive fictions, it makes sense for him to have favored subjects about whom little was known.

The *Historia Augusta*, one must admit, is in general not stylistically elevated and is sometimes quite poorly written. This points, I believe, to its occasional nature, and its anticipated small audience. Something similar can be seen in the massive corpus of works by Galen, who wrote some books for a broad audience, but many more for very specific circumstances, with specific individuals as the intended audience.¹ Only Galen's fame caused these one-offs to be collected and preserved. This helps explain their pedestrian style. Similarly, the pseudo-Plutarchan *Parallela Minora*, which we have speculated was also meant as a one-time parody or joke for an appreciative audience, is written in an odd, colloquial style. It was preserved only because it was erroneously included in the works of Plutarch by a compiler who presumably considered the thematic rather than the stylistic elements of the work. While a traditional, polished work would undergo several rounds of feedback, from recitation to distribution among friends, before it was ready for copying and "publication," the *Historia Augusta*, not meant to last beyond its initial unveiling, was left with its repetitiveness and awkwardness intact.² What caused it to slip out of the hands of its circle, and to be read and copied as an authentic historical work, cannot be known, but one factor in its survival after that point must have been simply the absence of a Latin work of history or biography that covered the second and third centuries. A similar game played with first-century history as its subject would have had much less chance of survival.

The *Historia Augusta* was the product of a very specific time. The turn of the fifth century was a great era of exegesis and other forms of reflection upon texts. This style of scholarly engagement did not persist, and when the *Historia Augusta* is used as a source in the mid-sixth century, its distinctive allusive fictions have been systematically effaced.

In his Gothic history, written in Latin at Constantinople in 551, Jordanes tells his reader about the parents and national origin of the emperor Maximinus the Thracian (*Get*. 83–88):

> Nam, ut dicit Symmachus in quinto suae historiae libro, Maximinus, inquiens, Caesar mortuo Alexandro ab exercitu effectus est imp., ex infimis parentibus in Thracia natus, a patre Gotho nomine Micca, matre Halana, quae Ababa dicebatur.

> For, as Symmachus says in the fifth book of his history, after Alexander died, Maximinus was made emperor by the army. He was born in Thrace of lowly parents, a Gothic father named Micca and an Alanic mother named Ababa.

There follows a summary of Maximinus's deeds as a soldier and, briefly, emperor.

We have seen this information before—the names Micca and Hababa were identified by Hohl as jokes that the *HA*-author derived from the Greek of Herodian

(*Maximin.* 1.5; Herodian 6.8.1). Further evidence that Jordanes's ultimate source was the *Historia Augusta* lies in the claim that Maximinus's mother was an Alan by ethnicity, although in reality the Alans were not found in the lands north of the empire until they were driven there by the Huns after 370.

The Symmachus cited here should presumably be identified with the statesman and historian Quintus Aurelius Memmius Symmachus, the grandson of the famous Symmachus who beseeched Gratian for the return of the Altar of Victory to the senate house. That he was a historian is clear from the work known as *Anecdoton Holderi*, which describes him as the author of a Roman history in seven books.[3] He was consul in 485, and was executed by Theodoric in 526, charged with treason with his son-in-law Boethius.

In his introduction, Jordanes tells us that the overall structure of his history is based on the *Gothic History* of Cassiodorus, written in the 520s or 530s, which he has supplemented with other Greek and Latin authors. Cassiodorus, the scholar and adviser to the Ostrogothic king Theodoric, died around 585. Opinions differ over whether Jordanes simply transcribed Cassiodorus's use of Symmachus or consulted the text of Symmachus himself. And of course it is impossible to know whether Jordanes or Cassiodorus truncated what he found in Symmachus. Still, it is worth noting what has been left out, by one or more of these authors.

These chapters of Jordanes include almost every detail from the *Two Maximini* 2–4: the future emperor's parents, his physical appearance (over eight feet tall), how he came to the attention of Severus through a variety of competitions against the Romans, and, subsequently, how he served under Caracalla but withdrew from imperial service out of disgust at the behavior of Elagabalus. Only this passage has been overlooked (4.1–3):

> Bibisse autem illum saepe in die vini Capitolinam amphoram constat, comedisse et quadraginta libras carnis, ut autem Cordus dicit, etiam sexaginta. quod satis constat, holeribus semper abstinuit, a frigidis prope semper, nisi cum illi potandi necessitas. udores saepe suos excipiebat et in calices vel in vasculum mittebat, ita ut duos vel tres sextarios sui sudoris ostenderet.

> It is agreed, moreover, that he often drank in a day a Capitoline amphora of wine, and ate forty pounds of meat, or, as Cordus says, even sixty. It seems sufficiently agreed, too, that he always abstained from vegetables, and almost always from cold things, except when he needed to drink. Often, he was collecting his sweat and putting it in cups or a small jar, and in this way he was exhibiting two or three pints of it.

The citation of Cordus is sufficient to make it clear that the *HA*-author is indulging his fancy for invention. The "Capitoline amphora," named for a standard measure preserved on the Capitoline, as the meter is preserved at Sèvres today, held about seven gallons of wine, so it is self-evidently ridiculous that Maximinus could have consumed that much. Hohl sees the adjective *Capitolinam* as a reference to the author "Julius Capitolinus," an authorial signal and joke that the amphora Maximinus supposedly drank was the creation of the author himself.[4] In Suetonius's *Tiberius* 42.2, in an account of the emperor's depravities that I earlier argued was a source for the *Historia Augusta*, we are told that the emperor favored an obscure candidate for the quaestorship because he consumed an entire amphora of wine at a dinner party. The parallel with the obscure barbarian Maximinus, who likewise impressed the emperor with his talents, is striking. And what of Maximinus's copious sweating? In Ammianus's description of the ceremonial entrance of Constantius II to Rome, and again as described in Constantius's obituary, the fact that the emperor never spat or wiped his nose in public is singled out for praise, creating the trope of bodily secretions as a way of evaluating an emperor (Amm. 16.10.10, 21.16.7). Constantius's obituary similarly mentions his abstention from fruit (21.16.7), which parallels the barbarous Maximinus's abstention from vegetables.

Symmachus or his successors have lost the key; they no longer recognize the intertexts needed to interpret the *Historia Augusta* correctly. Moreover, the use of nonbiblical allusions in historiography in general waned in the early medieval period. Although the *HA*-author's close contemporary, Orosius, still relies on his audience's familiarity with classical historiography and its intensive allusiveness, Jordanes, writing in learned circles in Constantinople in the mid-sixth century, can muster no more than a couple of Vergilian flourishes.[5] Gregory of Tours, writing in the second half of the sixth century, offers biblical allusions, but only the most infrequent references to Sallust or Vergil.[6] The so-called long late antiquity, reaching into the early Islamic era and including cultures and states ever further from the Mediterranean, may be a valid conceptual tool if we concentrate on religious, economic, and institutional history.[7] But the *Historia Augusta* is evidence for the discontinuity in literary history between the second and fifth centuries, on the one hand, and the sixth and eighth centuries, on the other.[8] The audience for historiographical prose no longer expected or desired a style that was deeply entwined with classical predecessors.

Isaac Casaubon, in his 1603 edition of the work that he named the *Scriptores Historiae Augustae*, engages the "authors" as normal biographers and does his best to explain away the work's many eccentricities, but he must sometimes admit its fallibility.[9] To the claim that Elagabalus was the first to use silver cookware, for example, including the *authepsa* that we have identified as a Ciceronian allusion, Casaubon, exasperated, states "sine dubio falsa sunt."[10] Without recognizing the allusive purpose of the passage, he corrects the historical claim with a list of many before Elagabalus who had used silver similarly. Edward Gibbon, also, can seem credulous in his engagement with the *Historia Augusta*. He accepts the letters and acclamations as authentic; he believes that Gordian traced his descent from Trajan and the Gracchi; he accepts that the Thirty Tyrants were authentic usurpers and that the tyrant Piso was a descendant of Cicero's son-in-law.[11] He recognizes, however, some of the work's flaws, criticizing, for example, the panegyric account of the reign of Alexander Severus, and noting, in his account of the assassination of Alexander, "I have softened some of the most improbable circumstances of this wretched biographer."[12]

But Gibbon, too, missed the mark. The *HA*-author is not a "wretched biographer," because he is not, really, a biographer. His failure to promote a political or religious agenda is not a flaw, because it was not his goal. The hypothesis that the *Historia Augusta* emerged in a circle of scholars interested in biography is plausible, if unprovable, derived from our knowledge of ancient reading and studying habits. But to imagine the work as a purposeful hoax is unfair to ancient readers. The ancients no doubt fall short of moderns in various ways, but the ability to recognize literary allusions to Cicero and Ammianus is not one of them. If the author had indeed set out seriously to deceive, he could have left modern historians in a very difficult place. A reasonably skillful and knowledgeable author filling in the gaps in his sources with plausible material, rather than making allusions to Cicero and Jerome, could have fooled his readers more often than not. Instead of filling gaps in sources, however, the *HA*-author boldly fabricates an alternative reality built from a range of literary and historiographical texts. We lack many of the details that we need to be full participants in his game, but accident has preserved for us a work that is valuable not only for the historical information it reproduces, however dimly, but also for its record of scholars at play in the early fifth century.

Notes

Introduction

1. On allusion in Ammianus in general, see G. Kelly, *Ammianus Marcellinus: The Allusive Historian* (Cambridge: Cambridge University Press, 2008). For examples of Ammianus's distortions for the sake of allusion, see F. Paschoud, "Se non è vero, è *ben trovato*: Tradition littéraire et vérité historique chez Ammien Marcellin," *Chiron* 20 (1990).

2. R. Syme, *The Historia Augusta: A Call of Clarity* (Bonn: Rudolf Habelt, 1971), 1. Cf. A. Chastagnol, *Histoire Auguste* (Paris: Robert Laffont, 1994), i: "certainement l'ouvrage le plus énigmatique que nous ait légué l'Antiquité"; A. Mehl, *Römische Geschichtsschreibung* (Stuttgart: W. Kolhammer, 2001), 147: "wohl das mysteriöseste Werk der antiken Literatur."

3. The best place to begin is Chastagnol, *Histoire Auguste*, ix–clxxxii; in English, A. Birley, "The Historia Augusta and Pagan Historiography," in *Greek and Roman Historiography in Latin Antiquity*, ed. G. Marasco (Leiden: Brill, 2003); Syme, *Call of Clarity*.

4. Thomson offers the intriguing parallel of the *Panegyrici Latini*: M. Thomson, *Studies in the* Historia Augusta (Brussels: Latomus, 2012), 25–28. Another parallel, perhaps, would be the various authors of the gospels; compilations of the books of the Bible first appear in the fourth century (cf. Euseb. *Vit. Const.* 4.36.2).

5. H. Dessau, "Über Zeit und Persönlichkeit der Scriptores Historiae Augustae," *Hermes* 24 (1889): 379–80.

6. L. Homo, "Les documents de l'Histoire Auguste et leur valeur historique," *Revue Historique* 151 (1926), 152 (1927).

7. E.g., F. Paschoud, *Histoire Auguste V.1: Vies d'Aurélien, Tacite* (Paris: Les Belles Lettres, 1996), 16 n. 9, 103.

8. J. N. Adams, "The Authorship of the HA," *Classical Quarterly* 22 (1972).

9. H. L. Zernial, *Über den Satzschluss in der Historia Augusta* (Berlin: Akademie-Verlag, 1956), 6 n. 1; some statistics are collected by A. W. de Groot, *Der Antike Prosarhythmus* (Groningen: J. B. Wolters, 1921), 111.

10. Chausson has argued not so much that Claudius was the ancestor of Constantine but that he could have been, given the lacunose state of our evidence. But the timing of the announcement is suspicious enough to encourage us to stick with the traditional historical reconstruction. F. Chausson, *Stemmata aurea: Constantin, Justine, Théodose; Revendications généalogiques et idéologie impériale au IVe siècle ap. J.-C.* (Rome: Bretschneider, 2007), 25–95.

11. *XII pan. lat.* 7.2; R. Syme, *Historia Augusta Papers* (Oxford: Clarendon Press, 1983), 66–68.

12. Dessau, "Über Zeit und Persönlichkeit," 344.

13. A. Chastagnol, *Recherches sur l'Histoire Auguste* (Bonn: Rudolf Habelt, 1970), 27–28; Paschoud, *Histoire Auguste V.1*, 63–64; P. Bruggisser, "Le char du préfet: Echos païens et chrétiens d'une polémique dans l'*Histoire Auguste* et chez Quodvultdeus," *HAC* 1991.

14. Dessau, "Über Zeit und Persönlichkeit," 348–59; R. Syme, *Emperors and Biography: Studies in the Historia Augusta* (Oxford: Clarendon Press, 1971), 1–16.

15. Jerome claims that Paula was descended from the Gracchi and Scipiones on her mother's side, from Agamemnon on her father's side; her husband Toxotius traced his descent to Aeneas. R. Syme, *Ammianus and the Historia Augusta* (Oxford: Clarendon Press, 1968), 162–63; Jer. *Ep.* 108.3–4.

16. Dessau, "Über Zeit und Persönlichkeit," 359–60.

17. T. Zawadzki, "Dioecesis Thraciarum, un indice de falsification dans l'Histoire Auguste," *BHAC* 1972/74 (1976): 323–32; Paschoud, *Histoire Auguste V.1*, 87–88.

18. Paschoud, *Histoire Auguste V.1*, 122.

19. Syme, *Ammianus and the Historia Augusta*, 61–62.

20. E.g., Paschoud, *Histoire Auguste V.1*, 79, 80 n. 54, 83, 94, 105; W. Eck, "Zum Konsulat in der *Historia Augusta*," *HAC* 1994: 119; T. D. Barnes, "Regional Prefectures," *BHAC* 1984/85 (1987); Syme, *Ammianus and the Historia Augusta*, 46.

21. E.g., J. Straub, *Studien zur Historia Augusta* (Bern: A. Francke, 1952), 7–39; Syme, *Ammianus and the Historia Augusta*, 112.

22. I return to the question of dating in chapter 4.

23. D. Rohrbacher, "The Sources of the *Historia Augusta* Re-examined," *Histos* 7 (2013); Syme, *Emperors and Biography*, 56; Chastagnol, *Histoire Auguste*, xxxvii–xlvi.

24. Chastagnol, *Histoire Auguste*, xlii–xlv.

25. See especially A. Birley, "The Lacuna in the Historia Augusta," *BHAC* 1972/74 (1976); S. Ratti, *Histoire Auguste IV.2: Vies des deux Valériens et des deux Galliens* (Paris: Les Belles Lettres, 2002), xix–xxviii.

26. Birley, "The Lacuna in the Historia Augusta," 57–58; Ratti, *Histoire Auguste IV.2*, xix–xxviii.

27. Chastagnol, *Histoire Auguste*, xliv–xlv.

28. F. Paschoud, "Raisonnements providentialistes dans l'Histoire Auguste," *BHAC* 1977/78 (1980): 164–65 n. 12.

29. D. den Hengst, *The Prefaces in the Historia Augusta* (Amsterdam: B. R. Grüner, 1981), 70–72.

30. Birley, "The Lacuna in the Historia Augusta."

31. D. den Hengst, review of Ratti, *Histoire Auguste IV.2*, in *Antiquité tardive* 13 (2005); reprinted in D. W. P. Burgersdijk and J. A. van Waarden, eds., *Emperors and Historiography* (Leiden: Brill, 2010), 195–99.

32. Schlumberger makes a strong case that the apparent lacuna at the beginning of the *HA* is also a contrivance of the author: J. Schlumberger, "Die Epitome de Caesaribus und die Historia Augusta," *BHAC* 1972/74 (1976).

33. Rohrbacher, "The Sources of the *Historia Augusta*," readily available online; see also T. D. Barnes, *The Sources of the* Historia Augusta (Brussels: Latomus, 1978), with T. D. Barnes, "The Sources of the Historia Augusta (1967-1992)," *HAC* 1995.

34. Bibliography in D. Rohrbacher, "Enmann's *Kaisergeschichte* from Augustus to Domitian," *Latomus* 68 (2009).

35. Victor: Dessau, "Über Zeit und Persönlichkeit," 363-67; E. Hohl, "Die Historia Augusta und die Caesares des Aurelius Victor," *Historia* 4 (1955); A. Chastagnol, "Zosime II, 38 et l'Histoire Auguste," *BHAC* 1964/65 (1966): 54-57; A. Chastagnol, "L'utilisation des 'Caesares' d'Aurelius Victor dans l'Histoire Auguste," *BHAC* 1966/67 (1968); A. Chastagnol, "Emprunts de l'Histoire Auguste aux Caesares d'Aurelius Victor," *Revue de Philologie* 41 (1967); den Hengst, *The Prefaces*, 111-13. Eutropius: esp. T. Damsholt, "Zur Benutzung von dem *Breviarium* des Eutrop in der *Historia Augusta*," *Classica et Mediaevalia* 25 (1964); also Dessau, "Über Zeit und Persönlichkeit," 368-70; Chastagnol, *Histoire Auguste*, lxviii-lxix.

36. A. Birley, "Marius Maximus, the Consular Biographer," *Aufstieg und Niedergang der römischen Welt* 2.34.3 (1997).

37. Chastagnol, *Histoire Auguste*, xli; F. Kolb, "Herodian in der Historia Augusta," *BHAC* 1972/74 (1976): 144-46.

38. Kolb, "Herodian in der Historia Augusta," 146-52.

39. F. Kolb, *Literarische Beziehungen zwischen Cassius Dio, Herodian und der Historia Augusta* (Bonn: Rudolf Habelt, 1972); Kolb, "Herodian in der Historia Augusta"; F. Kolb, "Cassius Dio, Herodian und die Quellen der Historia Augusta," *HAC* 1995.

40. Barnes, *The Sources of the* Historia Augusta, 108-11; F. Paschoud, "L'*Histoire Auguste* et Dexippe," *HAC* 1991.

41. Syme, *Emperors and Biographers*, 253 n. 3; Paschoud, "L'Histoire Auguste et Dexippe."

42. Paschoud, "L'Histoire Auguste et Dexippe," 240. See also J. Straub, "Calpurnia univiria," *BHAC* 1966/67 (1968): 102-4.

43. Rohrbacher, "The Sources of the *Historia Augusta*," 166-72. Eunapius: E. Hohl, "Vopiscus und die Biographie des Kaisers Tacitus," *Klio* 11 (1911): 189-91. Nicomachus Flavianus: W. Hartke, *Geschichte und Politik im spätantiken Rom* (Leipzig: Dieterich, 1940), 28-37; B. Bleckmann, *Die Reichskrise des III. Jahrhunderts in der spätantiken und byzantinischen Geschichtsschreibung* (Munich: Tuduv, 1992); F. Paschoud, *Histoire Auguste V.2: Vies de Probus, Firmus, Saturnin, Proculus et Bonose, Carus, Numérien et Carin* (Paris: Les Belles Lettres, 2002), xii-xix. Against Nicomachus Flavianus: Alan Cameron, *The Last Pagans of Rome* (Oxford: Oxford University Press, 2011), 627-90.

Chapter 1. Allusion in the *Historia Augusta*

1. On allusion in Latin poetry, I have found particularly stimulating the following: R. Thomas, "Virgil's *Georgics* and the Art of Reference," *Harvard Studies in Classical Philology* 90 (1986); J. Farrell, *Vergil's Georgics and the Traditions of Ancient Epic: The Art of Allusion in Literary Poetry* (New York: Oxford University Press, 1991); J. M. Pucci, *The Full-Knowing Reader* (New Haven: Yale University Press, 1998); S. Hinds, *Allusion and Intertext:*

Dynamics of Appropriation in Roman Poetry (Cambridge: Cambridge University Press, 1998); L. Edmunds, *Intertextuality and the Reading of Roman Poetry* (Baltimore: Johns Hopkins University Press, 2001).

2. E.g., D. S. Levene, *Livy on the Hannibalic War* (Oxford: Oxford University Press, 2010); T. A. Joseph, *Tacitus the Epic Successor: Virgil, Lucan, and the Narrative of Civil War in the Histories* (Leiden: Brill, 2012); J. F. Miller and A. J. Woodman, eds., *Latin Historiography and Poetry in the Early Empire: Generic Interactions* (Leiden: Brill, 2010); I. Marchesi, *The Art of Pliny's Letters: A Poetics of Allusion in the Private Correspondence* (Cambridge: Cambridge University Press, 2008); E. Finkelpearl, *Metamorphosis of Language in Apuleius: A Study of Allusion in the Novel* (Ann Arbor: University of Michigan Press, 1998).

3. Cic. *De or.* 2.350–60; Quint. *Inst.* 11; *Rhet. Her.* 3; J. P. Small, *Wax Tablets of the Mind: Cognitive Studies of Memory and Literacy in Classical Antiquity* (London: Routledge, 1997).

4. See, for example, R. Starr, "The Circulation of Literary Texts in the Roman World," *Classical Quarterly* 37 (1987); W. A. Johnson, *Readers and Reading Culture in the High Roman Empire* (Oxford: Oxford University Press, 2010), esp. 43–62; E. Valette-Cagnac, *La lecture à Rome: Rites et pratiques* (Paris: Éditions Belin, 1997), 111–69.

5. W. V. Harris, "Why Did the Codex Supplant the Book-Roll?," in *Renaissance Society and Culture: Essays in Honor of Eugene F. Rice, Jr.*, ed. J. Monfasani and R. G. Musto (New York: Italica, 1991).

6. E.g., W. Görler, "Vergilzitate in Ausonius' Mosella," *Hermes* 97 (1969); C. Ware, *Claudian and the Roman Epic Tradition* (Cambridge: Cambridge University Press, 2012); U. Keudel, *Poetische Vorläufer und Vorbilder in Claudians De Consulatu Stilichonis: Imitationskommentar* (Göttingen: Vandenhoeck & Ruprecht, 1970); I. Gualandri, *Aspetti della tecnica compositiva in Claudiano* (Milan: Istituto Editoriale Cisalpino, 1968).

7. M. Roberts, *The Jeweled Style: Poetry and Poetics in Late Antiquity* (Ithaca: Cornell University Press, 1989), 57.

8. Ware, *Claudian*, 10.

9. S. McGill, *Virgil Recomposed: The Mythological and Secular Centos in Antiquity* (New York: Oxford University Press, 2005).

10. See R. L. Wilken, "The Homeric Cento in Irenaeus, 'Adversus Haereses' I, 9, 4," *Vigiliae Christianae* 21 (1967).

11. "hoc tum die uno et addita lucubratione properatum modo inter liturarios meos cum repperissem" ("I found this book, composed hastily in a single day and some candlelight, among my drafts"). All translations are mine unless otherwise noted.

12. G. Kelly, *Ammianus Marcellinus*.

13. C. Salemme, *Similitudini nella storia: Un capitolo su Ammiano Marcellino* (Naples: Loffredo, 1989), 45–46. Translation and emphasis in the following passage is G. Kelly's: *Ammianus Marcellinus*, 207–9.

14. G. Kelly, *Ammianus Marcellinus*, 209.

15. Cf. Joseph Farrell on Vergil's use of allusion, in an Internet posting quoted by Edmunds, *Intertextuality*, 153–54: "My proposal is that in the presence of a great many

phenomena (I think mainly of intertextual ones, such as allusions to Homer or self-quotations), we are encouraged to look for more of the same and in fact rewarded for doing so. That is to say, the more obvious, and obviously intended aspects of Vergil's allusive program encourage the reader to look further for less obvious, less obviously intended examples as well. . . . By writing in this way, I would suggest, Vergil sets in motion a process whereby he actively enlists the reader's cooperation in creating, or better, discovering intertextual relationships between the texts in question."

16. F. Paschoud, "Quelques mots rares comme éventuels témoins du niveau de style de l'*Histoire Auguste* et des lectures de son auteur," in *Historia testis: Mélanges d'épigraphie, d'histoire ancienne et de philologie offerts à Tadeusz Zawadzki*, ed. Marcel Piérart and Olivier Curty (Fribourg: Éditions Universitaires, 1989).

17. McGill, *Virgil Recomposed*, 27. Cf. Thomas, "Virgil's *Georgics*," 174: "Methodologically there is one chief danger in a study such as this, that is, the problem of determining when a reference is really a reference, and when it is merely an accidental confluence, inevitable between poets dealing with a shared or related language. In part the resolution of this problem lies in that most perilous quality of the mind, judgment, but at the same time two absolute criteria will be applied in what follows: the model must be one with whom the poet is demonstrably familiar, and there must be a reason of some sort for the reference—that is, it much be susceptible of interpretation, or meaningful."

18. The challenges in doing so are clear: T. D. Barnes, "Some Persons in the Historia Augusta," *Phoenix* 26 (1972).

19. Dessau, "Über Zeit und Persönlichkeit," 348–57; A. von Domaszewski, *Die Personnennamen bei den Scriptores historiae Augustae* (Heidelberg: Carl Winters Universitätbuchhandlung, 1918).

20. H. Peter, "Die römischen sogenannten Dreissig Tyrannen," *Abhandlungen der Königlich-sächsischen Gesellschaft der Wissenschaften, philologisch-historische Klasse* 27 (1909): 181.

21. T. Honoré, "Scriptor Historiae Augustae," *Journal of Roman Studies* 77 (1987): 172 n. 274.

22. Von Domaszewski, *Die Personnennamen*, 11.

23. Den Hengst, *The Prefaces*, 68–69, 106–7.

24. A. R. Birley, "'Trebellius Pollio' and 'Flavius Vopiscus Syracusius,'" HAC 2002.

25. E. Hohl, "Vopiscus und Pollio," *Klio* 12 (1912).

26. Paschoud, *Histoire Auguste V.1*, xxvi.

27. Von Domaszewski, *Die Personnennamen*, 11.

28. Birley, "'Trebellius Pollio.'"

29. A. Chastagnol, "Le Capitole dans l'Histoire Auguste," *BHAC* 1986/89 (1991).

30. Von Domaszewski, *Die Personnennamen*, 13.

31. Von Domaszewski, *Die Personnennamen*, 13.

32. B. Baldwin, "The *Vita Avidii*," *Klio* 58 (1976).

33. Perhaps inspired by Pedanius Fuscus, mentioned in *Hadr.* 23.2.

34. Chastagnol, *Histoire Auguste*, civ.

35. Syme, *Historia Augusta Papers*, 98–108.

36. There are four entries in *PIR³*: C. Suetonius Paulinus, cos. 66; the biographer; the biographer's father; and Suetonius Optatianus from the *Historia Augusta*.

37. T. D. Barnes, "Publilius Optatianus Porfyrius," *American Journal of Philology* 96 (1975).

38. W. Levitan, "Dancing at the End of the Rope: Optatian Porfyry and the Field of Roman Verse," *Transactions of the American Philological Association* 115 (1985): 266.

39. F. Paschoud, "Noms camouflés d'historiens du 4e siècles dans l'*Histoire Auguste*," *Historia* 44 (1995).

40. S. H. Rutledge, *Imperial Inquisitions: Prosecutors and Informants from Nero to Domitian* (London: Routledge, 2001), 253–54.

41. Translations of this description with phrases like "esclave des honneurs," or "handmaiden of honours," are typical but seem to me senseless.

42. C. F. Konrad, "Cotta off Mellaria and the Identities of Fufidius," *Classical Philology* 84 (1989): 128–29.

43. B. Maire, *Gargilius Martialis: Les remèdes tirés des légumes et des fruits* (Paris: Les Belles Lettres, 2002).

44. On the other hand, the *HA*-author may simply have unearthed the name of Gargilius Martialis in a later scholastic context—he is cited in Servius's commentary on the *Georgics*, for example (at 4.148)—and both references may be fraudulent. Paschoud, *Histoire Auguste V.2*, 59.

45. B. Shaw, "Sabinus the Muleteer," *Classical Quarterly* 57 (2007).

46. See Servius, Philargyrius, and Schol. Bern. on *Ecl.* 4; R. Syme, "Pollio, Saloninus and Salonae," *Classical Quarterly* 31 (1937).

47. *Alex.* 14.6, 48.7, 64.5; *Aur.* 12.4.

48. Paschoud, *Histoire Auguste V.1*, 93; von Domaszewski, *Die Personnennamen*, 21–22.

49. I return to this subject in chapter 3.

50. Syme, *Ammianus and the Historia Augusta*, 167.

51. F. Graebner, "Eine Zosimosquelle," *Byzantinische Zeitschrift* 14 (1905): 126–27, thought this was a mistake; E. Hohl, "Die 'gotische Abkunft' des Kaisers Maximinus Thrax," *Klio* 34 (1942), recognized that it was a joke.

52. Paschoud, *Histoire Auguste V.1*, 138–39.

53. Syme, *Emperors and Biography*, 5.

54. F. Dunand, "Les *Deliaca* de l'*Histoire Auguste*," *Bulletin de la Faculté des Lettres de Strasbourg* 47 (1968).

55. Dunand, "Les *Deliaca*."

56. H. Dessau, "Über die S.H.A.," *Hermes* 27 (1892): 589.

57. L. Calpurnius Piso Caesoninus, cos. 58, was the father of the Calpurnia who married Julius Caesar. On allusion to the *In Pisonem*, see Paschoud on *Aur.* 13.1 and *Tac.* 13.4, *Histoire Auguste V.1*, 95, 298.

58. Paschoud, *Histoire Auguste V.2*, 308 n. 7.

59. G. R. Throop, "Ancient Literary Detractors of Cicero," *Washington University Studies* 1 (1913/14).

60. Den Hengst, *The Prefaces*, 90.

61. E. Courtney, *The Fragmentary Latin Poets* (Oxford: Clarendon Press, 1993), 26 (*fr.* 30).

62. Cf. *Av. Cass.* 5.6, a line of Ennius probably derived from Cic. *Rep.* 5.2.

63. Paschoud, *Histoire Auguste V.2*, 214–15.

64. E. Gibbon, *The Decline and Fall of the Roman Empire*, ed. J. B. Bury (London: Methuen & Co., 1909), 1.333.

65. See M. S. Dowling, *Clemency and Cruelty in the Roman World* (Ann Arbor: University of Michigan Press, 2006), esp. 78–89.

66. Syme, *Emperors and Biography*, 251–53. No other extant source claims that the republican Marius was an ironworker.

67. J. Lafaurie, "L'empire Gaulois: Apport de la numismatique," *Aufstieg und Niedergang der römischen Welt* 2.2 (1975): 927–29.

68. F. Paschoud, *Histoire Auguste IV.3: Vies des trente tyrans et de Claude* (Paris: Les Belles Lettres, 2011), 79–80.

69. Syme, *Historia Augusta Papers*, 41–42.

70. H. W. Bird, "Suetonian Influence in the Later Lives of the Historia Augusta," *Hermes* 99 (1971): 132–33; Paschoud, *Histoire Auguste V.2*, 347, 366, 384.

71. Compare what the author says about Gordian I (*Gord.* 3.2). As a youth, the future emperor is said to have written poems with the same titles as the poems written by Cicero. In the list that follows (*Marius*, *Aratus*, *Alcyonae*, *Uxorius*, and *Nilus*), the first three refer to actual works of Cicero and the last two are probably invented.

72. A. Chastagnol, "Trois études sur la Vita Cari," *BHAC* 1972/74 (1976): 82.

73. *PIR* A 1453.

74. On iambic didactic: Alan Cameron, "Poetry and Literary Culture," in *Approaching Late Antiquity: The Transformation from Early to Late Empire*, ed. S. Swain and M. Edwards (Oxford: Oxford University Press, 2004), 333–39.

75. H. Dessau, review of Hasebroek, *Die Fälschung der Vita Nigri und Vita Albini in den Scriptores Historiae Augustae*, 391; D. den Hengst, "'The Plato of Poets': Vergil in the Historia Augusta," in Romane memento: *Vergil in the Fourth Century*, ed. R. Rees (London: Duckworth, 2004), 168.

76. P. P. Courcelle, *Les Confessions de Saint Augustin dans la tradition littéraire: Antécédents et postérité* (Paris: Études Augustiniennes, 1963), 133–63; Y. de Kisch, "Les Sortes Vergilianae dans l'Histoire Auguste," *Mélanges d'archéologie et d'histoire* 82 (1970); N. Horsfall, "Apuleius, Apollonius of Tyana, Bibliomancy: Some Neglected Dating Criteria," *HAC* 1995: 175–78; P. van der Horst, "*Sortes*: Sacred Books as Instant Oracles in Late Antiquity," in *The Use of Sacred Books in the Ancient World*, ed. L. V. Rutgers et al. (Leuven: Peeters, 1998).

77. W. E. Klingshirn, "Defining the *Sortes Sanctorum*: Gibbon, Du Cange, and Early Christian Lot Divination," *Journal of Early Christian Studies* 10 (2002).
78. Van der Horst, "*Sortes*," 164–68.
79. Klingshirn, "Defining the *Sortes*," 124–26.
80. Horsfall's paraphrase ("Apuleius," 176), "In 400, he tells Januarius it is better—just—to use the Gospels rather than pagan literature for such ends," is incorrect and leaves the impression that the pagan practice was widespread. In fact, Augustine tells Januarius that using the Bible to predict the future is preferable to "the consultation of demons" ("ad daemonia consulenda")—that is, going to pagan oracular sites.
81. De Kisch, "Les *Sortes*."
82. Pucci, *The Full-Knowing Reader*, 43.

Chapter 2. The *Historia Augusta* and the Ancient Reader

1. See, for example, F. Leo, *Die griechisch-römische Biographie nach ihrer literarischen Form* (Leipzig: Teubner, 1901), 234–53; B. McGing and J. Mossman, "Introduction," in *The Limits of Ancient Biography*, ed. B. McGing and J. Mossman (Swansea: Classical Press of Wales, 2006), and the other chapters in that collection; J. Geiger, *Cornelius Nepos and Ancient Political Biography* (Stuttgart: Franz Steiner, 1985), 9–29; C. Pelling, "Biographical History? Cassius Dio on the Early Principate," in *Portraits: Biographical Representation in the Greek and Latin Literature of the Roman Empire*, ed. M. J. Edwards and S. Swain (Oxford: Clarendon Press, 1997); J. Marincola, "Genre, Convention, and Innovation in Greco-Roman Historiography," in *The Limits of Historiography: Genre and Narrative in Ancient Historical Texts*, ed. C. S. Kraus (Leiden: Brill, 1999), esp. 318–20.

2. T. Duff, *Plutarch's Lives: Exploring Virtue and Vice* (Oxford: Clarendon Press, 1999), 14–22; see also C. Cooper, "'The Appearance of History': Making Some Sense of Plutarch," in *Daimonopylai: Essays in Classics and the Classical Tradition Presented to Edmund G. Berry*, ed. R. B. Egan and M. Joyal (Winnipeg: University of Manitoba Centre for Hellenic Civilization, 2004).

3. R. G. Lewis, "Suetonius' 'Caesares' and Their Literary Antecedents," *Aufstieg und Niedergang der römischen Welt* 2.33.5 (1991).

4. D. L. Selden, "Genre of Genre," in *The Search for the Ancient Novel*, ed. J. Tatum (Baltimore: Johns Hopkins University Press, 1994), esp. 39–40; R. K. Hack, "The Doctrine of Literary Forms," *Harvard Studies in Classical Philology* 27 (1916). Plato, in *Leges* 700–701, describes the dangers to the state of mixing genres; Quintilian, in *Inst.* 10.2.22, claims that "sua cuique proposito lex, suus decor est: nec comoedia in coturnos adsurgit, nec contra tragoedia socco ingreditur" ("Each branch of literature has its own laws and its own appropriate character. Comedy does not seek to increase its height by the buskin and tragedy does not wear the slipper of comedy"). Cf. Hor. *Ars P.* 73–118.

5. R. A. Burridge, *What Are the Gospels? A Comparison with Graeco-Roman Biography* (Cambridge: Cambridge University Press, 1992), 28.

6. See especially C. K. Rothschild, "Irony and Truth: The Value of *De Historia Conscribenda* for Understanding Hellenistic and Early Roman Period Historiographical Method," in *Die Apostelgeschichte im Kontext antiker und frühchristlicher Historiographie*, ed. J. Frey et al. (Berlin: Walter de Gruyter, 2009).

7. See D. A. Russell, "*De Imitatione*," in *Creative Imitation and Latin Literature*, ed. D. West and T. Woodman (Cambridge: Cambridge University Press, 1979).

8. T. G. Rosenmeyer, "Ancient Literary Genres: A Mirage?," *Yearbook of Comparative and General Literature* 34 (1985); M. J. Edwards, "Gospel and Genre: Some Reservations," in McGing and Mossman, *The Limits*.

9. S. Freyne, "Mark's Gospel and Ancient Biography," in McGing and Mossman, *The Limits*, 72; Burridge, *What Are the Gospels?*, 38. See also B. Gentili and G. Cerri, *History and Biography in Ancient Thought* (Amsterdam: J. C. Gieben, 1988).

10. C. Fry, "*Suetonianus quidam*: L'auteur de l'*Histoire Auguste* en utilisateur du style suétonien," *HAC* 2010; E. Birley, "'Tales of My Grandfather,'" *BHAC* 1975/76 (1978).

11. Dio 53.19; J. Marincola, *Authority and Tradition in Ancient Historiography* (Cambridge: Cambridge University Press, 1997), 86–95.

12. Discussions with bibliography in M. Kleijwegt, "Caligula's 'Triumph' at Baiae," *Mnemosyne* 47 (1994); S. J. V. Malloch, "Gaius' Bridge at Baiae and Alexander-*Imitatio*," *Classical Quarterly* 51 (2001). The event is also discussed by Dio (59.16.11–17), Josephus (*AJ* 19.6), and Seneca (*De Brevitate Vitae* 18.5–6).

13. "affirmasset non magis Gaium imperaturum quam per Baianum sinum equis discursurum."

14. Malloch, "Gaius' Bridge," 206–7.

15. A. Chastagnol, "Quatre études sur la Vita Cari," *BHAC* 1977/78 (1980): 50–59; A. Rösger, "Vopiscus und das Authentizitätsproblem (Car. 4, 1–5, 3)," *BHAC* 1986/89 (1991); Paschoud, *Histoire Auguste V*.2, 337–43.

16. J. Gascou, *Suétone historien* (Paris: de Boccard, 1984), 544.

17. Why this list of places: Illyricum, Carthage, Milan, Aquileia? It is tempting to follow Chastagnol in noting first that Onesimus has been taken from Jerome's *Ep.* 3 to Rufinus (see chapter 3), and that Jerome was born in Illyricum, Rufinus at Aquileia; and, second, that the two remaining places are closely associated with other important radical Christians: Augustine from Africa and Ambrose, bishop of Milan. Chastagnol, "Quatre études," 50–59.

18. For the phrase, see Chastagnol, "Quatre études," 60–65.

19. V. Neri, "La caratterizzazione fisica degli imperatori nell' *Historia Augusta*," *HAC* 1998; D. Rohrbacher, "Physiognomics in Roman Imperial Biography," *Classical Antiquity* 29 (2010).

20. *Iul.* 45.1, *Aug.* 79.1–3, *Tib.* 68.1–3, *Calig.* 3.1, 50.1, *Claud.* 30, *Nero* 51, *Galb.* 3.3, 21, *Otho* 12.1, *Vit.* 17.2, *Vesp.* 20, *Tit.* 3.1, *Dom.* 18.

21. T. D. Barnes, "Ultimus Antoninorum," *BHAC* 1970 (1972).

22. And cf. 24.3, Vitellius; 31.5, Nero; 33.1, Tiberius, Caligula, and Nero; 34.1, Nero, Vitellius, and Caligula.

23. The columns below show the parallels:

Vitellius	Elagabalus
pike liver	mullet viscera
pheasant brain	pheasant head
peacock brain	peacock head
flamingo tongue	flamingo brain
lamprey milt	partridge eggs
	thrush brain

24. R. Turcan, *Histoire Auguste III.1: Vies de Macrin, Diaduménien, Héliogabale* (Paris: Les Belles Lettres, 1993), 199.

25. G. Mader notes the "reasonable suspicion that the rogue scholar was humorously 'improving' on his source." "History as Carnival, or Method and Madness in the *Vita Heliogabali*," *Classical Antiquity* 24 (2005): 147–48.

26. Bird, "Suetonian Influence in the Later Lives of the Historia Augusta."

27. A. Birley, "Marius Maximus, the Consular Biographer."

28. On the importance of style for historiography, see, for example, Diod. Sic. 20.2.1; Livy, *pref.* 2; Sall. *Cat.* 3.2; Livy 6.20.8; Plin., *Ep.* 7.4.3: T. P. Wiseman, *Clio's Cosmetics: Three Studies in Greco-Roman Literature* (Totowa, NJ: Rowman and Littlefield, 1979), 29. Cf., for examples of the absence of eloquence, Solin, *pref.* 2; Palladius 1.1.18; Pompon. 1.1; and T. Janson, *Latin Prose Prefaces: Studies in Literary Conventions* (Stockholm: Almqvist & Wiksell, 1964), 124–41.

29. Cf. *Pesc. Nig.* 8.6, 12.6; *Macr.* 11.4, 14.2; *Diad.* 7.3; *Alex.* 14.4, 38.6; *Maximin.* 9.4; F. Clover, "The Historia Augusta and the Latin Anthology," *BHAC* 1986/89 (1991).

30. This feature of the *Historia Augusta* alone makes it implausible that the author of the work is a poet, even an undistinguished one, as Thomson has argued: M. Thomson, "*Logodaedalia*: Ausonius and the *Historia Augusta*," in *Studies in Latin Literature and Roman History XIV*, ed. C. Deroux (Brussels: Latomus, 2008).

31. T. J. Luce, "Ancient Views on the Causes of Bias in Historical Writing," *Classical Philology* 84 (1989).

32. G. Kelly, "The Sphragis and Closure of the *Res Gestae*," in *Ammianus after Julian: The Reign of Valentinian and Valens in Books 26–31 of the* Res Gestae, ed. J. Den Boeft, J. W. Drijvers, and Daniel den Hengst (Leiden: Brill, 2007). Kelly shows that Ammianus is likely familiar with the similar language at the end of Eutropius ("quae nunc non tam praetermittimus, quam ad maiorem scribendi diligentiam reservamus," 10.18). Both passages are parodied at the end of the *Quad. Tyr.* (15.10): "nam Diocletianus et qui sequuntur stilo maiore dicendi sunt" ("for Diocletian and those who came after him must be described in a grander style").

33. Hor. *Epist.* 1.3.19; Jer., *Prologus in Didymi libro de Spiritu sancto*, with N. Adkin, "Ambrose and Jerome: The Opening Shot," *Mnemosyne* 46 (1993).

34. Marincola, *Authority and Tradition*, 53.

35. Marincola, *Authority and Tradition*, 91–92.

36. C. W. Fornara, "The Prefaces of Ammianus Marcellinus," in *Cabinet of the Muses: Essays on Classical and Comparative Literature in Honor of Thomas G. Rosenmeyer*, ed. M. Griffith and D. J. Mastronarde (Atlanta: Scholars Press, 1990).

37. G. Avenarius, *Lukians Schrift zur Geschichtsschreibung* (Meisenheim am Glan: Anton Hain, 1954), 127–30; B. Mouchová, *Untersuchungen über die Scriptores Historiae Augustae* (Prague: Univerzita Karlova, 1975), 12–18; den Hengst, *The Prefaces*, 44–46.

38. Chastagnol, *Histoire Auguste*, cix–cx.

39. In general, R. Turcan, "Les monuments figurés dans l'*Histoire Auguste*," *HAC* 1991.

40. T. P. Wiseman, *Historiography and Imagination* (Exeter: University of Exeter Press, 1994), 37–48; Marincola, *Authority and Tradition*, 101–3.

41. G. Kelly, *Ammianus Marcellinus*, 225–30.

42. Den Hengst, *The Prefaces*, 104, citing Symm. *Ep.* 4.34.4; Claud. *De Bello Gothico* 231–32.

43. Paschoud, *Histoire Auguste V.1*, 66.

44. Marincola, *Authority and Tradition*, 107–12; Diod. Sic. 2.32.4.

45. Johnson, *Readers*, 131–36.

46. J. Burian, "*Fides historica* als methodologischer Grundsatz der *Historia Augusta*," *Klio* 59 (1977).

47. Burian, "*Fides historica*," 297.

48. While scholars have noted the parallels between the *Historia Augusta* and some of these works, few conclusions have been offered. See especially F. Paschoud, "*Mendacii splendor*: Formes d'entrée en matière et protestations de véridicité dans la littérature de fiction," *Latomus* 54 (1995); Syme, *Historia Augusta Papers*, 1–11.

49. See in particular J. R. Morgan, "Fiction and History: Historiography and the Novel," in *A Companion to Greek and Roman Historiography*, ed. J. Marincola (Malden, MA: Blackwell, 2007); W. Hansen, "Strategies of Authentication," in *The Ancient Novel and Beyond*, ed. S. Panayotakis, M. Zimmerman, and W. H. Keulen (Leiden: Brill, 2003); J. R. Morgan, "Make-Believe and Make Believe: The Fictionality of the Greek Novels," in *Lies and Fiction in the Ancient World*, ed. C. Gill and T. P. Wiseman (Exeter: University of Exeter Press, 1993).

50. R. D. Luginbill, "Chariton's Use of Thucydides' *History* in Introducing the Egyptian Revolt: *Chaireas and Callirhoe* 6.8," *Mnemosyne* 53 (2000): 1.

51. J. Alvares, "Chariton's Erotic History," *American Journal of Philology* 118 (1997).

52. R. Hunter, "History and Historicity in the Romance of Chariton," *Aufstieg und Niedergang der römischen Welt* 2.34.2 (1993). Cf. W. Bartsch, "Der Charitonroman und die Historiographie" (Diss., Leipzig, 1934); T. Hägg, "*Callirhoe* and *Parthenope*: The Beginnings of the Historical Novel," *Classical Antiquity* 6 (1987); I. Ramelli, "Caritone e la storiografia greca: Il *Romanzo di Calliroe* come romanzo storico antico," *Acme* 53 (2000); S. D. Smith, *Greek Identity and the Athenian Past in Chariton: The Romance of Empire* (Groningen: Barkhuis, 2007), esp. 153–98.

53. See L. Kim, *Homer between History and Fiction in Imperial Greek Literature* (Cambridge: Cambridge University Press, 2010), 140–74; A. Bartley, "The Implications of the

Reception of Thucydides within Lucian's 'Vera Historia,'" *Hermes* 131 (2003); A. Georgiadou and D. H. J. Larmour, *Lucian's Science Fiction Novel*, True Histories: *Interpretation and Commentary* (Leiden: Brill, 1998); A. Camerotto, *Le metamorfosi della parola: Studi sulla parodia in Luciano di Samosata* (Pisa: Instituti Editoriali e Poligrafici Internazionali, 1998); E. Fuchs, *Pseudologia: Formen und Funktionen fiktionaler Trugrede in der griechischen Literatur der Antike* (Heidelberg: Universitätsverlag C. Winter, 1993), 189–236.

54. K. Ni-Mheallaigh, "Pseudo-Documentarism and the Limits of Ancient Fiction," *American Journal of Philology* 129 (2008): 404.

55. S. Merkle, "The Truth and Nothing but the Truth: Dictys and Dares," in *The Novel in the Ancient World*, ed. G. Schmeling (Leiden: Brill, 1996), 566.

56. Ni-Mheallaigh, "Pseudo-Documentarism."

57. S. Stephens, "Fragments of Lost Novels," in Schmeling, *The Novel in the Ancient World*, 674–80; J. Romm, "Novels beyond Thule: Antonius Diogenes, Rabelais, Cervantes," in Tatum, *The Search for the Ancient Novel*. The mythographer Acusilaos of Argos claimed to derive his knowledge from bronze tablets that his father dug up (*Suda* A 942 Adler).

58. Meyer was the first to offer a detailed demonstration of Damis's fictionality: E. Meyer, "Apollonios von Tyana und die Biographie des Philostratos," *Hermes* 52 (1917). Bowie powerfully restated and expanded the case: E. L. Bowie, "Apollonius of Tyana: Tradition and Reality," *Aufstieg und Niedergang der römischen Welt* 2.16.2 (1978), supported by M. Dzielska, *Apollonius of Tyana in Legend and History* (Rome: Bretschneider, 1986); J. A. Francis, "Truthful Fiction: New Questions to Old Answers on Philostratus' *Life of Apollonius*," *American Journal of Philology* 119 (1998). Arguments in favor of the actual existence of Damis are strained: F. Grosso, "La 'Vita di Apollonio di Tiana' come fonte storica," *Acme* 7 (1954); S. Jackson, "Apollonius and the Emperors," *Hermathena* 137 (1984); G. Anderson, *Philostratus: Biography and Belles Lettres in the Third Century A.D.* (London: Croom Helm, 1986). Against Anderson in particular, see M. J. Edwards, "Damis the Epicurean," *Classical Quarterly* 41 (1991).

59. S. Merkle, "Telling the Truth of the Trojan War: The Eyewitness Account of Dictys of Crete," in Tatum, *The Search for the Ancient Novel*.

60. Francis offers thoughts on what fictional truth means for the *Historia Augusta* in "Truthful Fiction."

61. A. Mehl, *Römische Geschichtsschreibung* (Stuttgart: W. Kolhammer, 2001), 147. Put somewhat differently by Dessau, "Über die S.H.A.," 605: "Ich muss es ablehnen, in Allem und Jedem, was unser Autor sich erlaubt hat, eine *ratio* finden zu wollen; er wird manches ohne die Spur einer solchen gethan haben; dafür war es eben ein obscurer Fälscher."

62. T. Birt, *Das antike Buchwesen in seinem Verhältniss zur Literatur* (Berlin: W. Hertz, 1882), 342–70.

63. B. A. van Groningen, "ΕΚΔΟΣΙΣ," *Mnemosyne* 16 (1963); Starr, "The Circulation of Literary Texts in the Roman World"; J. W. Iddeng, "*Publica aut Peri!* The Releasing and Distribution of Roman Books," *Symbolae Osloenses* 81 (2006); P. White, "Bookshops in the Literary Culture of Rome," in *Ancient Literacies: The Culture of Reading in Greece and Rome*, ed. W. A. Johnson and H. N. Parker (Oxford: Oxford University Press, 2009).

64. As expressed, for example, in J. Straub, "Senaculum, id est mulierum senatus," *BHAC* 1964/65 (1966): 238-39.

65. N. Baynes, *The Historia Augusta: Its Date and Purpose* (Oxford: Clarendon Press, 1926).

66. T. Honoré, "*Scriptor Historiae Augustae*"; Cameron, *Last Pagans*, 778.

67. Syme, *Ammianus and the Historia Augusta*, 183.

68. Syme, *Ammianus and the Historia Augusta*, 184.

69. Syme, *Emperors and Biography*, 3.

70. Syme, *Emperors and Biography*, 8.

71. Syme, *Emperors and Biography*, 14-15.

72. Syme, *Ammianus and the Historia Augusta*, 2.

73. Syme, *Historia Augusta Papers*, 128.

74. Smith wrote two books announcing and analyzing his discovery: *Clement of Alexandria and a Secret Gospel of Mark* (Cambridge: Harvard University Press, 1973) and *The Secret Gospel: The Discovery and Interpretation of the Secret Gospel According to Mark* (New York: Harper & Row, 1973). An early colloquy on the authenticity of the text is W. Wuellner, ed., *Longer Mark: Forgery, Interpretation, or Old Tradition* (Berkeley: Center for Hermeneutical Studies, 1975). The *Journal of Early Christian Studies* 11 (2003) offers a number of responses to the controversy, as does *Biblical Archaeology Review* 35 (2009). Two books seek to expose Smith as a fraud: S. C. Carlson, *The Gospel Hoax: Morton Smith's Invention of Secret Mark* (Waco, TX: Baylor University Press, 2005), and P. Jeffery, *The Secret Gospel of Mark Unveiled: Imagined Rituals of Sex, Death, and Madness in a Biblical Forgery* (New Haven: Yale University Press, 2007). Brown has been a firm defender of Smith and the gospel: see, e.g., S. G. Brown, *Mark's Other Gospel: Rethinking Morton Smith's Controversial Discovery* (Waterloo, ON: Wilfrid Laurier Press, 2005) and "The Question of Motive in the Case against Morton Smith," *Journal of Biblical Literature* 125 (2006).

75. Carlson, *The Gospel Hoax*, 59-61. Note that this specific charge is successfully refuted by H. Shanks, "Restoring a Dead Scholar's Reputation," *Biblical Archaeology Review* 35 (2009): 60.

76. C. E. Murgia, "Secret Mark: Real or Fake?," in Wuellner, *Longer Mark*, 35-40.

77. Birger Pierson quoted in H. Shanks, "Morton Smith—Forger," *Biblical Archaeology Review* 35 (2009): 50. Cf. "The result, and probably the intent . . . is humorous" in Murgia, "Secret Mark," 40.

78. H. C. Youtie, "Callimachus in the Tax Rolls," in *Scriptiunculae*, vol. 2 (Amsterdam: A. M. Hakkert, 1973).

79. Syme, *Ammianus and the Historia Augusta*, 186.

80. Syme, *Ammianus and the Historia Augusta*, 35.

81. P. van Minnen, "House-to-House Enquiries: An Interdisciplinary Approach to Roman Karanis," *Zeitschrift für Papyrologie und Epigraphik* 100 (1994).

82. I have found particularly useful on this subject the précis by D. Konstan, "The Active Reader in Classical Antiquity," *Argos* 30 (2006), and W. A. Johnson's full-scale study, *Readers and Reading Culture in the High Roman Empire*.

83. A. K. Gavrilov, "Techniques of Reading in Classical Antiquity," *Classical Quarterly* 47 (1997).

84. H. G. Snyder, *Teachers and Texts in the Ancient World: Philosophers, Jews and Christians* (London: Routledge, 2000), 19–30.

85. Cf. Galen, *In librum Hippocratis de natura humana* 3.4, on the customary discussion following the reading of the treatise.

86. See esp. *De Vita Contemplativa* 75–79; *De Somniis* 2.127; Snyder, *Teachers and Texts*, 123–37; Luke 2:46 shows Jesus in learned discussion with teachers in the Temple, and in Bethlehem, and see Luke 4:16–21, where Jesus reads and expounds upon a passage of Isaiah before being thrown out of Nazareth by his outraged interlocutors.

87. Plutarch, *How a Young Man Should Listen to Poems* 26b; Konstan, "The Active Reader," 2 (tr. Konstan).

88. G. Roskam, "Educating the Young . . . Over Wine? Plutarch, Calvinus Taurus, and Favorinus as Convivial Teachers," in *Symposion and Philanthropia in Plutarch*, ed. J. R. Ferreira et al. (Coimbra: Centro de Estudos Clássicos e Humanísticos da Universidade de Coimbra, 2009), 375.

89. Johnson, *Readers*, 32–73, quotation at 45.

90. Johnson, *Readers*, 98–136.

91. Johnson, *Readers*, 108–9.

92. S. P. Mattern, *Galen and the Rhetoric of Healing* (Baltimore: Johns Hopkins University Press, 2008), 11.

93. R. Lim, *Public Disputation, Power, and Social Order in Late Antiquity* (Berkeley: University of California Press, 1995).

94. Lim, *Public Disputation*, 70–108.

95. R. Hercher, Über die Glaubwürdigkeit der neuen Geschichte des Ptolemaus Chennus (Leipzig: Teubner, 1856); A. Chatzis, *Der Philosoph und Grammatiker Ptolemaios Chennos* (Paderborn: F. Schöningh, 1914); K.-H. Tomberg, *Die Kainé Historia des Ptolemaios Chennos: Eine literarhistorische und quellenkritische Untersuchung* (Bonn: Rudolf Habelt, 1968); Alan Cameron, *Greek Mythography in the Roman World* (Oxford: Oxford University Press, 2004), 134–59.

96. Cameron, *Greek Mythography*, 159.

97. M. Hose, "Ptolemaios Chennos und das Problem der Schwindelliteratur," in *In Pursuit of "Wissenschaft": Festschrift für William M. Calder III zum 75. Geburtstag*, ed. S. Heilen et al. (Zürich: Olms, 2008). Hose, unfortunately, does not seem to have been familiar with Cameron's work.

98. Compare the discussion of Anna Perenna in book 3 of Ovid's *Fasti*, another example of the presentation of mutually exclusive mythological examples by a witty author for a knowing audience.

99. Cameron, *Greek Mythography*, 141.

100. In a similar way, Peirano demonstrates that a number of early imperial pseudepigraphic works can be read as "creative supplements" and responses to canonical texts. For example, the *Ciris* answers a question that Vergil asked in *Georgics* 6.74, and Tibullus's

mention of his present poverty has spurred the pseudo-Tibullus *Panegyricus Messallae* to narrate his earlier life. I. Peirano, *The Rhetoric of the Roman Fake: Latin* Pseudepigrapha *in Context* (Cambridge: Cambridge University Press, 2012), 10 and passim.

101. Cameron, *Greek Mythography*, 137–40.

102. Cameron, *Greek Mythography*, 128.

103. F. Jacoby, "Die Überlieferung von Ps. Plutarchs Parallela Minora und die Schwindelautoren," *Mnemosyne* 8 (1940); J. Schlereth, *De Plutarchi quae feruntur parallelis minoribus* (Freiburg: Herder, 1931); J. Boulogne, *Plutarque: Oeuvres Morales*, vol. 4 (Paris: Les Belles Lettres, 2002), 221–75; A. Cameron, *Greek Mythography*, 127–34.

104. Cf. S. Luria, "Entstellungen des Klassikertextes bei Stobaios," *Rheinisches Museum* 78 (1929): 94 n. 3: "Mir scheint wahrscheinlicher, dass wir hier eine später missverstandene Parodie im Stil der lukanischen 'echten Geschichten' vor uns haben, als dass das Werk als eine ernstliche Mystifikation aufzufassen sei."

105. See M. Heath, *Menander: A Rhetor in Context* (Oxford: Oxford University Press, 2004), 244–53.

106. Cameron, *Greek Mythography*, 127–28.

107. Cameron, *Greek Mythography*, 133.

108. D. Obbink, "Readers and Intellectuals," in *Oxyrhynchus: A City and Its Texts*, ed. A. K. Bowman et al. (London: Egypt Exploration Society, 2007); cf. Johnson, *Readers*, 179–99.

109. Chastagnol, *Histoire Auguste*, 1106–7. Chastagnol, indeed, also offers as a parallel Gellius 19.13 on the use of the words *nanus* and *pumilio* to refer to a dwarf.

110. Mattern, *Galen*, 50.

111. Cf. Paschoud, *Histoire Auguste IV.3*, x.

112. Pucci, *The Full-Knowing Reader*, 53–63.

113. The notion of "interpretative communities" was first championed by S. Fish, *Is There a Text in This Class? The Authority of Interpretive Communities* (Cambridge: Harvard University Press, 1980); see also U. Eco, *The Role of the Reader* (Bloomington: Indiana University Press, 1979), 3–43.

Chapter 3. Religion in the *Historia Augusta*

1. M. Salzman, *The Making of a Christian Aristocracy* (Cambridge: Harvard University Press, 2002).

2. A. de Kisch, "Sur quelques omina imperii dans l'Histoire Auguste," *Revue des études latines* 51 (1973). Livian material in the *Historia Augusta* may derive from the excerptor Julius Obsequens: Cameron, *Last Pagans*, 757; T. Pekáry, "Statuen in der Historia Augusta," *BHAC* 1968/69 (1970).

3. A. R. Birley, "Religion in the *Historia Augusta*," *HAC* 1991.

4. Syme, *Ammianus and the Historia Augusta*, 139.

5. Early proponents of this narrative include J. Geffcken, *Der Ausgang des griechisch-römischen Heidentums* (Heidelberg: C. Winter, 1920); A. Alföldi, *A Festival of Isis in Rome*

under the Christian Emperors of the IVth Century (Budapest: Institute of Numismatics and Archaeology of the Pazmany University, 1937); A. Alföldi, *Die Kontorniaten: Ein verkanntes Propagandamittel der stadtrömische Aristokratie in ihrem Kampfe gegen das christliche Kaisertum* (Budapest: O. Harassowitz, 1942/43); H. Bloch, "A New Document of the Last Pagan Revival in the West, 393-394 A.D," *Harvard Theological Review* 38 (1945).

6. J. Straub, *Heidnische Geschichtsapologetik in der christlichen Spätantike: Untersuchungen über Zeit und Tendenz der Historia Augusta* (Bonn: Rudolf Habelt, 1963).

7. W. Speyer, *Büchervernichtung und Zensur des Geistes bei Heiden, Juden und Christen* (Stuttgart: Anton Hiersemann, 1981).

8. Speyer, *Büchervernichtung*, 134.

9. See in particular the many passages of Jerome and Augustine on Porphyry in R. Berchman, *Porphyry against the Christians* (Leiden: Brill, 2005), 155-91.

10. J.-P. Callu and M. Festy, "Alternatives historiennes: De l'*Historia Alexandri* à *Historia Augusta*," *HAC* 2010.

11. A recurrent argument of Cameron, *Last Pagans*, esp. 100-107.

12. Cameron, *Last Pagans*, 198-205.

13. E.g., Chastagnol, *Histoire Auguste*, cxxxii-cl.

14. A. Chastagnol, "Quelques thèmes bibliques dans l'Histoire Auguste," *BHAC* 1979/81 (1983): 118.

15. K. H. Schwarte, "Das angebliche Christengesetz des Septimius Severus," *Historia* 12 (1963); T. D. Barnes, "Legislation against the Christians," *Journal of Roman Studies* 58 (1968); A. R. Birley, *Septimius Severus: The African Emperor* (New Haven: Yale University Press, 1989), 135.

16. J. Straub, "Zur Ordination von Bischöfen und Beamten in der christlichen Spätantike: Ein Reformvorschlag der Historia Augusta?" in *Mullus: Festschrift Theodor Klauser*, ed. A. Stuiber and A. Hermann (Münster: Aschendorffsche Buchdruckerei, 1964).

17. Also the conclusion of S. A. Stertz, "Christianity in the *Historia Augusta*," *Latomus* 36 (1977): 708-9.

18. Paschoud, *Histoire Auguste V.2*, 234-37.

19. F. Paschoud, "Le Tyran Fantasmé: Variations de l'*Histoire Auguste* sur le thème de l'usurpation," in *Usurpationen in der Spätantike*, ed. F. Paschoud and J. Szidat (Stuttgart: Franz Steiner Verlag, 1997).

20. T. Optendrenk, *Die Religionspolitik des Kaisers Elagabal im Spiegel der Historia Augusta* (Bonn: Rudolf Habelt, 1969), 54-56, 132-33; F. Paschoud, "L'intolérance chrétienne vue et jugée par les païens," *Cristianesimo nella storia* 11 (1990): 566-71; L. Ruggini, "Elagabalo, Costantino e i culti 'siriaci' nella *Historia Augusta*," *HAC* 1991.

21. R. Turcan, "Héliogabale précurseur de Constantin?," *Bulletin de l'Association Guillaume Budé* 47 (1988).

22. The malleability of the evidence is suggested by the fact that Baynes, *The Historia Augusta: Its Date and Purpose*, 101, 139, felt that Elagabalus was a stand-in for Constantius II.

23. More broadly, it is particularly noteworthy, as Mader explains, that Elagabalus in general is portrayed as a stock Roman tyrant, not a weird religious fanatic, by the *HA*-author. Mader, "History as Carnival, or Method and Madness in the *Vita Heliogabali*."

24. Barnes, "Ultimus Antoninorum," 62.

25. Straub, *Heidnische Geschichtsapologetik*, 190; Optendrenk, *Die Religionspolitik*, 54–56; F. Paschoud, "Zosime 2, 29 et la version païenne de la conversion de Constantin," *Historia* 20 (1971); Ruggini, "Elagabalo," 136–37; F. Paschoud, *Zosime: Histoire Nouvelle*, 2nd ed. (Paris: Les Belles Lettres, 2000), 234–40; A. Baldini, "Varie su Zosimo, 2, 29 e la *Vita Heliogabali* della *Historia Augusta*," *HAC* 2010.

26. J. M. C. Toynbee and J. B. Ward-Perkins, *The Shrine of St. Peter and the Vatican Excavations* (London: Longmans, Green, 1956); G. Townend, "The Circus of Nero and the Vatican Excavations," *American Journal of Archaeology* 62 (1958).

27. Paschoud, *Histoire Auguste V.1*, 137; H. Brandt, "Die 'heidnische Vision' Aurelians (*H.A. A* 24, 2-8) und die 'christliche Vision' Konstantins des Grossen," *HAC* 1995. Chastagnol may be correct in seeing echoes of Jerome in the language used to describe this vision, however: A. Chastagnol, "Le supplice inventé par Avidius Cassius: Remarques sur l'Histoire Auguste et la lettre 1 de Saint Jérôme," *BHAC* 1970 (1972).

28. *Against Hierocles* 4, with A. Mendelson, "Eusebius and the Posthumous Career of Apollonius of Tyana," in *Eusebius, Christianity, and Judaism*, ed. H. W. Attridge and G. Hata (Detroit: Wayne State University Press, 1992).

29. C. P. Jones, "Apollonius of Tyana in Late Antiquity," in *Greek Literature in Late Antiquity*, ed. S. F. Johnson (Aldershot: Ashgate, 2006), 61–62: "There is a tendency in modern scholarship to be over-influenced by Eusebius' *Against Hierocles*, and to suppose that Apollonius was always and everywhere the hero of a 'pagan reaction,' and by the same token an object of fear or detestation on the part of Christians. The truth is rather that for non-Christian Greeks, and especially philosophers, he was in the first place an embodiment of their ancestral culture. Even educated Christians in both East and West recognized aspects of him that recalled the Christian 'philosophy.'"

30. Philost. *VA* 4.45, with Paschoud, *Histoire Auguste V.1*, 141.

31. Ratti, *Histoire Auguste IV.2*, xxxvi–xlvi.

32. Straub, *Heidnische Geschichtsapologetik*, 1–52.

33. Alan Cameron, review of Straub, *Heidnische Geschichtsapologetik*, in *Journal of Roman Studies* 55 (1965).

34. A. Chastagnol, "Le septième jour dans l'Histoire Auguste," *BHAC* 1975/76 (1978).

35. Chastagnol, "Zosime II, 38 et l'Histoire Auguste."

36. Syme, *Ammianus and the Historia Augusta*, 139, 173–74; A. Birley, "Religion," 34.

37. Should we conclude that the *HA*-author is sneering at followers of Serapis?

38. Syme, *Ammianus and the Historia Augusta*, 174: "not easy to attest, so it happens. But one can adduce 'Reverens' and 'Reverentius.'"

39. A. Chastagnol, "Le poète Claudien et l'Histoire Auguste," *Historia* 19 (1970): 459.

40. In chapter 4 I return to the *HA*-author's engagement with eunuchs, which I suggest represents an allusion to Ammianus.

41. A. Chastagnol, "Études sur la *Vita Cari*: Les *editores* romains et la dilapidation de patrimoines sénatoriaux," *HAC* 1996.

42. J. N. D. Kelly, *Jerome: His Life, Writings and Controversies* (New York: Harper & Row, 1975); S. Rebenich, *Hieronymus und sein Kreis: Prosopographische und sozialgeschichtliche*

Untersuchungen (Stuttgart: Franz Steiner Verlag, 1992); S. Rebenich, *Jerome* (Routledge: London, 2002); A. Fürst, *Hieronymus: Askese und Wissenschaft in Spätantike* (Freiburg: Herder, 2003).

43. A. Cain, *The Letters of Jerome: Asceticism, Biblical Exegesis, and the Construction of Christian Authority in Late Antiquity* (Oxford: Oxford University Press, 2009), 13–42. See also M. Vessey, "Jerome's Origen: The Making of a Christian Literary *Persona*," *Studia Patristica* 28 (1993).

44. Rebenich, *Hieronymus*, 85–98.

45. J. Fontaine, "L'aristocratie occidentale devant le monarchisme aux IVème et Vème siècles," *Rivista di storia e letteratura religiosa* 15 (1979).

46. Cameron, *Last Pagans*, 211–12.

47. D. Hunter, *Marriage, Celibacy, and Heresy in Ancient Christianity: The Jovinianist Controversy* (Oxford: Oxford University Press, 2007), 54–55.

48. D. S. Wiesen, *St. Jerome as a Satirist: A Study in Christian Latin Thought and Letters* (Ithaca: Cornell University Press, 1964), 65–112.

49. S. Lunn-Rockliffe, *Ambrosiaster's Political Theology* (Oxford: Oxford University Press, 2007), 105. Cf. M.-P. Bussières, *Ambrosiaster: Contre le païens et Sur le destin* (Paris: Éditions du Cerf, 2007).

50. H. Vogels, "Ambrosiaster und Hieronymus," *Revue bénédictine* 66 (1956); Lunn-Rockliffe, *Ambrosiaster's*, 19–26; Cain, *The Letters of Jerome*, 51–67; D. Hunter, *Marriage*, 159–70.

51. See also *Apol.* 2.42: "cum iam a plurimis legerentur et offenderentur pene omnes" ("They were read by a great many people, and almost every one was offended by them").

52. Cameron, *Last Pagans*, 745.

53. Cameron, *Last Pagans*, 748.

54. See E. Coleiro, "St. Jerome's Lives of the Hermits," *Vigiliae Christianae* 11 (1957); P. Harvey, "Saints and Satyrs: Jerome the Scholar at Work," *Athenaeum* 86 (1998); R. Wisniewski, "*Bestiae Christum loquuntur* ou des habitants du désert et de la ville dans la *Vita Pauli* de Saint Jérôme," *Augustinanum* 40 (2000); S. Weingarten, *The Saint's Saints: Hagiography and Geography in Jerome* (Leiden: Brill, 2005); P. Leclerc, E. M. Morales, and A. de Vogüé, eds. *Jérôme: Trois vies de moines* (Paris: Éditions du Cerf, 2007); S. Rebenich, "Inventing an Ascetic Hero: Jerome's Life of Paul the First Hermit," in *Jerome of Stridon: His Life, Writings and Legacy*, ed. A. Cain and J. Lössl (Burlington, VT: Ashgate, 2009).

55. Weingarten, *The Saint's Saints*, 83–105; T. D. Barnes, *Early Christian Hagiography and Roman History* (Tübingen: Mohr Siebeck, 2010), 170–82.

56. B. Schmeidler, "Die Scriptores Historiae Augustae und der heilige Hieronymus," *Philologische Wochenschrift* 31 (1927).

57. Cameron, review of Straub, *Heidnische Geschichtsapologetik*, 244.

58. For the priority of Jerome: Straub, *Heidnische Geschichtsapologetik*, 81–105; D. den Hengst, *The Prefaces*, 122–27; T. D. Barnes, "Jerome and the Historia Augusta," *HAC* 1991; Chastagnol, *Histoire Auguste*, xciii–xciv; F. Paschoud, "Symmaque, Jérôme et l'Histoire Auguste," *Museum Helveticum* 57 (2000). For the priority of the *HA*: N. Adkin, "The Historia Augusta and Jerome Again," *Klio* 79 (1997); Cameron, *Last Pagans*, 761–70.

59. Paschoud, *Histoire Auguste V.2*, 49.

60. Cameron, *Last Pagans*, 771.

61. G. Mussies, "Marnas God of Gaza," *Aufstieg und Niedergang der römischen Welt* 2.18.4 (1990); F. Trombley, *Hellenic Religion and Christianization c. 370–529*, 2 vols. (Leiden: Brill, 1993), 1.187–282.

62. Weingarten, *The Saint's Saints*, 138. Barnes has recently argued that our only Greek literary source for Marnas, the *Life of Porphyry* by Mark the Deacon, bishop of Gaza, was written no earlier than the middle of the sixth century: Barnes, *Early Christian Hagiography*, 260–83.

63. Cain, *The Letters of Jerome*.

64. Victor 37.3, *Epit. de Caes.* 37.2; Eutr. 9.17.1; Barnes, "Some Persons in the Historia Augusta," 150–51.

65. Cameron, silently changing his name from Onasimus to Onesimus, states that he was a "real historian" who "wrote on Constantine" (Cameron, *Last Pagans*, 781). In fact, the *Suda* states that he was active in the time of Constantine, that he was the son of a sophist and father of a sophist, and that he was the author of five named rhetorical works and "declamations, encomiums, and many other things."

66. A. Chastagnol, *Recherches*, 72–85; A. Chastagnol, "Autour de la 'sobre ivresse' de Bonosus," *BHAC* 1972/74 (1976).

67. Chastagnol, *Recherches*, 74–75.

68. E. Alföldi-Rosenbaum, "Apicius, De re coquinaria and the Vita Heliogabali," *BHAC* 1970 (1972): 5–10.

69. Straub, "Senaculum, id est mulierum senatus."

70. Chastagnol, *Histoire Auguste*, xcv–xcvi; E. G. Hinson, "Women Biblical Scholars in the Late Fourth Century: The Aventine Circle," *Studia Patristica* 23 (1997).

71. Turcan, *Histoire Auguste III.1*, 165–66.

72. Chastagnol, *Recherches*, 15.

73. Chastagnol, *Recherches*, 85.

74. Paschoud, *Histoire Auguste V.2*, 284. A portion of *Ep.* 22 also finds echoes in a pseudo-technical discussion in the life of Firmus: Chastagnol, *Recherches*, 96. Ratti points to a number of linguistic parallels between descriptions of Gallienus's luxurious behavior and those criticized in *Ep.* 22, although the language of luxury is so commonplace that none seems definitive to me: Ratti, *Histoire Auguste IV.2*, xlviii–lii.

75. Straub, "Calpurnia univiria."

76. Chastagnol, *Histoire Auguste*, xciv–xcv.

77. J. Schwartz, "Arguments philologiques pour dater l'Histoire Auguste," *Historia* 15 (1966): 464.

78. Straub, "Calpurnia univiria," 107–8.

79. Chastagnol, "Quelques thèmes bibliques," 122–25.

80. Den Hengst, *The Prefaces*, 87–88; B. Treucker, "Kriterien der Aktualisierung in der Historia Augusta," *BHAC* 1964/65 (1966): 276–77.

81. Syme, *Emperors and Biography*, 25–26.

82. Syme, *Emperors and Biography*, 12–13, 169.

83. Paschoud, "Symmaque."

84. J. Schlumberger, "'Non scribo sed dicto' (HA T 33, 8): Hat der Autor der Historia Augusta mit Stenographen gearbeitet?," *BHAC* 1972/74 (1976).

85. A. Souter, "Portions of an Old-Latin Text of St. Matthew's Gospel," in *Quantulacumque: Studies Presented to Kirsopp Lake*, ed. R. P. Casey, S. Lake, and A. K. Lake (London: Christophers, 1937).

86. P. Jay, *L'Exégèse de Saint Jérôme d'après son* Commentaire sur Isaïe (Paris: Études Augustiniennes, 1985), 80.

87. Paschoud, *Histoire Auguste V.2*, 146–50.

88. I return to this theme in chapter 4.

89. Straub, *Heidnische Geschichtsapologetik*, 106–24.

90. Quoted in M. Weinfeld, "Hillel and the Misunderstanding of Judaism in Modern Scholarship," in *Hillel and Jesus: Comparative Studies of Two Major Religious Leaders*, ed. J. H. Charlesworth and L. J. Johns (Minneapolis: Fortress Press, 1997), 64.

91. K. Hönn, *Quellenuntersuchungen zu den Viten des Heliogabalus und des Severus Alexander* (Teubner: Leipzig, 1911), 102.

92. L. R. Palmer, *The Latin Language* (London: Faber and Faber, 1954), 187.

93. Straub, *Heidnische Geschichtsapologetik*, 149–66.

94. Straub, *Heidnische Geschichtsapologetik*, 151–52.

95. Straub, *Heidnische Geschichtsapologetik*, 170–79.

96. F. Paschoud, "L'auteur de l'Histoire Auguste, est-il un apostat?," in *Consuetudinis Amor: Fragments d'histoire romaine offerts à J. P. Callu*, ed. F. Chausson and E. Wolff (Rome: Bretschneider, 2003).

97. Paschoud, "Raisonnements providentialistes dans l'Histoire Auguste"; Paschoud, *Histoire Auguste V.1*, 125–29.

98. See Cameron, *Last Pagans*, 33–56. See also G. W. Bowersock, "From Emperor to Bishop: The Self-Conscious Transformation of Political Power in the Fourth Century A.D.," *Classical Philology* 81 (1986).

99. On the *senatus consultum*, see J. Béranger, "Les sénatus-consultes dans l'Histoire Auguste," *BHAC* 1984/85 (1987).

100. Paschoud, *Histoire Auguste V.1*, 127, quotes Livy 27.34.7: "sed tum quoque aut verbo adsentiebatur aut pedibus in sententiam ibat."

101. Paschoud, *Histoire Auguste V.1*, 98.

102. E.g., J. Schwartz, "Une fantasie impie dans l'*Histoire Auguste*," *Revue d'histoire et de philosophie religieuses* 69 (1989); Chastagnol, "Le supplice inventé par Avidius Cassius," 102–4; A. Alföldi, "Zwei Bemerkungen zur Historia Augusta," *BHAC* 1963 (1964): 1–3; S. Ratti, "Réponses de l'*Histoire Auguste* aux apologistes Tertullien et Lactance," *Museum Helveticum* 59 (2002): 235–37; V. Neri, "Considerazioni sul tema della *luxuria* nell' *Historia Augusta*," *HAC* 1999: 222; and Syme, *Ammianus and the Historia Augusta*, 83, refuted by J. F. Gilliam, "Firmus and the Crocodiles," *BHAC* 1977/78 (1980).

103. F. Paschoud, "Le diacre Philippe, l'eunuque de la reine Candace et l'auteur de la vita Aureliani," *BHAC* 1975/76 (1978): 147–51.

Chapter 4. Imperial History Reimagined

1. Eck, "Zum Konsulat in der *Historia Augusta*"; V. Neri, "Il populus Romanus nell'Historia Augusta," *HAC* 1995; G. W. Bowersock, "Arabs and Saracens in the Historia Augusta," *BHAC* 1984/85 (1987); J. Béranger, "L'idéologie impériale dans l'Histoire Auguste," *BHAC* 1972/74 (1976).
2. Chastagnol, *Histoire Auguste*, cli–clxxiv.
3. J. Matthews, *The Roman Empire of Ammianus* (London: Duckworth, 1989), 20–27.
4. D. den Hengst, "*Verba, non res*: Über die Inventio in den Reden und Schriftstücken in der Historia Augusta," *BHAC* 1984/85 (1987): 170–74; Paschoud, *Histoire Auguste V.1*, 88–89.
5. Straub, *Studien zur Historia Augusta*, 19–39.
6. N. Lenski, "*Initium mali Romano imperio*: Contemporary Reactions to the Battle of Adrianople," *Transactions of the American Philological Association* 127 (1997).
7. Paschoud, *Histoire Auguste IV.3*, 284–86.
8. Chastagnol, *Recherches*, 86–89.
9. Syme, *Ammianus and the Historia Augusta*, 37–38.
10. A. Birley, "Further Echoes of Ammianus in the *Historia Augusta*," *HAC* 1991. On a smaller scale, Schwartz prefigured both Birley's and den Hengst's work by pointing out a number of parallels in phraseology and detail between Ammianus book 31 and the *Claudius*: J. Schwartz, "Sur la date de L'Histoire Auguste," *BHAC* 1966/67 (1968).
11. Paschoud, *Histoire Auguste V.1*, 71.
12. Paschoud demonstrates the fictitious nature of Aurelian's campaign, without connecting it to the Ammianus passage: Paschoud, *Histoire Auguste V.1*, 76–77.
13. Syme, *Ammianus and the Historia Augusta*, 56–59.
14. Syme, *Ammianus and the Historia Augusta*, 57.
15. Chastagnol, *Recherches*, 92.
16. Burian, "*Fides historica* als methodologischer Grundsatz der *Historia Augusta*," 287.
17. Syme, *Ammianus and the Historia Augusta*, 60–68; cf. W. Schmid, "Die Koexistenz von Sarapiskult und Christentum im Hadrianbrief bei Vopiscus," *BHAC* 1964/65 (1966); Syme, *Emperors and Biography*, 17–29.
18. Syme, *Ammianus and the Historia Augusta*, 41–42.
19. Syme, *Ammianus and the Historia Augusta*, 42; cf. Ratti, *Histoire Auguste IV.2*, 46.
20. Ratti, *Histoire Auguste IV.2*, lv–lvi.
21. Straub, *Heidnische Geschichtsapologetik in der christlichen Spätantike*, 53–80.
22. Syme, *Ammianus and the Historia Augusta*, 36.
23. R. von Haehling, "Der obstessende Kaiser—Ein Paradigma für Luxuria in der Tyrannentopik der Historia Augusta," *BHAC* 1986/89 (1991).
24. D. Rohrbacher, "Why Didn't Constantius II Eat Fruit?," *Classical Quarterly* 55 (2005).
25. Paschoud, *Histoire Auguste V.1*, 97–98.

26. O. Seeck, "Studien zur Geschichte Diocletians und Constantins iii: Die Entstehungszeit der H.A.," *Jahrbücher für classische Philologie* 36 (1890): 632.

27. W. Hartke, *Römische Kinderkaiser: Eine Strukturanalyse römischen Denkens und Daseins* (Berlin: Akademie Verlag, 1951), 342–43.

28. Baynes, *Historia Augusta*, 18; cf. N. Baynes, "The Date of the Composition of the Historia Augusta," *Classical Review* 38 (1924).

29. Baynes, *Historia Augusta*, 57.

30. Dessau, "Über Zeit und Persönlichkeit, 355–58.

31. T. Mommsen, "Die Scriptores Historiae Augustae," *Hermes* 25 (1890): 228–29.

32. Baynes, *Historia Augusta*, 24–28.

33. Baynes, *Historia Augusta*, 20.

34. K. F. Stroheker, "Princeps clausus: Zu einigen Berührungen der Literatur des fünften Jahrhunderts mit der Historia Augusta," *BHAC* 1968/69 (1970); see also A. Chastagnol, "Autour du thème du *princeps clausus*," *BHAC* 1982/83 (1985).

35. H. Scholten, *Der Eunuch in Kaisernähe: Zur politischen und sozialen Bedeutung des praepositus sacri cubiculi im 4. und 5. Jahrhundert n. Chr.* (Frankfurt am Main: Peter Lang, 1995); P. Guyot, *Eunuchen als Sklaven und Freigelassene in der griechisch-römischen Antike* (Stuttgart: Klett-Cotta, 1980).

36. T. Zawadzki, "Encore sur les buts et la date de composition de l'Histoire Auguste," *Studii clasice* 5 (1963).

37. Chastagnol, "Autour"; H. Stern, *Date et destinaire de l'Histoire Auguste* (Paris: Les Belles Lettres, 1953).

38. Alan Cameron, "Eunuchs in the *Historia Augusta*," *Latomus* 24 (1965); C. L. Murison, "Cassius Dio on Nervan Legislation: Nieces and Eunuchs," *Historia* 53 (2004); Guyot, *Eunuchen als Sklaven und Freigelassene*, 121–29.

39. S. Tougher, "Ammianus and the Eunuchs," in *The Late Roman World and Its Historian: Interpreting Ammianus Marcellinus*, ed. J. W. Drijver and D. Hunt (London: Routledge, 1999).

40. Cf. Barnes, "Ultimus Antoninorum," 64.

41. K.-P. Johne, *Kaiserbiographie und Senatsaristokratie: Untersuchungen zur Datierung und sozialen Herkunft der Historia Augusta* (Berlin: Akademie-Verlag, 1976), 105–19.

42. Pupienus and Sabinus: Johne, *Kaiserbiographie*, 117.

43. Cf. K.-P. Johne, "Die Biographie des Gegenkaisers Censorinus: Ein Beitrag zur sozialen Herkunft der Historia Augusta," *BHAC* 1972/74 (1976).

44. T. Honoré, "Lawyers and Government in the 'Historia Augusta,'" *Iura* 42 (1991); J. Straub, "Juristische Notizen in der Historia Augusta," *BHAC* 1976/76 (1978); D. Liebs, "Alexander Severus und das Strafrecht," *BHAC* 1977/78 (1980); D. Liebs, "Strafrechtliches in der Tacitusvita," *BHAC* 1979/81 (1983); D. Liebs, "OM 13.1 und das Reskriptenwesen der HA," *BHAC* 1982/83 (1985); D. Liebs, *Die Jurisprudenz im spätantiken Italien: 260–640 n. Chr.* (Berlin: Duncker & Humblot, 1987), 104–19.

45. Honoré, "Lawyers," 29–34.

46. Cf. P. de Jonge, *Philological and Historical Commentary on Ammianus Marcellinus XVII* (Groningen: Bouma's Boekhuis, 1977), 235.

47. H. Dessau, "Die Überlieferung der S.H.A.," *Hermes* 29 (1894).
48. Hartke, *Geschichte und Politik im spätantiken Rom*, 106-12.
49. Syme, *Ammianus and the Historia Augusta*, 75-76. The story of a storm weakening the enemy before the battle comports with the actual events of the Frigidus (Ambrose *Enarrationes in XII psalmos Davidicos* 36.15). The claim that a wind repulsed the weapons of the enemy during the battle represents a later elaboration by Claudian (*III Cons. Hon.* 94-95) and Rufinus (*Historia Ecclesiastica* 11.33). Cameron, *Last Pagans*, 112-17.
50. S. Ratti, "394: Fin de la rédaction de l'*Histoire Auguste?*," *Antiquité tardive* 16 (2008): 339-40.
51. Herennius Modestinus, pupil of Ulpian, *Digest* 47.2.52.20; Julius Titianus, Serv. at *Aen.* 4.42; Auson. *Grat. act.* 7.31.
52. Syme, *Emperors and Biography*, 11; Syme, *Ammianus and the Historia Augusta*, 77.
53. F. Paschoud, "Claude II aux Thermopyles?: À propos de HA *Claud.* 16, 1, Zosime 5, 5 et Eunape, *Vitae Soph.* 7, 3, 4-5," in *Institutions, société et vie politique dans l'Empire romain au IVe siècle ap. J.-C.*, ed. M. Christol and S. Demougin (Rome: Ecole Française de Rome, 1992); W. J. Cherf, "The Thermopylae Garrison of *Vita Claudii* 16," *Classical Philology* 88 (1993).
54. Paschoud, *Histoire Auguste V.1*, xvi.
55. "Une bonne part des actes religieux énumérés par Silanus . . . n'ont, selon la tradition, rien à faire avec une consultation des Livres Sibyllins." Paschoud, *Histoire Auguste V.1*, 126.
56. Cameron, *Last Pagans*, 213-18.
57. Paschoud, *Histoire Auguste V.1*, xvi; Johne, *Kaiserbiographie*, xx.
58. Syme, *Ammianus and the Historia Augusta*, 9-10; Matthews, *Roman Empire*, 23-27.
59. Amm. 31.2; Jer. *Adversus Iovinianum* 2.7 (393), *Ep.* 60.17 (396), *Ep.* 77.8 (400), *Commentariorum in Esaiam* 7.21 (408); O. J. Maenchen-Helfen, "The Date of Ammianus Marcellinus' Last Books," *American Journal of Philology* 76 (1955).
60. D. Rohrbacher, "Jerome, an Early Reader of Ammianus Marcellinus," *Latomus* 65 (2006).
61. For example, Stein feels that the vigor with which Ammianus defends the religious neutrality of Valentinian means that he must be writing not under Theodosius but under Eugenius: E. Stein, *Histoire du Bas-Empire* (Amsterdam: Adolf M. Hakkert, 1968), 215; see also A. Demandt, *Zeitkritik und Geschichtsbild im Werk Ammians* (Bonn: Rudolf Habelt, 1965), 148-51; Hartke, *Römische Kinderkaiser*, 72-73.
62. J. N. D. Kelly, *Jerome: His Life, Writings and Controversies*, 190, 192, 215, 222, 272.
63. Chastagnol, "Le poète Claudien et l'Histoire Auguste."
64. Chastagnol, "Trois études sur la Vita Cari," 75-80.
65. Paschoud and den Hengst accept some use of Claudian: e.g., Paschoud, *Histoire Auguste V.2*, 64-65, 400-404; D. den Hengst, "The Author's Literary Culture," *HAC* 1991: 169-70. Döpp is not convinced: S. Döpp, *Zeitgeschichte in Dichtungen Claudians* (Wiesbaden: Franz Steiner Verlag, 1980), 59 n. 63. Ratti argues against the use of Claudian: Ratti, "394," 342-44.

66. The same holds true, I think, for Paschoud's recent "preuve assez convaincante" of the use of Claudian. The coincidence of names of some barbarian tribes in an invented list in the *Claudius* (6.2–3) with names in two separate works of Claudian (*In Eutropium* 2.153–54; *Cons. Stil.* 1.94) permits too many other possible explanations to be definitive. Paschoud, *Histoire Auguste IV.3*, 274–75.

67. A. Chastagnol, "Végèce et l'Histoire Auguste," *BHAC* 1971 (1974).

68. M. B. Charles, *Vegetius in Context: Establishing the Date of the Epitoma Rei Militaris* (Stuttgart: Franz Steiner Verlag, 2007).

69. D. den Hengst, review of F. Paschoud, *Histoire Auguste V.1*, in *Antiquité tardive* 6 (1998); Syme, *Ammianus and the Historia Augusta*, 75.

70. Ratti, "394," 341–42.

71. Cameron, *Last Pagans*, 772–75.

72. Hartke, *Römische Kinderkaiser*, esp. 190–242.

73. Paschoud, *Histoire Auguste V.1*, xv. See also Syme, *Ammianus and the Historia Augusta*, 74; Chastagnol, *Histoire Auguste*, clxi–clxii.

74. Cameron, *Last Pagans*, 750–53.

75. E.g., Ambrose *Hexameron* 5.68 with L. Ruggini, "Il vescovo Ambrogio e la Historia Augusta: Attualità di un topos politico-litterario," in *Atti del Colloquio patavino sulla Historia Augusta*, ed. J. Straub (Rome: Bretschneider, 1963); Symm. *Or.* 3.

76. O. Seeck, "Politische Tendenzgeschichte im 5. Jahrhundert n. Chr.," *Rheinisches Museum* 49 (1912).

77. V. Neri, "L'imperatore come *miles*: Tacito, Attalo e la datazione dell'Historia Augusta," *HAC* 2002.

78. J. Matthews, *Western Aristocracies and Imperial Court A.D. 364–425* (Oxford: Oxford University Press, 1975), 270–300.

79. Zos. 6.7.1: καὶ κατὰ τὸ κελευόμενον Ἄτταλον, ὄντα ὕπαρχον τῆς πόλεως, εἰς τὸν βασίλειον ἀναβιβάζουσι θρόνον ("just as they had been ordered, they set Attalus, who was prefect of the city, upon the emperor's throne"). Olympiodorus *fr.* 6 Blockley: ἕνα τινὰ τῶν κατὰ τὴν Ῥώμην ἐπιδόξων (Ἄτταλος ἦν ὄνομα αὐτῷ) τὴν ἐπαρχότητα τότε διέποντα εἰς βασιλέα ἀνηγόρευσεν ("He proclaimed emperor one of the Roman nobles named Attalus, who at the time was prefect of the city"). Socrates *Hist. eccl.* 7.10.5: καταπαίζων τε τῆς βασιλείας ἀναδείκυσί <τινα> βασιλέα ὀνόματι Ἄτταλον ("[Alaric,] in mockery of the imperial dignity, proclaimed one Attalus emperor"). Sozom. *Hist. eccl.* 9.8.1: βιάζεται Ῥωμαίους βασιλέα ψηφίσασθαι τὸν Ἄτταλον, ὕπαρχον ὄντα τότε τῆς πόλεως ("compelled the Romans to elect Attalus, who was prefect of the city, as emperor").

80. Chastagnol, *Histoire Auguste*, clxii.

81. L. Ruggini, "*De Morte Persecutorum* e polemica antibarbarica nella storiografia pagan e Cristiana: A proposito della disgrazia di Stilicone," *Rivista di storia e letteratura religiosa* 4 (1968).

82. Paschoud, *Histoire Auguste V.2*, xxiii–xxvi.

83. Paschoud, *Histoire Auguste V.2*, xxv.

84. Eutropius 9.17: "Hic cum bella innumera gessisset, pace parata dixit brevi milites necessarios non futuros."

85. B. Pottier, "Un pamphlet contre Stilichon dans l'*Histoire Auguste*: La vie de Maximin le Thrace," *Mélanges de l'Ecole française de Rome* 117 (2005).

86. R. MacMullen, "The Roman Concept Robber-Pretender," *Revue internationale des droits de l'antiquité* 10 (1963).

87. Mommsen, "Scriptores," 229.

88. Cameron, *Last Pagans*, 753.

89. An argument first made by Otto Hirschfeld, "Die Abfassungszeit der Sammlung der Scriptores Historiae Augustae," in *Kleine Schriften* (Berlin: Wiedemann, 1913), 889-90.

90. Dessau, "Über Zeit und Persönlichkeit," 338-39.

91. Birley, "Further Echoes," 53-54.

92. First suggested by Seeck, "Politische Tendenzgeschichte."

93. Bird argues that the *HA*-author suspected that Constantine's lineage was invented and was making fun of it, which would add further irony to the theme: H. W. Bird, "The *Historia Augusta* on Constantine's Lineage," *Arctos* 31 (1997).

Afterword

1. Johnson, *Readers*, 85-91.

2. On *recitatio*, see K. Quinn, "The Poet and His Audiences in the Augustan Age," *Aufstieg und Niedergang der römischen Welt* 2.30.1 (1982); Valette-Cagnac, *La lecture à Rome: Rites et pratiques*, 111-69; F. Dupont, "*Recitatio* and the Space of Public Discourse," in *The Roman Cultural Revolution*, ed. T. Habinek and A. Schiesaro (Cambridge: Cambridge University Press, 1997); Johnson, *Readers*, 42-56.

3. "historiam . . . Romanam septem libris edidit." See A. Galonnier, "*Anecdoton Holderi* ou *Ordo Generis Cassiodororum*: Introduction, édition, traduction et commentaire," *Antiquité tardive* 4 (1996).

4. E. Hohl, "Capitolina Amphora," *Hermes* 52 (1917).

5. P. Van Nuffelen, *Orosius and the Rhetoric of History* (Oxford: Oxford University Press, 2012); B. Swain, "Jordanes and Virgil: A Case Study of Intertextuality in the *Getica*," *Classical Quarterly* 60 (2010).

6. M. Heinzelmann, *Gregory of Tours: History and Society in the Sixth Century*, tr. C. Carroll (Cambridge: Cambridge University Press, 2001), 94-152; G. Halsall, "The Preface to Book V of Gregory of Tours' Histories: Its Form, Context and Significance," *English Historical Review* 122 (2007).

7. On the "long" late antiquity, see A. Giardina, "Esplosione di tardoantico," *Studi storici* 40 (1999); Averil Cameron, "The 'Long' Late Antiquity: A Late Twentieth-Century Model," in *Classics in Progress: Essays on Ancient Greece and Rome*, ed. T. P. Wiseman (Oxford: Oxford University Press, 2002); A. Marcone, "A Long Late Antiquity? Considerations on a Controversial Periodization," *Journal of Late Antiquity* 1 (2008); C. Ando, "Decline, Fall, and Transformation," *Journal of Late Antiquity* 1 (2008).

8. Cf. J. H. W. G. Liebeschuetz, *Decline and Fall of the Roman City* (Oxford: Oxford University Press, 2001), 340.

9. I. Casaubon, *Historiae Augustae scriptores sex, Aelius Spartianus, Iulius Capitolinus,*

Aelius Lampridius, Vulcatius Gallicanus, Trebellius Pollio, et Flavius Vopiscus (Paris: Ambrosius et Hieronymus Drouart, 1603).

10. Casaubon, *Historiae Augustae*, 331.

11. Gibbon, *Decline and Fall*: letters, e.g. 1.190 n. 22, 1.201 n. 50, 1.205 n. 61; acclamations 1.195 n. 35; Gordian 1.189–90; Thirty Tyrants 1.295–300.

12. Gibbon, *Decline and Fall*, 1.168 n. 89, 1.171 n. 95; quotation at 1.185 n. 6.

Bibliography

Primary Sources

Ammianus Marcellinus. In W. Seyfarth, *Ammiani Marcellini Rerum Gestarum Libri Qui Supersunt*. Leipzig: Teubner, 1978.
Ausonius, *Cento Nuptialis*. In R. P. H. Green, *Decimi Magni Ausonii Opera*, 145–54. Oxford: Oxford University Press, 1999.
Cicero, *Brutus*. In H. Malcovati, *M. Tulli Ciceronis Scripta quae Manserunt Omnia*, fasc. 4: *Brutus*. Leipzig: Teubner, 1970.
Cicero, *Pro Sexto Roscio*. In A. R. Dyck, *Cicero Pro Sexto Roscio*. Cambridge: Cambridge University Press, 2010.
Diomedes, *Ars Grammatica*. In H. Keil, *Grammatici Latini*, vol. 1. Leipzig: Teubner, 1857.
Herodian. In C. R. Whittaker, *Herodian in Two Volumes*. Cambridge: Harvard University Press, 1969.
Horace, *Odes*. In D. R. Shackleton Bailey, *Q. Horatius Flaccus Opera*. Berlin: Walter de Gruyter, 2008.
Horace, *Satires*. In D. R. Shackleton Bailey, *Q. Horatius Flaccus Opera*. Berlin: Walter de Gruyter, 2008.
Jerome, *Against Jovinian*. In Migne, *PL*, vol. 23.
Jerome, *Commentary on Isaiah*. In *CCSL*, vols. 73–73A.
Jerome, *Commentary on Matthew*. In *CCSL*, vol. 77.
Jerome, *Contra Rufinum*. In *CCSL*, vol. 79.
Jerome, *Epistles*. In *CCSL*, vols. 54–56.
Jerome, *Life of Hilarion*. In P. Leclerc, E. M. Morales, and A. de Vogüé, *Jérôme: Trois vies de moines: Paul, Malchus, Hilarion*. Paris: Éditions du Cerf, 2007.
Jordanes, *Getica*. In T. Mommsen, *Iordanis Romana et Getica*. MGH AA, vol. 5.1. Berlin, 1882.
Juvenal, *Satires*. In W. V. Clausen, *A. Persi Flacci et D. Iuni Iuvenalis Saturae*. Oxford: Oxford University Press, 1992.
Olympiodorus of Thebes. In R. C. Blockley, *The Fragmentary Classicising Historians of the Later Roman Empire*, vol. 2. Liverpool: Francis Cairns, 1983.
Philostorgius. In J. Bidez, *Philostorgius: Kirchengeschichte*. Berlin: Akademie Verlag, 1972.
Plutarch, *Life of Alexander*. In K. Ziegler, *Plutarchi Vitae Parallelae 2.2*. Leipzig: Teubner, 1968.

Pseudo-Plutarch, *Parallel Lives*. In J. Boulogne, *Plutarque: Oeuvres morales*, vol. 4. Paris: Les Belles Lettres, 2002.
Ptolemy Chennos. In R. Henry, *Photius: Bibliothèque*, vol. 3. Paris: Les Belles Lettres, 1962.
Quintilian, *Institutio Oratoria*. In M. Winterbottom, *M. Fabi Quintiliani Institutionis Oratoriae Libri Duodecim*. Oxford: Clarendon Press, 1970.
Rufinus, *Apology*. In *CCSL*, vol. 20.
Sacerdos, *Artes Grammaticae*. In H. Keil, *Grammatici Latini*, vol. 6. Leipzig: Teubner, 1874.
Sallust, *Bellum Catilinae*. In L. D. Reynolds, *C. Sallusti Crispi Catilina Iugurtha Historiarum Fragmenta Selecta Appendix Sallustiana*. Oxford: Oxford University Press, 1991.
Sallust, *Histories*. In L. D. Reynolds, *C. Sallusti Crispi Catilina Iugurtha Historiarum Fragmenta Selecta Appendix Sallustiana*. Oxford: Oxford University Press, 1991.
Scholia in Iuvenalem. In P. Wessner, *Scholia in Iuvenalem vetustiora collegit*. Leipzig: Teubner, 1931.
Socrates. In G. C. Hansen, *Sokrates: Kirchengeschichte*. Berlin: Akademie Verlag, 1995.
Sozomen. In G. C. Hansen, *Sozomenus: Kirchengeschichte*. Turnhout: Brepols, 2004.
Suetonius. In M. Ihm, *C. Suetoni Tranquilli Opera*, vol. 1. Stuttgart: Teubner, 1958.
Symmachus, *Relatio 3*. In R. Klein, *Der Streit um den Victoriaaltar: Die dritte Relatio des Symmachus und die Briefe 17, 18 und 57 des Mailänder Bischofs Ambrosius*. Darmstadt: Wissenschaftliche Buchgesellschaft.
Vergil, *Aeneid*. In G. B. Conte, *P. Vergilius Maro Aeneis*. Berlin: Walter de Gruyter, 2009.
Zosimus. In F. Paschoud, *Zosime: Histoire Nouvelle*. Paris: Les Belles Lettres, 1989.

Secondary Sources

Adams, J. N. "The Authorship of the HA." *Classical Quarterly* 22 (1972): 186–94.
Adkin, N. "Ambrose and Jerome: The Opening Shot." *Mnemosyne* 46 (1993): 364–76.
———. "The Historia Augusta and Jerome Again." *Klio* 79 (1997): 459–67.
Alföldi, A. *Die Kontorniaten: Ein verkanntes Propagandamittel der stadtrömische heidnischen Aristokratie in ihrem Kampfe gegen das christliche Kaisertum*. Budapest: O. Harassowitz, 1943.
———. *A Festival of Isis in Rome under the Christian Emperors of the IVth Century*. Budapest: Institute of Numismatics and Archaeology of the Pazmany University, 1937.
———. "Zwei Bemerkungen zur Historia Augusta." *BHAC* 1963 (1964): 1–8.
Alföldi-Rosenbaum, E. "Apicius, De re coquinaria and the Vita Heliogabali." *BHAC* 1970 (1972): 5–10.
Alvares, J. "Chariton's Erotic History." *American Journal of Philology* 118 (1997): 613–29.
Anderson, G. *Philostratus: Biography and Belles Lettres in the Third Century A.D.* London: Croom Helm, 1986.
Ando, C. "Decline, Fall, and Transformation." *Journal of Late Antiquity* 1 (2008): 31–60.
Avenarius, G. *Lukians Schrift zur Geschichtsschreibung*. Meisenheim am Glan: Anton Hain, 1954.

Baldini, A. "Varie su Zosimo, 2, 29 e la *Vita Heliogabali* della *Historia Augusta*." *HAC* 2010: 13–35.
Baldwin, B. "The *Vita Avidii*." *Klio* 58 (1976): 101–19.
Barnes, T. D. *Early Christian Hagiography and Roman History*. Tübingen: Mohr Siebeck, 2010.
———. "Jerome and the *Historia Augusta*." *HAC* 1991: 19–28.
———. "Legislation against the Christians." *Journal of Roman Studies* 58 (1968): 32–50.
———. "Publilius Optatianus Porfyrius." *American Journal of Philology* 96 (1975): 173–86.
———. "Regional Prefectures." *BHAC* 1984/85 (1987): 13–24.
———. "Some Persons in the Historia Augusta." *Phoenix* 26 (1972): 140–82.
———. *The Sources of the* Historia Augusta. Brussels: Latomus, 1978.
———. "The Sources of the Historia Augusta (1967–1992)." *HAC* 1995: 1–34.
———. "Ultimus Antoninorum." *BHAC* 1970 (1972): 53–74.
Bartley, A. "The Implications of the Reception of Thucydides within Lucian's 'Vera Historia.'" *Hermes* 131 (2003): 222–34.
Bartsch, W. "Der Charitonroman und die Historiographie." Diss., Leipzig, 1934.
Baynes, N. "The Date of the Composition of the Historia Augusta." *Classical Review* 38 (1924): 165–69.
———. *The Historia Augusta: Its Date and Purpose*. Oxford: Clarendon Press, 1926.
Béranger, J. "Les sénatus-consultes dans l'Histoire Auguste." *BHAC* 1984/85 (1987): 25–53.
———. "L'idéologie impériale dans l'Histoire Auguste." *BHAC* 1972/74 (1976): 29–54.
Berchman, R. *Porphyry against the Christians*. Leiden: Brill, 2005.
Bird, H. W. "The *Historia Augusta* on Constantine's Lineage." *Arctos* 31 (1997): 9–17.
———. "Suetonian Influence in the Later Lives of the Historia Augusta." *Hermes* 99 (1971): 129–34.
Birley, A. R. "Further Echoes of Ammianus in the *Historia Augusta*." *HAC* 1991: 53–58.
———. "The Historia Augusta and Pagan Historiography." In *Greek and Roman Historiography in Late Antiquity*, edited by G. Marasco, 127–50. Leiden: Brill, 2003.
———. "The Lacuna in the Historia Augusta." *BHAC* 1972/74 (1976): 55–62.
———. "Marius Maximus, the Consular Biographer." *Aufstieg und Niedergang der römischen Welt* 2.34.3 (1997): 2678–757.
———. "Religion in the *Historia Augusta*." *HAC* 1991: 29–52.
———. *Septimius Severus: The African Emperor*. New Haven: Yale University Press, 1989.
———. "'Trebellius Pollio' and 'Flavius Vopiscus Syracusius.'" *HAC* 2002: 33–48.
Birley, E. "'Tales of My Grandfather.'" *BHAC* 1975/76 (1978): 91–98.
Birt, T. *Das antike Buchwesen in seinem Verhältniss zur Litteratur*. Berlin: W. Hertz, 1882.
Bleckmann, B. *Die Reichskrise des III. Jahrhunderts in der spätantiken und byzantinischen Geschichtsschreibung*. Munich: Tuduv, 1992.
Bloch, H. "A New Document of the Last Pagan Revival in the West, 393–394 A.D." *Harvard Theological Review* 38 (1945): 199–244.
Boulogne, J. *Plutarque: Oeuvres Morales*, vol. 4. Paris: Les Belles Lettres, 2002.
Bowersock, G. W. "Arabs and Saracens in the Historia Augusta." *BHAC* 1984/85 (1987): 71–80.

———. "From Emperor to Bishop: The Self-Conscious Transformation of Political Power in the Fourth Century A.D." *Classical Philology* 81 (1986): 298–307.

Bowie, E. L. "Apollonius of Tyana: Tradition and Reality." *Aufstieg und Niedergang der römischen Welt* 2.16.2 (1978): 1652–99.

Brandt, H. "Die 'heidnische Vision' Aurelians (*H.A. A* 24, 2–8) und die 'christlische Vision' Konstantins des Grossen." *HAC* 1995: 107–18.

Brown, S. G. *Mark's Other Gospel: Rethinking Morton Smith's Controversial Discovery*. Waterloo, ON: Wilfrid Laurier Press, 2005.

———. "The Question of Motive in the Case against Morton Smith." *Journal of Biblical Literature* 125 (2006): 351–83.

Bruggisser, P. "Le char du préfet: Echos païens et chrétiens d'une polémique dans l'*Histoire Auguste* et chez Quodvultdeus." *HAC* 1991: 93–100.

Burian, J. "*Fides historica* als methodologischer Grundsatz der *Historia Augusta*." *Klio* 59 (1977): 285–98.

Burridge, R. A. *What Are the Gospels? A Comparison with Graeco-Roman Biography*. Cambridge: Cambridge University Press, 1992.

Bussières, M.-P. *Ambrosiaster: Contre le païens et Sur le destin*. Paris: Éditions du Cerf, 2007.

Cain, A. *The Letters of Jerome: Asceticism, Biblical Exegesis, and the Construction of Christian Authority in Late Antiquity*. Oxford: Oxford University Press, 2009.

Callu, J.-P., and M. Festy. "Alternatives historiennes: De l'*Historia Alexandri* à *Historia Augusta*." *HAC* 2010: 117–33.

Cameron, Alan. "Eunuchs in the *Historia Augusta*." *Latomus* 24 (1965): 155–58.

———. *Greek Mythography in the Roman World*. Oxford: Oxford University Press, 2004.

———. *The Last Pagans of Rome*. Oxford: Oxford University Press, 2011.

———. "Poetry and Literary Culture." In *Approaching Late Antiquity: The Transformation from Early to Late Empire*, edited by S. Swain and M. Edwards, 327–54. Oxford: Oxford University Press, 2004.

———. Review of J. Straub, *Heidnische Geschichtsapologetik*. *Journal of Roman Studies* 55 (1965): 240–50.

Cameron, Averil. "The 'Long' Late Antiquity: A Late Twentieth-Century Model." In *Classics in Progress: Essays on Ancient Greece and Rome*, edited by T. P. Wiseman, 165–91. Oxford: Oxford University Press, 2002.

Camerotto, A. *Le metamorfosi della parola: Studi sulla parodia in Luciano di Samosata*. Pisa: Instituti editoriali e poligrafici internazionalii, 1998.

Carlson, S. C. *The Gospel Hoax: Morton Smith's Invention of* Secret Mark. Waco, TX: Baylor University Press, 2005.

Casaubon, I. *Historiae Augustae scriptores sex: Aelius Spartianus, Iulius Capitolinus, Aelius Lampridius, Vulcatius Gallicanus, Trebellius Pollio, et Flavius Vopiscus*. Paris: Ambrosius et Hieronymus Drouart, 1603.

Charles, M. B. *Vegetius in Context: Establishing the Date of the Epitoma Rei Militaris*. Stuttgart: Franz Steiner Verlag, 2007.

Chastagnol, A. "Autour de la 'sobre ivresse' de Bonosus." *BHAC* 1972/74 (1976): 91–112.

———. "Autour du thème du *princeps clausus*." *BHAC* 1982/83 (1985): 149–61.
———. "Emprunts de l'Histoire Auguste aux Caesares d'Aurelius Victor." *Revue de Philologie* 41 (1967): 85–97.
———. "Études sur la *Vita Cari*: Les *editores* romains et la dilapidation de patrimoines sénatoriaux." *HAC* 1996: 165–84.
———. *Histoire Auguste*. Paris: Robert Laffont, 1994.
———. "Le Capitole dans l'Histoire Auguste." *BHAC* 1986/89 (1991): 21–30.
———. "Le poète Claudien et l'Histoire Auguste." *Historia* 19 (1970): 444–63.
———. "Le septième jour dans l'Histoire Auguste." *BHAC* 1975/76 (1978): 133–40.
———. "Le supplice inventé par Avidius Cassius: Remarques sur l'Histoire Auguste et la lettre 1 de Saint Jérôme." *BHAC* 1970 (1972): 95–108.
———. "L'utilisation des 'Caesares' d'Aurelius Victor dans l'Histoire Auguste." *BHAC* 1966/67 (1968): 53–66.
———. "Quatre études sur la Vita Cari." *BHAC* 1977/78 (1980): 45–72.
———. "Quelques thèmes bibliques dans l'Histoire Auguste." *BHAC* 1979/81 (1983): 115–26.
———. *Recherches sur l'Histoire Auguste*. Bonn: Rudolf Habelt, 1970.
———. "Trois études sur la Vita Cari." *BHAC* 1972/74 (1976): 75–90.
———. "Végèce et l'Histoire Auguste." *BHAC* 1971 (1974): 59–80.
———. "Zosime II, 38 et l'Histoire Auguste." *BHAC* 1964/65 (1966): 43–78.
Chatzis, A. *Der Philosoph und Grammatiker Ptolemaios Chennos*. Paderborn: F. Schöningh, 1914.
Chausson, F. *Stemmata aurea: Constantin, Justine, Théodose; Revendications généalogiques et idéologie imperial au IVe siècle ap. J.-C.* Rome: Bretschneider, 2007.
Cherf, W. J. "The Thermopylae Garrison of *Vita Claudii* 16." *Classical Philology* 88 (1993): 230–36.
Clover, F. "The Historia Augusta and the Latin Anthology." *BHAC* 1986/89 (1991): 31–40.
Coleiro, E. "St. Jerome's Lives of the Hermits." *Vigiliae Christianae* 11 (1957): 161–78.
Cooper, C. "'The Appearance of History': Making Some Sense of Plutarch." In *Daimonopylai: Essays in Classics and the Classical Tradition Presented to Edmund G. Berry*, edited by R. B. Egan and M. Joyal, 33–55. Winnipeg: University of Manitoba Centre for Hellenic Civilization, 2004.
Courcelle, P. P. *Les Confessions de Saint Augustin dans la tradition littéraire: Antécédents et postérité*. Paris: Études Augustiniennes, 1963.
Courtney, E. *The Fragmentary Latin Poets*. Oxford: Clarendon Press, 1993.
Damsholt, T. "Zur Benutzung von dem *Breviarium* des Eutrop in der *Historia Augusta*." *Classica et Mediaevalia* 25 (1964): 138–50.
Demandt, A. *Zeitkritik und Geschichtsbild im Werk Ammians*. Bonn: Rudolf Habelt, 1965.
Dessau, H. "Die Überlieferung der S.H.A." *Hermes* 29 (1894): 393–416.
———. Review of J. Hasebroek, *Die Fälschung der Vita Nigri und Vita Albini in den Scriptores Historiae Augustae*. *Wochenschrift für klassische Philologie* 35 (1918): 389–93.
———. "Über die S.H.A." *Hermes* 27 (1892): 561–605.

———. "Über Zeit und Persönlichkeit der Scriptores Historiae Augustae." *Hermes* 24 (1889): 337–92.
Domaszewski, A. von. *Die Personennamen bei den Scriptores historiae Augustae*. Heidelberg: Carl Winters Universitätbuchhandlung, 1918.
Döpp, S. *Zeitgeschichte in Dichtungen Claudians*. Wiesbaden: Franz Steiner Verlag, 1980.
Dowling, M. S. *Clemency and Cruelty in the Roman World*. Ann Arbor: University of Michigan Press, 2006.
Duff, T. *Plutarch's Lives: Exploring Virtue and Vice*. Oxford: Clarendon Press, 1999.
Dunand, F. "Les *Deliaca* de l'*Histoire Auguste*." *Bulletin de la Faculté des Lettres de Strasbourg* 47 (1968): 151–55.
Dupont, F. "*Recitatio* and the Space of Public Discourse." In *The Roman Cultural Revolution*, edited by T. Habinek and A. Schiesaro, 45–59. Cambridge: Cambridge University Press, 1997.
Dzielska, M. *Apollonius of Tyana in Legend and History*. Rome: Bretschneider, 1986.
Eck, W. "Zum Konsulat in der *Historia Augusta*." *HAC* 1994: 109–20.
Eco, U. *The Role of the Reader*. Bloomington: Indiana University Press, 1979.
Edmunds, L. *Intertextuality and the Reading of Roman Poetry*. Baltimore: Johns Hopkins University Press, 2001.
Edwards, M. J. "Damis the Epicurean." *Classical Quarterly* 41 (1991): 563–66.
———. "Gospel and Genre: Some Reservations." In *The Limits of Ancient Biography*, edited by B. McGing and J. Mossman, 51–62. Swansea: Classical Press of Wales, 2006.
Farrell, J. *Vergil's Georgics and the Traditions of Ancient Epic: The Art of Allusion in Literary Poetry*. New York: Oxford University Press, 1991.
Finkelpearl, E. *Metamorphosis of Language in Apuleius: A Study of Allusion in the Novel*. Ann Arbor: University of Michigan Press, 1998.
Fish, S. *Is There a Text in This Class? The Authority of Interpretive Communities*. Cambridge: Harvard University Press, 1980.
Fontaine, J. "L'aristocratie occidentale devant le monarchisme aux IVe et Ve siècles." *Rivista di storia e letteratura religiosa* 15 (1979): 28–53.
Fornara, C. W. "The Prefaces of Ammianus Marcellinus." In *Cabinet of the Muses: Essays on Classical and Comparative Literature in Honor of Thomas G. Rosenmeyer*, edited by M. Griffith and D. J. Mastronarde, 163–72. Atlanta: Scholars Press, 1990.
Francis, J. A. "Truthful Fiction: New Questions to Old Answers on Philostratus' *Life of Apollonius*." *American Journal of Philology* 119 (1998): 419–41.
Freyne, S. "Mark's Gospel and Ancient Biography." In *The Limits of Ancient Biography*, edited by B. McGing and J. Mossman, 63–75. Swansea: Classical Press of Wales, 2006.
Fry, C. "*Suetonianus quidam*: L'auteur de l'*Histoire Auguste* en utilisateur du style suétonien." *HAC* 2010: 135–52.
Fuchs, E. *Pseudologia: Formen und Funktionen fiktionaler Trugrede in der griechischen Literatur der Antike*. Heidelberg: Universitätsverlag C. Winter, 1993.
Fürst, A. *Hieronymus: Askese und Wissenschaft in Spätantike*. Freiburg: Herder, 2003.
Gascou, J. *Suétone historien*. Paris: de Boccard, 1984.

Galonnier, A. "*Anecdoton Holderi* ou *Ordo Generis Cassiodororum*: Introduction, édition, traduction et commentaire." *Antiquité tardive* 4 (1996): 299–312.

Gavrilov, A. K. "Techniques of Reading in Classical Antiquity." *Classical Quarterly* 47 (1997): 56–73.

Geffcken, J. *Der Ausgang des griechisch-römischen Heidentums*. Heidelberg: C. Winter, 1920.

Geiger, J. *Cornelius Nepos and Ancient Political Biography*. Stuttgart: Franz Steiner, 1985.

Gentili, B., and G. Cerri. *History and Biography in Ancient Thought*. Amsterdam: J. C. Gieben, 1988.

Georgiadou, A., and D. H. J. Larmour. *Lucian's Science Fiction Novel,* True Histories: *Interpretation and Commentary*. Leiden: Brill, 1998.

Giardina, A. "Esplosione di tardoantico." *Studi storici* 40 (1999): 157–80.

Gibbon, E. *The Decline and Fall of the Roman Empire*. Edited by J. B. Bury. 7 vols. London: Methuen & Co., 1909–14.

Gilliam, J. F. "Firmus and the Crocodiles." *BHAC* 1977/78 (1980): 97–102.

Görler, W. "Vergilzitate in Ausonius' Mosella." *Hermes* 97 (1969): 94–114.

Graebner, F. "Eine Zosimosquelle." *Byzantinische Zeitschrift* 14 (1905): 87–159.

Groningen, B. A. van. "ΕΚΔΟΣΙΣ." *Mnemosyne* 16 (1963): 1–17.

Groot, A. W. de. *Der Antike Prosarhythmus*. Groningen: J. B. Wolters, 1921.

Grosso, F. "La 'Vita di Apollonio di Tiana' come fonte storica." *Acme* 7 (1954): 333–532.

Gualandri, I. *Aspetti della tecnica compositiva in Claudiano*. Milan: Istituto editoriale cisalpino, 1968.

Guyot, P. *Eunuchen als Sklaven und Freigelassene in der griechisch-römischen Antike*. Stuttgart: Klett-Cotta, 1980.

Hack, R. K. "The Doctrine of Literary Forms." *Harvard Studies in Classical Philology* 27 (1916): 1–65.

Haehling, R. von. "Der obstessende Kaiser—Ein Paradigma für Luxuria in der Tyrannentopik der Historia Augusta." *BHAC* 1986/89 (1991): 93–106.

Hägg, T. "*Callirhoe* and *Parthenope*: The Beginnings of the Historical Novel." *Classical Antiquity* 6 (1987): 184–204.

Halsall, G. "The Preface to Book V of Gregory of Tours' Histories: Its Form, Context and Significance." *English Historical Review* 122 (2007): 297–317.

Hansen, W. "Strategies of Authentication." In *The Ancient Novel and Beyond*, edited by S. Panayotakis et al., 301–14. Leiden: Brill, 2003.

Harris, W. V. "Why Did the Codex Supplant the Book-Roll?" In *Renaissance Society and Culture: Essays in Honor of Eugene F. Rice, Jr.*, edited by J. Monfasani and R. G. Musto, 71–85. New York: Italica, 1991.

Hartke, W. *Geschichte und Politik im spätantiken Rom*. Leipzig: Dieterich, 1940.

———. *Römische Kinderkaiser: Eine Strukturanalyse römischen Denkens und Daseins*. Berlin: Akademie Verlag, 1951.

Harvey, P. "Saints and Satyrs: Jerome the Scholar at Work." *Athenaeum* 86 (1998): 36–56.

Heath, M. *Menander: A Rhetor in Context*. Oxford: Oxford University Press, 2004.

Heinzelmann, M. *Gregory of Tours: History and Society in the Sixth Century*. Translated by C. Carroll. Cambridge: Cambridge University Press, 2001.

Hengst, D. den. "The Author's Literary Culture." *HAC* 1991: 161–70.

———. "'The Plato of Poets': Vergil in the *Historia Augusta*." In *Romane memento: Vergil in the Fourth Century*, edited by R. Rees, 172–88. London: Duckworth, 2004.

———. *The Prefaces in the Historia Augusta*. Amsterdam: B. R. Grüner, 1981.

———. Review of F. Paschoud, *Histoire Auguste V.1*, in *Antiquité tardive* 6 (1998): 415–19. Reprinted in *Emperors and Historiography*, edited by D. W. P. Burgersdijk and J. A. van Waarden, 200–208. Leiden: Brill, 2010.

———. Review of S. Ratti, *Histoire Auguste IV.2*, in *Antiquité tardive* 13 (2005): 432–34. Reprinted in *Emperors and Historiography*, edited by D. W. P. Burgersdijk and J. A. van Waarden, 195–99. Leiden: Brill, 2010.

———. "*Verba, non res*: Über die Inventio in den Reden und Schriftstücken in der Historia Augusta." *BHAC* 1984/85 (1987): 157–74.

Hercher, R. *Über die Glaubwürdigkeit der neuen Geschichte des Ptolemaus Chennus*. Leipzig: Teubner, 1856.

Hinds, S. *Allusion and Intertext: Dynamics of Appropriation in Roman Poetry*. Cambridge: Cambridge University Press, 1998.

Hinson, E. G. "Women Biblical Scholars in the Late Fourth Century: The Aventine Circle." *Studia Patristica* 23 (1997): 319–24.

Hirschfeld, O. "Die Abfassungszeit der Sammlung der Scriptores Historiae Augustae." In *Kleine Schriften*, 887–91. Berlin: Wiedemann, 1913.

Hönn, K. *Quellenuntersuchungen zu den Viten des Heliogabalus und des Severus Alexander*. Teubner: Leipzig, 1911.

Hohl, E. "Capitolina Amphora." *Hermes* 52 (1917): 472–75.

———. "Die 'gotische Abkunft' des Kaisers Maximinus Thrax." *Klio* 34 (1942): 264–89.

———. "Die Historia Augusta und die Caesares des Aurelius Victor." *Historia* 4 (1955): 220–28.

———. "Vopiscus und die Biographie des Kaisers Tacitus." *Klio* 11 (1911): 178–229.

———. "Vopiscus und Pollio." *Klio* 12 (1912): 474–82.

Homo, L. "Les Documents de l'Histoire Auguste et leur valeur historique." *Revue historique* 151 (1926): 161–98; 152 (1926): 1–31.

Honoré, T. "Lawyers and Government in the 'Historia Augusta.'" *Iura* 42 (1991): 13–41.

———. "Scriptor Historiae Augustae." *Journal of Roman Studies* 77 (1987): 156–76.

Horsfall, N. "Apuleius, Apollonius of Tyana, Bibliomancy: Some Neglected Dating Criteria." *HAC* 1995: 169–78.

Hose, M. "Ptolemaios Chennos und das Problem der Schwindelliteratur." In *In Pursuit of "Wissenschaft": Festschrift für William M. Calder III zum 75. Geburtstag*, edited by S. Heilen et al., 177–96. Zürich: Olms, 2008.

Hunter, D. *Marriage, Celibacy, and Heresy in Ancient Christianity: The Jovinianist Controversy*. Oxford: Oxford University Press, 2007.

Hunter, R. "History and Historicity in the Romance of Chariton." *Aufstieg und Niedergang der römischen Welt* 2.34.2 (1993): 1055–86.

Iddeng, J. W. "*Publica aut Peri!* The Releasing and Distribution of Roman Books." *Symbolae Osloenses* 81 (2006): 58–84.

Jackson, S. "Apollonius and the Emperors." *Hermathenea* 137 (1984): 25–32.

Jacoby, F. "Die Überlieferung von Ps. Plutarchs Parallela Minora und die Schwindelautoren." *Mnemosyne* 8 (1940): 73–144.

Janson, T. *Latin Prose Prefaces: Studies in Literary Conventions.* Stockholm: Almqvist & Wiksell, 1964.

Jay, P. *L'exégèse de Saint Jérôme d'après son* Commentaire sur Isaïe. Paris: Études Augustiniennes, 1985.

Jeffery, P. *The Secret Gospel of Mark Unveiled: Imagined Rituals of Sex, Death, and Madness in a Biblical Forgery.* New Haven: Yale University Press, 2007.

Johne, K.-P. "Die Biographie des Gegenkaisers Censorinus: Ein Beitrag zur sozialen Herkunft der Historia Augusta." *BHAC* 1972/74 (1976): 131–42.

———. *Kaiserbiographie und Senatsaristokratie: Untersuchungen zur Datierung und sozialen Herkunft der Historia Augusta.* Berlin: Akademie-Verlag, 1976.

Johnson, W. A. *Readers and Reading Culture in the High Roman Empire.* Oxford: Oxford University Press, 2010.

Jones, C. P. "Apollonius of Tyana in Late Antiquity." In *Greek Literature in Late Antiquity*, edited by S. F. Johnson, 49–64. Aldershot: Ashgate, 2006.

Jonge, P. de. *Philological and Historical Commentary on Ammianus Marcellinus XVII.* Groningen: Bouma's Boekhuis, 1977.

Joseph, T. A. *Tacitus the Epic Successor: Virgil, Lucan, and the Narrative of Civil War in the* Histories. Leiden: Brill, 2012.

Kelly, G. *Ammianus Marcellinus: The Allusive Historian.* Cambridge: Cambridge University Press, 2008.

———. "The Sphragis and Closure of the *Res Gestae.*" In *Ammianus after Julian: The Reign of Valentinian and Valens in Books 26–31 of the* Res Gestae, edited by J. Den Boeft et al., 219–41. Leiden: Brill, 2007.

Kelly, J. N. D. *Jerome: His Life, Writings and Controversies.* New York: Harper & Row, 1975.

Keudel, U. *Poetische Vorläufer und Vorbilder in Claudians De Consulatu Stilichonis: Imitationskommentar.* Göttingen: Vandenhoeck & Ruprecht, 1970.

Kim, L. *Homer between History and Fiction in Imperial Greek Literature.* Cambridge: Cambridge University Press, 2010.

Kisch, Y. de. "Les *Sortes Vergilianae* dans l'Histoire Auguste." *Mélanges d'archéologie et d'histoire* 82 (1970): 321–62.

———. "Sur quelques omina imperii dans l'Histoire Auguste." *Revue des études latines* 51 (1973): 190–207.

Kleijwegt, M. "Caligula's 'Triumph' at Baiae." *Mnemosyne* 47 (1994): 652–71.

Klingshirn, W. E. "Defining the *Sortes Sanctorum*: Gibbon, Du Cange, and Early Christian Lot Divination." *Journal of Early Christian Studies* 10 (2002): 77–130.

Kolb, F. "Cassius Dio, Herodian und die Quellen der Historia Augusta." *HAC* 1995: 179–92.

———. "Herodian in der Historia Augusta." *BHAC* 1972/74 (1976): 143–52.

———. *Literarische Beziehungen zwischen Cassius Dio, Herodian und der Historia Augusta.* Bonn: Rudolf Habelt, 1972.
Konrad, C. F. "Cotta off Mellaria and the Identities of Fufidius." *Classical Philology* 84 (1989): 119–29.
Konstan, D. "The Active Reader in Classical Antiquity." *Argos* 30 (2006): 5–16.
Lafaurie, J. "L'empire Gaulois: Apport de la numismatique." *Aufstieg und Niedergang der römischen Welt* 2.2 (1975): 853–1012.
Leclerc, P., E. M. Morales, and A. de Vogüé, edd. and trs. *Jérôme: Trois vies de moines: Paul, Malchus, Hilarion.* Paris: Éditions du Cerf, 2007.
Lenski, N. "*Initium mali Romano imperio*: Contemporary Reactions to the Battle of Adrianople." *Transactions of the American Philological Association* 127 (1997): 129–68.
Leo, F. *Die griechisch-römische Biographie nach ihrer litterarischen Form.* Leipzig: Teubner, 1901.
Levene, D. S. *Livy on the Hannibalic War.* Oxford: Oxford University Press, 2010.
Levitan, W. "Dancing at the End of the Rope: Optatian Porfyry and the Field of Roman Verse." *Transactions of the American Philological Association* 115 (1985): 245–69.
Lewis, R. G. "'Suetonius' 'Caesares' and Their Literary Antecedents." *Aufstieg und Niedergang der römischen Welt* 2.33.5 (1991): 3623–74.
Liebeschuetz, J. H. W. G. *Decline and Fall of the Roman City.* Oxford: Oxford University Press, 2001.
Liebs, D. "Alexander Severus und das Strafrecht." *BHAC* 1977/78 (1980): 115–47.
———. *Die Jurisprudenz im spätantiken Italien: 260–640 n. Chr.* Berlin: Duncker & Humblot, 1987.
———. "OM 13.1 und das Reskriptenwesen der HA." *BHAC* 1982/83 (1985): 221–37.
———. "Strafrechtliches in der Tacitusvita." *BHAC* 1979/81 (1983): 151–71.
Lim, R. *Public Disputation, Power, and Social Order in Late Antiquity.* Berkeley: University of California Press, 1995.
Luce, T. J. "Ancient Views on the Causes of Bias in Historical Writing." *Classical Philology* 84 (1989): 16–31.
Luginbill, R. D. "Chariton's Use of Thucydides' *History* in Introducing the Egyptian Revolt: *Chaireas and Callirhoe* 6.8." *Mnemosyne* 53 (2000): 1–11.
Lunn-Rockliffe, S. *Ambrosiaster's Political Theology.* Oxford: Oxford University Press, 2007.
Luria, S. "Entstellungen des Klassikertextes bei Stobaios." *Rheinisches Museum* 78 (1929): 81–104.
MacMullen, R. "The Roman Concept Robber-Pretender." *Revue internationale des droits de l'antiquité* 10 (1963): 221–25.
Mader, G. "History as Carnival, or Method and Madness in the *Vita Heliogabali*." *Classical Antiquity* 24 (2005): 131–72.
Maenchen-Helfen, O. J. "The Date of Ammianus Marcellinus' Last Books." *American Journal of Philology* 76 (1955): 384–99.
Maire, B. *Gargilius Martialis: Les remèdes tirés des légumes et des fruits.* Paris: Les Belles Lettres, 2002.

Malloch, S. J. V. "Gaius' Bridge at Baiae and Alexander-*Imitatio*." *Classical Quarterly* 51 (2001): 206–17.

Marchesi, I. *The Art of Pliny's Letters: A Poetics of Allusion in the Private Correspondence*. Cambridge: Cambridge University Press, 2008.

Marcone, A. "A Long Late Antiquity? Considerations on a Controversial Periodization." *Journal of Late Antiquity* 1 (2008): 4–19.

Marincola, J. *Authority and Tradition in Ancient Historiography*. Cambridge: Cambridge University Press, 1997.

———. "Genre, Convention, and Innovation in Greco-Roman Historiography." In *The Limits of Historiography: Genre and Narrative in Ancient Historical Texts*, edited by C. S. Kraus, 281–324. Leiden: Brill, 1999.

Mattern, S. P. *Galen and the Rhetoric of Healing*. Baltimore: Johns Hopkins University Press, 2008.

Matthews, J. *The Roman Empire of Ammianus*. London: Duckworth, 1989.

———. *Western Aristocracies and Imperial Court A.D. 364–425*. Oxford: Oxford University Press, 1975.

McGill, S. *Virgil Recomposed: The Mythological and Secular Centos in Antiquity*. New York: Oxford University Press, 2005.

McGing, B., and J. Mossman. "Introduction." In *The Limits of Ancient Biography*, edited by B. McGing and J. Mossman, ix–xx. Swansea: Classical Press of Wales, 2006.

Mehl, A. *Römische Geschichtsschreibung*. Stuttgart: W. Kolhammer, 2001.

Mendelson, A. "Eusebius and the Posthumous Career of Apollonius of Tyana." In *Eusebius, Christianity, and Judaism*, edited by H. W. Attridge and G. Hata, 510–22. Detroit: Wayne State University Press, 1992.

Merkle, S. "Telling the Truth of the Trojan War: The Eyewitness Account of Dictys of Crete." In *The Search for the Ancient Novel*, edited by J. Tatum, 183–96. Baltimore: Johns Hopkins University Press, 1994.

———. "The Truth and Nothing but the Truth: Dictys and Dares." In *The Novel in the Ancient World*, edited by G. Schmeling, 563–80. Leiden: Brill, 1996.

Meyer, E. "Apollonios von Tyana und die Biographie des Philostratos." *Hermes* 52 (1917): 371–424.

Miller, J. F., and A. J. Woodman, eds. *Latin Historiography and Poetry in the Early Empire: Generic Interactions*. Leiden: Brill, 2010.

Mommsen, T. "Die Scriptores Historiae Augustae." *Hermes* 25 (1890): 228–92.

Morgan, J. R. "Fiction and History: Historiography and the Novel." In *A Companion to Greek and Roman Historiography*, edited by J. Marincola, 553–64. Malden, MA: Blackwell, 2007.

———. "Make-Believe and Make Believe: The Fictionality of the Greek Novels." In *Lies and Fiction in the Ancient World*, edited by C. Gill and T. P. Wiseman, 175–229. Exeter: University of Exeter Press, 1993.

Mouchová, B. *Untersuchungen über die Scriptores Historiae Augustae*. Prague: Univerzita Karlova, 1975.

Murgia, C. E. "Secret Mark: Real or Fake?" In *Longer Mark: Forgery, Interpretation, or Old Tradition*, edited by W. Wuellner, 35–40. Berkeley: Center for Hermeneutical Studies, 1975.

Murison, C. L. "Cassius Dio on Nervan Legislation: Nieces and Eunuchs." *Historia* 53 (2004): 343–55.

Mussies, G. "Marnas God of Gaza." *Aufstieg und Niedergang der römischen Welt* 2.18.4 (1990): 2412–57.

Neri, V. "Considerazioni sul tema della *luxuria* nell'*Historia Augusta*." *HAC* 1999: 217–40.

———. "Il populus Romanus nell'Historia Augusta." *HAC* 1995: 219–68.

———. "La caratterizzazione fisica degli imperatori nell'*Historia Augusta*." *HAC* 1998: 249–68.

———. "L'imperatore come miles: Tacito, Attalo e la datazione dell'Historia Augusta." *HAC* 2002: 373–96.

Ni-Mheallaigh, K. "Pseudo-Documentarism and the Limits of Ancient Fiction." *American Journal of Philology* 129 (2008): 403–31.

Obbink, D. "Readers and Intellectuals." In *Oxyrhynchus: A City and Its Texts*, edited by A. K. Bowman et al., 271–86. London: Egypt Exploration Society, 2007.

Optendrenk, T. *Die Religionspolitik des Kaisers Elagabal im Spiegel der Historia Augusta*. Bonn: Rudolf Habelt, 1969.

Palmer, L. R. *The Latin Language*. London: Faber and Faber, 1954.

Paschoud, F. "Claude II aux Thermopyles? À propos de HA *Claud*. 16, 1, Zosime 5, 5 et Eunape, *Vitae Soph*. 7, 3, 4–5." In *Institutions, société et vie politique dans l'Empire romain au IVe siècle ap. J.-C.*, edited by M. Christol and S. Demougin, 21–28. Rome: Ecole française de Rome, 1992.

———. *Histoire Auguste IV.3: Vies des trente tyrans et de Claude*. Paris: Les Belles Lettres, 2011.

———. *Histoire Auguste V.1: Vies d'Aurélien, Tacite*. Paris: Les Belles Lettres, 1996.

———. *Histoire Auguste V.2: Vies de Probus, Firmus, Saturnin, Proculus et Bonose, Carus, Numérien et Carin*. Paris: Les Belles Lettres, 2002.

———. "L'auteur de l'Histoire Auguste, est-il un apostat?" In *Consuetudinis Amor: Fragments d'histoire romaine offerts à J. P. Callu*, edited by F. Chausson and E. Wolff, 362–68. Rome: Bretschneider, 2003.

———. "Le diacre Philippe, l'eunuque de la reine Candace et l'auteur de la vita Aureliani." *BHAC* 1975/76 (1978): 147–51.

———. "Le Tyran Fantasmé: Variations de l'*Histoire Auguste* sur le thème de l'usurpation." In *Usurpationen in der Spätantike*, edited by F. Paschoud and J. Szidat, 87–98. Stuttgart: Franz Steiner Verlag, 1997.

———. "L'*Histoire Auguste* et Dexippe." *HAC* 1991: 217–70.

———. "L'intolérance chrétienne vue et jugée par les païens." *Cristianesimo nella storia* 11 (1990): 545–77.

———. "*Mendacii splendor*: Formes d'entrée en matière et protestations de véridicité dans la littérature de fiction." *Latomus* 54 (1995): 262–78.

———. "Noms camouflés d'historiens du 4e siècles dans l'*Histoire Auguste*." *Historia* 44 (1995): 502–4.

———. "Quelques mots rares comme éventuels témoins du niveau de style de l'*Histoire Auguste* et des lectures de son auteur." In *Historia testis: Mélanges d'épigraphie, d'histoire ancienne et de philologie offerts à Tadeusz Zawadzki*, edited by Marcel Piérart and Olivier Curty, 217–28. Fribourg: Éditions universitaires, 1989.

———. "Raisonnements providentialistes dans l'Histoire Auguste." *BHAC* 1977/78 (1980): 163–78.

———. "*Se non è vero, è ben trovato*: Tradition littéraire et vérité historique chez Ammien Marcellin." *Chiron* 20 (1990): 37–54.

———. "Symmaque, Jérôme et l'Histoire Auguste." *Museum Helveticum* 57 (2000): 173–82.

———. *Zosime: Histoire Nouvelle*. 2nd ed. Paris: Les Belles Lettres, 2000.

———. "Zosime 2, 29 et la version païenne de la conversion de Constantin." *Historia* 20 (1971): 334–53.

Peirano, I. *The Rhetoric of the Roman Fake: Latin* Pseudepigrapha *in Context*. Cambridge: Cambridge University Press, 2012.

Pekáry, T. "Statuen in der Historia Augusta." *BHAC* 1968/9 (1970): 151–72.

Pelling, C. "Biographical History? Cassius Dio on the Early Principate." In *Portraits: Biographical Representation in the Greek and Latin Literature of the Roman Empire*, edited by M. J. Edwards and S. Swain, 117–44. Oxford: Clarendon Press, 1997.

Peter, H. "Die römischen sogenannten Dreissig Tyrannen." *Abhandlungen der Königlich-sächsischen Gesellschaft der Wissenschaften, philologisch-historische Klasse* 27 (1909): 179–222.

Pottier, B. "Un pamphlet contre Stilichon dans l'*Histoire Auguste*: La vie de Maximin le Thrace." *Mélanges de l'Ecole française de Rome* 117 (2005): 223–67.

Pucci, J. M. *The Full-Knowing Reader*. New Haven: Yale University Press, 1998.

Quinn, K. "The Poet and His Audiences in the Augustan Age." *Aufstieg und Niedergang der römischen Welt* 2.30.1 (1982): 75–180.

Ramelli, I. "Caritone e la storiografia greca: Il *Romanzo di Calliroe* come romanzo storico antico." *Acme* 53 (2000): 43–62.

Ratti, S. *Histoire Auguste IV.2: Vies des deux Valériens et des deux Galliens*. Paris: Les Belles Lettres, 2000.

———. "Réponses de l'*Histoire Auguste* aux apologistes Tertullien et Lactance." *Museum Helveticum* 59 (2002): 229–37.

———. "394: Fin de la rédaction de l'*Histoire Auguste*?" *Antiquité tardive* 16 (2008): 335–48.

Rebenich, S. *Hieronymus und sein Kreis: Prosopographische und sozialgeschichtliche Untersuchungen*. Stuttgart: Franz Steiner Verlag, 1992.

———. "Inventing an Ascetic Hero: Jerome's Life of Paul the First Hermit." In *Jerome of Stridon: His Life, Writings and Legacy*, edited by A. Cain and J. Lössl, 13–28. Burlington, VT: Ashgate, 2009.

———. *Jerome*. London: Routledge, 2002.

Roberts, M. *The Jeweled Style: Poetry and Poetics in Late Antiquity.* Ithaca: Cornell University Press, 1989.
Rohrbacher, D. "Enmann's *Kaisergeschichte* from Augustus to Domitian." *Latomus* 68 (2009): 709–19.
———. "Jerome, an Early Reader of Ammianus Marcellinus." *Latomus* 65 (2006): 422–24.
———. "Physiognomics in Roman Imperial Biography." *Classical Antiquity* 29 (2010): 94–119.
———. "The Sources of the *Historia Augusta* Re-examined." *Histos* 7 (2013): 146–80.
———. "Why Didn't Constantius II Eat Fruit?" *Classical Quarterly* 55 (2005): 323–36.
Romm, J. "Novels beyond Thule: Antonius Diogenes, Rabelais, Cervantes." In *The Search for the Ancient Novel*, edited by J. Tatum, 101–16. Baltimore: Johns Hopkins University Press, 1994.
Rosenmeyer, T. G. "Ancient Literary Genres: A Mirage?" *Yearbook of Comparative and General Literature* 34 (1985): 74–84.
Rösger, A. "Vopiscus und das Authentizitätsproblem (Car. 4, 1–5, 3)." *BHAC* 1986/89 (1991): 179–82.
Roskam, G. "Educating the Young . . . Over Wine? Plutarch, Calvinus Taurus, and Favorinus as Convivial Teachers." In Symposion *and* Philanthropia *in Plutarch*, edited by J. R. Ferreira et al., 269–83. Coimbra: Centro de Estudos Clássicos e Humanísticos da Universidade de Coimbra, 2009.
Rothschild, C. K. "Irony and Truth: The Value of *De historia conscribenda* for Understanding Hellenistic and Early Roman Period Historiographical Method." In *Die Apostelgeschichte im Kontext antiker und frühchristlicher Historiographie*, edited by J. Frey et al., 277–91. Berlin: Walter de Gruyter, 2009.
Ruggini, L. "*De Morte Persecutorum* e polemica antibarbarica nella storiografia pagana e Cristiana: A proposito della disgrazia di Stilicone." *Rivista di storia e letteratura religiosa* 4 (1968): 433–47.
———. "Elagabalo, Costantino e i culti 'siriaci' nella *Historia Augusta*." *HAC* 1991: 123–46.
———. "Il vescovo Ambrogio e la Historia Augusta: Attualità di un topos politico-letterario." In *Atti del Colloquio patavino sulla Historia Augusta*, edited by J. Straub, 68–79. Rome: Bretschneider, 1963.
Russell, D. A. "*De Imitatione.*" In *Creative Imitation and Latin Literature*, edited by D. West and T. Woodman, 1–16. Cambridge: Cambridge University Press, 1979.
Rutledge, S. H. *Imperial Inquisitions: Prosecutors and Informants from Nero to Domitian.* London: Routledge, 2001.
Salemme, C. *Similitudini nella storia: Un capitolo su Ammiano Marcellino.* Naples: Loffredo, 1989.
Salzman, M. *The Making of a Christian Aristocracy.* Cambridge: Harvard University Press, 2002.
Schlereth, J. *De Plutarchi quae feruntur parallelis minoribus.* Freiburg: Herder, 1931.
Schlumberger, J. "Die Epitome de Caesaribus und die Historia Augusta." *BHAC* 1972/74 (1976): 201–20.

———. "'Non scribo sed dicto' (HA T 33, 8): Hat der Autor der Historia Augusta mit Stenographen gearbeitet?" *BHAC* 1972/4 (1976): 221-38.
Schmeidler, B. "Die Scriptores Historiae Augustae und der heilige Hieronymus." *Philologische Wochenschrift* 31 (1927): 955-60.
Schmid, W. "Die Koexistenz von Sarapiskult und Christentum in Hadrianbrief bei Vopiscus." *BHAC* 1964/5 (1966): 153-84.
Scholten, H. *Der Eunuch in Kaisernähe: Zur politischen und sozialen Bedeutung des praepositus sacri cubiculi im 4. und 5. Jahrhundert n. Chr.* Frankfurt am Main: Peter Lang, 1995.
Schwarte, K. H. "Das angebliche Christengesetz des Septimius Severus." *Historia* 12 (1963): 185-208.
Schwartz, J. "Arguments philologiques pour dater l'Histoire Auguste." *Historia* 15 (1966): 454-65.
———. "Sur la date de L'Histoire Auguste." *BHAC* 1966/67 (1968): 91-100.
———. "Une fantasie impie dans l'*Histoire Auguste*." *Revue d'histoire et de philosophie religieuses* 69 (1989): 481-83.
Seeck, O. "Politische Tendenzgeschichte im 5. Jahrhundert n. Chr." *Rheinisches Museum* 49 (1912): 208-24.
———. "Studien zur Geschichte Diocletians und Constantins iii: Die Entstehungszeit der H.A." *Jahrbücher für classische Philologie* 36 (1890): 609-39.
Selden, D. L. "Genre of Genre." In *The Search for the Ancient Novel*, edited by J. Tatum, 39-64. Baltimore: Johns Hopkins University Press, 1994.
Shanks, H. "Morton Smith—Forger." *Biblical Archaeology Review* 35 (2009): 49-53, 86-87.
———. "Restoring a Dead Scholar's Reputation." *Biblical Archaeology Review* 35 (2009): 59-61, 90-91.
Shaw, B. "Sabinus the Muleteer." *Classical Quarterly* 57 (2007): 132-38.
Small, J. P. *Wax Tablets of the Mind: Cognitive Studies of Memory and Literacy in Classical Antiquity*. London: Routledge, 1997.
Smith, M. *Clement of Alexandria and a Secret Gospel of Mark*. Cambridge: Harvard University Press, 1973.
———. *The Secret Gospel: The Discovery and Interpretation of the Secret Gospel According to Mark*. New York: Harper & Row, 1973.
Smith, S. D. *Greek Identity and the Athenian Past in Chariton: The Romance of Empire*. Groningen: Barkhuis, 2007.
Snyder, H. G. *Teachers and Texts in the Ancient World: Philosophers, Jews and Christians*. London: Routledge, 2000.
Souter, A. "Portions of an Old-Latin Text of St. Matthew's Gospel." In *Quantulacumque: Studies Presented to Kirsopp Lake*, edited by R. P. Casey, S. Lake, and A. K. Lake, 349-54. London: Christophers, 1937.
Speyer, W. *Büchervernichtung und Zensur des Geistes bei Heiden, Juden und Christen*. Stuttgart: Anton Hiersemann, 1981.
Starr, R. "The Circulation of Literary Texts in the Roman World." *Classical Quarterly* 37 (1987): 213-23.

Stein, E. *Histoire du Bas-Empire*. Amsterdam: Adolf M. Hakkert, 1968.
Stephens, S. "Fragments of Lost Novels." In *The Novel in the Ancient World*, edited by G. Schmeling, 655–83. Leiden: Brill, 1996.
Stern, H. *Date et destinaire de l'Histoire Auguste*. Paris: Les Belles Lettres, 1953.
Stertz, S. A. "Christianity in the *Historia Augusta*." *Latomus* 36 (1977): 694–715.
Straub, J. "Calpurnia univiria." *BHAC* 1966/67 (1968): 101–18.
———. *Heidnische Geschichtsapologetik in der christlichen Spätantike: Untersuchungen über Zeit und Tendenz der Historia Augusta*. Bonn: Rudolf Habelt, 1963.
———. "Juristische Notizen in der Historia Augusta." *BHAC* 1975/76 (1978): 195–216.
———. "Senaculum, id est mulierum senatus." *BHAC* 1964/65 (1966): 221–40.
———. *Studien zur Historia Augusta*. Bern: A. Francke, 1952.
———. "Zur Ordination von Bischöfen und Beamten in der christlichen Spätantike: Ein Reformvorschlag der Historia Augusta?" In *Mullus: Festschrift Theodor Klauser*, edited by A. Stuiber and A. Hermann, 336–45. Münster: Aschendorffsche Buchdruckerei, 1964.
Stroheker, K. F. "Princeps clausus: Zu einigen Berührungen der Literatur des fünften Jahrhunderts mit der Historia Augusta." *BHAC* 1968/69 (1970): 273–83.
Swain, B. "Jordanes and Virgil: A Case Study of Intertextuality in the *Getica*." *Classical Quarterly* 60 (2010): 243–49.
Syme, R. *Ammianus and the Historia Augusta*. Oxford: Clarendon Press, 1968.
———. *Emperors and Biography: Studies in the Historia Augusta*. Oxford: Clarendon Press, 1971.
———. *The Historia Augusta: A Call of Clarity*. Bonn: Rudolf Habelt, 1971.
———. *Historia Augusta Papers*. Oxford: Clarendon Press, 1983.
———. "Pollio, Saloninus and Salonae." *Classical Quarterly* 31 (1937): 39–48.
Thomas, R. "Virgil's *Georgics* and the Art of Reference." *Harvard Studies in Classical Philology* 90 (1986): 171–98.
Thomson, M. "*Logodaedalia*: Ausonius and the *Historia Augusta*." In *Studies in Latin Literature and Roman History XIV*, edited by C. Deroux, 445–75. Brussels: Latomus, 2008.
———. *Studies in the* Historia Augusta. Brussels: Latomus, 2012.
Throop, G. R. "Ancient Literary Detractors of Cicero." *Washington University Studies* 1 (1913–14): 19–41.
Tomberg, K.-H. *Die Kainé Historia des Ptolemaios Chennos: Eine literarhistorische und quellenkritische Untersuchung*. Bonn: Rudolf Habelt, 1968.
Tougher, S. "Ammianus and the Eunuchs." In *The Late Roman World and Its Historian: Interpreting Ammianus Marcellinus*, edited by J. W. Drijver and D. Hunt, 64–73. London: Routledge, 1999.
Townend, G. "The Circus of Nero and the Vatican Excavations." *American Journal of Archaeology* 62 (1958): 216–18.
Toynbee, J. M. C., and J. B. Ward-Perkins. *The Shrine of St. Peter and the Vatican Excavations*. London: Longmans, Green, 1956.
Treucker, B. "Kriterien der Aktualisierung in der Historia Augusta." *BHAC* 1964/65 (1966): 273–92.
Trombley, F. *Hellenic Religion and Christianization c. 370–529*. 2 vols. Leiden: Brill, 1993.

Turcan, R. "Héliogabale précurseur de Constantin?" *Bulletin de l'Association Guillaume Budé* 47 (1988): 38–52.

———. *Histoire Auguste III.1: Vies de Macrin, Diaduménien, Héliogabale*. Paris: Les Belles Lettres, 1993.

———. "Les monuments figurés dans l'*Histoire Auguste*." *HAC* 1991: 287–310.

Valette-Cagnac, E. *La lecture à Rome: Rites et pratiques*. Paris: Éditions Belin, 1997.

Van der Horst, P. "*Sortes*: Sacred Books as Instant Oracles in Late Antiquity." In *The Use of Sacred Books in the Ancient World*, edited by L. V. Rutgers et al., 143–74. Leuven: Peeters, 1998.

van Minnen, P. "House-to-House Enquiries: An Interdisciplinary Approach to Roman Karanis." *Zeitschrift für Papyrologie und Epigraphik* 100 (1994): 227–51.

Van Nuffelen, P. *Orosius and the Rhetoric of History*. Oxford: Oxford University Press, 2012.

Vessey, M. "Jerome's Origen: The Making of a Christian Literary *Persona*." *Studia Patristica* 28 (1993): 135–45.

Vogels, H. "Ambrosiaster und Hieronymus." *Revue bénédictine* 66 (1956): 14–19.

Ware, C. *Claudian and the Roman Epic Tradition*. Cambridge: Cambridge University Press, 2012.

Weinfeld, M. "Hillel and the Misunderstanding of Judaism in Modern Scholarship." In *Hillel and Jesus: Comparative Studies of Two Major Religious Leaders*, edited by J. H. Charlesworth and L. J. Johns, 56–70. Minneapolis: Fortress Press, 1997.

Weingarten, S. *The Saint's Saints: Hagiography and Geography in Jerome*. Leiden: Brill, 2005.

White, P. "Bookshops in the Literary Culture of Rome." In *Ancient Literacies: The Culture of Reading in Greece and Rome*, edited by W. A. Johnson and H. N. Parker, 268–87. Oxford: Oxford University Press, 2009.

Wiesen, D. S. *St. Jerome as a Satirist: A Study in Christian Latin Thought and Letters*. Ithaca: Cornell University Press, 1964.

Wilken, R. L. "The Homeric Cento in Irenaeus, 'Adversus Haereses' I, 9, 4." *Vigiliae Christianae* 21 (1967): 25–33.

Wiseman, T. P. *Clio's Cosmetics: Three Studies in Greco-Roman Literature*. Totowa, NJ: Rowman and Littlefield, 1979.

———. *Historiography and Imagination*. Exeter: University of Exeter Press, 1994.

Wisniewski, R. "*Bestiae Christum loquuntur* ou des habitants du désert et de la ville dans la *Vita Pauli* de Saint Jérôme." *Augustinianum* 40 (2000): 105–44.

Wuellner, W., ed. *Longer Mark: Forgery, Interpretation, or Old Tradition*. Berkeley: Center for Hermeneutical Studies, 1975.

Youtie, H. C. "Callimachus in the Tax Rolls." In *Scriptiunculae*, vol. 2: 1035–41. Amsterdam: A. M. Hakkert, 1973.

Zawadzki, T. "Dioecesis Thraciarum, un indice de falsification dans l'Histoire Auguste." *BHAC* 1972/74 (1976): 323–32.

———. "Encore sur les buts et la date de composition de l'Histoire Auguste." *Studii clasice* 5 (1963): 249–58.

Zernial, H. L. *Über den Satzschluss in der Historia Augusta*. Berlin: Akademie-Verlag, 1956.

Index

Aaron, 120
Abraham, 92, 96, 120
Achilles, 78–79, 104–7, 120
Acholius, 27–28, 148
Acta Alexandrinorum, 76
Actium, 37
Acusilaos of Argos, 188n57
Adrianople, 135–40, 145, 169
Ad Salices, 136–37, 139
Aelius (life), 5, 6, 8, 12
Aelius Cesettianus, 152
Aemilianus, 9
Aemilius Parthenianus, 5
Aeneas, 44, 145, 178n15
Africa, 154, 165–66
Africanus, 142
Agamemnon (character in Petronius), 77
Agamemnon (mythological figure), 178n15
Alamanni, 165–66
Alans, 7, 139–40, 172–73
Alaric, 155, 161–64, 167–68
Alexander (of Macedon), 48, 59, 104–7
Alexander Severus (emperor): and Acholius, 27; and Apollonius, 96; and Christianity, 92–93, 99; dedicates pearls to Venus, 119; and Delian gifts, 31–32; and Elagabalus, 58; and eunuchs, 151; extraordinary memory of, 28; and fancy dress, 120; and Gargilius Martialis, 26; and the Golden Rule, 126–28; as Honorius, 167; and interest rates, 99; in Jordanes, 172; and Julian, 147–50; *lararium* of, 92, 96, 98, 120; and the law, 99, 153; and Marnas, 108–11; and the *princeps clausus*, 150; prophecy of divinization, 128; star omen at birth, 128–29; suffocates Verconius Turninus, 129; and Vergilian oracle, 42, 44
Alexander Severus (life): addressed to Constantine, 6; and Ammianus, 171; and Gibbon, 175; paired with *Elagabalus*, 8, 30, 58; use of *KG* and Herodian, 13, 16, 171
Alexandria, 75–76, 79, 110
Alfenus, 19–20
Altar of Victory: Ambrose against, 28, 88, 129–32; removal by Gratian, 130–32; Symmachus for, 173
Alypius, 43
Ambervalia, 130
Ambrose: against the Altar of Victory, 28, 88, 129–30; on boy emperors, 162; and Milan, 185n17; silent Bible reading, 76; as source for *HA*, 103, 129–30, 132–33
Ambrosiaster, 102
Amburbium, 130
Ammianus Marcellinus: on Adrianople, 136–40, 145; on bias in history, 61–62; and the date of the *HA*, 8, 146, 157–58, 162; date of the *Res Gestae* of, 157–58; and depiction of Alexander Severus in the *HA*, 146–50; on eunuchs, 151–52; and Fabius Marcellinus, 25, 45; on the Franks, 141; on fruit consumption, 144; on the Gauls, 141; and Gellius, 18–20; 25; as a general source for allusion for the *HA*, 15–16, 20, 85, 134–53, 169–71, 174–75; on Julian's invasion of Persia, 67–68; on the kidnapping of Constantina, 140–41, 168; on law, 153; on military crowns, 144–45; on obelisks, 66; on religion, 87, 94; and Sallust, 25, 45; on the Sibylline books, 155; on triviality in history, 63; on the urban prefect, 152; use of allusion, 3, 18–20
Ammonius, 41

Index

ancilia, 38
ancilla, 25
andiktes, 75
Anecdoton Holderi, 173
Anicii, 7, 159
Antinous, 26
Antioch, 112, 136–38, 156
Antium, 52
Antoninus Pius (emperor), 6, 36, 63–64
Antoninus Pius (life), 8
Antonius Diogenes, 71
Antony, 43, 104
Antony, Mark, 22, 119
Apamea, 43
Apennines, 42
Aper, 51
Apicius, 54, 114
Apollinaris, 40
Apollinaris, Aurelius, 40, 42
Apollo, 42, 87, 130, 145
Apollonius of Tyana, 71, 96–98, 120
Apuleius, 17, 71, 104
Aquileia, 52, 113
Arabs, 134–36
Aramaic, 67
Arca Caesarea, 129
Arcadius, 99, 151, 161–62, 165
Archilochus, 41
Aristarchus, 82
Aristonicus of Alexandria, 79
Aristonicus of Tarentum, 79
Armenia, 136–37, 139, 143
Armenian, 135–36
Arnobius of Sicca, 132
Artemisia, 78
ascetic, 91, 102
asceticism, 104, 133
Asia Minor, 29
Aspetos, 79
astrologers, 89, 93–94, 121
Atlas Mountains, 143
Attalus, Priscus, 163–64, 166–67
Atticus, 59
Augustine: on Apollonius of Tyana, 98; on Apuleius, 71; on astrology, 43; on biblical sortition, 44, 184n80; and Carthage, 185n17; compared with Jerome, 171; on the Golden Rule, 127; on Porphyry, 192n9; on silent reading, 76
Augustus: and Christ, 126; and Claudius, 6; and clemency, 36; conquest of Mediterranean, 125; and Cornelius Gallus, 94; and heir Marcellus, 44; letter of, in Suetonius, 52
Aurelian (emperor): accession, 51; and Apollonius, 100–101; birth, 53, 140; on Bonosus, 112–13; and the consultation of the Sibylline books, 130–31; death, 159; defeat of Sarmatians in Illyricum, 140; era of, 82–83, 156; on Firmus, 83; and grandson Aurelianus, 32; letter of Valerian to, 135–39; mosaic of, 67; success against Goths, 144; and the treachery of Heraclammon, 29–30
Aurelian (life): categorization of, 9; dedication of, 7; introduction of, 7, 22, 59, 140, 152; Vopiscus on, 83–84, 105
Aurelianus, 32
Aureolus, 12, 25, 60, 156
Auruncians, 19
Ausonius, 17, 18
authepsa, 31–32, 45, 175
Aventine, 116
Avidius Cassius (Caesar), 36, 99
Avidius Cassius (life), 6, 8, 12, 36

Baal, 108
Baiae, 50–51
Balbinus, 30
Balbus, Cornelius, 30
Balbus Cornelius Theophanes, 30
Basilica of St. Peter, 96
Bassus, 82–83
Beroea, 137–38
Berosus, 121
Bibaculus, 41
Bible: allusion to, 17; allusion to, in the *HA*, 89, 103, 129; on boy emperors, 126; Jerome as commentator on, 123–24, 128–29; maximum human age allotted in, 121; prophetic consultation of, 43–44; silent reading of, 76
Bituriges, 141
Blesilla, 116
Boethius, 173

Index

Bologna, 67
Bonosus (friend of Jerome), 102, 113–15
Bonosus (usurper): drinking, 112–14; father of, 155; one of the *Quad. Tyr.*, 122; usurpation, 111–14; wife of, 118, 139
Brahman Indians, 122
breviaria, 11, 85
Britain, 169
Byzantine, 77–78
Byzantium, 135, 139, 156

Caesar Vopiscus, 23
Caesonini, 118
Caligula: and Elagabalus, 54–56, 96; birthplace, debate over, 27, 52; bridges the Bay of Baiae, 50–51
Callimachus, 75–6
Calpurnia, 33, 118–20
Calpurnius, Julius, 40
Calpurnius Siculus, 40
Calvisius Taurus, Lucius, 76
Caninus Rebilus, Gaius, 38
Capelianus, 154
Capitoline: amphora, 173–74; games, 22; hill, 23, 34, 96, 99, 157; oak, 22; trio, 131
Capitolinus, Julius: and the Capitoline amphora, 174; one of the *HA*-author's pseudonyms, 4–5, 22; origin of name, 23; praised for truthfulness, 49–50
Capitolinus, M. Manlius, 23
Capri, 55, 150
Caracalla (emperor), 96, 143–44, 173
Caracalla (life), 8, 137
Carinus (emperor): as Gratian, 166; dedicatee of Nemesianus, 40; Fabius Ceryllianus historian of, 27; games of, 69; jeweled clothing of, 40; portrayed badly by *KG*, 39, 167; strews rooms with roses, 156; swims with melons, 3, 144
Carioviscus, 135–36
carrago, 138–39
Carthage, 135n15
Carthaginians, 44, 52, 153
Carus (emperor): accession, 51; birthplace, debate over, 27, 32–34, 52, 113, 156; Fabius Ceryllianus historian of, 27, 52–53; father of Numerian, 39; games of, 69; poem on deeds of, 39–41; as Valentinian I, 166–67
Carus, Carinus, and Numerian, 9, 57, 111, 122
Cascellius, 19–20
Cassiodorus, 173
catafractarii, 138–39
Catilinarian conspiracy, 29
Catiline (of Sallust), 77
Cato, 26, 104–5
Catullus, 41
Ceionii, 7, 72
Ceionius Albinus, 152
Ceionius Iulianus, 82–83
Celsinus, 104–5
Censorinus, 67, 118, 152
cento, 18, 43
Cento Nuptialis, 18
Ceryllianus, Fabius, 27, 52
Cerylus, 27
Characters in Comedy, 82
Chariton, 70
Chilo, Q. Annius, 29
Chrysogonus, 30–31
Cicero: on Alexander the Great, 107; on archaic religion, 44; and the clausula *esse videatur*, 34, 38; and Coelius Antipater, 26; and the date of the *HA*, 156; *HA* allusions to, 14, 21–23, 29–35, 39, 45, 50, 73, 103, 111, 131, 133, 175; Hadrian prefers Cato to, 26; on historiography, 59, 62; and Marcus Fonteius, 84; on memorization, 17; as office holder, 32; and the phrase *maiores nostri*, 33; Pliny alludes to, 17; poems by, 183n71; quoted by *HA*, 37–38; quoted by Jerome, 121; son-in-law of, 175; style of, 39
Cilicia, 32–33
Circesium, 67
clarissimus, 24
Claudian: allusive, 17; and eunuchs, 101; and the date of the *HA*, 157, 199n65, 200n66; defends Stilicho, 167; uses term *Getae*, 7; writes historical epic, 40
Claudius (emperor): assumption of power, 145; and the house of Constantine, 6–7, 61, 73, 140, 146, 169, 177n10; death, 120–21; finger strength of, 38; letter to Regalianus, 69;

223

Index

Claudius (emperor) (*continued*)
likened to Scipio, 34; military success, 140; panegyric of, 6, 34–35, 61; at Thermopylae, 155; Vergilian oracles for, 42

Claudius (life): addressed to Constantius Chlorus, 6–7; and Ammianus, 140; categorization of, 9, 13; inspired by marriage of Gratian and Constantina, 73, 168; Vopiscus on, 84

Claudius (urban prefect), 140
Clement of Alexandria, 74–75, 82
Cleopatra, 118–19
clibinarii, 139
Clitarchus, 59
Clodius, 23, 32
Clodius Albinus (usurper), 42, 44, 53, 144
Clodius Albinus (life), 5–6, 8, 12, 13
codex, 17, 43
Coelius Antipater, 26
Collection of Greek and Roman Parallel Stories (Parallela Minora), 79–82
Cologne, 67, 112, 114
Commentary on Isaiah, 103, 157
Commentary on Matthew, 103, 124, 126–29, 157
Commodus (emperor), 57, 63, 160, 164
Commodus (life), 5, 8
Concordia, 132
Constans I, 161
Constans II, 168
Constantia, Flavia Maxima, 74, 104, 168
Constantine I (the Great): addressed by *HA*-author, 4, 6, 72, 95; claim of descent from Claudius, 6–7, 169, 177n10, 201n93; and Elagabalus, 95–96; era of, 112; and eunuchs, 151; house of, 6, 140, 146, 168; and Onesimus, 195n65; suppression of the work of Porphyry by, 90; tax policies, 100; vision of the cross, 98
Constantine III (Flavius Claudius Constantinus), 168–69
Constantinian dynasty, 74, 140, 146, 159
Constantinople: Byzantium as, 139; Constantine's transfer of temple statuary to, 96; imperial residence, 156; Jordanes at, 172, 174; Priscian at, 170; Valens in, 137–38
Constantius I Chlorus, 6, 7, 61, 113

Constantius II: daughter of, 168; Elagabalus as, 192n22; entrance to Rome of, in Ammianus, 174; and eunuchs, 151; and fruit consumption, 144, 174; and Julian's rations, 149; and *KG*, 11; and law of provisioning, 153; and Sapor, 143; and Silvanus, 141; and the obelisk, 145; and usurpation, 150
Consualia, 108, 111
Consus, 108, 111
Contra Symmachum, 130
Cordus, Junius or Aelius: claimed as a source for the *HA*, 5; criticized, 63–65, 69, in Jordanes, 173–74
Corinth, 155
Corinthian, 31–32
Corippus, 40
Cornicula, Annius, 61
Coruncianus, 19
Crete, 70–71
Ctesias, 68
Cumae, 42
Curiatii, 80
Curius, 19
Curius Fortunatianus, 65
Cybele, 101
Cyprus, 105–6
Cyrus, 148

Dacia Ripensis, 53
Dalmatia, 27, 113
Damasus, 111
Damis, 71, 98
Daniel, 105–6
Decii, 10, 34
Decius (emperor) 10, 155
Deioces, 150
Delian, 31–32
Delphic Oracle, 43–44
Demodice, 80
Demodicus, 80–81
Demostratus, 80
De viris illustribus, 102, 111, 157
Dexippus, 11–13, 154
Diadumenianus (Caesar), 5, 53
Diadumenianus (life), 8, 13

Index

Diana, 40
Dictys of Crete, 70–71, 98
Didius Julianus (emperor), 58, 153, 156
Didius Julianus (life), 8
Dio Cassius, 51, 62
Diocletian: addressed by *HA*-author, 4, 6, 72; Baths of, 67; and Carinus, 39; and eunuchs, 151; as fierce pagan champion, 166; and the grandfather of the *HA*-author, 51; seizure of power, 51, 145–46; wears jeweled slippers, 117
Diomedes, 120
Domitian, 25, 39, 56–57, 150
Drako, 78
Dynamius, 141

Egeria, 81
Egyptian: books as evidence, 83–84; chewing gum made of papyrus, 35; Karanis, 75; in the letter of Hadrian, 93–94, 122, 142–43; letters on the tomb of Gordian, 67; monasticism, 104, 112; obelisk, 66; priests in Herodotus, 68; Serapeum, 157; usurpation of Firmus, 82–84
Elagabalus (emperor): and the banquet of Vitellius, 55; as Constantine, 95–96; as Constantius II, 192n22; and eunuchs, 151–52; and flavored swimming pools, 114; and the obelisk, 145; pardons corrupt Septimius Arabianus, 109–10; and perverted cookware, 31–32, 45, 174–75; plots against Alexander, 44; searches for well-endowed men, 156; and the *senaculum*, 115–17; shaved pubic hair, 3; slandered, 58; and *spintriae*, 54–55; and Suetonian emperors, 54–56, 171; threatens Judaism, Christianity, 92; villainous, 8, 45, 54, 148, 156–57, 173, 192n23; youthfulness responsible for bad behavior, 164
Elagabalus (life): addressed to Constantine, 6; as a fruitful site for allusion, 54; and Macrinus, Diadumenianus, 13; Marius Maximus as source for, 11–12; Marius Maximus not a source for, 16, 171; paired with *Alexander Severus*, 8, 30; theme of indecency, 65

Encolpius, 109–10
Ennius, 26, 34
ephemeris, 25
Ephemeris belli Troiani, 70
Epictetus, 76
Epigenes, 121
Epiphanius, 104–6
Epirus, 79
Episcopalian, 75
Epitome rei militaris, 157
Erasistratus, 77
esse videatur, 33
Etruscan, 67
Eucherius, 165, 167
Eugamius, 154
Eugenius: allusions to, 154, 158; defeated by Theodosius, 88, 162–63; and Eugamius, 154; history writing under, 157, 199n61; and miraculous wind, 154; raised to purple, 88
Eunapius, 14, 89, 96
eunuchs, 100–101, 151–52, 165, 168
Eupompus, 78
euripus, 114–15
Eusebius (of Caesarea), 98
Eusebius Scholasticus, 41
Eustochium, 116–18, 122
Eutherius, 151
Eutropius (eunuch), 101
Eutropius (historian): and *KG*, 11, 13, 30, 34, 37, 146; and *Marcus*, 146; source for the *HA*, 11, 85, 170; and Trajan, 66; and Valens, 66
Evander, 19

Fabillus, 154
Fabius Marcellinus: attributed with life of Trajan, 66; 150; evokes Ammianus Marcellinus, 25, 50; paired with Gargilius Martialis, 26; praised for truthfulness, 49–50
Fabius Sossianus, 82–83
Fabricius, 19
Faltonii, 72
Faltonius Probus Alypius, 164
Faustina, 36
Favorinus, 18–19, 77, 82

Felicio, 100–101
Festus, 25
Firmus: consumed ostrich, 69; existence doubted, 57; known as Cyclops, 35; legitimacy debated, 82–84; one of the *Quad. Tyr.*, 9, 122; physiognomic portrait of, 53; supports army on glue, 35–36
Florian, 67, 105, 166
Fonteius, Marcus, 82–84
Formiae, 36
Fortuna, 42
Franks, 141, 165–66
Frigeridus, 136–37, 139
Frigidus, 88–91, 154, 158, 163
Fritigern, 139
Frontinus, 13
Fufia Caninia (Lex), 153
Fufidius, 25
Furius Maecius Gracchus, 164

Gaetulicus, Gnaeus Lentulus, 52
Gainea, 41
Galba, 53
Galen, 73, 77, 84, 171–72
Galla Placidia, 168
Gallic invasion, 105, 141, 143
Gallic Wars, 48
Gallienus (emperor): and Christianity, 99; criticized, 62, 84, 195n74; death, 156; and Palfurius Sura, 25; son of, 27; sycophantic praise of, 61–62; usurpers under, 10
Gallienus (life), 6
Gallus (Caesar), 24
Gallus, Cornelius, 94
Gallus Antipater, 25–26, 45
Gargilianus, 27
Gargilius Martialis, 26, 49–50
Gaudianus, 100–101
Gaudiosus, 100
Gaul: birthplace of Carus, 34, 113; Clodius Albinus in, 44; Julian Caesar in, 149, 153; and Marcus Fonteius, 84; and the name Gallicanus, 23; Valentinian II in, 151
Gauls, 44, 94, 141, 143
Gaza, 108, 110–11, 122
Gellius (historian), 104–5

Gellius, Aulus: in Ammianus, 18–20; and booksellers, 73; community of readers depicted by, 17, 68, 77, 82, 85; discussion of unusual words in, 139
Germanicus, 52–53
Germans, 67, 114, 155
Gerontius, 155
Geta (emperor), 156
Geta (life), 6, 8, 13, 39
Getica (*Gothic History* of Jordanes), 28, 172
Gildo, 161
Golden Rule, 126–29
Gordian I: games, 66; and Gibbon, 175; physiognomic portrait, 53; poems, 183n71; tombstone, 67–68, 154
Gordian II, 144, 154
Gordian III, 9–10, 13, 100
Goth/Gothic: at Adrianople, 136, 138–39; Alaric, 162; ancestry of Maximinus, 7, 172; Aurelian conqueror of, 144; Cassiodorus, history of, 173; *Getae* as, 7; Gordian conqueror of, 67; Hunila, 118, 139–40; Jordanes, history of, 172
Gothic History (Cassiodorus), 173
Gracchan, 122
Gracchi, 7, 26, 175, 178n15
Gratian: antipagan activities, 88–89, 132, 173; and Carinus, 166; child emperor, 161–62, 165; marriage with Constantina, 74, 140, 168
Gregory of Tours, 174
gymnosophists, 122

Hababa, 28–29, 45, 172
Hadrian (emperor): and Antinous, 26; archaic literary tastes, 25–26, 45; as a good emperor, 160–61; letter of, 93, 122, 142–43; and Suetonius, 62; and Vergilian oracles, 42, 85
Hadrian (life), 8, 12, 20
Haldagates, 135–36
Hariomundus, 135–36
Hebrew, 67, 124, 127
Hebrew Questions on Genesis, 121
Helena, 95
Heliodorus, 68
Heraclammon, 29
Heracles, 78

Herennianus, 141
Herodian: not exploited by the *HA*, 13, 16, 167, 171; as source for the *HA*, 8–13, 85
Herodotus: commentary of Aristarchus on, 82; and Egypt, 68, 143; and epigraphy, 70; founder of history, 62; on monarchical sequestration, 150; in Ptolemy the Quail, 78
Heroicus, 71
Hierocles, 98
Hilaria, 7
Hilarion, 104–6, 108
Hildomundus, 135–36
Hillel, 128
Hippias, 148
Hipponax, 41
Historia contra paganos, 89
Homer, 104–6, 146
Homeric: knowledge, 79; revisionism, 70; sortition, 43–44
Honorius: from 408 to 410, 162–63; and Alexander Severus, 167; as boy emperor, 161, 165; at Ravenna, 156; recognized Constantine III, 169; sequestered, 151
Horace: in Ammianus, 20; on clemency, 37; as iambic poet, 41
Horatii, 19–20, 80
Hunila, 118, 139–40
Huns, 7, 139–40, 157, 173
Hypsicrates, 82

Illyricans, 52
Illyricum, 52, 125, 140, 185n17
Interamna, 165
interficere, 5
Irenaeus, 18
Isaiah, 103, 123–26, 129
Isis, 31
Islamic, 174
Italian, 141
Italicus, 108
Italy, 19, 138
Ituraean, 135–36
Iuverna, 165–66

Jerome: as author of allusive prologues, 108; birthplace, 185n17; commentaries of, 123–29; and date of Ammianus, 157; and date of *HA*, 8, 146, 157–58, 162; letters of, 111–22; radical ascetic, 101–3; saint's lives of, 104–10; as source of allusion for *HA*, 3, 14, 16, 20, 85, 103, 170–71;
Jerusalem, 74
Jesus, 74, 96, 117, 128–29
Jews: and biblical sortition, 43; books of, 121; criticized in letter of Hadrian, 93–94, 122; debates with Christians, 77; distinct from Samaritans, 8; and the Golden Rule, 126–28; once-married women praised by, 119; ordination of priests, 93; reading sacred texts, 76; Severan ban on conversion, 91–92; Sibylline books of, 156; threats of Elagabalus against, 92
John (the Baptist), 106
John Lydus, 82
Jordanes, 28, 172–74
Josephus, 51
Joshua, 117
Jotapianus, 10
Jovian, 167
Judaism, 87, 91
Julia Domna, 71
Julian (emperor): and Alexander, 146–51, 169, 171; in Ammianus, 10, 61, 67, 144–51, 153, 155, 167, 169, 171; as author, 90; bestows crowns, 144–45; death, 10; era of, 62; and Flavius Claudius Constantinus, 168; half brother of, 24; Probus as a symbol for, 166–67; quotes Homer, 146; and Sibylline books, 155; theory of Baynes about, 73, 146–47, 168
Julian (son of Constantine III), 168
Julianus (physician), 77
Julia Symiamira, 95, 115
Julius Caesar: and clemency, 36; *Commentaries*, 13, 22; father-in-law of, 182n57; lives of, 5, 48; wife of, 119
Junius, Gaius, 33
Junius Tiberianus: criticizes historians, 59, 131; identity of, 7; provides linen books, 68; as urban prefect, 152
Juno, 119, 131
Jupiter, 42, 99, 109–10, 131
Juvenal, 12, 21–22

Kaiseraugst, 120
Kaisergeschichte (*KG*): and the *Alexander Severus*, 13; on Balbinus, 30; on Bonosus, 112, 114; on Carinus, 39, 166; on Carus, 166; on Claudius, 34–35; on Constantine, 95; defined, 11; on Diocletian, 117; on Gallienus, 99; as a general source for the *HA*, 13, 85, 170; in the *Marcus*, 146; on Numerian, 39; on Probus, 166; on the urban prefect, 152; on the usurper Marius, 37–38; on Valerian, 99
Karanis, 75
kerkos, 79
Kerkusera, 79
Kritolaus, 80–81

Lactantius, 132, 168
Lampridia, 24
law: of Alexander, 110, 149; ancient, in Ammianus, 19; Arcadian against usury, 99; in Cicero, 32; *HA*-author's knowledge of limited, 150, 152–53; imposition of Roman, 125; of Julian, 149; against monks, 102; of Moses, 128; natural, 127; Roman, 161, 166; Samaritans and Jews separate in, 8; of the *senaculum*, 115; against Stilicho, 167; Theodosian limiting interest rate, 99
Leonidas, 155
Libanius, 157
libraries, 68, 74, 85, 90
libri lintei, 68
Licinius, 68, 145
Life of Antony, 104
Life of Apollonius of Tyre, 71
Life of Hilarion: date, 104, 107; in *De viris illustribus*, 157; as evidence for the cult of Marnas, 110; preface parodied, 115, 132; and the *Probus*, 104–8; *sagmarius* in, 117; as a scholarly biography, 129; as a source of allusion for the *HA*, 103–11
Life of Malchus, 157
Life of Paul, 103, 133
Livy: accused of lying, 59, 131; independence of, 62; praised for eloquence, 49–50; on Sibylline books, 155; as a source of omens, 87; uncertainty of, 81

Lucian: *How to Write History*, 48, 82; *Teacher of Rhetoric*, 79; *True Histories*, 70–71
Lucilius, 41
Lucius, 104
Luke, 76
Lycophron, 79

Macrinus (emperor), 5, 95
Macrinus (life), 6, 8
Macrobius, 82
Maecia, 7
Maecianus, 117–18
Maecii, Furii, 118
Maecius, 7
Maecius Faltonius Nicomachus, 159–62, 164–65
Maeonius Astyanax, 28
Magna Mater, 145
maiores nostri, 32–33
Majorian, 151
Malchus, 105
Mallius Chilo, 29
Mamurius Veturius, 38
Manichaeans, 77
Manlius Chilo, Q., 29
Marcella, 111, 116
Marcellus, 42, 44
Marcomanni, 156
Marcus Aurelius (emperor): clemency of, 36; Cordus historian of, 63–64; death, 13; praises Pertinax, 12, 57
Marcus Aurelius (life): addressed to Diocletian, 6; categorized, 8; in the *Commodus*, 5; paired with Avidius Cassius, 12; presumption of authenticity, 20; use of *KG* in, 146
Marinus Pacatianus, 10
Marius (republican general), 37–38
Marius (usurper), 37–39
Marius Maximus: on Apollonius, 96; on Caracalla, 40; on the city prefect, 152; on Didius Julianus, 58; on Elagabalus, 16, 54, 71; on Gargilius Martialis, 26; as a general source for the *HA*, 11–13, 57, 85; on Hadrian, 25, 45; on lawyers, 153; on omens, 87; on Palfurius Sura, 25; praised for truthfulness, 49–50; and Suetonius, 48, 53; on Trajan, 65
Mark, 74

Index

Mark the Deacon, 195n62
Marnas, 108–11, 122, 171
Mars, 38
Martial, 26–27
Matthew, 43, 103, 123–24, 126–29
Maxentius, 95
Maximianus, 6, 105
Maximinus I (Thrax): abstained from vegetables, 144; illustrated victories of, 67; in Jordanes, 172–74; parents of, 28, 45; reign of, 9, 84; son of, 153; as Stilicho, 167
Maximinus II (Daia), 145
Maximinus the Younger, 154, 167
Maximus, Marcus Clodius Pupienus, 12
Maximus and Balbinus, 6, 9, 13, 167
Mediterranean, 125, 174
Melanthias, 137–38
memorization, 17
Menander, 27, 76
Mercurius, 143
Mesopotamia, 135–36, 143
Messalla, 101, 140
Micca, 28–29, 45, 172
Milan, 52, 67, 88, 156
Minerva, 132
Mithridates, 143
mnemon, 93
mnemonicum, 28
Modestinus, 153–54
Moesia, 53
monastic, 102, 112, 116
monasticism, 102, 104, 108
Montanus, 100–101
Moor, 94
Morton Salt Company, 75
Moses, 117, 120–21, 128
"Mystic Mark," 74
Myths of Tragedy, 82

Nemesianus (conspirator), 40
Nemesianus, Olympius (poet), 39–40
Nepos, 62
Nero: and Elagabalus, 54, 56, 96, 171; as a boy emperor, 160, 164; time of, 70
Nerva, 12, 135
Nestor, 78

New History (Ptolemy), 77
Nicephorium, 42
Nicomachi, 90, 168
Nicomachus Flavianus: as author, 14, 90, 96, 98; as senator, 88–89, 162
Nicomachus Flavianus the Younger, 90, 164
Nicomedia, 156–57
Nicopolis, 135–39
Noemon the Carthaginian, 79
Notitia Dignitatum, 138
Numa, 42, 81
Numerian: absent from allegory, 167; dedicatee of Nemeisianus, 40; Fabius Ceryllianus historian of, 27; games, 69; in the *KG*, 39; literary talent, 39, 42, 45; murderer of, 51; son of Carus, 9, 57

Ocean, 166
Odysseus, 78
occidere, 5
Odenathus, 28
Olympius, 167
omen: of the birth of Alexander, 128; frequent in *HA*, 87; from Livy, 87; in Matthew, 129
On Bringing up Blood, 77
Onasimus, 112
Onesimus, 52, 112–13, 185n17, 195n65
Optatianus Porphyrius, Publilius, 24
Oresta, 145
Orosius, 7, 89, 174
Orpheus, 92, 96, 120
Ostrogothic, 173
Otho, 52, 54
Outis, 78
Ovid, 17, 39, 190n98
Oxyrhynchus, 82

Palfurius Sura, 25
Palmyra, 29
Pammachius, 122
panegyric: of Alexander Severus, 175; of Carus, 42; of Claudius, 6, 34–35, 61, 121, 155; collection of, as precedent for multiple authorship, 177n4; of Constantine, 168; contrasted with history, 61; of Gallienus, 61; of Majorian, 151; of Scipio Africanus, 34

Pannonia Secunda, 142
Pannonian, 97
Panpin, 75
Parallela Minora (falsely attributed to Plutarch), 79–82, 172
Parthians, 165–66
Patriarch, 94
Paul (apostle), 43, 120
Paul (centenarian), 121
Paul (holy man), 104
Paula, 122, 178n15
Paulina, 122
Pedanius Fuscus, 181n33
Pelasgians, 19
Peloponnesus, 155
Perinthus, 139–40
Persia: archives of, 68; Gordian's tomb in, 67; Julian's campaign in, 145, 155; Sapor, king of, 143; Valens sends Victor to, 137; war of Probus with, 125; Xerxes, emperor of, 78
Persians: battle with Greeks, 78; capture Valerian, 9–10; Carus fights, 34; Roman jurisdiction over, 166
Pertinax (emperor), 57, 144
Pertinax (life), 8, 12
Pescennius Niger (usurper), 53
Pescennius Niger (life), 5–8, 12
Petronius Probus, 146, 157, 159, 168
Petronius Probus, Flavius Anicius 159
Pharisees, 166
Pheneans, 80
Philemon, 154
Philip, 9, 10, 66
Philippi, 67
Philo, 76
Philostorgius, 164
Philostratus, 71, 98
Phoenician, 70–71
Phrygian, 84, 101
physiognomy, 53–54, 58
Piso (usurper), 67, 175,
Pisones, 33, 118–19
Platonist, 76
Pliny the Elder, 21, 35–36, 52, 119
Pliny the Younger, 17, 77
Plotinus, 76, 90

Plutarch: on Alexander, 47–48, 63–64; *Parallela Minora*, falsely attributed to, 79–80; on poetry, 76
Pollio, Asinius, 22, 27
Pompeius Theophanes, 30
Pompey, Gnaeus, 30, 66
pons Aureoli, 12
Pontus, 105
Porphyry, 76, 90
Postumii, 7
Praeneste, 42, 44
princeps clausus, 150–51
Priscian, 170
Priscus, Lucius, 10
Probi, 72, 146, 159
Probus (emperor): accession, 51; death lamented, 52, 112; defeated Bonosus, 112; displays probity, 5; generals trained by, 100; life of, by Onesimus, 112; praised, 61, 104–5, 131; Proculus's revolt against, 141; prophecy of descendants, 72, 146, 158–59; utopianism of, 125
Probus (life): allegorical interpretation of, 166–67; categorization of, 9; Onesimus unmentioned in, 112; precedes *Quad. Tyr.*, 111; uses term *Getae*, 7
Procopius, 25
Proculus: ancestry, 141; deflowered a hundred virgins, 3, 117–18, 141, 169; family of, 141; Onesimus historian of, 113; part of *Quad. Tyr.*, 9, 122; usurpation, 141
Profuturus, 136–37
prose rhythm, 6
protector, 143
Protesilaus, 71
Protrepticus, 8
Prudentius, 130
pseudo-Plutarch, 81, 172
Ptolemy the Quail, 77–79
Punic Wars, 105
Puteoli, 50

quadriga, 122
Quadrigae Tyrannorum: defined, 9; fictional nature, 57; origin of name, 122; parallels with Suetonius, 57

Index

Quartinus, 118
Quintilian, 17, 81
Quirinal, 115–16

Radagaisus, 155
Ravenna, 156
rebellio, 21
Regalianus, 69
Res Gestae (Ammianus), 134, 143, 147, 157
Reverendus, 100–101
Rheximachus, 80
Rhine, 114
Rhodope, 137–38
Richomeres, 136–37
Rome (city): in Ammianus, 140, 152; Caligula and, 53; Capitol at, 157; Carus's birthplace, 32, 52; Cicero's exile from, 32; Constantius's entrance to, in Ammianus, 174; events at, between 408 and 410, 169; Gordian and, 67; *HA*-author favors, 156; Jerome and, 102–3, 111, 114, 116, 118; obelisk brought to, 145; and the *praefectus urbi*, 152; sack of, 157; siege of, 162–63; temples in, 31
Romulus, 81, 108
Rostra, 34
Rufinus, 102, 112–13
Rufius Celsus, 82–83
Rutilius Namatianus, 112

Sabine, 87, 108, 111
sagmarius, 117
Salamis (island), 78
Salamis (on Cyprus), 105–6
Sallust: accused of lying, 59, 131; allusions to, in *HA*, 39, 45; *Catiline* of, read aloud, 77; on Fufidius, 25; in Gregory of Tours, 174; Hadrian prefers Coelius to, 26; independence of, 62; in Jerome and the *HA*, 104–7; praised for eloquence, 49–50; and Tacitus, 17
Salonae, 27
Salonina, 27
Saloninus, 27, 62
Salvius Iulianus, 152
Samaritans, 8, 91–94, 122
Samso, 117, 141

Samson, 117
Sapor, 143
Saracens, 135–36
Sarmatians: bows of, 69; Gordian conqueror of, 67; prediction of rule over, 165–66; Theodosius fights, 140; virgins from, 117
Saturninus, 9, 52, 94, 122
satyr, 104
Scipio: ancestor of Paula, 178n15; born from snake, 81; Cicero on the death of, 121; Claudius and, 34–35
Scylla, 106
Scyros, 79
Scythian, 9, 156
Sebastian, 137–38
"Secret Mark," 74
Secular Games, 9
semibarbarus, 168
senaculum, 115–16
Seneca, 51, 59
Septicius Clarus, 62
Septimius (biographer), 109–10
Septimius Arabaianus, 109–11
Septuagint, 124
Serapammon, 100–101
Serapeum, 110, 157
Serapis, 31, 93–94, 110, 122
Servius, 117
Servius *auctus*, 13
Severus (life), 6, 8, 13
Severus, Septimius (emperor): abstemious, bean-eating, 144; in acclamations, 163; banned conversion to Christianity or Judaism, 91; defeat of Clodius Albinus, 44; in Jordanes, 173; as severe, 5
Severus Archontius, 83
Sibylline: books, 130, 155–56; oracles, 68; verses, 42
Sicanians, 19
Sicily/Sicilians, 23, 32
Sidonius, 98
Silvanus, 141, 169
Simonides, 148
Sirmium, 53, 140, 142, 156
Smith, Morton, 74–76
Socrates (Egyptian tax official), 76
Sozomen, 104, 166

Index

Spain, 105
Sparta/Spartans, 29, 155
Spartianus, Aelius, 4–5, 24
spinthria/spintria, 54–55
Statius Valens, 66
Stilicho: burned Sibylline books, 155–56; death, 162; father of Eucherius, 165; Maximinus as, 167–68; and the Peloponnesus, 155; ruled on behalf of Honorius, 161–62, 164
Stobaeus, 82
Stoic, 76
Strange History (Ptolemy), 77
Suetonius: biographical principle, 39; on Caesar's campaigns, 48; dedication of work to Septicius Clarus, 62; and Elagabalus, 54–56; general source of allusion for the *HA*, 3, 39, 49–58, 73, 151, 171; grandfather of, 51–52; *HA* written in the style of, 14; and imperial birthplaces, 52–53; introduced subject of imperial finger strength into biography, 38; life of Terence, 23; Marius Maximus followed, 12; offered genealogical information on emperors, 12; and physiognomics, 153; praised for restraint, 65; praised for truthfulness, 49–50; rarity of name of, 24; on religion, 87; on Tiberius, 150
Suetonius Optatianus, 24–25
Sulla, 25, 30
Sulpicius Alexander, 150–51
Sunday, 99
Symmachus, 7, 89, 163
Symmachus the Younger (Quintus Aurelius Memmius Symmachus), 172–74
symposium, 76–77
synagogue, 76
Syrian, 99

Tacitus (emperor): accession, 51, 156; and Aelius Cesettianus, 152; as Attalus, 163; eats lettuce, 144; prophecy of descendants, 166; senatorial decree of, 68; statue of, 67; Suetonius Optatianus as biographer of, 24; warned against boy emperors, 159–61, 164
Tacitus (historian): accused of lying, 59, 131; alludes to Sallust, 17; and bias in historiography, 61–62; praised for eloquence, 49–50

Tacitus (life), 9, 105
Taprobane, 165–66
Tarentum, 79
technopaegnia, 24
Tegeans, 80
Temple of Peace, 84–85
Tertullian, 132
Tertullus, 163
tetrarch, 6
Tetrici, 67
Thebes, 145
Theocritus, 77
Theodore, 75
Theodoric, 173
Theodosian era, 146, 158, 162, 168
Theodosius I: accession, 162; allegorical representation of, 167; antipagan legislation of, 88–89; baptized by Acholius, 28; condemned Annales of Nicomachus Flavianus, 90; constraints of writing history under, 157, 199n61; death, 161; defeats Nicomachus Flavianus, 162; fights Sarmatians, 140–41
Theodosius II, 90, 99, 165
Thermopylae, 155
Thersagoras, 82
Thessalonica, 28
Thetis, 79
Thirty Tyrants: authored by Trebellus Pollio, 21; champions truth over eloquence, 60; contains short accounts of usurpers, 9–10; draws on Jerome, 123, 126, 129; fictional nature of, 16; flaunts unnamed authorities, 66; Gibbon and, 175; on the proper behavior of women, 118; slanders Gallienus, 62
Thrace: birthplace of Maximinus, 7, 28, 172; fourth-century changes in, 7; Gothic noblewomen in, 139–40; and Valens, 136–37
Thrasyllus, 51
Three Gordians, 6, 9, 13, 167
Thucydides, 62
Tiberius: amazing finger strength of, 38; astrologer of, 51; era of, 67; favored heavy drinker, 174; seceded to Capri, 150; sexual perversions of, 54–55; tormented grammarians, 78
Tibullus, 190n100

Index

Timesitheus, 100
Titianus, 154
Titus (emperor), 39, 57
Titus (usurper), 118
To a Variety of Friends (Jerome), 111
To Marcella, 111
Toxotius, 7, 122, 178n15
Trajan: ancestor of Gordian, 175; Cordus as biographer of, 64; Fabius Marcellinus as biographer of, 149; four biographers of, 66; mingles with subjects, 150; renowned for virtue, 6, 160–61; succeeded by Hadrian, 42; and Ulpius Crinitus, 139
Trajanus (general in Ammianus), 136–38, 139
Trebatius, 19–20
Trebellius Pollio: author of late lives, 8; in the *Aurelian*, 7; and the *Claudius*, 6; and the lacuna, 10; one of the *HA*-author's pseudonyms, 4; origin of name, 21–22
Trebonius Gallus, 9
Trier, 156
Trimalchio, 77
Tritannus, 35
Trogus, 49–50, 59, 131
Troilus, 41
Trojan War, 70–71, 140
Troy, 28, 44
Two Gallieni, 9, 62
Two Maximini, 6, 9, 13, 167
Two Valerians, 9–10, 143
Tyana, 97

Ulpian, 153
Ulpian Library, 68–69, 97–98
Ulpius Crinitus, 135–36, 139
Ulpius Silanus, 130
Uranius Antoninus, 10

Valens (emperor): and Adrianople, 136–40, 145; age of, 63; in Ammianus, 63, 135–40, 145; dedicatee of Eutropius, 66
Valens (usurper), 84
Valentinian I, 28, 63, 166
Valentinian II, 150, 161–62, 165
Valentinian III, 90, 151, 158
Valerian (Caesar), 67, 156

Valerian (emperor): and Acholius, 27; on Aurelian, 68, 135, 144–45; captured by Persians, 9, 143; and Ceionius Albinus, 152; death, 9–10; persecuted Christians, 10, 99; on stockpiling provisions, 139; on Trajan, 139; usurpers under, 10
Valerius, 81
Valerius Marcellinus, 25, 65
Varius (name of Elagabalus), 54
Varro, 35–36, 121
Vatican, 96
Vegetius, 157–58
Velenus, 143
Velsolus, 143
Venus, 44, 118–19
Verconius Turninus, 129
Verennianus, 141
Vergil: alluded to by Apuleius, 17; ancient texts of, 73; *cento* from, 18; as a general source of allusion for the *HA*, 14, 42, 50; Hadrian prefers Ennius to, 25; in Jerome, 104; in Jordanes, 174; and Numerian, 42; quoted by Diocletian, 145; scholarly commentaries on, 27, 123; *sortes*, 42–45, 85, 171; and Theocritus, 77; use of allusion, 180n15
Verona, 158
Verres, 32
verse: on Aureolus, 60; historical epic, 41; Homeric, 43–44, 146; of Horace, 36; iambos, 41; inscription, 12; of Numerian, 39, 42; of Optatianus, 24; prophetic, on Alexander, 128; Sibylline, 42; *sortes*, 42–43; translated from Greek, 60, 98;
Verus (emperor), 5
Verus (life), 5–6, 8
Verus, Aurelius, 66
Vespasian: banished Palfurius Sura, 25; forum of, 84; mocked Cerylus, 27; sons of, 39, 57
Vestal Virgins, 119
Victor (*mag. eq.*), 136–37
Victor, Aurelius: in Ammianus, 157; with the cognomen Pinius, 25; and the date of the *HA*, 8; and the *KG*, 11, 13, 37; source of the *HA*, 85, 170; wrote life of Trajan, 66
Victoria (goddess), 132
Victoria (usurper), 156

233

Index

Victorini, 67
vir illustris, 7
Vitellius, 54–55
Viturgia, 141
Volusianus, 9
vopiscus, 23
Vopiscus Syracusanus, Flavius: conversation with Junius Tiberianus, 7; and the lacuna, 10; one of the *HA*-author's pseudonyms, 4, 9; origin of name, 23; praises Trebellius Pollio, 22; in the Probus, 104, 107
Vulcacius Gallicanus (Volcacius, Vulcatius), 4, 5, 23–24

Vulcacius Rufinus, 24
Vulcacius Sedigitus, 23
Vulcatius Terentianus, 23

Wonders beyond Thule, 71

Xerxes, 50, 78

Zaitha, 67
Zenobia, 29, 53
Zeus, 108
Zonaras, 13
Zosimus, 11, 96, 163

Index Locorum

Ambrose
   Enarrationes in XII psalmos Davidicos
      36.15, 199n49
   Epistles
      15 and 16, 28
      18, 129
      18.7, 130
      18.10, 130
   Hexameron
      5.68, 200n75
Ammianus Marcellinus
      14.11.3, 151
      15.3.6, 143
      15.3.7, 142
      15.5.1, 63
      15.5.5, 141
      15.5.9, 147
      15.5.15, 141
      15.5.22, 141
      15.7, 94
      15.8.7, 146
      15.12.1, 94, 141
      16.1.3, 61
      16.2.5, 138
      16.5.3, 149
      16.5.5, 147
      16.5.7, 147
      16.5.8, 148
      16.7.4, 152
      16.10.8, 139
      16.10.10, 174
      16.12.7, 139
      16.12.63, 139
      17.4, 66, 145
      17.5.3, 143
      17.8.2, 153

      17.9.2, 153
      18.1.7, 155
      18.4.2–4, 151
      18.5.4, 151
      18.8.11, 141
      19.12.14, 143
      20.4.12, 149
      21.10.6, 157
      21.16.7, 144, 174
      22.3, 148
      22.4.1–2, 148
      22.4.10, 148
      22.6.1, 94
      22.6.16, 145
      22.9.11, 150
      22.10.3, 149
      22.10.4, 149
      22.10.7, 149
      22.11.4, 94
      22.16.12, 157
      22.16.23, 94
      23.3.3, 145
      23.3.7, 145
      23.5.7, 67
      23.5.9, 67
      23.5.10, 67
      24.4.24, 145
      25.4.19–21, 149
      25.4.22, 148
      26.1, 62, 69
      26.1.1, 63
      26.6.16, 25
      27.11, 157
      29.1, 89
      29.6.7, 140, 168
      29.6.15, 140–41

Index Locorum

Ammianus Marcellinus (*continued*)
    29.6.15–16, 140
    29.6.17, 140
    31.2, 199n59
    30.4.11–12, 19
    31.4.8–11, 139
    31.5.15, 140
    31.6.3, 139
    31.6.8, 140
    31.7.1, 139
    31.7.2, 139
    31.7.5, 139
    31.7.7, 138–39
    31.7.16, 139
    31.11.1, 139
    31.11.1–2, 136–38
    31.13.18, 139
Apicius
    1.1, 114
    1.3, 114
    1.4, 114
Arnobius
  Adversus gentes
    1.52, 98
    2.71, 121
Augustine
  Conf.
    4.3.5, 43
    8.12.29, 43
  De civ. D.
    18.18, 71
  Epistles
    55.37, 44
    138.18, 98
Aurelius Victor
    26–27, 12
    32–33, 99
    33.9, 37
    34.2, 34
    37.3, 195n64
    39.3, 117
Ausonius
  Grat. act.
    7.31, 199n51
Babylonian Talmud
  Tractate Shabbat
    31a, 128

Bible
  Deut.
    34:7, 121
  Ex.
    28:4, 120
    39:1–2, 120
  Gen.
    6:3, 121
  Isa.
    2:4, 125
    3:4, 126
  Lk.
    2:46, 190n86
    4:16–21, 190n86
    6:31, 127
    10:27, 127
  Matt.
    2, 129
    7:12, 127
    26:52, 129
    28:18, 128
  Rom.
    13:13–14, 43
Callimachus
    Pfeiffer *fr.* 177, line 33, 75
Censorinus
  De Die Natali
    17, 121
Cicero
  Arch.
    24, 107
  Att.
    3.4, 32
    7.7.6, 30
  Balb.
    57, 30
  Brut.
    11.42, 59
  Cat.
    1.2, 111
    1.9, 111
    3.14, 29
  Clu.
    23, 24
    89–96, 33
  De or.
    2.217, 23

2.217–97, 23
2.350–60, 180n3
Div.
1.98, 42
2.85, 42
Dom.
7, 23
Fam.
7.30.1, 38
Flac.
15, 131
17, 131
Phil.
6.11, 22
11.11, 23
Planc.
95–96, 32
Rep.
5.2, 183n62
Rosc. Am.
46.133, 30
Verr.
2.4.131, 32
Claudian
Cons. Hon.
94–95, 199n49
Cons. Stil.
1.94, 200n66
De Bello Gothico
231–32, 187n42
In Eutropium
2.153–54, 200n66
Codex Theodosianus
2.8.1, 99
7.1.12, 128
7.4.5, 153
7.16.1, 167
9.6.12, 89
9.42.22, 167
11.1.6, 7
Digest
47.2.52.20, 199n51
Dio Cassius
51.22.2, 119
59.16.11–17, 185n12
72.18.3–4, 63
73.13.1, 58

77.18.4, 96
78.40.4, 44
80.7, 156
Diodorus Siculus
2.32.4, 187n44
20.2.1, 186n28
Diomedes
Keil, *Gramm. Lat.* 1.485.11–17, 41
Epitome de caesaribus
34.4, 34
37.2, 195n64
Eunapius
VS
472, 102
Eusebius
Vit Const.
4.36.2, 177n4
Eutropius
9.2, 12
9.2.1, 30
9.7–8, 99
9.9.2, 37
9.11.2, 34
9.17, 200n79
9.17.1, 195n64
9.26, 117
10.18, 186n32
Galen
Against Julianus
2.2 18A.253K, 77
In librum Hippocratis de natura humana
3.4, 190n85
Libr. Propr.
1 19.14K, 77
Gellius
1.10.1–2, 19
1.26, 76
2.22, 82
3.1, 77
3.3.1, 23
4.1.1, 18
5.6.8, 145
5.6.17, 145
9.9, 77
17.3, 24
19.13, 191n109

Heliodorus
> Aeth.
>> 2.38, 68

Herodian
> 6.8.1, 28, 173
> 7.1.9–10, 118
> 7.10.4, 30
> 8.8.4, 30

Herodotus
> 1.99, 150
> 6.184, 143
> 8.88.3, 78

Historia Augusta
> Ael.
>> 2.9, 5
>> 4.1, 42
>
> Alex.
>> 3, 147
>> 4.2, 117
>> 4.6, 42
>> 13.5, 129
>> 14.3–4, 128
>> 14.4, 186n29
>> 14.5, 42
>> 14.6, 148
>> 15.1, 148–49
>> 15.2, 149
>> 15.6–17.4, 149
>> 16.3, 149
>> 17.4, 108
>> 18.1, 149
>> 21.6–8, 149
>> 23.4–7, 151
>> 24.3–5, 100
>> 24.4, 9
>> 26.8, 31
>> 29.2, 96, 120
>> 36.2, 129
>> 37.7, 26
>> 37.8, 26
>> 37.9, 26
>> 38.2, 26
>> 38.6, 186n29
>> 40.6–11, 120
>> 43.5–6, 99
>> 44.9, 32
>> 45.4–5, 152
>> 47.1, 153
>> 47.2, 149
>> 48, 150
>> 48.6, 25, 66
>> 51.3, 119
>> 51.5, 149
>> 51.6–8, 126–27
>> 56.5, 139
>> 66, 150
>> 66.3–67.1, 151
>> 67.1, 168
>
> Aur.
>> 1.1, 140
>> 1.4, 66
>> 1.7, 68
>> 2.1–2, 59, 131
>> 3.1, 140
>> 3.1–2, 53
>> 6.3, 140
>> 8.1, 68
>> 9.2, 152
>> 10.2, 139
>> 10.3, 139
>> 10.3–11.6, 135–36
>> 11.1, 139
>> 11.3, 139
>> 11.4, 139
>> 11.5–7, 139
>> 11.6, 138
>> 13.3, 144
>> 14.2, 28
>> 14.6, 28, 182n47
>> 15.4–6, 101
>> 16–17, 109–10
>> 18.4–20.8, 130
>> 18.5–21.4, 155
>> 19–20, 28
>> 20.2, 131
>> 20.5, 130
>> 22.4, 92
>> 23.1, 29
>> 23.4, 29
>> 24.3–9, 96–98
>> 29.2, 92
>> 34.4, 139
>> 42.4, 32
>> 42.6, 10

43, 150
43.1–4, 151
43.6–7, 92
45.6, 93
48.7, 182n47
49.6, 92
64.5, 28, 182n47

Av. Cass.
3.3, 5
5.6, 183n62
6.2–3, 99
6.4, 158
11.2–8, 36

Car.
3.5, 10
4.2, 112
4.3, 27
4.4, 156
4.5, 113
4.6, 32
4.6–7, 32–33
5.2–3, 33–34
5.3, 52
6.6, 40
7.3, 112
8.4, 40
11.1–2, 39–40
13.4, 50, 145–46
13.4–15.5, 51
14.1, 50
15.1, 50
15.5, 50
16.1, 112
17.1, 40, 117
17.3, 112, 144, 156
17.6, 113
19.2, 69
20.4–21.1, 101

Carac.
5.7, 143
5.8, 143
7.1, 143

Claud.
2.3, 6
2.4–5, 120–21
3.1, 61
3.3–5, 34

5.3, 156
5.4, 25
6.2–3, 200n66
6.5, 61
6.6, 138
7.7, 34
8.1, 140
8.2, 61, 138–39
8.5, 139
8.6, 138
10, 6
10.1–6, 43
10.13, 69
11.5, 61
13, 53
13.3, 140
13.5, 38
16, 155
16.1, 140
16.2, 139
17, 57

Clod. Alb.
1.4, 5
5, 42
5.3–4, 87
11.2, 144

Comm.
1.1, 5
10.2, 50
15.4, 12
18–19, 57
18.2, 12

Diad.
3, 53
7.3, 186n29

Did. Iul.
1, 152
1.2, 156
3.8, 58

Elag.
1.1, 54
1.2, 152
3.4, 95
3.5, 8, 92, 94
4.3–4, 115–16
5.1, 156
5.3, 157

Historia Augusta (*Elag.*) (*continued*)
    6.6, 145
    6.7–8, 95
    7.5–7, 95
    15.7, 96
    18.4, 54
    19.3, 31
    19.8, 56
    23.1, 96
    20.4, 56
    20.6, 55
    21.5, 56
    21.6, 114
    23.4, 117
    23.8, 56
    24.3, 185n22
    24.7, 145
    30.8, 58
    31.5, 185n22
    31.7, 56
    32.6, 9
    32.8, 56
    33.1, 54, 185n22
    34.1, 185n22
    34.2–3, 65
Gall.
    4.8, 156
    13.9, 138
    14.9, 156
    17.2, 62
    18.3, 25
    19.3, 27
    19.8, 62
    21.3, 27
Geta
    3.1, 156
Gord.
    1.1–5, 10
    2.2, 122
    3.2, 183n71
    3.7, 66
    6, 53
    11.7, 167
    11.9, 167
    11.10, 167
    16.2, 154
    21.1, 144
    21.4, 64–65
    21.5, 23
    23.7–25.3, 151
    25.1–3, 100–101
    25.3, 100
    31.1, 10
    33.1–4, 9
    34.2–3, 67
    34.5, 68
Hadr.
    2.8, 42
    10.2, 149
    14.6, 26
    16.3, 25–26
    23.3, 181n33
Macr.
    1.1, 63–64
    1.4, 69, 141
    4.2, 25
    11.4, 186n29
    14.2, 186n29
Marc.
    1.6, 12
    25.10, 12
Max. et Balb.
    1.1–2, 10
    1.4, 167
    2.11, 167
    4.5, 25, 50, 65
    7.3, 30
    17.1, 167
    17.2, 167
    17.6, 167
Maximin.
    1.5, 28, 173
    4.1, 144
    4.1–3, 173
    4.2, 144
    7.5, 167
    9.4, 186n29
    12.10–11, 67
    15.9, 167
    16.5, 167
    18.2, 167
    20.8, 167

26.2, 167
27.5, 154
27.6–7, 122
Pert.
2.8, 12, 57
8.2, 57
12.2, 144
15.8, 12, 57
Pesc. Nig.
1.3, 24
2.7, 153
8.6, 43, 186n29
11.1, 149
12.6, 186n29
Prob.
1.1–6, 104–5
1.3, 66
1.6, 59
2.7, 25, 26, 49–50
12.7, 132
20.1–6, 124–25
21.2, 61
22.1, 61
22.3, 100
24.2–3, 146, 158–59
24.6–8, 122
24.8, 9
Quad. Tyr.
1.1, 50, 66
2.1–2, 82–83
3.2, 35
3.4, 43
4, 53
4.2, 35, 69
7.4–5, 93–94
7.5, 8
8, 93
8.2–4, 94
8.3, 8
8.7, 94
8.10, 142
9.4, 50, 52
12.1, 141
12.3, 141
12.4, 117
12.6, 141

12.7, 117, 141
13.1, 112–13
13.5, 141
14.1, 113, 155
14.2, 113
14.3, 112–13
14.4, 112–13
14.5, 112, 114
15.1, 114
15.3–7, 139
15.4, 118
15.5, 50
15.9, 69
15.10, 186n32
Sev.
4.6, 144
14.12–13, 57
17.1, 91
19.8, 144
Tac.
5.1–2, 163
5.3–7.1, 159–61
6.5, 126
7.2, 152
8.1–2, 68
10.7, 153
11.2, 144
11.7, 24
15.1, 68
15.1–5, 165–66
16.4, 166
18.5, 156
18.6, 156
Tyr. Trig.
1.1, 60
1.2, 66
3.2, 66
6.4, 66
7.2, 67
8.2, 37
11.4–5, 12
11.6–7, 60
12.3, 28
13.2, 66
15.5, 28
15.7, 66

Index Locorum

Historia Augusta (*Tyr. Trig.*) (*continued*)
    18.1–3, 66
    18.13, 66
    21.6, 67
    24.1, 66
    25, 67
    25.3, 50
    30, 53
    31.4, 66
    31.7–10, 84
    31.7–12, 118
    31.8, 156
    32, 118
    32.3, 66
    32.5–6, 118–19
    33, 118
    33.1, 118, 152
    33.4, 67
    33.7–8, 123
    33.8, 60
  Valer.
    1.1–4, 143
    8.3, 67, 156
    8.5, 10

Homer
  Il.
    2.135, 24
    5.83, 146
    16.334, 146
    20.477, 146

Horace
  Ars P.
    73–118, 184n4
    371, 20
  Carm.
    1.3.23–24, 43
    1.17.13–14
    4.8.13, 34
  Epist.
    1.3.19, 186n33
  Epod.
    10.1–2, 41
  Sat.
    2.1.4, 20
    2.3.230, 20

Jerome
  Adv. Iovinian.
    1.47, 116
    2.7, 199n59
  Apology against Rufinus
    1.16, 23
    2.5, 103, 116
  Chron.
    293d, 91
  Commentary on Isaiah
    7.21, 199n59
    17, 110
  De vir. ill.
    135, 157
  Epistles
    3, 102
    3.4.1, 115
    3.4.3, 113
    3.4–5, 113
    3.5.3, 114
    10, 121
    22.3, 117
    22.11.1, 118
    22.12.1, 117
    22.13, 116
    22.13.1, 117
    22.15, 116
    22.15.1, 118
    22.16, 116
    22.19, 117
    22.24, 117
    22.28, 117
    22.41, 117
    29.5.3, 120
    41.4, 101
    43.4, 116
    49, 119
    49.15, 120
    52.2, 121
    52.13.3, 122
    53.1.2–4, 98
    53.7, 43
    53.9.2, 122
    60.17, 199n59
    66.2.2, 122

70.2, 23
71.7, 124
77.8, 199n59
107.1.2, 122
107.2.2, 122
107.2.3, 110, 122
107.8, 122
108.3–4, 178n15
123.16.2, 168
Hebrew Questions on Genesis
6:3, 121
Prologus in Didymi libro de Spiritu sancto
186n33
Vit. Hilar.
1.1–8, 105–6
8.1–7, 108
11.3–4, 108
11.11–13, 108–9
Jordanes
Getica
83–88, 172
Josephus
AJ
19.6, 185n12
Juvenal
6.385–88, 22
6.512–13, 101
Lactantius
De mort. pers.
18.13, 168
Div. inst.
2.13, 121
5.3.7–21, 98
Libanius
Epistles
1063, 157
Or.
30.8–10, 102
Livy
pref. 2, 186n28
1.20.3, 119
1.45.4, 87
6.20.8, 186n28
27.34.7, 196n100

Lucian
Teacher of Rhetoric
17, 79
Lycophron
Alex.
240–41, 79
Manilius
3.560–80, 121
Martial
1.67, 27
4.56, 26
5.29, 26
Nemesianus
Cyn.
92, 40
Olympiodorus
fr. 6 Blockley, 163, 200n79
Origo Gentis Romanae
10.2, 23
Ovid
Fast.
3.383–84
Palladius
1.1.18, 186n28
Panegyrici Latini
7.2, 178n11
Paulus
Sent.
5.23.18, 89
Persius
2.69, 32
Petronius
48, 77
Philo
De Somniis
2.127, 190n86
De Vita Contemplativa
75–79, 190n86
Philostorgius
12.3, 164
Philostratus
Her.
30.1, 71
33.1, 71

Plato
> Leg.
>> 700–701, 184n4

Pliny the Elder
> 7.47, 23
> 7.81, 35
> 7.153–59, 121
> 9.119–21, 119
> 13.72, 35
> 13.82, 35
> 34.9, 32
> 36.74, 96

Pliny the Younger
> Epistles
>> 6.17, 77
>> 7.4.3, 186n28
> Pan.
>> 49.1, 150

Plutarch
> How a Young Man Should Listen to Poems
>> 26b, 190n87
> Vit. Alex.
>> 1.1.2–3, 47

Pomponius
> 1.1, 186n28

Porphyry
> Plot.
>> 13.10–17, 76

ps.-Plutarch
> Parallela Minora
>> 305a, 80
>> 309d–e, 80

Quintilian
> Inst.
>> 2.4.18, 81
>> 10.2.18, 34
>> 10.2.22, 184n4
>> 11, 180n3

Rhetorica ad Herennium
> 3, 180n3

Rufinus
> Apology
>> 2.5, 103
>> 2.42, 194n51
> Hist. eccl.
>> 11.33, 199n49

Rutilius Namatianus
> 1.439–52, 102
> 1.515–26, 102
> 2.41–60, 155

Sacerdos
> Keil, Gramm. Lat.
>> 6.494.27–28, 34

Sallust
> Cat.
>> 3.2, 107, 186n28
>> 8.4, 107
>> 17.3, 20
>> 50.4, 29
> Hist.
>> 1.55.21, 25
> Iug.
>> 85.1, 38

Scholia ad Iuvenalem
> 4.53, 25

Seneca
> Brev. vit.
>> 18.5–6, 185n12
> Q Nat.
>> 7.16, 59

Servius
> In Aen.
>> 4.42, 199n51
>> 4.653, 121
>> 8.285, 38
> In Ecl.
>> 4.1, 27, 182n46
> In G.
>> 4.148, 182n44

Sidonius
> Carm.
>> 5.358, 151
> Epistles
>> 8.3.4–6, 98

Socrates
> 1.9, 90
> 6.6.35–7, 40–1
> 7.10.5, 200n79

Solinus
> pref. 2, 186n28

Sozomen
> 5.25.1, 155

       9.8.1, 200n79
       9.8.2, 164
Suda
   A 942, 188n57
   O 327, 112
Suetonius
   Aug.
       9, 48
       79.1–3, 185n20
   Calig.
       3.1, 185n20
       8, 27
       16.1, 55
       19, 50
       19.3, 51
       22.3, 55
       32.3, 56
       37.1, 56
       50.1, 185n20
   Claud.
       30, 185n20
   Dom.
       18, 185n20
       22.1, 56
   Galba
       3.3, 185n20
       5.1, 116
   Iul.
       45.1, 185n20
       56, 22
       76.2, 38
   Nero
       11.1, 96
       15.2, 38
       20–21, 56
       22.3–24.1, 56
       27.2, 56
       31.3, 56
       51, 185n20
   Otho
       10, 50, 52
       12.1, 185n20
   Tib.
       15, 67
       42.2, 174
       43.1, 55

       68.1, 38
       68.1–3, 185n20
       70, 79
   Tit.
       3.1, 185n20
       3.2, 39
   Vesp.
       20, 185n20
       23.1. 27
   Vit.
       13.2, 55
       17.2, 185n20
Sulpicius Alexander
   at Gregory of Tours *Hist.* 2.9, 150–51
Symmachus
   Epistles
       4.34.4, 187n42
       7.18, 163
   Or.
       3, 200n75
   Relat.
       3, 129
       3.3, 130
       3.8, 28
       3.9, 130
       4, 7
Tacitus
   Ann.
       3.65.1–2, 62
       4.32.1, 62
       14.4.4, 96
   Dial.
       17.4, 121
       22.7, 34
Valerius Maximus
   2.2.6, 116
Varro
   Ling.
       5.166, 116
Vegetius
   Mil.
       2.24, 157
Vergil
   Aen.
       1.265, 43
       1.278, 43

Vergil (*Aen.*) (*continued*)
    1.381, 43
    6.848–54, 42
    6.857–8, 42
    6.869, 43
    6.869–70, 42
    6.882–83, 42
    8.808–12, 42
    10.830, 145
Catal.
    10.7, 27

G.
    6.74, 190n100

Zosimus
    1.16.1, 154
    2.29.5, 96
    4.54.1, 154
    5.31.3, 167
    5.32, 167
    5.44.1, 163
    6.7.1, 200n79
    6.7.3, 166

WISCONSIN STUDIES IN CLASSICS

Patricia A. Rosenmeyer, Laura McClure,
Mark Stansbury-O'Donnell, and Matthew Roller

Series Editors

Romans and Barbarians: The Decline of the Western Empire
E. A. Thompson

A History of Education in Antiquity
H. I. Marrou
Translated from the French by George Lamb

Accountability in Athenian Government
Jennifer Tolbert Roberts

Festivals of Attica: An Archaeological Commentary
Erika Simon

Roman Cities: Les villes romaines
Pierre Grimal
Edited and translated by G. Michael Woloch

Ancient Greek Art and Iconography
Edited by Warren G. Moon

Greek Footwear and the Dating of Sculpture
Katherine Dohan Morrow

The Classical Epic Tradition
John Kevin Newman

Ancient Anatolia: Aspects of Change and Cultural Development
Edited by Jeanny Vorys Canby, Edith Porada, Brunilde Sismondo Ridgway, and Tamara Stech

Euripides and the Tragic Tradition
Ann Norris Michelini

Wit and the Writing of History: The Rhetoric of Historiography in Imperial Rome
Paul Plass

The Archaeology of the Olympics: The Olympics and Other Festivals in Antiquity
Edited by Wendy J. Raschke

Tradition and Innovation in Late Antiquity
Edited by F. M. Clover and R. S. Humphreys

The Hellenistic Aesthetic
Barbara Hughes Fowler

Hellenistic Sculpture I: The Styles of ca. 331–200 B.C.
Brunilde Sismondo Ridgway

Hellenistic Poetry: An Anthology
Selected and translated by Barbara Hughes Fowler

Theocritus' Pastoral Analogies: The Formation of a Genre
Kathryn J. Gutzwiller

Rome and India: The Ancient Sea Trade
Edited by Vimala Begley and Richard Daniel De Puma

Kallimachos: The Alexandrian Library and the Origins of Bibliography
Rudolf Blum
Translated by Hans H. Wellisch

Myth, Ethos, and Actuality: Official Art in Fifth Century B.C. Athens
David Castriota

Archaic Greek Poetry: An Anthology
Selected and translated by Barbara Hughes Fowler

Murlo and the Etruscans: Art and Society in Ancient Etruria
Edited by Richard Daniel De Puma and Jocelyn Penny Small

The Wedding in Ancient Athens
John H. Oakley and Rebecca H. Sinos

The World of Roman Costume
Edited by Judith Lynn Sebesta and Larissa Bonfante

Greek Heroine Cults
Jennifer Larson

Flinders Petrie: A Life in Archaeology
Margaret S. Drower

Polykleitos, the Doryphoros, and Tradition
Edited by Warren G. Moon

The Game of Death in Ancient Rome: Arena Sport and Political Suicide
Paul Plass

Polygnotos and Vase Painting in Classical Athens
Susan B. Matheson

Worshipping Athena: Panathenaia and Parthenon
Edited by Jenifer Neils

Hellenistic Architectural Sculpture: Figural Motifs in Western Anatolia and the Aegean Islands
Pamela A. Webb

Fourth-Century Styles in Greek Sculpture
Brunilde Sismondo Ridgway

Ancient Goddesses: The Myths and the Evidence
Edited by Lucy Goodison and Christine Morris

Displaced Persons: The Literature of Exile from Cicero to Boethius
Jo-Marie Claassen

Hellenistic Sculpture II: The Styles of ca. 200–100 B.C.
Brunilde Sismondo Ridgway

Personal Styles in Early Cycladic Sculpture
Pat Getz-Gentle

The Complete Poetry of Catullus
Catullus
Translated and with commentary by David Mulroy

Hellenistic Sculpture III: The Styles of ca. 100–31 B.C.
Brunilde Sismondo Ridgway

*The Iconography of Sculptured Statue Bases in the Archaic and
    Classical Periods*
Angeliki Kosmopoulou

Discs of Splendor: The Relief Mirrors of the Etruscans
Alexandra A. Carpino

Mail and Female: Epistolary Narrative and Desire in Ovid's "Heroides"
Sara H. Lindheim

Modes of Viewing in Hellenistic Poetry and Art
Graham Zanker

Religion in Ancient Etruria
Jean-René Jannot
Translated by Jane K. Whitehead

A Symposion of Praise: Horace Returns to Lyric in "Odes" IV
Timothy Johnson

Satire and the Threat of Speech: Horace's "Satires," Book 1
Catherine M. Schlegel

Prostitutes and Courtesans in the Ancient World
Edited by Christopher A. Faraone and Laura K. McClure

Asinaria: The One about the Asses
Plautus
Translated and with commentary by John Henderson

Ulysses in Black: Ralph Ellison, Classicism, and African American Literature
Patrice D. Rankine

Imperium and Cosmos: Augustus and the Northern Campus Martius
Paul Rehak
Edited by John G. Younger

Ovid before Exile: Art and Punishment in the "Metamorphoses"
Patricia J. Johnson

Pandora's Senses: The Feminine Character of the Ancient Text
Vered Lev Kenaan

Nox Philologiae: Aulus Gellius and the Fantasy of the Roman Library
Erik Gunderson

New Perspectives on Etruria and Early Rome
Edited by Sinclair Bell and Helen Nagy

The Image of the Poet in Ovid's "Metamorphoses"
Barbara Pavlock

Responses to Oliver Stone's "Alexander": Film, History, and Cultural Studies
Edited by Paul Cartledge and Fiona Rose Greenland

The Codrus Painter: Iconography and Reception of Athenian Vases in the Age of Pericles
Amalia Avramidou

The Matter of the Page: Essays in Search of Ancient and Medieval Authors
Shane Butler

Greek Prostitutes in the Ancient Mediterranean, 800 BCE–200 CE
Edited by Allison Glazebrook and Madeleine M. Henry

Sophocles' "Philoctetes" and the Great Soul Robbery
Norman Austin

Oedipus Rex
Sophocles
A verse translation by David Mulroy, with introduction and notes

The Slave in Greece and Rome
John Andreau and Raymond Descat
Translated by Marion Leopold

Perfidy and Passion: Reintroducing the "Iliad"
Mark Buchan

The Gift of Correspondence in Classical Rome: Friendship in Cicero's "Ad Familiares" and Seneca's "Moral Epistles"
Amanda Wilcox

Antigone
Sophocles
A verse translation by David Mulroy, with introduction and notes

Aeschylus's "Suppliant Women": The Tragedy of Immigration
Geoffrey W. Bakewell

Couched in Death: "Klinai" and Identity in Anatolia and Beyond
Elizabeth P. Baughan

Silence in Catullus
Benjamin Eldon Stevens

Odes
Horace
Translated with commentary by David R. Slavitt

Shaping Ceremony: Monumental Steps and Greek Architecture
Mary B. Hollinshead

Selected Epigrams
Martial
Translated with notes by Susan McLean

The Offense of Love: "Ars Amatoria," "Remedia Amoris," and "Tristia" 2
Ovid
A verse translation by Julia Dyson Hejduk, with introduction and notes

Oedipus at Colonus
Sophocles
A verse translation by David Mulroy, with introduction and notes

Women in Roman Republican Drama
Edited by Dorota Dutsch, Sharon L. James, and David Konstan

Dream, Fantasy, and Visual Art in Roman Elegy
Emma Scioli

Agamemnon
Aeschylus
A verse translation by David Mulroy, with introduction and notes

Trojan Women, Helen, Hecuba: Three Plays about Women and the Trojan War
Euripides
Verse translations by Francis Blessington, with introduction and notes

Echoing Hylas: A Study in Hellenistic and Roman Metapoetics
Mark Heerink

Horace between Freedom and Slavery: The First Book of "Epistles"
Stephanie McCarter

The Play of Allusion in the "Historia Augusta"
David Rohrbacher

www.ingramcontent.com/pod-product-compliance
Lightning Source LLC
Chambersburg PA
CBHW070839160426
43192CB00012B/2242